SAINTS

INSPIRATION AND GUIDANCE FOR EVERY DAY OF THE YEAR

SAINTS

INSPIRATION AND GUIDANCE FOR EVERY DAY OF THE YEAR

weldon**owen**

weldon**owen**

CEO Raoul Goff
VP Publisher, Weldon Owen Roger Shaw
Associate Publisher Mariah Bear
Editorial Director Katie Killebrew
VP Creative Chrissy Kwasnik
VP Manufacturing Alix Nicholaeff
Art Director Allister Fein
Senior Production Manager Greg Steffen

Produced by Weldon Owen
an imprint of Insight Editions
P.O. Box 3088
San Rafael, CA 94912
www.weldonowen.com

Work © Weldon Owen International 2021

ISBN: 978-1-68188-748-7

Printed in Turkey

First printed in 2021
2021 2022 2023 2024 · 10 9 8 7 6 5 4 3 2 1

CONTENTS

This book is organized chronologically, divided into monthly sections, following the calendar year. In order to find a particular saint's feast day, readers should consult the Index, which references each saint by date.

FOREWORD

In order to offer the most comprehensive coverage of these exemplary men and women, we feature celebrated saints from all quarters, including those listed on the General Roman Calendar, the Liturgical Calendar for the Dioceses of the United States of America, and those on the Lectionary of the Church of England. In addition, other luminaries have been added, including many Eastern Orthodox, local, and modern saints.

Where appropriate, a few individuals who are not saints, but whose lives significantly contributed to the corpus of saintly activity and achievement (and who might currently be under consideration for beatification or canonization), have also been included in the book. With some 20,000 saints to choose from, we may well be guilty of omissions that some might deem significant. Within the scope and confines of the current volume, however, we hope we have done justice, in the spirit of ecumenism, to the many and various facets of what is now a truly global faith.

WHAT MAKES A SAINT?

Three decades ago, *The Catholic Encyclopedia* included around 5,000 saints. Some of their lives were recorded in detail, while some remained barely identifiable from mere scraps of information, hearsay, and legend. During the pontificates of Pope John Paul II (1978-2005) and Benedict XVI (2005-2013), the roster grew exponentially; a tidal wave of saints was admitted to the canon, swelling the total to around 20,000. In addition, the Church of England, while carefully treading an ecumenical line in its selection of saints old and new alongside many worthy characters in its list of observances, has admitted a new list of 20th-century martyrs.

The first Christian saints were those immediately involved with the life and ministry of Christ—in effect His family members, first disciples, and immediate associates, As Christianity grew and spread within both the Eastern and Western Roman Empires—driven by the missionary impetus of Christ's Apostles—a new and practically innumerable host of "martyrs" were created as the new creed collided with long-standing pagan beliefs and traditions and the imperial persecution of Christians. The practice of inviting martyrdom, sadly not unfamiliar in the modern world, was almost certainly part of the Christian regimen at the time. Martyrdom has continued into the present day: missionary activity produced a huge number of martyrs, as did the global expansion of Christianity in the wake of European colonialism and the European wars of religion sparked by the Reformation.

A new category of saint, the "confessor," emerged after the emperor Constantine decreed Christianity to be the official religion of the Roman Empire in 323. Many of these saints came to prominence as theologians, bishops, archbishops, and patriarchs involved in steering the passage, development, outreach, and consolidation of the Church. In more recent years, many worthy people have been added to the canon of sainthood by their sheer selfless good work, and their foundation of, and support for, religious orders dedicated to the care and education of the less fortunate.

HAGIOGRAPHY

The urge to record and celebrate the achievements and sacrifices of saints dates back to at least the 3rd century AD. One of the most important hagiographers was St. Jerome (Sept. 30), although his was only one of a wide range of martyrologies and calendars of saints' feast days. The *Martyrologium of Usuard*, dating from the mid-9th century, attempted an encyclopedic listing. From the early Middle Ages, a literary tradition of recounting the lives of the more lively and popular saints emerged. Perhaps the most famous example was Jacobus de Voragine's *Legenda Aurea (The Golden Legend)*, completed in around 1266.

The most important list of saints is *The Roman Martyrology*. It was assembled from a wide range of sources with a sense of scientific and historical purpose in 1583 under the auspices of Pope Gregory XIII. It has been revised several times over the last four centuries and remains the main repository of information concerning the canon of saints, at least for the Western churches.

THE PATH TO SAINTHOOD

Saints tended to be adopted and recognized on a local level for the first thousand years or so of Christianity. Often sainthood was a product of veneration by a saint's contemporaries, peers, and successors, although increasingly the recognition of a saint was in the gift of the local bishop. During this period, relics (and the possession of them) also became an important aspect of veneration.

The many saints who entered the canon in the first millennium of Christian history are referred to as doing so "Pre Congregation." The more formal process of recognition evolved from the 10th century as successive bishops of Rome began to assert their exclusive right to recognize saints. Pope Alexander III (d.1181) began a more formal process for the papal recognition of sainthood; this came to involve an advisory "congregation" of senior churchmen. However, the earliest version of the modern rigorous examination of a candidate's worthiness for papal consideration or approval was only introduced in 1634. Today, this involves three main processes: veneration, beatification, and canonization. Central to these processes is the Congregation for the Causes of Saints, which originated in the 17th century as the Congregation of Sacred Rites, but was reformed in 1969 with the specific task of carefully assessing all the evidence and providing the pontiff with reliable advice in making a decision.

Veneration The first stage is usually petitioned at a local or parochial level. The title "Venerable" is applied to those whose beatification has been accepted in principle if not fully decreed, pending further investigation.

Beatification The second level involves a deeper testing of the evidence of the candidate's sanctity, and at least one attested miracle as a result of the individual's intercession is required. Exceptions may be made in the case of martyrdom or exceptional sanctity. A person who has been beatified acquires the title "Blessed."

Canonization The third and final stage of elevation to sainthood is the outcome of a long evaluation of evidence—biographical, testimonial, and otherwise—and the detailed appraisal of whether God has indeed performed miracles due to the saint's intercession. In recent years, this has relied increasingly on medically approved "miracles," such as the scientifically inexplicable recovery from an untreatable or terminal condition. The "incorruption" of a saint's remains, a convincing qualification in previous centuries, is now regarded as less reliable.

THE LITURGICAL CALENDAR BEGINS EVERY YEAR DURING THE MONTH OF NOVEMBER ON THE FIRST SUNDAY OF ADVENT AND RUNS THROUGH TO THE SOLEMNITY OF CHRIST.

Liturgical Calendars

Each denomination has its own liturgical calendar that lists particular days of observance for major feasts, many of which include saints' days. They do not always accord, and on an annual basis saints' feast days may be shifted or ignored if they coincide with a more important fixture on the calendar.

In addition, the calendars themselves may be affected by considerations like the paschal feast days linked to Easter.

For the purposes of this volume, the editors have included all those saints (canonized, beatified, or listed as significant contributors to the body of Christian faith) that are included on the following liturgical calendars (although there are provisions within these calendars for local observances, many of which have also been included):

The General Roman Calendar Established in 1969, and only minimally revised since then, the Calendar lists Optional Memorials, Obligatory Memorials, Feasts, and Solemnities. It allocates only about half of the days in a year to feasts for specific saints, although many more appear on *The Roman Martyrology*.

The General Roman Calendar also provides appendices for local feast days that it approves in various countries around the world (for example, St. Patrick in Ireland, or St. Elizabeth Ann Seton in the United States).

The Lectionary of the Church of England In many instances this accords with the General Roman Calendar, but it also includes teachers of the Faith, bishops and other pastors, members of religious communities, missionaries, Christian rulers, reformers, and others recognized uniquely by the Church of England.

The Liturgical Calendar for the Dioceses of the United States of America Based upon the General Roman Calendar, this includes a number of saints unique to North America.

MILESTONES OF CHRISTIANITY

In the two thousand-plus years since the birth of Jesus—and the flowering of a movement devoted to his teachings—Christianity has expanded from a handful of devoted-but-localized congregants to a massive worldwide institution that outnumbers all other faiths. Today's Roman Catholic Church, with approximately 1.3 billion baptized followers, gave rise to a number of splinter sects, including the Eastern Orthodox Church, with roughly 220 million followers, and the many Protestant denominations, with possibly one billion aherents collectively. The passing centuries have also witnessed significant ecclesiastical events, the rise of certain historical figures, and philosophical upheavals that combined to reshape the doctrines of the evolving Church.

JOHN THE BAPTIST
Born to an elderly Jewish couple, John's future endeavors as a prophet of the Messiah were foretold by the angel Gabriel. John preached of this glorious coming in the lower Jordan Valley and baptized many in the name of God, including Jesus himself, before he was beheaded at the order of Herod Antipas, against whom he had preached.

SAINT JOHN THE BAPTIST PREACHING IN THE WILDERNESS BY ANTON RAPHAEL

JESUS OF NAZARETH
Considered by many the Messiah, or Christ, awaited by the Jews, Jesus' coming was prophysied by a number of Old Testament figures, including Daniel, Ezekiel, Hosea, Isaiah, and Jeremiah. Born to the Virgin Mary around 4 BC in the Kingdom of Judea, Jesus worked as a carpenter, the trade of his earthly father, Joseph. He did not begin his ministry until the age of 30, but accomplished much between then and his death by crucifiction, including a number of miracles. His impact on the world, both theologically and philosophically, has been incalculable.

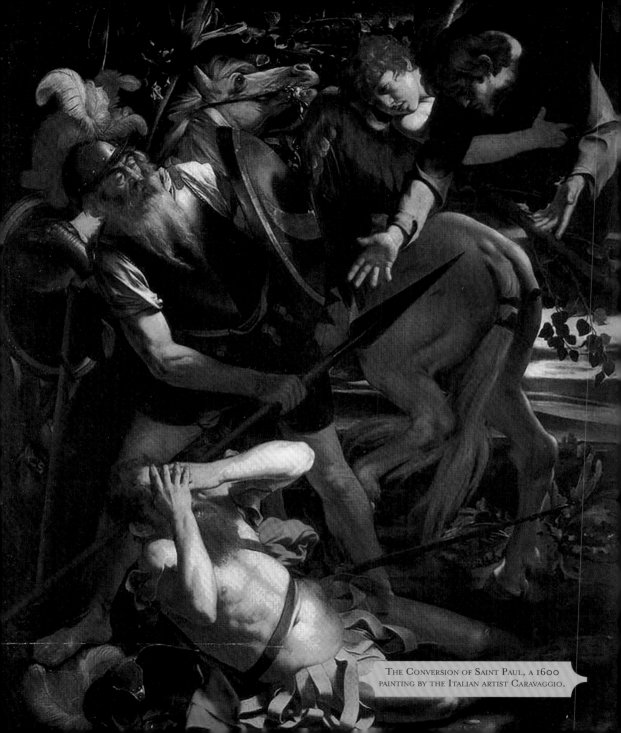

THE CONVERSION OF SAINT PAUL, A 1600
PAINTING BY THE ITALIAN ARTIST CARAVAGGIO.

CHURCH HIERARCHY

The Christian Church began with Jesus Christ and his Apostles, most of whom actually witnessed his ministry. After the Crucifiction and Resurrection, the Apostles appointed their successors, known as bishops, and they in turn appointed other bishops, a process known as Apostolic succession. These ambassadors for Christ were charged with the task of spreading Jesus' Word throughout the Levant, the Middle East, the Mediterranean, and beyond. It is from the ranks of these inspired holy men and women that many saints were first drawn.

MARTYRS

In the early days of the Church, practicing or preaching Christianity was a risky endeavor. Many pagan nations, including ocassionally Rome, outlawed the belief. Authorities imprisoned and tortured Jesus' followers to make them recant and often put them to death in gruesome spectacles. Early Christians who died for their faith were known as protomartyrs. Sadly, even today those spreading the Word of Christ in areas of political unrest may face a similar sacrifice.

CONVERSION OF SAUL

Saul of Tarsus was a Jewish Pharisee who "intensely persecuted" Christians. While traveling to Damascus to hunt down and arrest Christians, he was blinded by a flash of light from heaven and heard the voice of Jesus asking, "Why do you persecute me?" With his sight restored, Saul became Paul, a most energetic Apostle, who had a profound effect on the early church . . . and authored nearly half of the New Testament.

THE FIRST POPES

The exalted position of bishop of Rome was originally held by the Apostle Peter, also called Simon. Jesus proclaimed of him, "Thou art Peter, and upon this rock I will build my church." (Petrus was Latin for rock.) The majority of popes were based in Rome and later dwelled in a walled city, the Vatican, situated within Rome. Occasionally a second pope, called the antipope, was recognized by certain factions who wanted to replace the true pope.

16TH-CENTURY FRESCO DEPICTING CONSTANTINE I AND THE BISHOPS ATTENDING THE COUNCIL OF NICAEA

COUNCIL OF NICAEA

This ecumenical meeting of bishops was held in the city of Nicaea, modern Turkey, in 325 AD by Emperor Constantine I, who was the first Roman emperor to convert to Christianity. Its purpose was to attain consensus in the church by an assembly of its representatives. Its aim was to settle the issue of the divine nature of God the Son and his relationship to God the Father, which provoked the creation of the Nicene Creed.

THE GREAT SCHISM

A permanent break between the Eastern (Byzantine) and Western (Roman) Catholic Churches occurred due to a complex mix of religious disagreements and political conflicts. One significant religious disagreement between the two branches had to do with whether it was acceptable to use unleavened bread for the sacrament of Communion. The Eastern Church answers to the Patriarch of Constantinople.

PROTESTANT REFORMATION

Arising in 16th century Germany, this movement began in 1517 when priest and theologian Martin Luther published his *Ninety-five Theses*, a reaction against the sale of indulgences—by which clergy reduced the punishment meted out for sinning. Luther's actions sparked a much wider and lasting break with Catholicism and led to new denominational families such as Lutherans, Methodists, Baptists, and Pentacostals. More "fundamental" Protestant denominations like Evangelicals and Charismatics have surged in recent years.

THE INQUISITION

Originally an institution set up by the Roman Catholic Church to combat heresy, it lasted from the 1250s to the early 19th century. In Spain its main targets were Jewish or Muslim converts to Christianity suspected of reverting to their original faiths. Elsewhere, targets included Jews, scientist, witches, and Protestants. Inquisitors often resorted to violence or torture to elicit confessions and so many thousands of "admitted" heretics were killed, typically burned at the stake.

ROME 8 DECEMBER 1869. THE SOLEMN OPENING OF THE GREAT ECUMENIC COUNCIL

FIRST VATICAN COUNCIL

Held between 1869 and 1870, this gathering of ranking churchmen was convoked by Pope Pius IX to address contemporary problems such as the rising influences of rationalism, liberalism, and materialism. It included agreement, after heated debate, on the pope's jurisdiction over the whole Church and that his primacy included papal infallibility—meaning the pope's decisions are preserved free from error when he instructs that a doctrine is to be believed.

VATICAN II

Pope John XXIII convened this council from 1962 to 1965 in order to provide spiritual renewal, support unity, and to "modernize the Church after 20 centuries of life." Topics included changes in the Mass—turning the altar to face the congregation and foregoing Latin, the administering of the Sacraments, the role of laity in the Mass, and the Church's relationship to other denominations and to contemporary culture. Vatican II set in motion many changes that had unlooked-for effects on the Church.

POPE JOHN XXIII

JANUARY

The first month of the Julian and Gregorian calendars, January is associated with winter in the Northern Hemisphere and summer in the Southern. It is named after the double-faced Roman deity Janus, god of the doorway.

Christian festivals during this month include the Circumcision, falling on the eighth day after the Nativity, and Epiphany which, on January 6, celebrates the Adoration of the Magi on the twelfth day of Christmas. For the Eastern Churches, where it is known as Theophany, the date is associated with the Baptism of Christ (and was the day upon which Christ's Nativity was originally celebrated). In some traditions, Epiphany forms a period of the liturgical calendar lasting until the beginning of Lent. In the West, it marks the beginning of the first period of Ordinary Time.

THE BLESSED VIRGIN MARY IS THE SINGLE MOST POPULAR FIGURE IN WESTERN ART. OFTEN GLORIFIED, OFTEN OVERWHELMED BY ATTENDANTS, HERE GIOVANNI BATTISTA SALVI DA SASSOFERRATO'S SIMPLE VISION OF A DEVOTED WOMAN (C.1650) REFLECTS HER ESSENTIAL PURITY.

Mary

Christ's mother, the most important and widely revered saint in the Christian canon, is celebrated on the first day of the year, known formally as the Solemnity of Mary, Mother of God. The numerous days in the ecclesiastical calendar previously devoted to her were rationalized at the Second Vatican Council (1962–65), and in 1969 the General Roman Calendar assigned this day as hers alone. The Blessed Virgin Mary still reappears throughout the Christian calendar, however: feast days associated with her life include her Nativity on September 8; the Annunciation of Our Lord on March 25; the Nativity of Christ on December 25; the Presentation of the Lord on February 2; her Assumption on August 15, her principal feast day; and her Enthronement as the Queen of Heaven on August 22. Her mourning for her lost son is commemorated on September 15 as Our Lady of Sorrows (Mater Dolorosa). She has been adopted by innumerable local churches and cults worldwide, the most significant of these including pilgrimage centers, such as Lourdes, where Marian apparitions have occurred. The monastery of Montserrat in Catalonia even has a black Virgin (La Moreneta), as does the pilgrimage center of Czestochowa in Poland.

Underlying all this pomp and majesty is the enduring image of a humble Jewish village girl from Nazareth. In the New Testament, Mary—a girl selected by God to give birth to His son—first appears already betrothed to Joseph, a local carpenter. Both were of the lineage of King David. Although Mary only occasionally appears in the Gospels during the ministry of Jesus, she is understood to have been a continuing presence throughout His life, crucifixion, and resurrection. She is often regarded as His first disciple, and was with the Apostles when they were visited by the Holy Spirit on Pentecost. Her example of purity, chastity, humility, and devotion is one that nuns are enjoined to emulate.

In 449, the Second Council of Ephesus conjectured that if Jesus Christ is an indivisible part of the Holy Trinity, should Mary not therefore be acclaimed as the Mother of God? For the Orthodox churches, Mary became Theotokos (the God-bearer); in the West, the Mother of God. As a result, an outburst of Marian cults spread across the Christian world. Despite her stature in the church, the Blessed Virgin Mary remains the most accessible, approachable, and beloved of all the saints.

PATRON SAINT OF: *Benedictines, the Brothers Hospitallers, Cistertians, seafarers, fishmongers, harness makers, among many others*

STATUS: *Mother of God*

BORN: *c. 18 BC, Nazareth*

DIED: *c. 30–33 AD*

VENERATED BY: *Christianity, Islam*

CANONIZED: *Pre-Congregation*

SYMBOLS: *Blue mantle, crown of 12 stars, pregnant woman, roses, woman with child, woman trampling serpent, crescent moon, woman clothed with the sun, heart pierced by sword, rosary beads*

Hail Mary, Full of Grace, The Lord is with thee. Blessed art thou among women, and blessed is the fruit of thy womb, Jesus. Holy Mary, Mother of God, pray for us sinners now, and at the hour of death. Glory Be to the Father, and to the Son, and to the Holy Spirit. Amen.

Basil the Great

PATRON SAINT OF:
Russia, Cappadocia, Hospital administrators, Reformers, Monks, Education, Exorcism, Liturgists

STATUS: *Bishop*

BORN: *AD 329 Kayseri, Asia Minor (Turkey)*

DIED: *AD 379 Kayseri, Asia Minor*

VENERATED BY: *Eastern Orthodox Church, Oriental Orthodoxy, Roman Catholic Church, Anglican Communion, Lutheranism*

CANONIZED:
Pre-Congregation

SYMBOLS: *Vested as bishop, depicted as thin and ascetic with tapering black beard, wearing omophorion, holding Gospel or scroll a white Carthusian habit.*

Saint Basil, o great follower of God, help all as well as me. Defender of orthodoxy, defend us too, that follow your faith and stand beside you. . . .

Saint Basil, o miracle worker, father of our spirit, listen and hear your children's spirits in the name of Jesus Christ. Amen.

B asil was born to a strongly Christian family—his parents are both revered as saints in the Eastern Orthodox churches, as were his brothers St. Gregory of Nyssa (Jan. 10) and St. Peter of Sebaste. He was educated at home and then studied in Constantinople and Athens, where he met Gregory Nazianzen. They both entered a Christian community at Pontus, where Basil developed his teachings concerning monasticism. Eventually ordained around 362, he returned to Caesarea, where he developed a theological argument against Arianism, then the creed of the Roman emperor, Valens. This was the nontrinitarian belief that Jesus was the son of God, begotton by God the Father, but was distinct from the Father and subordinate to him; the Son was God the Son, but not co-eternal with God the Father.

Basil, known for his care of the poor and underprivileged, also established guidelines for monastic life, focusing on community, liturgical prayer, and manual labor.

THE THREE HOLY HIERARCHS (FROM THE LEFT), BASIL THE GREAT, JOHN CHRYSOSTOM AND GREGORY NAZIANZEN.

Geneviève

Born into a shepherding family in Nanterre, France, Geneviève moved to Paris after her parents died. She entered a nunnery there, apparently inspired to do so by St. Germanus of Auxerre (July 31). She had many visions of heavenly saints and angels, to the point where her enemies tried to drown her in a lake. Germanus himself intervened on her behalf. When the city was besieged by the Franks under Childeric in 464, she led a party from the city to gather food, her dedication winning the respect of Childeric and saving many lives. She subsequently is said to have converted his son, Clovis, in 496, who built the Church of the Holy Apostles in Paris in her memory. Earlier, in 451, her advocacy of peace and the power of prayer was also said to have saved Paris from the depredations of Attila the Hun's marauding army.

Geneviève's influence survived her: in 1129 an outbreak of ergot poisoning in Paris, caused by a grain fungus, was brought to an end when her relics were taken in procession to Notre-Dame Cathedral, an event still celebrated today.

PATRON SAINT OF: *Paris*

STATUS: *Nun, mystic*

BORN: *c. 419, Nanterre, Western Roman Empire*

DIED: *502–512, Paris, France*

VENERATED BY: *Roman Catholic Church, Eastern Orthodox Church*

CANONIZED: *Pre-Congregation*

SYMBOLS: *Candle*

Saint Genevieve, you who by the days before, penance and prayer, ensured the protection of Paris, intercede near God for us, for our country, for the devoted Christian hearts…. May your example be for us, an encouragement to always seek God and serve him through our brothers and sisters. Amen.

SAINT GENEVIEVE, SEVENTEENTH-CENTURY PAINTING, MUSÉE CARNAVALET, PARIS

Elizabeth Ann Seton

Regarded as creator of the US Catholic parochial school system, Elizabeth Ann Seton is the earliest born of the American saints. Elizabeth (née Bayley) was raised in a wealthy Episcopalian family, and married a merchant when she was 20, raising five children. She became involved in charitable social work and set up the Society for the Relief of Poor Widows and Children in 1797, but her husband suddenly became bankrupt, and then she herself was widowed.

She converted to Catholicism in 1805, and was invited to establish a girls' school in Baltimore. In 1809, she founded the Sisters of Charity of St. Joseph, the first homegrown American religious society, and another school for poor children in Emmitsburg, Maryland. She was elected superior and, with 18 companions, took her vows in 1810. By 1830, the Sisters were running orphanages and schools as far west as Cincinnati and New Orleans, and had established the first hospital west of the Mississippi in St. Louis.

PATRON SAINT OF:
Catholic schools, seafarers, widows, loss of a child or parent, Shreveport; Louisiana, and the State of Maryland

STATUS: *Widow, founder*

BORN: *August 28, 1774, New York, NY*

DIED: *January 4, 1821, Emmitsburg, Maryland*

VENERATED BY: *Roman Catholic Church*

CANONIZED: *1975*

SYMBOLS: *a pink flower, a book, a school, a rosary, a bible, and wheat*

Lord God, You blessed Elizabeth Seton with gifts of grace;

As wife and mother, educator and foundress,

So that she might spend her life in service to your people.

Through her example and prayers

May we learn to express our love for you

In love for our fellow men and women.

We ask this through our Lord Jesus Christ, your Son,

Who lives and reigns with you and the Holy Spirit,

One God, for ever and ever. Amen.

John Nepomucene Neumann

Born in Europe to German/Czech parents, John Nepomucene was named after the patron saint of Bohemia and was destined to enter the church. The Austro-Hungarian government suspended ordinations, however, so in 1836, John emigrated to the United States in order to undertake missionary work. He was ordained within three weeks of arriving in Manhattan and joined the Redemptorist Order—the first American priest to do so—in 1842, meanwhile preaching to fellow immigrants in New York State, Pittsburgh, and Baltimore. He was known for his frugality and owned only one pair of boots during his years in America.

John was naturalized in 1848, and appointed bishop of Philadelphia in 1852. At the time Philadelphia had a large and expanding Catholic immigrant population. Under his tenure a massive program of building was inaugurated (despite resistance from the "Know-Nothing" anti-Catholics), resulting in the completion of Baltimore's cathedral and the creation of almost 100 churches and 80 schools in Pennsylvania and Delaware. New parish churches were being completed at a rate of something like one per month.

PATRON SAINT OF:
Catholic education

STATUS: *Bishop, missionary*

BORN: *March 28, 1811, Bohemia, modern Czech Republic*

DIED: *January 5, 1860, Philadelphia, PA*

VENERATED BY: *Roman Catholic Church*

CANONIZED: *1977*

SYMBOLS: *Refemptionist habit with pectoral cross*

Passion of Christ, strengthen me. Strengthen me to carry my daily cross. Through the intercession of your servant, St. John Neumann, I ask that You lighten the burden that now weighs heavily on my heart. (Mention your intentions here) St. John Neumann, you had a special love for the sciences. Pray for all scientists, that through their studies, they may be led ever closer to God, the first cause and designer of all Creation. Holy Spirit, help me to recognize the gifts that You have given me. Help me to follow You more closely and lead others to You with those gifts. So, like St. John Neumann, I may become a saint using these gifts and walking a path that You have laid out for me. Amen.

The National Shrine of St. John Neumann lies under the altar of St. Peter the Apostle in Philadelphia, his remains encased in a glass reliquary.

André of Montreal

Born Alfred Bessette, Saint André of Montreal was revered for his miraculous healings. Illness followed André throughout his life, such that he was once rejected from the Congregation of the Holy Cross due to his frailty. At the insistence of the Archbishop at the time, he was later accepted, taking the name Brother André.

The greatest focus of Andrés work in the church was to care for the sick, and he quickly became known for his miraculous oil healings. André was deeply devoted to Saint Joseph, and would often recommend prayer to Saint Joseph to those who came to him for healing. His popularity as a healer grew over time, to the point that he received tens of thousands of letters each year from those seeking cures. Despite this, he remained humble, adamant that every healing was the work of Saint Joseph. After his death in 1937, his coffin was visited by over a million people.

PATRON SAINT OF:
Caregivers, the sick, healers

STATUS: *Healer, Porter to the Congregation of the Holy Cross*

BORN: *August 9, 1845, Quebec, Canada*

DIED: *January 6, 1937, Quebec, Canada*

VENERATED BY: *Roman Catholic Church (Canada and the United States), Congregation of the Holy Cross*

CANONIZED: *October 17, 2010*

SYMBOLS: *St. Joseph's oil, parchment*

Saint Brother André, you grant us the favor of realizing your dream and of making present in our day the heritage you left to the world. Help us to continue in the spirit of unconditional acceptance which you showed each person you met. May our presence here, our attitudes and our words always reflect the love and compassion which marked your whole life long. Saint Brother André, pray for us. Amen.

Raymond of Peñafort

This long-lived and distinguished churchman was born in Catalonia to a noble family with ties to the royal house of Aragon and received a doctorate in canon and civil law at the University of Bologna. He then returned to Barcelona, joining the newly formed Dominican Order to preach and study. He was called to Rome in 1230 by Pope Gregory IX, and began the task of collating conciliar and papal decrees into a standard reference work for canonical lawyers. At the age of 47, he received the habit.

Raymond returned to Catalonia in 1236 to become general of the Dominicans (1238–40) and establish the Inquisition in Iberia, focusing on the conversion of Muslims and Jews. He supported St. Thomas Aquinas (Jan. 28) in writing his *Summa contra Gentiles*, and seems to have been involved, with St. Peter Nolasco and James of Aragon, in founding the Mercedarian Order, a mendicant order established to rescue ransomed Christians during the Spanish Reconquista.

RAYMOND'S IMPORTANCE IN THE DEVELOPMENT OF THE CATHOLIC CHURCH IN IBERIA MADE HIM A POPULAR SUBJECT FOR VISIONARY PAINTINGS DURING THE COUNTER-REFORMATION PERIOD.

PATRON SAINT OF: *Canon laywers, other lawyers*

STATUS: *Priest, canonist.*

BORN: *c.1175, Vilafranca del Penedès, Catalonia, Spain*

DIED: *1275, Barcelona, Spain*

VENERATED BY: *Roman Catholic Church, Dominicans*

CANONIZED: *1601*

SYMBOLS: *Dominican robes; skimming across the sea with his cape forming both boat and sail.*

Let us pray. Glorious Saint Raymond of Peñafort, wise and holy patron,

Come to the aid of those entrusted to your care, and all who flee to your protection.

Intercede for us in our need, and help us through your prayers, example, and teaching, to proclaim the truth of the Gospel to all we meet.

And when we have reached the fullness of our years, we beseech you to guide us home to heaven, to live in peace with you, Our Mother Mary, and Our Lord Jesus Christ. Amen.

Laurence Giustiniani

Known also as Lawrence Justinian, he was admired for his humble piety, a trait he seems to have inherited from his devout mother. Although the Giustinianis were a senior patrician family in 14th-century Venice, their lineage included a number of saints. Laurence eschewed a secular career, intent on a life of prayer and charity. He joined a community of canons regular, where he was known for his poverty and mortification—wearing sackcloth and begging for food. At the time he was ordained, in 1407, the congregation was being transformed into one with a more active role in the community, and he rose to become prior general, reorganizing their constitution.

In 1433 he was made bishop of Castello, in the diocese of Venice, by Pope Eugene IV, one of the founders of the Monastery of San Giorgio. Laurence's organizational skills meant that in 1451 (against his will) he was proclaimed the first Patriarch of Venice, a post he held for more than four years. His ascetic writings were widely published after his death.

PATRON SAINT OF:
Venice

STATUS: *Bishop.*

BORN: *July 1, 1381, Venice Italy*

DIED: *Jan 8, 1456, Venice, Italy*

VENERATED BY: *Roman Catholic Church, Venetian Augustinians*

CANONIZED: *1690*

SYMBOLS: *Episcopal vestments*

Grant us, we beseech Thee O almighty God, to extinguish the flames of our evil dispositions, as Thou didst grant blessed Laurence to overcome the fires of his torments.

Through our Lord Jesus Christ, Thy Son, Who liveth and reigneth with Thee in the unity of the Holy Ghost, God, Forever and ever. Amen.

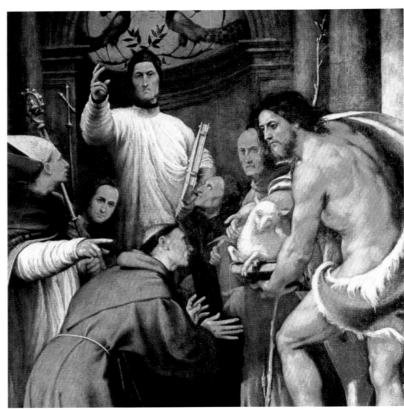

LAURENCE BLESSES THE ADORATION OF THE LAMB BY ST. FRANCIS AND JOHN THE BAPTIST.

Adrian of Canterbury

The chronicles of the Venerable Bede (May 25) attest that Adrian was a Greek-speaking North African Berber, who became abbot of a monastery near Monte Cassino in Italy. He was twice offered, and twice declined, the archbishopric of Canterbury by Pope Vitalian. Instead, he suggested a Greek monk named Theodore of Tarsus (Sept. 19) for the position. Papal assent was given, on condition that Adrian accompany Theodore to England because he had twice been to Gaul and knew the roads and best modes of traveling. They arrived in 668, and Adrian was immediately made the abbot of Sts. Peter and Paul Church (now St. Augustine's) in Canterbury. There he long survived his companion, continuing to preside over the monastery until his death. His great theological and linguistic knowledge helped to build the Canterbury monastic foundation into a major educational and missionary force in Britain. Adrian came to be regarded as a saint, and during restoration work on the monastery in 1091, his body was disinterred and found to be uncorrupted. His tomb became a major pilgrimage site, and many miraculous cures were claimed for the site.

STATUS: *Abbot.*

BORN: *c. 640, North Africa*

DIED: *C. 710, Canterbury, England*

VENERATED BY: *Roman Catholic Church*

CANONIZED: *Pre-Congregation*

Adrian, we ask your intercession with our Heavenly Father for the grace of wisdom. Pray that we might continue to learn and grow in our faith. May we seek true wisdom which leads to knowledge in the ways of God and His will for our lives. May this wisdom increase our love of Him and the furthering of His Kingdom. Amen.

Gregory of Nyssa

This saint came from a notable family of early Christians in Asia Minor. Along with his older brother, St. Basil the Great, and their friend, theologian Gregory of Nazianzus (both Jan. 2), he is remembered as one of the Cappadocian Fathers. Among other doctrines, they asserted the superiority of Christian teachings over those of traditional Greek philosophy. Although lacking the organization skills of Basil, and the contemporary influence of Gregory of Nazianzus, this learned theologian made significant contributions to the doctrine of the Trinity.

In 372, Gregory was consecrated Bishop of Nyssa, a remote city in eastern Anatolia near Armenia, where Arianism, a non-trinitarian belief, had taken hold. His most enduring contributions concerned the indivisible nature of the Trinity (central to the Nicene Creed, adopted at the Council of Constantinople, which Gregory attended in 381), the necessity of unquestioning faith in seeking to understand the infinity of God, the emulation of God through the example of Christ, and the importance of achieving this within a monastic community. Since the middle of the 20th century, a significant increase in interest in Gregory's works from the academic community, particularly his writings involving universal salvation, have resulted in challenges to many of the traditional interpretations of his theology.

STATUS: *Bishop*

BORN: *c.335, Neocaesarea, Cappadocia (modern Turkey)*

DIED: *c.395, Nyssa, Cappadocia*

VENERATED BY: *Eastern Orthodox Church, Roman Catholic Church, Oriental Orthodoxy, Anglicanism, Benedictines and Cistercians*

CANONIZED: *Pre-Congregation*

SYMBOLS: *Vested as a bishop*

Where are you pasturing your flock, O good Shepherd, who carry the whole flock on your shoulders? (For the whole of human nature is one sheep and you have lifted it onto your shoulders). Show me the place of peace, lead me to the good grass that will nourish me, call me by name so that I, your sheep, hear your voice, and by your speech give me eternal life. Answer me, you whom my soul love. Amen.

GREGORY OF NYSSA WAS OF PARAMOUNT IMPORTANCE TO THE DEVELOPMENT OF THE DOCTRINES OF THE EARLY CHURCH. HERE, HE IS DEPICTED IN AN 11TH-CENTURY MOSAIC.

Theodosius the Cenobiarch

Born in the same region as the Cappadocian fathers, Theodosius was attracted to the religious life as a boy (when his mother later became a nun, he acted as her spiritual father). He was especially drawn to the promise of the Holy Land. Emulating Abraham, he left his parents and friends behind for the love of God and set out for Jerusalem during the time of the Fourth Ecumenical Council of Chalcedon, in 451. Theodosius, determined to learn discipline before living in solitude, studied under the hermit abbot Longinus near the Tower of David in Jerusalem. He eventually settled in a mountaintop cave, praying at all times, and roping himself upright to prevent sleep. He fasted constantly and did not taste bread for 30 years.

His extreme asceticism gained him many admirers. As a result he formed a small community of monks near Bethlehem that tended to the sick, elderly, and mentally impaired. This is where Cenobiarch comes from, meaning "leader of those with a life in common." The community grew rapidly, attracting a mixture of different nationalities and cultures. It later became the Monastery of St. Theodosius.

PATRON SAINT OF:
File-makers

STATUS: *Monk, hermit, abbot.*

BORN: *c. 423, Cappadocia*

DIED: *c. 529, near Jerusalem*

VENERATED BY: *Roman Catholic Church, Eastern Orthodox Church*

CANONIZED:
Pre-Congregation

With the rivers of your tears, you have made the barren desert fertile. Through sighs of sorrow from deep within you, your labors have borne fruit a hundred-fold. By your miracles you have become a light, shining upon the world. O Theodosius, our Holy Father, pray to Christ our God, to save our souls. Amen.

MOSAIC OF THEODOSIUS THE CENOBIARCH

12

Marguerite Bourgeoys

Born in the Champagne region of France, Marguerite Bourgeoys was the first female saint of Canada. Born into a middle-class but socially connected family, her father was a candlemaker and coiner at the Royal Mint. Although not much interested in a holy life, she attended sodality sponsored by the local monastery of Notre-Dame, studying religion and pedagogy. In 1640, during a procession of Our Lady of the Rosary, she felt the calling to dedicate herself to the service of God. She soon became an advocate of educating children, especially girls.

Considering the European penchant for imperialism—and the more benign desire to bring redemption to those considered pagans—the governor of New France (Canada) sent out a call for teaching missionaries. Marguerite responded, and in 1653 she was sent to the small community of Ville-Marie, where she embraced her new role with devotion and zest. She not only formed bonds with the First Nations, she oversaw the construction of churches and schools, marking the beginning of public schooling in Montreal.

PATRON SAINT OF:
Orphans, those living in poverty, those rejected by religious orders

STATUS: *Missionary, teacher*

BORN: *1620, Troyes, France*

DIED: *1700, Montreal, Canada*

VENERATED BY: *Roman Catholic Church, Anglican Church of Canada*

CANONIZED: *1982*

O Mother Bourgeoys, you, whose compassionate power is ever increasing, show us your way of Truth, Faith and Holiness. Make us humble enough to abandon ourselves to the Will of God, generous enough to find in the Cross the joy of the Loving Giver. May your fidelity to Jesus in the Blessed Sacrament lead us ever nearer to this source of light and peace. May your spirit of openness help us to be concerned for our brothers and sisters throughout the world. Finally, may Our Lady of the Trinity, Father, Son and Holy Spirit, bring us to this unity of eternal grace to which God has called you for all eternity. Amen.

MARGUERITE BOURGEOYS EPITOMIZED THE COMBINATION OF TOUGH-MINDEDNESS AND SANCTITY THAT HAS BEEN THE HALLMARK OF SUCCESSFUL FEMALE MISSIONARIES DOWN THE AGES.

Hilary of Poitiers

Hilary was born to a patrician, pagan family in southwest France. He was educated in Latin and, unusually, Greek, almost exclusively the language of Christian texts. It was his reading of both languages that led to his conversion to Christianity. He was baptized in around 345; eight years later he was made bishop of Poitiers. He is significant as a champion of Nicene Trinitarianism, a doctrine widely accepted in the Eastern Church and making rapid inroads in the West where Arianism was still rife. Trinitarianism held that God the Father, God the Son, and God the Holy Spirit were "eternally co-existent," while Arians contended that Jesus, the son of God, not only had a separate existence, but had been "created" rather than always existing.

Inevitably, the dispute had a political element. In 356, St. Hilary's forceful arguments led to his exile, on the orders of the emperor Constantius II, to Phrygia in Asia Minor. Here, again arguing in favor of Trinitarianism, he wrote *De Trinitate*, one of the earliest Christian texts in Latin.

PATRON SAINT OF:
Lawyers, mothers, children with disabilities, invoked against snakebite

STATUS: *Bishop.*

BORN: *310 AD, Poitiers, France*

DIED: *367 AD, Poitiers, France*

VENERATED BY: *Roman Catholic Church, Eastern Orthodox Church, Anglican Communion, Lutheran Church, Oriental Orthodoxy*

CANONIZED:
Pre-Congregation

SYMBOLS: *Episcopal vestments, a mitre and crozier, and a beard, usually white and often long*

Father, keep us from vain strife of words. Grant to us constant profession of the Truth! Preserve us in a true and undefiled faith so that we may hold fast to that which we professed when we were baptized in the Name of the Father, Son and Holy Spirit, that we may have Thee for our Father, that we may abide in Thy Son and in the fellowship of the Holy Spirit. Through Jesus Christ, Our Lord. Amen.

Kentigern (Mungo)

I n Wales and England, the saint is known by his birth name, Kentigern; the name Mungo was an pet name stemming from the Gaelic words mo cha, or "dear one." The boy was reared by St. Serf, who was converting the Picts; it was he who called him Mungo. At 25, he began his missionary work in Strathclyde, building a church across the water from the site of an extinct volcano, a location that would become modern-day Glasgow. The mission was situated where the current Cathdral stands.

Mungo, whose ministry lasted 13 years, furnished an austere example of holy devotion, living a simple life in a small cell and making many converts. After pressure from an anti-Christian ruler, he relocated to Wales and founded the cathedral at Llanelwy. After a pilgrimage to Rome and evangelising in Galloway, he settled in Glasgow, where a large community formed around him.

PATRON SAINT OF:
Glasgow, Scotland, salmon, those accused of infidelity, invoked against bullies

STATUS: *Missionary, bishop, founder*

BORN: *518, Culross*

DIED: *13 January, 614, Glasgow (Feast day January 14 in Eastern Church)*

VENERATED BY: *Roman Catholic Church, Eastern Orthodox Church, Anglican Communion*

SYMBOLS: *Bishop with a robin on his shoulder; holding a bell and a fish with a ring in its mouth*

O God, who through the Bishop St Kentigern caused the light of the true faith to shine forth in all its splendour by the preaching of the word,grant, we pray, that by loyal adherence to the teaching of him whose venerable feast day we celebrate,we may attain the glory of everlasting light,through Christ our Lord. Amen.

THIS STAINED GLASS DETAIL OF MUNGO IS IN THE PARISH CHURCH OF THE HOLY TRINITY IN STRATFORD-UPON-AVON, ENGLAND.

Paul the Anchorite

K nown also as Paul of Thebes, this saint is said to have been the first Christian hermit. Seer and holy man, his life given over to fasting and prayer, Paul the Hermit exerted a potent influence on later generations. A high-born Christian of Greek-Egyptian heritage, Paul was orphanned at 15, then fled to the desert at age 22 to escape a round of Christian persecutions launched by the emperor Decius. There he remained, gaunt and bearded, living in a cave, clad in rags, until he died at the age of 113. A raven was said to have fed him, bringing him half a loaf of bread a day (a story reminiscent of Elijah in the Old Testament).

The best-known account of Paul's life was written by St. Jerome. It was Jerome who claimed that a later Egyptian monk, Antony of Egypt (Jan. 17), buried Paul with the help of two lions. Paul's retreat to a life of pious contemplation and hardship has also been regarded as a response—or rebuke—to the increasingly comfortable life in the service of God enjoyed by many Christians after Constantine's adoption of Christianity as the official faith of the Roman Empire.

PATRON SAINT OF:
San Pablo City, Philippines

STATUS: *Hermit*

BORN: *227 AD, Egypt*

DIED: *342 AD, Monastery of St. Paul the Anchorite*

VENERATED BY: *Roman Catholic Church, Eastern Orthodox Church, Oriental Orthodoxy, Anglican Communion*

CANONIZED:
Pre-Congregation

SYMBOLS: *Two lions, palm tree, raven*

O God, you called Saint Paul our Father to renounce the honors of this world by fleeing into the desert there to spend the rest of his life in contemplation on your holy name. Through his intercession, may we despise all earthly desires and seek love eternal alone.

We ask this through our Lord Jesus Christ, your Son, who lives and reigns with you and the Holy Spirit, one God, forever and ever. Amen.

SEER AND HOLY MAN, HIS LIFE GIVEN OVER TO FASTING AND PRAYER, PAUL THE HERMIT EXERTED A POTENT INFLUENCE ON LATER GENERATIONS. HE REMAINS THE ARCHETYPAL CHRISTIAN ASCETIC, DEPICTED HERE BY MATTIA PRETI (C.1660).

Berard of Carbio and Companions

Berard of Carbio was a thirteenth-century Franciscan friar executed with his four companions for promoting Christianity in Morocco. Together, they are venerated as the Franciscan protomartyrs, and their shrine is located at Igreja de Santa Cruz, Coimbra, Portugal.

Berard joined the newly formed Franciscan Order in 1213. When St. Francis decided his followers needed to extend their apostolic work, he sent Berard, with monks Peter and Otho, and two lay brothers, Adjustus and Accursius, to Muslim Morocco as missionaries. Only Berard could speak any Arabic. They visited Seville, Spain (still in Moorish hands), en route, but were arrested and expelled. In Morocco, they preached in the streets of Marrakesh, denouncing Muhammad. At first thought simply insane, they were eventually arrested and expelled. After returning and continuing their attempts at converting the Muslims, they were taken before the sultan. He personlly executed them, drawing his scimitar in anger and beheading them when they refused to renounce their own faith.

STATUS: *Martyrs.*

BORN: *Umbria, Italy*

DIED: *January 16, 1220, Morocco*

VENERATED BY: *Roman Catholic Church*

CANONIZED: *1481*

Lord God, You sanctified the beginnings of the Order of Friars Minor by the glorious struggle of Your holy martyrs Berard and companions. As they did not hesitate to give up their lives for You so may we bear staunch witness to You by our lives.

Gracious God, in every age you have sent men and women who have given their lives in witness to your love and truth. Inspire us with the memory of Berard and companions, whose faithfulness led to the way of the cross, and give us courage to bear full witness with our lives to your Son's victory over sin and death, for He lives and reigns with You and the Holy Spirit, one God, now and forever. Amen.

THE MARTYRS OF MARRAKESCH, FRANCISCAN FRIARS

Anthony of Egypt

Known also as Anthony the Great and Anthony of the Desert, he is widely regarded as the father of monasticism, which is why Anthony is sometimes referred to as the "Father of All Monks." He was born in Egypt to a wealthy Greek family, but upon his parents' death in about 270, he sold their estates and gave the proceeds to the poor. He became a hermit, initially under the guidance of an older mentor. Egyptian hermits tended to live in ancient, empty rock-cut tombs, caves, or ruined buildings in the desert. Antony assembled a number of followers and established the first monastery around 306—not a building dedicated to communal living such as those that are familiar today, but a loose community of mystics living in whatever shelter they could find.

The Desert Fathers would undertake manual labor or weave palm baskets to pay for food and clothing, but physical deprivation and relative isolation would often lead to hallucinatory torments. Despite this, Antony lived to a great age. He is invoked to heal skin diseases, and, furthermore, the pain of afflictions like ergotism and shingles was once referred to as St. Anthony's fire.

PATRON SAINT OF:
Basketmakers, gravediggers, hermits, monks, pigs, sufferers from skin disease, epileptics, ergotism, amputees

STATUS: *Abbot*

BORN: *251, near Memphis, Egypt*

DIED: *356, Mt. Kolzim, Egypt*

VENERATED BY: *Roman Catholic Church, Eastern Orthodox Church, Coptic Church*

CANONIZED: *Pre-Congregation*

SYMBOLS: *Tau Cross, pig, bell; often shown being tempted by demons*

Pray for us that we may become worthy to receive the promises of Jesus. Amen.

THE TEMPTATION OF ST. ANTONY WAS A POPULAR SUBJECT IN MEDIEVAL ART. HIERONYMUS BOSCH (C.1453–1516) RETURNED TO THE THEME SEVERAL TIMES: IN THIS RESTRAINED PAINTING THE HERMIT AND HIS PIG ARE SHOWN IN A NOT VERY ISOLATED WILDERNESS.

Margaret of Hungary

PATRON SAINT OF:
Hungary, Budapest

STATUS: *Princess*

BORN: *Januaary 27, 1242, Klis, Croatia*

DIED: *January 18, 1270, Margaret Island, Hungary*

VENERATED BY: *Roman Catholic Church, Dominicans*

CANONIZED: *1943*

SYMBOLS: *Holding a book or a lily, wearing a crown*

O God, the lover and guardian of chastity, by whose gifts Thy handmaid Margaret united the beauty of virginity and the merit of good works, grant we pray, that through the spirit of salutary penance we may be able to recover integrity of soul. Through Christ our Lord. Amen.

When Hungary was liberated from Tatar (Mongol) domination in 1241, King Béla IV and his wife swore that their next daughter would be devoted to God. They kept their promise, and Princess Margaret, their ninth child, was placed in the Dominican convent at Veszprém at the age of three. Six years later she was transferred to the Convent of the Blessed Virgin, built by her parents on Rabbit Island (now Margaret Island) on the Danube River at Buda. She spent the balance of her life there. As a mark of her deep devotion to God, she chastised herself frequently, wearing hairshirts, an iron girdle, and shoes spiked with nails, while performing the most menial tasks. She died at only 28, possibly as a result of her self-imposed deprivations. There were many early attempts to canonize her, but none was effective until 1943. Still, some 27 miracles were attributed to her, including raising people from the dead.

MARGARET, BEING OF ROYAL DESCENT, IS ALWAYS SHOWN WEARING A CROWN.

Wulfstan

Wulfstan was the son of landed gentry, but the family lost their property around the time of King Cnut. After years of study and encouragement from his tutors Wulfstan was ordained a priest in 1038 and joined a Benedictine monstery in Worcester. Due to his piety, chastity, and dedication he was appointed Bishop of Worcester in 1062. This was a time of great turmoil, when the English throne fell to invaders from Normany. Wulstan, a social reformer, struggled to bridge the gap between the old regime of his confidant Harold II, last crowned Anglo-Saxon king, and the harsh Norman regime of William the Conqueror. He was the only English-born bishop to retain his diocese for any significant time after the Conquest. He was also an outspoken critic of the slave trade and helped put an end to it in Bristol. He died after a prolonged illness. At Easter of 1158, King Henry II and his wife, Eleanor of Aquitaine, visited Worcester Cathedral and placed their crowns on Wulfstan's shrine, vowing never to wear them again.

SAINT WULFSTAN, BISHOP OF WORCESTER

PATRON SAINT OF: *Vegetarians, dieters*

STATUS: *Bishop*

BORN: *1008, Warwickshire, England*

DIED: *January 1095*

VENERATED BY: *Roman Catholic Church, Anglican Communion*

CANONIZED: *1203*

SYMBOLS: *Pastoral staff, which he refused to surrender*

Lord God, you raised up Wulfstan to be a bishop among your people and a leader of your Church: Help us, after his example, to live simply, to work diligently, and to make your kingdom known; through Jesus Christ our Lord. Amen.

Sebastian

20

PATRON SAINT OF:
*Archers, soldiers, athletes,
plague victims*

STATUS: *Martyr*

BORN: *c. 265*

DIED: *c. 300*

VENERATED BY: *Roman
Catholic Church, Eastern
Orthodox Church*

CANONIZED:
Pre-Congregation

SYMBOLS: *Portrayed nearly
nude, shot with arrows, or
simply an arrow*

*Glorious Sebastian, martyr and
saint,*

*I call on your strength and
courage to help me through this
difficult trial.*

*Your faith was so deep, a
multitude of arrows could not
finish you.*

*I ask for your intercession that
I may also survive that which
threatens to destroy my beliefs in
the mercy of Christ. Amen.*

Most accounts describe Sebastian as a Gaul (although St. Ambrose says he came from Milan) who volunteered to join the Roman army in around 283. He was promoted to captain in the Praetorian Guard, the imperial bodyguards. When, during the persecutions under the emperor Diocletian, it was discovered that Sebastian had comforted some of the Christian martyrs, was himself a Christian, and had actively converted others, Diocletian condemned him to be shot to death by his fellow archers. He was buried at a cemetery on the Appian Way, and the first church dedicated to him lies nearby.

The reason Sebastian is invariably represented as alive, despite being pierced by innumerable arrows, is simple: the arrows didn't kill him. Left for dead by his executioners, Sebastian was apparently healed by St. Irene, the wife of a fellow martyr, St. Castulus. Unfortunately, Diocletian was not to be denied, and Sebastian was subsequently clubbed to death. Sebastian's fate, and the fact that so little is known about him, indicates that his story is probably an amalgam of several incidents during the persecutions of Diocletian, but his story has become iconic.

THE REPRESENTATION OF SEBASTIAN IS IMMEDIATELY
RECOGNIZABLE; THE AGONY OF HIS ATTEMPTED
EXECUTION, AS A NEARLY NUDE YOUTH, BOUND TO
A TREE OR COLUMN, PIERCED BY ARROWS, BECAME A
POPULAR SUBJECT FOR RENAISSANCE PAINTERS SUCH AS
ANDREA MANTEGNA (C.1430–1506).

Agnes

The story of Agnes is simple: while little more than a girl, this beautiful daughter of a noble Roman refused marriage with the son of Prefect Sempronius due to her dedication to Christ. As this occurred during the Diocletian persecutions, she was sentenced to death, but was first dragged through the streets to a brothel to be defiled before her execution. When she was stripped, her hair miraculously grew to hide her nakedness, and those who assaulted her were struck blind. Her accuser, the prefect's son also fell dead, but he revived when she prayed for him. As a result she was released to face trial and was again found guilty. Tied to a stake, the wood would not burn, so she was stabbed in the neck and finally died. Her martyrdom occurred in the public Circus of Domitian, the modern-day site of the popular Piazza Navona in Rome.

She remains one of the best known of the early Roman martyrs, and is particularly popular in the Spanish-speaking world, where she is called Inés.

PATRON SAINT OF: *Gardeners, crops, young girls, the betrothed, rape victims, chastity*

STATUS: *Virgin, martyr.*

BORN: *c. 291 AD, Rome, Italy*

DIED: *c. 304, Rome, Italy*

VENERATED BY: *Roman Catholic Church, Eastern Orthodox Church, Anglican Communion, Lutheranism*

CANONIZED: *Pre-Congregation*

SYMBOLS: *Book, martyr's palm, lamb (due to the similarity of her name to agnus, Latin for lamb, although her name derives from the Greek term hagne, meaning chaste or pure)*

GRUESOME RECONSTRUCTIONS OF THE FATES OF MANY EARLY CHRISTIAN MARTYRS WERE DWELT UPON BY CATHOLIC ARTISTS FROM THE RENAISSANCE ONWARDS.

O glorious St. Agnes,

You served God in humility and confidence on earth and are now in the enjoyment of His beatific Vision in heaven because you persevered till death and gained the crown of eternal life.

Remember now the dangers that surround me in the vale of tears, and intercede for me in my needs and troubles.

Amen.

Vincent of Saragossa

Vincent, a protomartyr of Spain, spent much of his life in Saragossa, under the tutelage of Bishop Valerius, who also ordained him. Because Valerius had a speech impediment, Vincent often spoke for him. Vincent was appointed deacon of the city but, like St. Lawrence (Aug. 10), was arrested in Valencia, along with Valerius, during the persecutions of Diocletian in 304. He managed to convert his jailer, but when asked to throw the Scriptures into a fire, he refused, and was then roasted on a gridiron (again like St. Lawrence). Before Vincent was buried in Valencia, ravens apparently guarded his body.

His remains were later transported by sea to what is now Cape St. Vincent in Portugal, and they were transferred to Lisbon in 1173.

PATRON SAINT OF:
Vine growers (because he offers protection from frosts, common in January), wine and vinegar merchants, violations, abortions, Portugal, Lisbon, Valencia

STATUS: *Deacon, martyr*

BORN: *3rd century, Huesca, Spain*

DIED: *304, Valencia, Spain*

VENERATED BY: *Roman Catholic Church, Eastern Orthodox Church, Church of England*

SYMBOLS: *Gridiron/ griddle, ravens*

Almighty God, whose deacon Vincent, upheld by thee, was not Terrified by threats nor overcome by torments: Strengthen us, we beseech thee, to endure all adversity with invincible and steadfast faith; through Jesus Christ our Lord, who liveth and reigneth with thee and the Holy Spirit, one God, for ever and ever. Amen.

A 16TH-CENTURY IMAGE OF VINCENT .

Marianne Cope

Christened Maria Anna Barbara Koob in Hesse, Germany, Marianne Cope's family emigrated to the United States when she was three, and settled in Utica, New York. After working as a factory hand, she entered the Sister Order of St. Francis as a tertiary. She taught German immigrants for a decade, then became involved with hospital work in Syracuse, New York.

In 1883, responding to a call for help from King David Kalakaua, she and six other nuns traveled to Honolulu to care for sufferers from leprosy (Hansen's Disease). She initially worked in a hospital on Oahu, but in 1888 moved to the leper colony at Kalaupapa, where she cared for the victims and their families with Father Damien of Molokai (May 10). When he died she took over control of the colony. Several miraculous cures from the disease have been attributed to her.

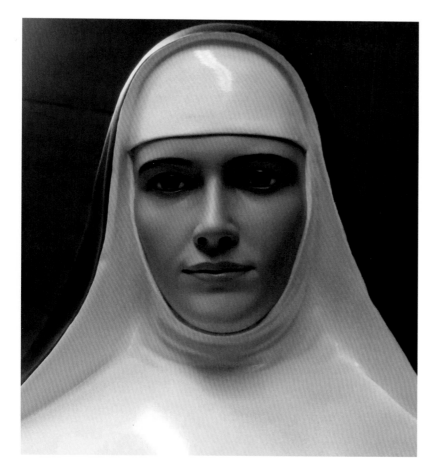

PATRON SAINT OF: *Leprosy sufferers, HIV/AIDS sufferers, outcasts, Hawaii*

STATUS: *Nun, missionary*

BORN: *1838, Heppenheim, Germany*

DIED: *1918, Kalaupapa, Hawaii*

CANONIZED: *2005*

VENERATED BY: *Roman Catholic Church, Hawaii*

All glory and praise be to you, Lord God almighty!

St. Marianne led a group of sisters/nurses to the Hawaiian Islands to care for the poor suffering souls afflicted with Hansen's disease (leprosy). In imitation of St. Marianne's self-sacrificing spirit, I ask for the grace to be more truly concerned with the welfare of others.

Through the intercession of St. Marianne, I ask that the petition of this Novena be granted in the name of Christ, our Lord. Amen.

Francis de Sales

Having studied in Paris, de Sales became a Doctor of Law at Padua, and was destined for a glittering diplomatic career. Instead, in 1593 he insisted on becoming ordained. His first task was hazardous: to convert the Calvinists of his native Chablais country in Savoy. He largely succeeded, becoming Bishop of Geneva in 1602. He was famed for the skill, gentleness, and persuasiveness of his preaching. He was an excellent administrator and writer; his Treatise on *The Love of God* and the *Introduction to the Devout Life* (for lay readers) were widely translated and remain in print today. He wrote many informal tracts. De Sales became friendly with Jane Frances de Chantal (Aug. 12), and helped her found the Order of the Visitation in 1610. His insistence that the devout life should be integrated with everyday life, and should be accessible to all, led to several congregations being established under his patronage, notably the Oblates of St. Francis de Sales and the Salesians of John Bosco.

PATRON SAINT OF:
Journalists, the deaf

STATUS: *Bishop, Doctor of the Church*

BORN: *1567, Annecy, France*

DIED: *622, Lyon, France*

VENERATED BY: *Roman Catholic Church*

CANONIZED: *1665*

SYMBOLS: *Represented as balding and bearded in bishop's robes, appears on the coat of arms of the Salesian Society*

My God, I give you this day. I offer you, now, all of the good that I shall do and I promise to accept, for love of you, all of the difficulty that I shall meet.

Help me to conduct myself during this day in a manner pleasing to you. Amen.

Dwynwen of Wales

Dwynwen was possibly a daughter of 5th century Welsh King Brychan Brycheiniog. She lived in Anglesey, and her name is still recalled in place names such as Ynys Llanddwyn and Porthddwyn in Wales and the church of Sen Adhwynn in Advent, Cornwall. The legend recounts that she fell in love with a young man name Maelon, who rejected her advances. She prayed to forget him and an angel gave her a potion for Maelon that turned him to ice. She then prayed for three things: that Maelon be thawed, that God protect all true lovers, and that she remain unmarried. All her requests were granted, and she became the patron saint of lovers, similar to St. Valentine. Afterward, she retreated to the the solitude of Ynys Llanddwyn off the west coast of Anglesey to become a hermit until she died, in about AD 460. St. Dwynwen's Church on Ynys Llanddwyn became an important shrine during the Middle Ages, and she is still venerated throughout Wales and Cornwall.

PATRON SAINT OF: *Lovers, sick animals*

STATUS: *Princess*

BORN: *c. 5th century*

DIED: *c. 5th century*

VENERATED BY: *Roman Catholic Church, Eastern Orthodox Church, Anglican Communion*

SYMBOLS: *Depicted as a young woman with long hair holding a miniature church*

Oh Blessed St. Dwynwen, you who knew pain and peace, division and reconciliation. You have promised to aid lovers and you watch over those whose hearts have been broken. As you received three boons from an Angel, intercede for me to receive 3 blessings to obtain my heart's desire, and if that is not God's will, a speedy healing from my pain; your guidance and assistance that I may find love with the right person, at the right time, and in a right way; and an unshakeable faith in the boundless kindness and wisdom of God and this I ask in the name of Jesus Christ our Lord. Amen.

Timothy and Titus

Noted as companions of St. Paul, very little is known about these two early bishops. They emerge as recipients of letters from Paul in the New Testament. Timothy was born at Lystra in Asia Minor, and like Paul was of Greco-Jewish parentage. He met Paul on the latter's second missionary journey, and accompanied him to its conclusion and also traveled with Paul on his third missionary journey. Paul tasked him with encouraging Greek Christian communities in Thessalonica, Corinth, and Philippi; he is often cited as the first bishop of Ephesus. A 4th-century account has him stoned to death by worshippers of Artemis for objecting to one of their festivals.

Titus was a Greek, probably born at Antioch, and he traveled with Paul and Barnabas (June 11) to Jerusalem to discuss with Peter (June 29) whether Gentile converts to Christianity should be circumcised. He then accompanied Paul to Ephesus, and interceded in Paul's dispute with the Christians of Corinth. Paul instructed him to organize Christian communities in Crete; Titus is regarded as the first bishop of Gortyna in Crete.

PATRON SAINTS OF:
Stomach disorders

STATUS: *Bishops (Timothy also a Martyr)*

BORN: *1st century AD*

DIED: *1st century AD (Timothy c. ad 97)*

VENERATED BY: *Roman Catholic Church, US Evangelical Lutheran Church*

CANONIZED:
Pre-Congregation

SYMBOLS: *Usually shown with miters, Timothy's crest reflects his death, showing rocks and a club*

God our Father,

You gave Your saints Timothy and Titus the courage and wisdom of the apostles:

may their prayers help us to live holy lives and lead us to heaven, our true home.

Through our Lord Jesus Christ, Your Son, who lives and reigns with you in the unity of the Holy Spirit, one God, for ever and ever.

Amen.

Angela Merici

Orphaned when they were young, Angela and her sister moved to Brescia. After her sister's death, Angela entered the Tertiary Franciscan Order, and became devoted to educating poor girls in the Christian tradition. Legend tells of her journeying to the Holy Land around 1524, losing her sight in Crete on the way, but regaining it at the same place upon her return. In 1535, having selected 12 other nuns, she established a house in Brescia under the patronage of St. Ursula (Oct. 21). The Ursulines wore lay clothing and continued Angela's work in educating girls and tending the poor. She was buried in the church of St. Afra, Brescia, which was destroyed by Allied bombing in WWII, but has now been restored as the Merician Centre.

PATRON SAINT OF: *Orphans, the handicapped, sickness*

STATUS: *Virgin, founder.*

BORN: *c.1470, Desenzano del Garda (then in the Republic of Venice), near Brescia, Italy*

DIED: *1540, Brescia, Italy*

VENERATED BY: *Roman Catholic Church*

CANONIZED: *1807*

SYMBOLS: *Cloak, ladder*

Give us the spirit and mind of Angela, that we may make a Gospel mark on our world as she did on hers. Like our spiritual guide and mother, may we do justice, love tenderly, and walk humbly with you all the days of our lives. Amen.

ST. ANGELA MERICI TEACHING BY PIETRO CALZAVACCA (MID 19TH-CENTURY)

Thomas Aquinas

The importance of Thomas Aquinas as a communicator and sharer of ideas cannot be overestimated. Principally known as a theologian, writer, and teacher, his great work, *Summa Theologica* (1268–1273) appraised the writings of many previous theologians and philosophers. It also offered an agenda for the Catholic Church at a time of considerable doctrinal and political instability.

Aquinas was educated at the Benedictine monastery of Monte Cassino, then at Naples University. Despite his noble family's opposition, he entered the Dominican Order of the Preachers in 1244. He continued his studies in Paris and Cologne, under Albertus Magnus. Between 1259 and 1268 he taught, studied, and wrote variously at Naples, Orvieto, Viterbo, and Rome, returning in his later years to Paris and Naples. His *Summa contra Gentiles*, a discussion of how Christianity might be argued to pagans, became a key text centuries later when overseas Christian missions began in earnest. His sheer output of writing was enormous (*Summa Theologica* was translated into English in 22 volumes), but in 1273 he suddenly stopped writing—possibly due to illness.

PATRON SAINT OF:
Catholic universities

STATUS: *Priest, Doctor of the Church*

BORN: *c.1225, Aquino, near Naples, Italy*

DIED: *1274, Fossanova, Terracina, Italy*

VENERATED BY: *Roman Catholic Church*

CANONIZED: *1323*

SYMBOLS: *Arms show the "Sun in Splendor" combined with the "All-Seeing Eye" referring directly to God*

Come, Holy Spirit, Divine Creator, true source of light and fountain of wisdom! Pour forth your brilliance upon my dense intellect, dissipate the darkness which covers me, that of sin and of ignorance. Grant me a penetrating mind to understand, a retentive memory, method and ease in learning, the lucidity to comprehend, and abundant grace in expressing myself. Amen.

Brother Juniper

The Servant of God, Brother Juniper, called "the renowned jester of the Lord," was one of the original followers of St. Francis of Assisi. In 1210, he was received into the Order of Friars Minor by St. Francis himself. "Would to God, my brothers, that I had a whole forest of such Junipers," Saint Francis would joke.

Several stories in the *Little Flowers of St. Francis* illustrate his generosity and simplicity. Once, when visiting a sick man, Juniper offered to perform any service. The man said he longed for a meal of pig's feet, and so Juniper found a pig in a field, cut off a foot, and cooked it for the man. When the pig's owner found out, he abused the Franciscans, calling them thieves and refusing repayment. St. Francis ordered Juniper to apologize. Juniper went to the farmer and cheerfully retold the tale. When the man reacted with anger, a confused Juniper simply repeated the story with great zeal, embraced him, and begged the man to donate the rest of the pig for the poor. At this display the owner's heart was changed. Juniper was also known for giving away his clothing—or that of other friars—to the half-naked people he met on the road.

STATUS: *Friar*

BORN: *Before 1210*

DIED: *January 29, 1258*

VENERATED BY: *Roman Catholic Church*

Brother Juniper, we can learn much from your lavish generosity and your humbleness of heart. Pray that we may be inspired to give until it hurts, to put others needs above our own, and to love God with our whole heart and soul. Amen.

SERVANT OF GOD BROTHER JUNIPER AND THE BEGGAR

Blessed Mary Angela Truszkowska

S ophia contracted tuberculosis at 16 and was sent to Switzerland to restore her health. Once recovered, Sophia joined the Society of St. Vincent de Paul and began ministering to the abandoned children and homeless of Warsaw, even opening a shelter. Eventually she joined the secular Third Order of St. Francis, taking the name Angela. In 1855 she rented a small house for the orphaned girls and elderly women.

On November 21, 1855, Angela and her cousin Clothilde Ciechanowska solemnly dedicated themselves to do the will of Christ while praying before Our Lady of Czestochowa. Thus, they founded the "Congregation of the Sisters of St. Felix of Cantalice." Sophia took the name Mary Angela. In Warsaw, the Sisters were often called the "Felicians," the name still used today. Mother Angela was scarcely 44 when she withdrew from active leadership due to increasing deafness. Yet she saw the order grow and expand, including missions to the United States among the sons and daughters of Polish immigrants.

STATUS: *Founder.*

BORN: *May 16, 1825, Kaliz, Poland*

DIED: *October 10, 1899, Krakov, Kingdom of Galicia and Lodomeria*

VENERATED BY: *Roman Catholic Church*

CANONIZED: *1993*

God our Father,

we praise and thank you for the gift of Blessed Mary Angela, who lived your will in faith and trust, and lived your love in service to others.

I pray, in confidence, that through her intercession you will grant me the favor which I request.

I ask this through Christ our Lord. Amen.

John Bosco

J ohn "Don" Bosco was the youngest of three brothers raised in poverty. He lost his farmhand father at age two, but his mother played a strong role in his upbringing and supported his ideals.

Bosco practiced juggling and worked at various crafts to fund his studies. He was ordained in 1841 and devoted himself to the young and poor. Bosco established the Society of St. Francis de Sales in 1859, and set up artisanal workshops to educate impoverished boys, teaching them bookbinding, printing, shoemaking, ironworking, and tailoring. The Salesian Teaching Order was formally approved in 1874 and soon spread around the world. The first mission was to Argentina in 1875, where Salesians evangelized the Patagonian Indians.

Don Bosco, Torino, 1880

PATRON SAINT OF: *Catholic publishers and editors, Catholic schools, schoolchildren, apprentices, laborers*

STATUS: *Priest, educator, founder.*

BORN: *August 16, 1815, Becchi, near Castelnuovo, Italy*

DIED: *January 31, 1888, Turin, Italy*

VENERATED BY: *Roman Catholic Church, Anglican Communion*

CANONIZED: *1934*

O glorious Saint John Bosco, who in order to lead young people to the feet of the divine Master and to mould them in the light of faith and Christian morality didst heroically sacrifice thyself to the very end of thy life and didst set up a proper religious Institute destined to endure and to bring to the farthest boundaries of the earth thy glorious work, obtain also for us from Our Lord a holy love for young people who are exposed to so many seductions in order that we may generously spend ourselves in supporting them against the snares of the devil, in keeping them safe from the dangers of the world, and in guiding them, pure and holy, in the path that leads to God. Amen.

FEBRUARY

The second month of the year, and one of the coldest in northern climes, February is traditionally associated with purification. February 2 is Candlemas, celebrated as a day of renewal, hope, and purification. This is when, tradition has it, if the weather is fair and frosty, severe wintry conditions are yet to come before spring. A high point in the month occurs on February 14, when Saint Valentine's Day is almost universally recognized as a day celebrating love and romance.

Shrove Tuesday, the day before Ash Wednesday, which inaugurates the 40-day pre-Easter Lenten fast, also frequently falls in February. The day is one of confession and atonement, the word "shrove" deriving from the act of shrivening—the absolution of sin. In much of the Christian world this is celebrated as Mardi Gras, Carnival, or "Fat Tuesday," a joyous festival often including parades and masked dancing and a final gustatory indulgence before the deprivations of Holy Month.

CARNIVAL OR THE MINUET BY THE VENETIAN PAINTER TIEPOLO (1727–1804) WONDERFULLY CAPTURES THE SPIRIT OF RELEASE, LIVELINESS, AND FRIVOLITY ASSOCIATED WITH THE MOMENT OF ABSOLUTION FROM SIN ON SHROVE TUESDAY.

Brigid of Kildare

With St. Patrick (March 17) and St. Columba (June 9), Brigid is one of three patron saints of Ireland. It is possible she was a pagan goddess rather than a Christian saint; her life overlaps closely with a number of pagan traditions from Ireland's Druidic past. Her feast day was an important pagan celebration, Imbolc, which heralded the coming of spring.

Brigid is said to have been the illegitimate daughter of a pagan chief called Dubhthach, her mother one of his slaves. She was known for her sweet disposition and piety, inspired in part by having heard the elderly St. Patrick preach. She became a nun and set about founding a series of convents, the most celebrated, founded perhaps in 470, was at what became Kildare, or Cill-Dara — "the church of the oak." The land on which the convent was built was given to her by the King of Leinster, who told Brigid she could have as much land as her cloak would cover. Once placed on the ground, the cloak miraculously grew to a vast size.

PATRON SAINT OF:
Ireland, County Kildare, babies, blacksmith, boatmen, illegitimate children, dairy workers, poets, printing presses, travelers

STATUS: *Virgin, abbess*

BORN: *c. 451, County Louth, Ireland*

DIED: *c.525, Kildare, Ireland*

VENERATED BY: *Roman Catholic Church, Eastern Orthodox Church, Anglican Communion*

CANONIZED:
Pre-Congregation

SYMBOLS: *Abbess with staff; lamp or candle flame over her head a white Carthusian habit*

O Jesus! Inexhaustible Fountain of compassion, Who by a profound gesture of Love, said from the Cross: "I thirst!" suffered from the thirst for the salvation of the human race. I beg of Thee O my Savior, to inflame in our hearts the desire to tend toward perfection in all our acts; and to extinguish in us the concupiscence of the flesh and the ardor of worldly desires. Amen.

SAINT BRIGID AS DEPICTED IN SAINT NON'S CHAPEL, ST DAVIDS, WALES.

Joan de Lestonnac

PATRON SAINT OF:
Abuse victims, people rejected by religious orders, widows

STATUS: *Foundress*

BORN: *December 27, 1556, Bordeaux, France*

DIED: *February 2, 1640, Bordeaux, France*

VENERATED BY: *Roman Catholic Church, Sisters of the Company of Mary*

CANONIZED: *1949*

Dear God, when life is not going my way, I want other people to make it right again. I sometimes choose to shower my unhappiness on whomever I meet. Help me to concentrate on your blessings this day so that I can be an inspiration to others and reflect my faith in you. Amen.

St. Joan de Lestonnac, niece of the French essayist Montaigne, was born in Bordeaux, France, in 1556. She was happily married at age seventeen and birthed four children, but her husband died suddenly in 1597. After her children were raised, she entered the Cistercian monastery at Toulouse. She was forced to leave the Cistertians when she developed health problems. She returned to Bordeaux with the idea of forming a new congregation, and several young girls joined her as novices. They ministered to victims of a plague that struck the region, and were determined to counteract the evils of heresy promulgated by Calvinism. Thus was formed the Congregation of the Religious of Notre Dame of Bordeaux. In 1608, Joan and her companions received the religious habit from the Archbishop of Bordeaux. Joan was elected superior in 1610, and many miracles occurred at her tomb.

Ansgar (Anskar, Oscar)

The son of a noble Frankish family, Ansgar was called the "Apostle of the North." He became an important figure in the expansion of Christianity from the 8th century onward to those parts of northern and central Europe that lay beyond the Roman Empire's former frontiers. After Charlemagne's brutal conquest of Saxony, extensive efforts were made by clergy to convert the lands farther north and east. As early as 820, Ansgar was sent to Jutland (modern Denmark). In 822, he helped establish a monastery at Corvey in Westphalia. In 829, he ventured to Birka in Sweden, where he built the country's first church. In 831, he was appointed archbishop of Hamburg, and oversaw all further missionary work in Denmark. Following a devastating Danish raid on Hamburg in 845, Ansgar was made bishop of Bremen, from where he continued his fearless missionary work until his death. Throughout his life he experienced a series of visions urging him, as he believed, to ensure that "salvation reached the ends of the earth."

PATRON SAINT OF: *Denmark; a crater on the Moon, Ansgarius, named after him*

STATUS: *Evangelist, bishop*

BORN: *September 8, 801, Picardy, France*

DIED: *February 3, 865, Bremen, Germany*

VENERATED BY: *Roman Catholic Church, Eastern Orthodox Church, Anglican Communion, Lutheranism*

CANONIZED: *Pre-Congregation*

SYMBOLS: *Bishop's miter and attire; carrying a model church*

God, You willed to send St. Ansgar to enlighten many peoples. Through his intercession, grant that we may walk in the light of Your truth. Amen.

THE 19TH-CENTURY STATUE OF ANSGAR IN HAMBURG, GERMANY.

Gilbert of Sempringham

The son of a minor Norman magnate, Gilbert became noted for his austerity and charitable works. As a youth, he was sent to Paris to study theology. (It is possible some sort of physical deformity kept him from becoming a knight, the normal goal of a noble son.) On his father's death in 1130, Gilbert used his inheritance to organize the Gilbertine Order, the only native monastic community established in England in the Middle Ages. It was unusual, too, in accepting both men and women. By the time of Gilbert's death at the improbably old age of 105, there were 13 foundations. Gilbert fell out of favor with the king, Henry II, for his supposed support of Thomas Becket (Dec. 29), but was eventually acquitted. In his old age, Gilbert also had to confront a revolt by lay brothers of the order, who complained of being overworked and underfed. By the time of its dissolution by Henry VIII, the order comprised 26 monasteries.

STATUS: *Founder*

BORN: *c.1083, Lincolnshire, England*

DIED: *1189, Lincolnshire, England*

VENERATED BY: *Roman Catholic Church, Church of England*

CANONIZED: *1202*

St. Gilbert, you started a custom within the Gilbertines called the plate of the Lord Jesus, where the best food was given to the poor and the religious ate the leftovers. This reflected your radical spirituality— you gave everything you could to the poor and kept back little for yourself. Pray that we may be inspired to be as generous not only with our material things, but with ourselves as well. Pray that we may share all of ourselves with those around us, serving them as we would serve Christ Himself. Commend us to God this day and for the rest of our lives. Amen.

Agatha

While the circumstances of her life remain almost entirely obscure, Agatha was one of the most venerated of the early Christian martyrs, the object of a cult that by the 6th century had become widespread.

According to legend, she was born to a noble family and dedicated herself to God from a young age, rejecting all men. Her persecution took place during the reign of Emperor Decius (250–253). A Roman magistrate, Quintianus, furious at having his advances spurned by the young and beautiful Agatha, first forced her to work in a brothel, then had her tortured, variously rolling her over live coals—in the process setting off an earthquake—and ordering that her breasts be hacked off with pincers. St. Peter himself is said to have healed her wounds in her cell. She died in prison and is buried at the Badia di Sant'Agata, Catania.

PATRON SAINT OF:
Sicily, Catania, nurses, firefighters, bakers; sufferers from breast cancer

STATUS: *Virgin, martyr*

BORN: *c. 231, Catania, Sicily*

DIED: *c. 251, Catania, Sicily*

VENERATED BY: *Roman Catholic Church, Eastern Orthodox Church*

CANONIZED:
Pre-Congregation

SYMBOLS: *Disembodied breasts, shears, tongs, loaves of bread.*

O Heavenly Father, who raised Agatha to the dignity of Sainthood, we implore Your Divine Majesty by her intercession to give us health of mind, body and soul. Free us from all those things which hold us bound to this earth, and let our spirit, like hers, rise to your heavenly courts. Amen.

AGATHA WAS FREQUENTLY DEPICTED WITH HER SUNDERED BREASTS ON A TRAY. THEIR RESEMBLANCE TO TWO LOAVES MAY BE WHY SHE IS ALSO THE PATRON SAINT OF BAKERS. THIS HEROIC IMAGE WAS PAINTED AROUND 1756 BY GIOVANNI BATTISTA TIEPOLO.

PATRON SAINT OF:
Japan

STATUS: *Martyr*

BORN: *c. 1562, Settsu
County, Japan*

DIED: *1597, Nagasaki,
Japan*

VENERATED BY: *Roman
Catholic Church*

CANONIZED: *1862*

SYMBOLS: *Palm, cross, spear*

God our Father,

*Source of strength for all your
saints, you led Paul Miki and his
companions through the suffering
of the cross to the joy of eternal life.*

*May their prayers give us courage
to be loyal until death in professing
our faith.*

*Through Jesus Christ, your Son,
who lives and reigns with you in the
unity of the Holy Spirit, one God,
for ever and ever.*

Amen.

Paul Miki and Companions

In 1549, seven years after the first Europeans had reached Japan, the Jesuit priest St. Francis Xavier (Dec. 3) led a mission to the country. The Japanese authorities were warily welcoming, seeing contact with the West as a means of increasing trade. As a result, a number of small Christian communities were founded. In time, other missionaries arrived. Paul Miki, the son of a high-ranking Japanese soldier, was among their converts and in 1582 entered the Jesuit seminary in Azuchi. He would emerge as a forceful and energetic preacher.

When the country's ruler, Toyotomi Hideyoshi, became convinced that the West intended to colonize Japan by exploiting Christianity as a means of infiltration, attitudes toward the missionaries hardened. In 1587, he outlawed the religion. In December 1596, Miki and six Franciscan missionaries, seventeen Japanese laymen, and two other Japanese Jesuits were arrested in Osaka and condemned to be crucified in Nagasaki.

They were crucified on February 5 on a hill overlooking the city, strapped to the crosses with ropes and chains, and then speared to death. The martyrs were defiant to the last. They chanted the "Te Deum" as they were led to their deaths. Paul Miki continued to preach to the assembled crowds even from his cross.

THE 26 MARTYRS OF NAGASAKI INCLUDED A NOTABLE FRANCISCAN MISSIONARY, PETER BAPTIST,
SHOWN AT THE CENTER OF THIS PAINTING OF THE EVENT.

Colette

Nicole Boilet was the daughter of a carpenter and his wife, who both prayed incessantly to St. Nicholas for a child. Her mother was 60 when she bore a daughter. Colette, who was a pious child who took pleasure in prayer, combined the worldly and the unworldly in unusual ways. Her chief claim to fame was as the founder of the Colettine Poor Clares, an order of nuns that attempted to restore the austerity of the original order of the Poor Clares, founded in 1212 by Saints Clare and Francis of Assisi. That she was imbued with a deep spirituality is clear. At only 21, having become a Franciscan tertiary, she became a hermit. It was then that she had a vision in which St. Francis instructed her to reform the Poor Clares. To do this, in 1406 she walked to Nice to petition the schismatic French pope, Benedict XIII, to support her. She founded 17 convents, the nuns enjoined to practice not merely "extreme poverty" but "perpetual fast and abstinence."

PATRON SAINT OF: *Women seeking to conceive, expectant mothers, sick children*

STATUS: *Virgin, foundress*

BORN: *January 13, 1381, Corbie, France*

DIED: *March 6, 1447, Ghent, Belgium*

VENERATED BY: *Roman Catholic Church, Franciscans*

CANONIZED: *1807*

O Blessed Jesus,

I dedicate myself to You in health, in illness, in my life, in my death, in all my desires, in all my deeds. So that,

I may never work henceforth except for Your glory, for the salvation of souls, and for that which You have chosen me.

From this moment on, dearest Lord, there is nothing which I am not prepared to undertake for love of You. Amen.

SAINT COLETTE (C. 1520), BY THE MASTER OF LOURINHÃ (NATIONAL MUSEUM OF ANCIENT ART, LISBON, PORTUGAL).

Josephine Bakhita

PATRON SAINT OF:
South Sudan; victims of human trafficking and slavery

STATUS: *Nun*

BORN: *1869, Darfur, Sudan*

DIED: *1947, Schio, Italy*

VENERATED BY: *Roman Catholic Church*

CANONIZED: *2000*

Saint Josephine Bakhita, as a child, you were sold as a slave and had to endure untold difficulties and suffering.

Once freed from your physical slavery, you found the true redemption in your encounter with Christ and his Church.

Oh, St. Bakhita, help those who are trapped in slavery; intercede on their behalf before God so that they are freed from the chains of captivity.

May God free anyone who has been enslaved by man.

Provide relief to those who survive slavery and allow them to see Him as a model of faith and hope.

Help all survivors to find healing for their wounds.

We beg you to pray and intercede for those who are enslaved among us.

Amen.

From around the age of seven, Sudanese Josephine Bakhita was kidnapped and sold into slavery. She suffered years of abuse and torture with multiple owners—one of them, an Ottoman soldier, had 60 separate patterns cut into her torso. Eventually she was given the name Bakhita, which meant "lucky."

In 1883, she was sold to an Italian diplomat, Callisto Legnani. Two years later he and his family returned to Italy, taking Bakhita with them. There she became nanny to Mimmina, daughter of the Michielis family. Around 1888, Bakhita and Mimmina were left in the care of the Daughters of Charity, in Venice, while the Michielis family traveled. In 1890, Bakhita was baptized into the Catholic Church—and was received by them as a nun in 1896. In 1902, the order sent her to Schio, north of Venice, where her humility, her willingness to please, and her extreme devotion were widely recognized. Soon her fame spread across Italy and she was called "La Nostra Madre Moretta" or "Our Little Brown Mother." During her final years, Josephine was severely ill. She retained her demure cheerfulness to the end, however, content to act "as the Master [God] desires." There were calls for her canonization almost from the moment of her death.

AS BEFITS THE MODESTY THAT WAS SO STRIKING A PART OF HER LIFE AT SCHIO, THERE ARE FEW IMAGES OF ST. JOSEPHINE BAKHITA. THIS IS THE BEST KNOWN.

Apollonia

Though little is known about her life, the circumstances of Apollonia's martyrdom are well documented for an early Christian saint. Described as parthénos presbytis, by Dionysus, Bishop of Alexandra, she was possibly a deaconess and therefore held in great esteem. She died during a series of riots in Alexandria that turned into an anti-Christian massacre. Along with other suspected Christians, Apollonia was seized by a group of men and her teeth were knocked out after she suffered a number of blows to her face. The rioters then threatened to burn her alive if she would not renounce Christianity. In response she flung herself into the flames. Given that she died of her own volition, concerns remained that she had committed suicide—considered a mortal sin by the Church—rather than suffering martyrdom. The matter was decisively settled in Apollonia's favor by St. Augustine of Hippo (Aug. 28) in the 5th century. It was pointed out that many female martyrs had chosen death over the renunciation of their faith or to preserve their chastity.

PATRON SAINT OF: *Dentists; sufferers from toothache; Elst, Belgium*

STATUS: *Virgin, martyr*

BORN: *c. 200*

DIED: *c. 249, Alexandria, Egypt*

VENERATED BY: *Roman Catholic Church, Church of England, Eastern Orthodox and Coptic churches*

CANONIZED: *Pre-Congregation*

SYMBOLS: *Tongs for pulling teeth, cross, martyr's palm*

O Glorious Apollonia, patron saint of dentistry and refuge to all those suffering from diseases of the teeth, I consecrate myself to thee, beseeching thee to number me among thy clients.

Assist me by your intercession with God in my daily work and intercede with Him to obtain for me a happy death. Pray that my heart like thine may be inflamed with the love of Jesus and Mary, through Christ our Lord. Amen.

O My God, bring me safe through temptation and strengthen me as thou didst our own patron Apollonia, through Christ our Lord. Amen.

THIS PORTRAIT OF SAINT APOLLONIA, SEEN HERE BEARING THE MARTYR'S PALM, WAS PAINTED BY FRANCISCO DE ZURBARÁN AND HANGS IN THE LOUVRE MUSEUM.

Scholastica

Scholastica was born in Umbria of wealthy parents, and while it was known that she was St. Benedict's sister, a later tradition claims she was his twin. Pious from a young age, she and her brother were raised together until he left to pursue studies in Rome.

Once a year she visited her brother close by his abbey, and they would spend the day worshiping together. One time, as she felt her death approaching, she entreated him to remain with her. When Benedict insisted on leaving, Scholastica prayed . . . and a wild storm blew in, forcing him to stay. "What have you done?" he cried. "I asked you and you would not listen, so I asked God and He did listen." Three days later Benedict saw her soul leave the earth and ascend to heaven. He had her body laid in the tomb he had prepared for himself.

PATRON SAINT OF:
Benedictine women's communities, school, books, convulsive children, invoked against storms

STATUS: *Virgin, sister of St. Benedict*

BORN: *c. 480, Nursia, Umbria, Italy*

DIED: *February 10, 543, near Monte Cassino, Italy*

VENERATED BY: *Catholic Church, Eastern Orthodox Church, Anglican Communion*

CANONIZED:
Pre-Congregation by St. Peter II

St. Scholastica, after you died, your brother saw your soul fly to God in the form of a dove. Pray that after our own deaths, we may rise as swiftly to God as you did, without languishing in Purgatory. Pray that we may give all of our hearts to God, so that He may be first and foremost in our lives. Lastly, pray that we may discern His will for our lives, so that we may complete the unique mission ordained for us on earth and serve our fellow brothers and sisters with great joy. Amen.

Blaise of Sebasate

One of the Fourteen Holy Helpers, St. Blaise was an early Christian martyr and one of the most popular medieval saints. Blaise was likely of noble birth and, after being educated in the Christian faith, was made bishop of Sebastia, Armenia. Although Christianity had been adopted as the state religion around 300 AD, Roman emperor Licinius began a persecution, and Blaise was discovered and apprehended. While imprisoned, he miraculously cured a boy from fatally choking. After being torn apart with wool combers' irons, Blaise was beheaded.

Subsequent legends claim that before Blaise became a bishop he was a physician possessed of wonderful healing power who performed numerous miracles, including the cure of diseased beasts. This accounts for his being the patron saint of wild animals. He was also venerated as the patron of sufferers from throat diseases. Blaise's cult spread throughout Christendom from the 8th century, and many churches, such as that in Dubrovnik, Croatia, are dedicated to him.

PATRON SAINT OF:
Sicily, Dubrovnik, veterinarians, wool combers, sufferers of throat disease

STATUS: *Bishop, martyr*

BORN: *c. late 200s, Sivas, Turkey*

DIED: *316 AD, Sivas, Turkey*

VENERATED BY: *Roman Catholic Church, Eastern Orthodox Church*

CANONIZED: *Pre-Congregation*

SYMBOLS: *Wax, taper, iron combs (instruments of his passion), or two crossed candles; sometimes represented in a cave with animals*

O glorious Saint Blaise, who by thy martyrdom didst leave to the Church a precious witness to the faith, obtain of us the grace to preserve within ourselves this divine gift, and to defend, without human respect, both by word and example, the truth of that same faith, which is so wickedly attacked and slandered in these our times...

St. Blaise, depicted with symbolic iron combs

Eulalia

Known also as Aulaire, Aulazia, Olalla, and Eularia, this co-patron saint of Barcelona was a 13-year-old Christian martyr from a noble Roman family. When Emperor Diocletian stepped up persecution of Christians, near the end of the Roman ban on Christianity, the governor of Barcelona, Daclian, enforced his decrees. Eulalia eloquently refused to deny her faith, and so she was stripped, flagellated, and tortured. When her open wounds were burned with torches, the flames blew back against her tormenters. She prayed that God would take her to heaven, and witnesses said that a dove flew from her mouth as she died.

Afterward, a sudden snowstorm covered her naked body like a cloak. Her body was originally interred in the church of Santa Maria de les Arenes (St. Mary of the Sands; now Santa Maria del Mar, or St. Mary of the Sea). It was hidden in 713 during the invasion of the Moors and not recovered until 878. In 1339, her remains were relocated to an alabaster sarcophagus in the crypt of the newly built Cathedral of Santa Eulalia.

PATRON SAINT OF:
Barcelona; sailors; invoked against drought

STATUS: *Virgin, martyr*

BORN: *c. 290, Spain*

DIED: *February 12, 303, Barcelona*

VENERATED BY: *Roman Catholic Church, Eastern Orthodox Church*

CANONIZED: *633*

SYMBOLS: *X-shaped cross, stake, dove*

Blessed martyr St. Eulalia, I come before you seeking your intercession on behalf of (name youth) who has run away or is missing. Pray a spirit of protection over him/her and pray that his/her parents be freed from fear and anxiety. . . . Eulalia, I have confidence in your intercession and trust in a favorable outcome.

PAINTING OF EULALIA WITH THE X-SHAPED "CROSS SALTIRE" IN BARCELONA CATHEDRAL

Catherine of Ricci

C atherine de' Ricci was among the most devout, even extreme, saints in a period notable for its extreme saints. As young as age six, she manifested an acute desire for prayer and contemplation. At 13, she became a member of the strict Dominican convent of San Vincenzo in Tuscany. She would remain at San Vincenzo for the rest of her life, in 1547 becoming its perpetual prioress.

Known as a mystic, for 12 years from the age of 20, at noon on every Thursday, she experienced a state of religious ecstacy that lasted for exactly 28 hours, in which she relived Christ's Passion. During this intense "mystical marriage" Catherine exhibited stigmata, the physical wounds to the hands and feet suffered by Christ during His Crucifixion. In order to increase her own physical suffering, Catherine reportedly wore a "sharp iron chain" around her neck. She was also given to bouts of rigorous fasting. Her letters to Pope Pius V and other Catholic leaders illustrate her courageous work for church reformation and constitute a rich contribution to spirituality and theological thought. She is also one of the "incorruptibles," saints whose bodies exhibited no sign of decay after their death.

PATRON SAINT OF: *The sick; invoked against illness*

STATUS: *Prioress, virgin.*

BORN: *April 23, 1522, Florence, Italy*

DIED: *February 2, 1590, Prato, Italy*

VENERATED BY: *Roman Catholic Church; Tuscany, Italy*

CANONIZED: *1746*

SYMBOLS: *Usually represented in ecstasy*

Almighty God, you brought our sister Catherine to holiness through her contemplation of your Son's passion. As we remember the dying and rising of your Son, help us to become courageous preachers and teachers of these mysteries. We ask this through our Lord Jesus Christ, your Son, who lives and reigns with you and the Holy Spirit, one God, for ever and ever. Amen.

Valentine

Despite his almost global recognition as the patron saint of love and romance, remarkably little is known about the real St. Valentine. He was a Roman (possibly a soldier or priest) who converted to Christianity and helped Christians to escape during the persecutions of Emperors Claudius or Valerian. He is said to have been martyred on the Flaminian Way in Rome, probably by crucifixion or burning.

Ancient martyrologies cite two Valentines on this day. The other was a bishop of Terni, Italy, who was also martyred in Rome, although his remains were translated to Terni. They may be one and the same person.

Valentine's cult of romantic gestures may relate to an ancient and widespread belief that, in the Northern Hemisphere, pairs of birds mate on February 14. Some scholars believe that the date relates to the Roman festival of Lupercalia, a springtime feast of purification, health, and fertility, which occurred on the ides of February (mid-month).

PATRON SAINT OF:
Beekeepers, lovers, the betrothed, those courting; Terni, Italy

STATUS: *Martyr*

BORN: *c.235*

DIED: *c.270*

VENERATED BY: *Roman Catholic Church*

CANONIZED:
Pre-Congregation

SYMBOLS: *Heart, heart pierced by arrow, pairs of birds.*

Dear Lord, who art high in the Heavens,

Giver of Love and Passion,

And He who strings the heart's cords,

Lead the Lovers this day, February ten plus four.

The day during the month of two,

When the date is the perfect number of God

Greater two souls and two hearts....

Amen.

St Valentine Kneeling in Supplication (David Teniers III, 1600s)

Claude de la Colombiere

C olombière was the Jesuit confessor of St. Margaret Mary Alacoque (Oct. 16) and, with her, helped to establish the Feast of the Sacred Heart of Jesus. He entered the Society of Jesus in 1658 and was ordained in 1675. He became the spiritual director of the nuns of the Monastery of the Visitation Sisters located next to the church. This was how he came to know Sr. Margaret Mary Alacoque and where he promoted the validity of her visions.

Later he was active in Restoration England, as confessor to the future King James II's wife, Mary of Modena, but was arrested for preaching treachery and imprisoned in appalling conditions. After an appeal from King Louis XIV, under whose protection he fell, Colombière was released and expelled from England. The imprisonment had ruined his health, however, and he died in Lyon two years later from a severe hemorrhage.

PATRON SAINT OF: *Devotion to the Sacred Heart of Jesus*

STATUS: *Priest, founder*

BORN: *January 2, 1641, near Lyon, France*

DIED: *15, 1682, Paray, France*

VENERATED BY: *Roman Catholic Church, Jesuits*

CANONIZED: *1992*

Men may deprive me of possessions and of honor; sickness may strip me of strength and the means of serving You. I may even lose Your grace by sin; but I shall never lose my hope. I shall keep it to the last moment of my life; and at that moment all the demons in hell will strive to tear it from me in vain. "In peace, in the selfsame, I will sleep and I will rest."

THE ARISTOCRATIC COLOMBIÈRE WAS A NOTED RHETORICIAN AND PREACHER.

Juliana

According to Bede, Juliana was the child of the pagan Africanus. She was nevertheless devoted to Christ and had been baptized in secret. When her father made plans to wed her to Eleusius, a Roman officer from Antioch, she embarked on an extended debate with the Devil, who encouraged her to honor his wishes. She later became famous for this exchange. Because she refused the offer of marriage during the persecutions of Emperor Maximian, her father turned her over to the governor. She managed to survive burning in a furnace and immersion in boiling oil, but was ultimately decapitated. Another Christian convert, Barbara, was martyred along with Juliana and also canonized. Not long after, a noblewoman named Sephonia came through Nicomedia and took Juliana's body with her to Italy and had it buried in Campania. In the early 13th century her remains were transferred to Naples.

PATRON SAINT OF: *Childbirth, sickness*

STATUS: *Virgin, martyr*

BORN: *c.285, Cumae, Italy*

DIED: *c.305, Nicomedia or Naples*

VENERATED BY: *Roman Catholic Church, Eastern Orthodox Church, Oriental Orthodoxy, Church of England*

CANONIZED: *Pre-Congregation*

SYMBOLS: *Shown with a winged devil on a chain, or fighting a dragon*

Lord God, You gave St. Juliana the crown of eternal joy because she gave her life rather than renounce the virginity she had promised in witness to Christ. Encouraged by her generosity, help us to rise out of the bondage of our earthly desires and attain to the glory of your kingdom. Grant this through our Lord Jesus Christ, your Son. Amen.

IN THIS GREEK ICON, JULIANA IS SHOWN BEARING THE DISTINCTIVE CROSS OF THE ORTHODOX CHURCH.

The Seven Servites

I n 1233, seven well-born Florentines founded the Order of Friar Servants of Mary, popularly known as the Servites. They united against the growing moral depravity of Florence, a rapidly expanding mercantile center. The confraternity retreated to a humble house outside the city and, devoting themselves to the Seven Sorrows of the Blessed Virgin, they practiced solitude, penance, and prayer. An abundance of visitors forced them to retreat farther from Florence, and they built a hermitage and simple church at Monte Senario. The confraternity claimed direct inspiration and instruction from the Blessed Virgin Mary. They later emerged from isolation as friars, actively working within the community.

Officially approved by Pope Benedict XI in 1304, they became, over the centuries, one of the most vigorous and far-reaching of the five original mendicant orders. Their feast was once celebrated on February 11, then the 12th, but in 1969 it was changed to February 17, the date of Alexis Falconeri's death. The son of a wealthy merchant, Alexis was the only Servite who was not a priest, believing he was not worthy of that honor. Yet it was his vision of Mary that inspired the formation of the Servites. He helped build the Servite church at Cafaggio as well as managing the day-to-day temporal affairs of the congregation.

STATUS: *Founders*

BORN: *Early 13th century, Florence*

DIED: *Mid-13th to early 14th century*

NAMES: *Buonfiglio (Bonfilius) Monaldi*

Giovanni Bonaiuncta

Benedict dell'Antello

Amadeus degli Amidei (Bartholomew)

Ricovere Uguccione (Hugh)

Geraldino Sostegni

Alexis Falconieri

CANONIZED: *1888, jointly*

Ye glorious Patriarchs, heroes of the highest sanctity, whereby ye were made worthy to be chosen by the very Mother of God to spread devotion to her sorrows.

Forsaking the world, in the savage caverns of Monte Senario ye did crucify your flesh with unheard of penances, and did nourish your spirit with constant meditation on the highest truths of our holy faith.

Amen.

THE MADONNA WITH THE SEVEN FOUNDERS OF THE SERVITE ORDER

Fra Angelico

Born Guido di Pietro in the Italian province of Tuscany, this extraordinarily gifted painter is known to us today as Fra Angelico. After training as a painter, Guido entered the Dominican Order in Fiesole in around 1418, taking the name Giovanni. He continued painting initially in the service of the order in Florence and Tuscany. He painted many Annunciations, created extensive cycles of paintings for San Marco, Florence. In 1445 he was called to Rome by Pope Eugene IV, but ended up working mainly for his successor Nicolas V, providing cycles of the lives of St. Stephen and St. Lawrence for Nicolas's chapel. He then worked in Orvieto, and returned to Florence in 1450, where he was by then the most celebrated painter of his age. Because his religious paintings were so spiritually transcendent and his piety was so well-known, he was given the sobriquet Angelico (Italian for "angelic") posthumously and also referred to as Beato (Italian for "blessed").

PATRON SAINT OF:
Catholic Artists

STATUS: *Friar, artist*

BORN: *c.1395, Tuscany, Italy*

DIED: *1455, Rome, Italy*

VENERATED BY: *Roman Catholic Church*

CANONIZED: *1982*

Blessed Fra Angelico, we ask your aid in reminding us to pray before we begin our work, offering it to the glory of God and as a means of attaining holiness. Help us to see God's beauty in everything around us, marveling at His care and attention in the smallest things and inspiring us to be as solicitous in our own tiny way to our humble deeds. Pray that we may sing of God's ineffable mercy and grace along with you in the loftiness of heaven. Amen.

FRA ANGELICO SHOWN IN WHAT IS BELIEVED TO BE A SELF PORTRAIT.

Barbatus of Benevento

Barbatus was born in the village of Vandano, where he received a Christian education and took holy orders as soon as he was able, being ordained in Marcona. Employed by the local bishop as a preacher, he discovered a talent for the task. In a region that was only barely Christian, he often had to warn his parishioners about the evils of worshipping the local idols, a golden viper and a walnut tree. When Benevento came under seige by Emperor Constans II, Barbatus encouraged his fearful flock to cut down the offending tree and then he melted the golden viper into a chalice for his church. He eventually convinced the Lombards and their prince, Romuald I, to convert to Christianity.

PATRON SAINT OF:
Benevento

STATUS: *Bishop*

BORN: *c. 610 Cerreto Sanitta, Italy*

DIED: *February 19, 682*

VENERATED BY: *Roman Catholic Church, Eastern Orthodox Church*

CANONIZED:
Pre-Congregation

SYMBOLS: *Crozier*

Mighty Lord, Saint Barbatus of Benevento was a priest with great zeal who fought against the superstitious beliefs of pagans. Though his own parishioners would not listen to him, the pagans did, renounced their sinful ways, and converted to the true Faith . . . Bless my own understanding of the supernatural. Teach me what is of You, and bring to light the superstitions I believe. Help me to let go of all deceptions, mistaken beliefs, and occult powers, and bring the Holy Spirit to me in the fullness of His power. Then guide me in setting others free from the ideas that do them harm. Saint Barbatus, pray for me. Amen.

BARBATUS OF BENEVENTO WAS A FIERY PREACHER WHOSE FLOCK TURNED ON HIM BECAUSE OF HIS ZEAL

20

PATRON SAINTS OF:
The sick

STATUS: *Visionaries*

BORN: *Francisco — June 11, 1908; Jacinta — March 11, 1910; Portugal*

DIED: *Francisco — April 3, 1919; Jacinta — February 20, 1920; Portugal*

VENERATED BY: *Roman Catholic Church; Portugal*

CANONIZED: *2017*

SYMBOLS: *Carrying a lamp and rosary*

Dear St. Francisco and St. Jacinta,

The children of the world would like to learn from you how to love more perfectly.

St Jacinta, teach us how to love one another, especially sinners.

Help us to pray and to make sacrifces for those who ofend Our Lord so deeply.

St Francisco, teach us your great love for the Sacred Heart of Jesus in the Holy Eucharist, hurt by the ingratitude of so many.

St. Francisco and St. Jacinta, pray for us, pray for all the children and families of the world! Amen.

Francisco and Jacinta Marto

Francisco de Jesus Marto and Jacinta de Jesus Marto were siblings from Aljustrel, a small hamlet near Fátima, Portugal. With their cousin Lúcia dos Santos (1907–2005), these peasant children witnessed three apparitions of the Angel of Peace in 1916 and several apparations of the Blessed Virgin Mary at Cove de Iria in 1917. The title Our Lady of Fátima was given to the Virgin Mary as a result, and the Sanctuary of Fátima became a major center of world Christian pilgrimage. Jacinta and Francisco spent what remained of their young lives in a daze of sanctity—Francisco plunged himself into rounds of solitary prayer, "to console Jesus for the sins of the world" and seven-year-old Jacinta, tormented by a vision of Hell revealed by the Virgin, became convinced she had to sacrifice herself in order to save sinners. Both died in the global influenza epidemic, Francisco first, but Jacinta developed pleurisy and lingered for several months before succumbing to a death she had already predicted.

AN OFFICIAL PORTRAIT OF FRANCISCO AND JACINTA MARTO

Peter Damian

Peter Damian was one of the outstanding reformers of the early medieval church. He was born into a large, poor family, and at age 28 he entered the austere Camaldolese Benedictine monastery at Fonte Avellana. By 1043 he had been appointed abbot. Appalled by the behavior of many in the clergy, he began a campaign of reform, addressing simony (the buying or selling of ecclesiastical offices) and the widespread abuse of the vows of celibacy. He also called for a strict evaluation of the role of the papacy. In 1057, he was made a cardinal by St. Gregory VII (May 25) and appointed Bishop of Ostia, but he nevertheless continued his reform work. He eventually appealed to be relieved of his episcopate and returned to Fonte Avellana to end his life in retreat and contemplation. Author Dante placed him in one of the highest circles of Paradiso as a great predecessor St. Francis of Assisi.

Although a harsh critic of others, Damian was also severe on himself—he wore a hair shirt, fasted frequently, and promoted the benefits of self-flagellation as a means of mortification.

STATUS: *Bishop, reformer*

BORN: *1007, Ravenna, Italy*

DIED: *1072, Faenza, Italy*

CANONIZED: *1828*

SYMBOLS: *Shown as a cardinal bearing a knotted rope; a pilgrim holding a papal bull; Benedictine monk's habit; flagellant's whip*

Grant, we pray, almighty God, that we may so follow the teaching and example of the Bishop Saint Peter Damian, that, putting nothing before Christ and always ardent in the service of your Church, we may be led to the joys of eternal light.

Through our Lord Jesus Christ, your Son, who lives and reigns with you in the unity of the Holy Spirit, one God, for ever and ever.

Amen.

PETER DAMIAN PORTRAYED BY FRANCESCO DEL ROSSI (IL SAVIATI, 1510–63) IN STA. MARIA DELLE CARCERI, ITALY. THE SAINT IS SHOWN BEARING A BOOK AND A WHIP FOR SELF-FLAGELLATION. THE ITALIAN POET DANTE RANKED DAMIAN AS A SIGNIFICANT PREDECESSOR OF ST. FRANCIS OF ASSISI IN HIS DIVINE COMEDY.

Margaret of Cortona

Margaret was an Italian penitent who was, by all accounts, a beautiful woman. Born a peasant, her mother died when she was young. She enjoyed the favors of a young knight and lived with him at Montepulciano for some ten years, bearing him a son out of wedlock. He was murdered when she was 26 and, rejected by her family, she was taken in by two women who offered Margaret and her son a home in the Etruscan hilltop town of Cortona. Pursued by poisonous gossip, she became repentant and took to very public acts of extreme self-mortification, including starvation, mutilation, and punishment of her son. Eventually, she was accepted as a Franciscan tertiary, devoting herself to acts of charity until her son grew up. He then became a Franciscan novitiate. Thereafter, Margaret became increasingly reclusive, and moved to the ruined church of St. Basil's outside the city walls. Here she gained a reputation as a savior of sinners through counseling and prayer. She was active in founding a paupers' hospital in Cortona. Her apparently incorrupt remains can still be seen in the church built for her over the ruins of St. Basil's at Cortona.

PATRON SAINT OF:
Single mothers, penitent prostitutes, sexual temptation, the falsely accused, the homeless, the insane

STATUS: *Penitent*

BORN: *1247, Laviano, Italy*

DIED: *1297, Cortona, Italy*

VENERATED BY: *Roman Catholic Church, Cortona*

CANONIZED: *1728*

SYMBOLS: *Lapdog; figure tending the sick*

O glorious St. Margaret, you embarked on a life of penance and poverty after you repented of your sins. Jesus touched your heart, and after imposing on yourself a rigorous life of fasting, Jesus talked and conversed with you, revealing to you his merciful heart that rejoices whenever a sinner returns to him.

On controlling your appetite for food, you managed to free yourself from all temptations, including those of the flesh of which you were a victim for many years. Listen then to our petitions. May you bring our petitions to Jesus. Amen.

Polycarp

Polycarp was significant in the development of the Early Church in Greek Asia Minor. He was a disciple of John the Evangelist (Dec. 27), and is regarded as one of the few direct links between the Apostles of the New Testament and the early Christian bishops. Along with Pope Clement I (Nov. 23), and Ignatius of Antioch (Oct. 17), Polycarp is regarded as one of the Apostolic Fathers of the Church. He became Bishop of Smyrna, where he defended the Christian orthodoxy against the various heresies of Gnosticism. His sole surviving written work, his Letter to the Philippians, was used as a liturgical text for several centuries.

At a considerable age, Polycarp was invited to Rome by Pope Anicetus to discuss the dating of Easter. Polycarp advocated the traditional (Eastern) link to the dating of the Jewish Passover. The two could not agree, but parted on good terms. Shortly after his return to Smyrna, a Roman youth, Germanicus, was killed at a "pagan" (possibly Christian) ceremony. In the ensuing confusion Polycarp was arrested and ordered to denounce his faith. He refused, and attempts were made to burn him at the stake, but surrounded by an ethereal blue light, the flames failed to vanquish him. He was eventually stabbed to death and his corpse successfully cremated.

PATRON SAINT OF:
Sufferers of earache or dysentery

STATUS: *Bishop, martyr.*

BORN: *c. 69 AD*

DIED: *c.155, Smyrna, modern Turkey*

VENERATED BY: *Roman Catholic Church, Eastern Orthodox Church*

CANONIZED:
Pre-Congregation

SYMBOLS: *Wearing a pallium, often holding a book; frequently surrounded by flames*

God of all creation, you gave your bishop Polycarp the privilege of being counted among the saints who gave their lives in faithful witness to the gospel. May his prayers give us the courage to share with him the cup of suffering and to rise to eternal glory. We ask this through our Lord Jesus Christ, your Son. Amen.

POLYCARP'S VALIANT APPROACH TO MARTYRDOM OVERSHADOWED HIS THEOLOGICAL STATUS. WHEN HIS ACCUSERS CAME TO HIS FARMHOUSE TO ARREST HIM, HE OFFERED THEM SUPPER BEFORE CALMLY DENYING THEIR DEMANDS TO APOSTATIZE.

John Theristus

John Theristus (for "reaper") was born in Sicily. During a Saracen raid in Calabria, his father, a Byzantine farmer named Arconte di Cursano, was killed and his mother taken as a slave. She gave birth among the Saracens in Palermo, but John was raised as a Christian. At 14 he escaped from his captors and fled to Monasterace, Italy. Dressed as a saracen, he was questioned by the bishop; John said he was seeking baptism, but the cleric subjected him to many trials before completing the sacrament. John felt drawn to the Benedictine monks who dwelled in the caves around Stylus and was eventually admitted into their community. His virtue, piety, and charity soon elevated him to abbot.

One night during the local harvest, while John was bringing bread and wine to the farmers, a great storm blew up and threatened the vital crops. John's prayers saved the harvest, holding off the storm until all the wheat could be gathered. This was the source of his nickname.

STATUS: *Monk*

BORN: *1049, Palermo, Italy*

DIED: *1129, Calabria, Italy*

VENERATED BY: *Roman Catholic Church, Eastern Orthodox Church*

O God, who gave St. John Theristus the fortitude to escape from his infidel captors and seek baptism in Italy, we ask that You instill in us the courage to reject our own mortal frailties and the faith to seek out affirmation of our faith in both strange and familiar lands. This we ask in the name of Jesus Christ, our Lord. Amen.

Walburga

Walburga was the daughter of St. Richard, a West Saxon king. Not only was her father canonized, but both of her brothers, Willibald (July 7) and Winibald, were also saints, as was her uncle, Boniface (June 5), who was the foremost Anglo-Saxon missionary of the period, largely responsible for bringing Christianity to Germany. It was in response to a plea from Boniface that Walburga went to Germany in around 748, where she became abbess of both the monastery and the convent at Heidenheim. She became trained in medicine, and was notable for writing, in Latin, the lives of her brothers, who were also active in Germany.

In 870, her remains were removed from Heidenheim and reburied in the Benedictine convent, today the Abbey of St. Walburgs, at Eichstätt in Bavaria. There, it was discovered that holy oil—in reality water produced naturally—was running from her tomb. It has continued to flow and is still bottled by the nuns at Eichstätt.

PATRON SAINT OF: *Storms, sailors, rabies; protection of crops*

STATUS: *Abbess, missionary*

BORN: *c. 710, Devon, England*

DIED: *777, Heidenheim, Germany*

VENERATED BY: *Roman Catholic Church, Benedictines, in Germany*

CANONIZED: *Pre-Congregation*

SYMBOLS: *Crown, crozier, phial of oil, three ears of corn*

Oh holy virgin, St. Walburga, mercifully you lead all the sick and helpless who implore your help to Jesus, your Divine Spouse.

He is the Good Samaritan who will heal them all.

Lead me also to Him, and ask for my deliverance from the troubles that afflict me; be my consoler and helper, for you can and will help me if it be God's will.

Full of confidence I ask this favor, and when you have helped me I will not cease to thank you,

O blessed St. Walburga.

SAINT WALPURGA ~ PAINTING BY THE MASTER OF MESSKIRCH, C. 1535–40.

Isabelle of France

Isabelle of France was a French princess, the daughter of Louis VIII and of Blanche of Castile. She was a younger sister of the great king Louis IX—who would become St. Louis. As a girl she was known for her fervent prayers and fasting. She also loved acquiring knowledge, studying Latin so that she could comprehend the works of the Church Fathers. She rejected a number of notable suitors, preferring to consecrate her virginity and life to God. When the pope wrote to her, asking her to marry the King of Jerusalem to create a Christian alliance, she humbly declined. She often invited the poor to dinner and served them before eating herself and in the evening visited the sick and poor.

In 1256, she founded the nunnery in Longchamp named the Monastery of the Humility of the Blessed Virgin Mary in the Forest of Rouvray (the Bois de Boulogne), west of Paris. Yet she never joined the community; ill health prevented her from following the nun's rule of life, plus that way she was allowed to keep her wealth, enabling her to support the nuns and give to the poor.

PATRON SAINT OF:
Patroness of the sick

STATUS: *Princess, foundress*

BORN: *March 1225*

DIED: *February 23, 1270*

VENERATED BY: *Roman Catholic Church, Poor Clares, Franciscans*

CANONIZED: *1696*

Dear Lord, we thank You for giving us St. Isabel of France as an example of holiness. Help us to imitate the virtue she showed in her deep spirit of poverty. St. Isabel of France, you were born to a family of the highest rank. Though you could have led a luxurious lifestyle, you chose instead to live simply and to devote your life to God. Please bring my petitions before God Whom you served so devotedly! Amen.

St. Isabelle at the Church of Saint-Germain l'Auxerrois in Paris, a Neo-Gothic replica of the original statue

Gabriel of Our Lady of Sorrows

Gabriel of Our Lady of Sorrows, born Francesco Possenti, was the 11th child of a professional family with 13 children. Gabriel only discovered his spiritual vocation, fiercely resisted by his father, after a series of illnesses and nearly being shot while hunting. In 1856, he joined the Passionists, an Italian contemplative and missionary congregation founded in 1720 by St. Paul of the Cross (Oct. 19). Although his life in the monastery at Morrovalle was not extraordinary, from the start, he was a model novitiate, exceptionally studious, and scrupulous in the execution of his spiritual duties. He was especially known for his devotion to the Virgin Mary. Three years later, he fell ill with tuberculosis. The certainty that he would die young only increased his already profound sanctity. He died from the wasting disease at the age of 23 in the retreat at Isola del Gran Sasso. Two miracles are ascribed to him: the inexplicable healings of Maria Mazzarella from pulmonary tuberculosis and periostitis, and the instantaneous cure of Dominic Tiber from an inoperable hernia.

PATRON SAINT OF: *Students, seminarians*

STATUS: *Novitiate*

BORN: *March 1, 1838, Assisi, Italy*

DIED: *February 27, 1862, Isola, Italy*

VENERATED BY: *Roman Catholic Church*

CANONIZED: *1920*

SYMBOLS: *Passionist habit and sign*

O God, Who didst teach blessed Gabriel to have the sorrows of Thy most dear Mother in perpetual remembrance, and through her didst glorify him with the fame of holiness and miracles; grant unto us, by his intercession and example, so to share the sorrows of Thy Mother that we may be saved by her maternal protection: Who livest and reignest world without end. Amen.

THROUGHOUT HIS BRIEF CAREER AS A PASSIONIST, ST. GABRIEL'S SPIRITUAL MENTOR WAS FATHER NORBERT, HERE SEEN WITH ST. GABRIEL (WHITE SYMBOL ON ROBE). HE WAS PRESENT AT GABRIEL'S BEATIFICATION IN ROME BY PIUS X IN 1908.

Hilarius

28

STATUS: *Pope*

BORN: *November 19, 461, Sardinia*

DIED: *February 29, 468, Rome*

VENERATED BY: *Roman Catholic Church*

CANONIZED: *Pre-Congregation*

St. Hilarius, I pray that you, who supported church unity and who became bishop of Rome, and who worked to ensure that the highest leaders in the land acknowledged the authority of your role as head of the Church, will inspire me with your boundless energy to stand against those who would slander or oppress me for my faith. This I pray in the name of Jesus Christ.

Amen.

Born in Sardinia, Hilarius (or Hilary), became a guardian of church unity. He was archdeacon to Pope Leo I and fought for the rights of the Roman See. In 449, Hilarius and Bishop Julius of Puteoli served as papal legates to the Second Council of Ephesus, meant to decide whether Patriarch Flavian of Constantinope had justly excommunicated Eutyches for allegedly refusing to admit "two natures"—both divine and human—in Christ. Hilarius carried a letter from Leo supporting the Patriarch. Although the head notary declared the pope's letter should be read first, the Council proceeded to condemn Flavian, and Leo's letter was not read. Hilarius, speaking for Leo, pronounced the single Latin word, "Contradicitur," thus annulling Flavian's sentence. This displeased Pope Dioscorus I of Alexandria, and soon after Flavian died from injuries caused by followers of Dioscurus. Hilarius himself became pope in 461 and continued the policy of Leo I, who had obtained from Emperor Valentinian III a confirmation of the supremacy of the bishop of Rome. Hilary used his position to strengthen ecclesiastical government in Gaul and Spain and to construct many Roman churches.

Oswald of Worcester

Oswald of Worcester was of Danish military descent, and related to Odo of Canterbury, who played a key part in his education. Odo sent him to study at the strict Benedictine monastery at Fleury, France, where he was ordained. After returning to England, Oswald became bishop of Worcester in 962, and in 972 was elevated to Archbishop of York, the second-most senior churchman in England. While in high office, he did much to introduce monastic practices in England, founding Westbury-on-Trym near Bristol and Ramsey, Huntingdonshire. From these, several other houses were established in the diocese of Worcester. Oswald is also known for promoting learning among the clergy in his diocese, bringing in instructors from Fleury. He died while washing the feet of the poor, a Lenten custom. Numerous miracles were attributed to him and a vigorous cult developed after his death. St. Oswald is a leap year saint. He died on February 29, making his feast day "leap day." When it is not a leap year, the celebration is transferred to February 28.

STATUS: *Archbishop, founder*

BORN: *c. 925, Denmark or England*

DIED: *992, Worcester, England*

VENERATED BY: *Roman Catholic Church, Western Orthodoxy, Anglican Communion*

CANONIZED: *Pre-Congregation*

Almighty ever-living God, who chose blessed Oswald to preside as Bishop over your holy people, we pray that, by his merits, you may bestow on us the grace of your loving kindness. Through our Lord Jesus Christ, your Son, who lives and reigns with you in the unity of the Holy Spirit, one God, for ever and ever.

Amen.

MARCH

March is the third month of the Gregorian calendar. Named for Mars, the Roman god of war, it can be suitably harsh, weatherwise. It includes two key festivals in the British Isles: Saint David's Day for the patron saint of Wales (March 1), and Saint Patrick's Day for the patron saint of Ireland (March 17). Both are robustly celebrated with feasting, drink, and song. A more solemn festival is the Annunciation of the Blessed Virgin Mary on March 25, which is especially important in the Eastern Orthodox calendar. In Europe, Mother's Day traditionally falls on the fourth Sunday in Lent, and was originally an occasion upon which workers and domestic servants could travel home to their mother churches and visit their families. The festival of Easter does, on occasion, fall within March, when it may neatly coincide with the beginning of spring at the Northern Hemisphere's vernal equinox.

THE ANNUNCIATION, THE REVELATION TO THE BLESSED VIRGIN MARY BY THE ARCHANGEL GABRIEL THAT SHE HAD BEEN CHOSEN TO BE THE MOTHER OF CHRIST, IS ONE OF THE CENTRAL EPISODES IN THE CHRISTIAN STORY. IT WAS A POPULAR SUBJECT AMONG RENAISSANCE ARTISTS, INCLUDING FRA ANGELICO (FEB. 18), WHO PAINTED SEVERAL VARIATIONS OF THE SCENE.

David

S t. David (Dewi Sant in Welsh) is the patron saint of Wales and among the best-known saints, with more than 50 churches dedicated to him. While he clearly existed and appears to have been a forceful preacher, teacher, and missionary, his life remains clouded. The earliest account was compiled some 500 years after his death, likely to justify the Welsh Church's independence from that of England. He studied scripture under St. Paulinus of Wales, whom the youthful David cured of blindness brought on by "excessive weeping through prayer."

David later traveled widely, establishing 12 monasteries, among them those at Glastonbury and Bath. His regime was austere: monks were expected to engage in manual labor; speech was largely forbidden; personal possessions were not allowed; and no meat was consumed (thus David represents vegetarians). Nicknamed Aquaticus ("water drinker"), David would immerse himself in freezing water to aid contemplation. He is reputed to have made pilgrimages to Rome and Jerusalem, where the patriarch himself appointed him an archbishop.

PATRON SAINT OF: *Wales, Pembrokeshire, poets, vegetarians*

STATUS: *Bishop.*

BORN: *c. 500, Pembrokeshire, Wales*

DIED: *March 1, 589, St. David's, Wales*

VENERATED BY: *Roman Catholic Church, Eastern Orthodox Church, US Episcopal Church*

CANONIZED: *1123*

SYMBOLS: *Shown in abbot's robes, usually accompanied by a dove, perhaps standing on a hillock*

You chose to live a simple life, and helped others whose lives were simple not through choice but circumstances. Pray that I may consider my choices and live more simply in order to make a big difference to others.

Show me the way to make small tasks occasions of prayer. Kindle in me a love of God so that in everything I do, I will keep that spirit of prayer.

Amen.

EARLY IMAGES OF DAVID ARE RARE. HERE THE SAINT IS DEPICTED WITH A DOVE IN A FINE 19TH-CENTURY STAINED-GLASS WINDOW IN THE CHURCH OF GREAT ST. MARY'S, CAMBRIDGE, ENGLAND.

Agnes of Bohemia

This notable medieval European saint was the daughter of Ottokar I of Bohemia. She spurned her royal background to embrace a life of what Pope John Paul II, who canonized her, called "heroic charity." Betrothed to a number of princes as a child, Agnes determined she wanted no part of a political marriage. With the aid of Pope Gregory IX she dedicated herself to God and lived a life of "austerity and virginity." After a lengthy correspondence with St. Clare (Aug. 11), in 1231 Agnes founded a branch of the Poor Clares in Prague, with five nuns sent to her from Clare in Assisi. Agnes then built a monastery and a hospital, also dedicated to St. Francis (Oct. 4). In 1238 she organized a lay group working in the hospital as a new military order, dedicated to nursing, known as the Knights of the Cross with the Red Star. The following year Agnes handed over all her responsibilities to these monastic knights.

Her willing embrace of poverty and her habit of tending to the poor herself, with no menial task beneath her attentions, encouraged large numbers of high-born Bohemian women to dedicate themselves to similar good works.

PATRON SAINT OF:
Czech Republic

STATUS: *Princess, nun, abbess, foundress*

BORN: *June 20, 1205, Prague, modern Czech Republic*

DIED: *March 2, 1282, Prague, modern Czech Republic*

VENERATED BY: *Roman Catholic Church, Order of St. Clare*

CANONIZED: *1989*

SYMBOLS: *Depicted as a reflective and benevolent figure*

. . . St. Agnes, you embraced the Franciscan way of life even though you were born to royalty. Pray that we may learn to be poor in spirit and rich in virtue. St. Agnes, you took on the meanest duties in the convent. Pray that we may offer our daily mundane tasks to God with great love. St. Agnes, you followed the narrow way that leads to life, pray that we too, may carry our crosses with Christ until we reach our heavenly reward. Amen.

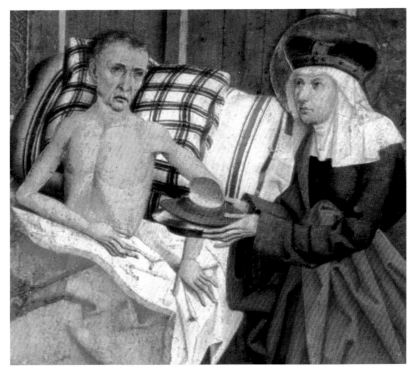

A PRIMITIVE LATE 15TH-CENTURY BOHEMIAN PAINTING OF ST. AGNES TENDING THE SICK. EVEN ONCE SHE HAD BEEN APPOINTED MOTHER SUPERIOR OF THE PRAGUE CLARES IN 1234, ST. AGNES PERSONALLY COOKED FOR THE SICK IN HER HOSPITAL.

Katherine Drexel

Born in Philadelphia, Pennsylvania, of Dutch descent, Katharine Drexel put aside her privileged life to become a pioneer in providing education and justice for Native Americans and African Americans in the first half of the 20th century. She began life as a society heiress; her wealthy father, a successful and philanthropic banker, left her a legacy worth in excess of $100 million (by today's values). Under the influence of Pope Leo XIII, Katharine became a nun and, in 1891, founded the Sisters of the Blessed Sacrament as an order dedicated to missionary work within the Native American and black communities.

She established her first missionary school in Santa Fe, New Mexico, in 1894, and went on to found a further 11 such schools on various Indian reservations. In addition, Katharine used her wealth to found, staff, and support nearly 60 schools, as well as orphanages, across the rural areas and inner cities of the Deep South, at a time when African Americans did not have access to a basic education. She was instrumental in establishing the school in New Orleans that would later evolve into Xavier University, the only black Roman Catholic college in the United States.

PATRON SAINT OF: *Philanthropists, racial justice*

STATUS: *Missionary, foundress*

BORN: *November 26, 1858, Philadelphia, USA*

DIED: *March 3, 1955, Bensalem, USA*

VENERATED BY: *Roman Catholic Church*

CANONIZED: 2000

SYMBOLS: *Depicted with children of color at her side*

Ever loving God, you called Saint Katharine Drexel to teach the message of the Gospel and to bring the life of the Eucharist to the Black and Native American peoples. By her prayers and example, enable us to work for justice among the poor and oppressed. Draw us all into the Eucharistic community of your Church, that we may be one in you. Grant this through our Lord Jesus Christ, your Son, who lives and reigns with you and the Holy Spirit, one God, for ever and ever. Amen.

THIS LIFE-SIZE STATUE OF KATHARINE ACCOMPANIED BY AN AFRICAN-AMERICAN BOY AND A NATIVE AMERICAN GIRL IS IN THE BASILICA OF THE NATIONAL SHRINE OF THE IMMACULATE CONCEPTION IN WASHINGTON, D.C.

MARCH

Casimir "the Peacemaker"

Casimir Jagiellion, the patron saint of both Poland and Lithuania, was the second son of Casimir IV, King of Poland. In 1471, at the request of Hungarian nobles, Casimir's father sent him to Hungary at the head of a large army. After political upheaval in their country, some Hungarians were unhappy with their new king, Matthias Corvinus, and wanted the young Casimir to replace him. Casimir would not wage war, however, and returned home. He refused to fight against fellow Christians and so remained a lifelong conscientious objector. He also turned away from all kingly pursuits and refused an arranged marriage with the daughter of the Holy Roman Emperor Frederick III, preferring to dedicate himself to a life of prayer, humility, and chastity. Suffering from illness throughout his life, Casimir finally succumbed to tuberculosis. Miracles were reported at Casimir's tomb in Vilnius, the Lithuanian capital, where his relics still rest today.

PATRON SAINT OF:
*Bachelors, kings, princes, youth;
Poland, Lithuania*

STATUS: *Prince*

BORN: *October 3, 1458,
Kraków, Poland*

DIED: *March 4, 1484,
Grodno, Lithuania*

VENERATED BY: *Roman
Catholic Church*

CANONIZED: *1521 or
1602*

SYMBOLS: *Lily, grand ducal
cap, absence of sword*

*O God, who didst preserve thy
servant Casimir constant and
faithful in thy service amidst
the delights of a court, and the
attractive allurements of the world,
grant, we beseech thee, that by his
intercession thy people may despise
the transitory things of the world
and eagerly pursue things which
are eternal: through Jesus Christ
our Lord. Amen.*

THE CULT OF CASIMIR IS PARTICULARLY STRONG AMONG THE POLISH AND LITHUANIAN IMMIGRANT COMMUNITIES OF NORTH AMERICA. THIS ELABORATE ALTAR DEDICATED TO HIM IS IN ST. CASIMIR CHURCH, CLEVELAND, OHIO.

John Joseph of the Cross

Born Carlo Gaetano Calosirto, this son of a noble family was a model of virtue, even as a child. He entered the Franciscan Order at age 16, taking the name John Joseph of the Cross. In 1674, he was sent to Afila to found a convent and performed much of the construction himself. He could afford fine clothes, but out of respect for the poor, he preferred simple clothing. He also fasted constantly, abstained from wine, and slept only three hours each night. Ordained a monk in 1677, he took to the contemplative life and was accounted the first Italian to follow the reform movement of Spanish Franciscan St. Peter of Alcantara.

Although John Joseph preferred to live the modest life of his order, he held several positions of authority, including vicar provincial of the Alcantarine Reform in Naples.

PATRON SAINT OF: *Naples, Ischia*

STATUS: *Priest, confessor*

BORN: *August 15, 1654, Ischia, Italy*

DIED: *March 5, 1739, Naples, Italy*

VENERATED BY: *Roman Catholic Church, Franciscans*

CANONIZED: *1839*

SYMBOLS: *Sometimes represented levitating*

St. John Joseph, we ask today for your mighty intercession, to pray for us that we learn humility and seek an attitude of service so we, too, may follow in the footsteps of Jesus. In His Mighty Name we pray, Amen.

Chrodegang of Metz

Born to a noble Frankish family, Chrodegang acted as chief minister under kings Charles Martel and Pepin III. He was named bishop of Metz in 742. Following the murder of Boniface (June 5) he received the pallium (an ecclesiastical vestment) from Pope Stephen and became responsible for church reform throughout the Frankish empire. In 748 he founded Gorze Abbey, near Metz, and also established St. Peter's Abbey on the Moselle River.

Among his contributions, he introduced Roman liturgy and Gregorian chant to the Frankish church and is responsible for the Rule of Chrodegang, a guide based on St. Benedict for how Catholic secular clergy and canons—priests attached to a diocese—should live in the community. This rule was widely circulated and gave impetus to the spread of community life among the secular clergy. It is likely that the Rule of Chrodegang was carried by Irish monks to their native land from the monasteries of northeastern Gaul.

PATRON SAINT OF:
Metz, Germany

STATUS: *Bishop*

BORN: *c. 712 near Liège, modern Belgium*

DIED: *766, Metz, Germany*

VENERATED BY: *Roman Catholic Church, Eastern Orthodox Church*

CANONIZED:
Pre-Congregation

SYMBOLS: *Often depicted wearing the white, Y-shaped lambswool pallium*

Blessed Chrodegang, who created your Rule for communities of clergy based on the work of St. Benedict, please guide me as I embark on a new group endeavor: let me lead where needed, furnish ideas when necessary, and heed the leadership of others when appropriate. Give me patience toward others and patience toward myself during the times I may falter. In Jesus' name I pray. Amen.

Perpetua, Felicity, and Companions

T he religious significance of Perpetua and Felicity has endured for almost two millennia: their feast day can be found in a Roman calendar dating from 354 and their names are still recited in the Roman Canon in Catholic churches today. Four men—Saturus, Saturninus, Secundus, and Revocatus—were martyred with them, yet it is the two women who are remembered most vividly.

Both were married catechumens (Church initiates), imprisoned for their beliefs during the persecutions of Septimius Severus. The 22-year-old Perpetua was a respectable matron with an infant son; Felicity was her pregnant slave, who gave birth in prison. They were all sent to die in the arena, where leopards and bears attacked the men. A heifer tossed Perpetua and Felicity on its horns, goring Perpetua and crushing Felicity. Perpetua, in a religious ecstasy, overlooked her wounds and pulled Felicity to her feet. As the crowd called for their deaths, Perpetua and Felicity, and the surviving Saturninus and Revocatus, were killed by gladiators.

PATRON SAINT OF:
Perpetua: death of children, sterility, birth of sons, widows; Felicity: cattle, death of children

STATUS: *Martyrs*

BORN: *c.180, Carthage, modern Tunisia*

DIED: *203, Carthage, modern Tunisia*

VENERATED BY: *Roman Catholic Church, Eastern Orthodox churches, US Episcopal Church, Lutheran Church*

CANONIZED:
Pre-Congregation

SYMBOLS: *Wild cows, spiked ladder, Perpetua often guarded by a dragon*

O St. Perpetua, Your father brought your infant son to the prison to persuade you to apostatize, but you held firm in your faith. . . . Pray that we may lead others to Christ by our joyful and lively faith. Saints Perpetua and Felicity, you now reside in heaven with our Savior; pray that we will one day see Him face to face. Amen.

A 19TH-CENTURY MOSAIC SHOWING PERPETUA AND FELICITY BEING AWARDED THE PALMS OF MARTYRDOM.

John of God

This saint's life was beset with tragedy and strife, but in the end his good works gave him ease. As a child, John worked as a shepherd in Portugal. As a young man he moved to Spain, joining a wild band of mercenaries and fighting in several campaigns for Charles V. At around age 40, he experienced a religious revelation and traveled south, determined to work among Christian slaves in Moorish North Africa, inviting martyrdom. He was deterred by a Franciscan monk, and turned to an itinerant life distributing printed religious texts and images in Andalusia. He finally settled in Granada. A sermon by John of Ávila (May 10) provoked in him such an extreme fervor for religious penitence that he was committed to an insane asylum.

It would be John of Ávila, once again, who visited and saved him, encouraging John to care for the poor and sick, given his experience with his fellow inmates in the asylum. He went on to establish a hospital in Granada and formed the Hospitaller Order of St. John of God, which attracted many voluntary supporters.

PATRON SAINT OF:
Nurses, hospitals, booksellers, publishers, printers, alcoholics, firefighters; Tultepec (Mexico), Montemoro Novo (Portugal)

STATUS: *Priest, founder*

BORN: *1495, Montemoro Novo, Portugal*

DIED: *1550, Granada, Spain*

VENERATED BY: *Roman Catholic Church, US Episcopal Church, US Evangelical Lutheran Church*

CANONIZED: *1690*

SYMBOLS: *Crown of thorns, heart, an alms box, holding a pomegranate, two bowls hung around his neck and a basket with a halo of seven stars; always depicted wearing a white Carthusian habit*

St. John of God you possessed a holy zeal that led you to follow God with a heart brimming with love. You were quick to serve others and follow God's promptings in your life. Amen.

A DRAMATIC PAINTING OF ST. JOHN OF GOD RECEIVING INSPIRATION FROM AN ANGEL, BY THE SPANISH BAROQUE PAINTER MURILLO (C.1617–82).

Francesca of Rome

Francesca dei Roffredeschi was born to a noble family that lived in Trastevere, Rome. Although eager to become a nun, her parents married her at age 13 to the commander of the papal troops, who was often away campaigning. They had six children, but lost two to the plague, after which Frances adopted a vow of continence, reduced her diet to bread and occasional vegetables, and began helping the poor and sick. Many aristocratic women of Rome were inspired to follow her example.

During this time of the Great Schism, the papacy was divided, and Rome was largely in ruins, filled with bandits. In this hostile city, Frances is said to have been guided through the streets by her guardian angel, bearing a lamp. She eventually founded the Benedictine Oblates of Mary, and following her husband's death Frances became the superior. Frances enjoyed ecstasies and visions, predicting the end of the Schism and the restoration of papal supremacy. Her remains are now near her convent, in the church of Santa Francesca Romana overlooking the Forum.

PATRON SAINT OF: *Automobile drivers, cab drivers, death of children, lay people, people ridiculed for their piety, widows*

STATUS: *Oblate, founder*

BORN: *1384, Rome, Italy*

DIED: *March 7, 1440, Rome, Italy*

VENERATED BY: *Roman Catholic Church*

CANONIZED: *1608*

SYMBOLS: *In Benedictine robes, often carrying basket of food with guardian angel bearing a branch of oranges or a lamp*

St. Frances of Rome, you fed the poor from a miraculous refilling of grain in your husband's stores; pray that we may have complete confidence in God's loving providence. St. Frances, your guardian angel visibly followed you everywhere. Pray that we may heed our guardian angels' advice and that they protect us from harm. You had a frightening vision of hell; intercede for today and every day, that we may avoid sin at all costs and order our lives according to the will of God. St. Frances, you were a loving wife and mother; pray for all families in this confusing and chaotic time. Amen.

FRANCES RECEIVING APPROVAL FOR HER COMMUNITY FROM POPE EUGENE IV IN 1433.

40 Martyrs of Sebaste

I n 320 AD, Roman emperor Licinius ordered that every Christian in the Roman army must renounce his religion on pain of death, but 40 soldiers at Sebaste in Cappadocia (Turkey) refused to sacrifice to Roman idols. In the middle of winter, these soldiers were stripped naked and left overnight on a frozen lake. A heated bathhouse was even built at the lake's edge as an incentive to apostatize. By morning, all except one, St. Melito, were dead. Melito's mother carried her son behind the cart full of the soldiers' bodies until he died, and then she placed him with the others. The bodies of the soldiers were burned and their ashes thrown into the waters. The earliest account of their martyrdom was likely given by Bishop Basil of Caesarea (370–379) in a homily offered on their feast day.

PATRON SAINT OF:
Persecuted Christians

STATUS: *Martyrs*

BORN: *Late 3rd century*

DIED: *320, Sebaste, modern Turkey*

VENERATED BY: *Roman Catholic Church, Eastern Orthodoxy, Oriental Orthodoxy, Lutheran Church, Anglican Church*

CANONIZED:
Pre-Congregation

SYMBOLS: *Normally shown naked, en masse, freezing; crown of martyrdom; martyr's palm*

O God, who set the feet of your devout missionaries on treacherous paths as they sought to share your Holy Word with the outside world, give me an understanding of how they faced danger and even death with constancy in their hearts and ultimate faith in their heavenly reward. This I pray in the name of Jesus Christ, your Son. Amen.

THIS SUPERB BAS-RELIEF IVORY CARVING CONVEYS THE CHILLY FATE OF THE SOLDIERS OF SEBASTE.

Eulogius of Cordoba

Eulogius was one of the many Martyrs of Córdoba, Christians who suffered in Moorish Andalusia. During the early 700s, Muslims conquered a portion of southern Spain, establishing Cordoba as their capital. Initially, Christians living there were allowed freedom to worship providing they paid tribute. Eulogius's brother, Joseph, even rose to a high rank within the government of ruler Abd-er Rahman II. But around 850, a fierce persecution began and many Christians, accused of abusing the name of Mohammed or conspiring against the Arabs, were killed or forced to flee. Eulogius, offspring of a landed family, was a higly esteemed priest and the head of an ecclesiastical school. When a young Moorish convert, the future St. Leocritia, fled her angry family, it was Eulogius who sheltered her. But they were found out and arrested. The priest had been chosen as the next Archbishop of Toledo, but could not be consecrated due to his imprisonment. He was publicly beheaded shortly thereafter.

PATRON SAINT OF:
Carpenters and coppersmiths

STATUS: *Martyr*

BORN: *c. 800 AD, Córdoba*

DIED: *March 11, 857 AD, Córdoba*

VENERATED BY: *Roman Catholic Church, Eastern Orthodox Church*

CANONIZED:
Pre-Congregation

SYMBOLS: *Shown with martyr's crown or martyr's palm*

Give me the courage to strive for the highest goals, to flee every temptation to be mediocre. Enable me to aspire to greatness, as St. Eulogius, and to open my heart with joy to Your call to holiness. Amen.

THE MARTYRDOM OF SAINT EULOGIUS OF CORDOBA, AT CORDOBA CATHEDRAL, BY AN UNKNOWN ARTIST OF THE 17TH CENTURY.

Louise de Marillac

Loving and compassionate God, we celebrate with great joy the faith and works of our patroness St. Louise de Marillac. Instill in us the fire of her love, the tenacity of her belief, and the tenderness of her care for the most abandoned. Draw us together into the light of your presence and help us to trust in the power of your Spirit, leading us to ever closer to you, who live and reign forever and ever. Amen.

K nown also as Louise Le Gras, she co-founded the Daughters of Charity along with St. Vincent de Paul. Louise was born in Picardy, claimed as the natural daughter of Louis de Marillac, Lord of Ferrires. Her uncle was a courtier of the queen, Maria de Medici—she never knew her mother—and so she lived and was educated among the French aristocracy. After she was denied entry to the Capuchin nuns, her family arrange a marriage with Queen Marie's secretary, Antoine Le Gras. She had a happy domestic life, bore one son, and did ministery work in her parish.

When Antoine died in 1525, Louise took her son and moved near Vincent de Paul, who became her her spiritual mentor. The two soon realized that the current system of wealthy ladies aiding the poor was creating tension. They determined that aristocratic women should raise the funds, but that those of similar rank to the poor should minister to them. Any young country women willing to aid the needy were thus sent to Paris, to work under Vincent's Ladies of Charity, which became the nucleus of the Daughters of Charity.

Leander of Seville

W hen people recite the Nicene Creed at Mass—"I believe in one god, the Father almighty maker of heaven and earth"—they should think of this saint, who introduced the practice in the sixth century. He believed it reinforced the faith of his congregation and acted as an antidote to heretical views.

Although Leander's family espoused Arianism, a doctrine denying the divinity of Christ, he himself was a fervent Christian. He began his life in the Church as a Benedictine monk and spent three years in study and prayer. He was made Bishop of Seville in 579, founding a school there that became a center of Catholic learning, while working steadily to defeat anti-Christian heresies. This created a conflict with the Visigoth king, Liuvigild, an advocate of Arianism. Forced into exile in Byzantium, he petitioned Emperor Tiberius II Constantine to take up arms against the Arians, but to no avail. When Liuvigild died, Leander returned from Byzantium to work with and eventually convert the new king, Recarred. After Leander's death, his brother, St. Isidore the encyclopedist, succeeded him as bishop. Their sister Florentina, an abbess, was also a saint.

STATUS: *Bishop, Doctor of the Church*

BORN: *c. 534*

DIED: *March 13, 600 or 601*

VENERATED BY: *Roman Catholic Church, Eastern Orthodox Church*

CANONIZED: *Pre-Congregation*

SYMBOLS: *Episcopal attire*

St. Leander, you worked tirelessly for the conversion of your Arian rulers. Pray with us for our political rulers, that they may embrace Judeo-Christian values and act on behalf of the people for those values. St. Leander, you came from a family of saints. Please intercede for all of our loved ones who have drifted away from the faith. St. Leander, you were a good servant who invested your talents wisely. Pray that we may have the grace of final perseverance. Amen.

SAN LEANDRO BY BARTOLOMÉ ESTEBAN PEREZ MURILLO

Matilda of Ringelheim

Matilda of Ringelheim became the first Ottonian queen after her husband became King Henry I of East Francia. Her eldest son, Otto I, restored the Holy Roman Empire in 962, while Matilda founded several spiritual institutions and women's convents.

Born into a noble family, Matilda was raised by her grandmother, an abbess in Saxony. One sister married the king of West Francia and her brother became Bishop of Châlons-sur-Marne. Matilda herself married Henry "the Fowler," Duke of Saxony and eventual King of the Franks. Their first-born, Otto, would become the future emperor. She was extremely pious, righteous, and charitable and performed many acts of mercy. After Henry I died in 926, she founded an abbey in Quedlinburg, where he was buried. When Otto sued her for the property included in her widow's dowry, she was forced into exile. Otto's wife later secured a reconciliation, and Matilda returned with her possessions restored.

PATRON SAINT OF:
A number of eponymous churches and a hospital in Germany

STATUS: *Queen*

BORN: *c. 892, Enger, Saxony*

DIED: *March 14, 968, Quendinburg, Saxony*

VENERATED BY: *Eastern Orthodox Church, Roman Catholic Church*

CANONIZED: *Possibly by acclamation*

SYMBOLS: *Shown holding a purse or alms*

St. Matilda, noble queen, you knew both great happiness, leading a pious life with your children . . . and also great suffering after being exiled by your son. Yet you reconciled with him, providing us with an example of how important it is to seek and restore amity with those we love. We thank you for your devotion and faith. Amen.

Longinus

Longinus is the unnamed Roman soldier who pierced Christ's side with his spear at the Crucifixion. Although the event is mentioned only in the Gospel of St. John, all three other Gospels describe a centurion who, upon Christ's death, proclaims that He must have been the Son of God. The spearman and the centurion have become fused in the apocryphal legend of Longinus.

The name Longinus is probably derived from the Greek longche, spear. His story was often embellished, including in Voragine's *Golden Legend*. It seems that Longinus's revelation on Golgotha immediately converted him. Thereafter, he is described, much like St. George, as a traveling Christian knight errant, bearing his spear. In some accounts he was martyred in Cappadocia (Turkey).

His cult emerged in the 6th century, as did the cult of the "Spear of Destiny" in Jerusalem. Stories concerning his relics developed during the Middle Ages. The "Lance of Longinus" features in several Holy Grail legends. A fragment of a spearhead discovered in the Holy Land during the Crusades is a revered relic in St. Peter's, Rome.

PATRON SAINT OF:
The blind and people with poor eyesight, labor, power, and good discernment

STATUS: *Penitent, martyr*

BORN: *Early 1st century AD*

DIED: *Mid–1st century AD*

VENERATED BY: *Roman Catholic Church, Eastern Orthodox Church, Armenian Apostelic Church*

CANONIZED:
Pre-Congregation

SYMBOLS: *In centurion's uniform, or on horseback, in knight's armor bearing a spear*

Dear Blessed Saint Longinus, your benevolence is absolute, and your devotion to God is admirable. You are an example of what I want to follow in life as a Christian devotee. So I need you to give me forgiveness and guide each of my steps towards spiritual healing and the kingdom of heaven....

THE STATUE OF SAINT LONGINUS BY BERNINI IN SAINT PETER'S BASILICA

Abraham Kidunaia

S tated in a biography written by his friend, St. Ephram, Abraham was born to a wealthy family some time during the late third century in either Cappadocia or Mesopotamia (accounts vary). After receiving a thorough education, his family convinced him to make an advantageous marriage. He escaped this fate by explaining to his soon-to-be bride his desire to live as a hermit. He retired to a rural cell, walling up his door, leaving only a small opening for food. When he inherited his parents fortune, he gave it all to the poor, establishing his reputation as a holy man. Many flocked to him for guidance.

Abraham was finally ordained by the Bishop of Edessa in order to undertake the conversion of local pagans, and he duly smashed their idols and altars. For three years he was driven back and persecuted, but he finally succeeded in gaining their trust. Fearing a desire for material things, he returned to his cell for 50 years, until his death. Abraham is especially venerated in Eastern Orthodox churches.

STATUS: *Priest, hermit*

BORN: *Cappdocia or Mesopotamia*

DIED: *360 AD, Assos, Asia Minor (modern Turkey)*

VENERATED BY: *Roman Catholic Church, Eastern Orthodox Church, Oriental Orthodoxy*

CANONIZED: *Pre-Congregation*

Blessed St. Abraham Kidunaia, inspire us, after your many long years of holy solitude, to put away worldy things and mundane pursuits, and to reconnect with the flame of faith that dwells within us. Let us seek insights that nourish our spirits and restorative thoughts that calm our souls. This we pray in the name of Jesus Christ. Amen.

MINIATURE FROM THE MENOLOGION OF BASIL II

Patrick

S t. Patrick is credited with the conversion of Celtic Ireland, an island never colonized by Rome. The patron saint of Ireland alongside Sts. Columba and Brigid (June 9, Feb. 1), he may be the best known of national patron saints, his fame spread by generations of Irish migrants. Typical of many Dark Ages saints, any historical truth is embroidered with later legends. St. Patrick's legends include using a shamrock—subsequently the country's national symbol—to illustrate the Trinity and his expulsion of snakes, symbols of evil, from Ireland.

Patrick was born a Christian in Britain, in Wales or Scotland, and at 16 was abducted by Irish raiders and carried to Ireland. Forced to work as a shepherd, in the process he discovered a latent spirituality. After fleeing slavery in Ireland, he traveled to France, where he was ordained and performed missionary work before Celestine I made him a bishop and sent him to Ireland to "gather the Irish into the one fold of Christ." His work brought him into conflict with local chiefs and kings, along with Druids and other religious leaders. Yet he asserted that he had not only "baptized thousands," but had established numerous chapels and convents.

PATRON SAINT OF:
Ireland, New York, Boston, Nigeria, engineers

STATUS: *Bishop, missionary*

BORN: *c.387/390, Britain*

DIED: *c.463/469, Ireland*

VENERATED BY: *Roman Catholic Church, Lutheran Church*

CANONIZED:
Pre-Congregation

SYMBOLS: *Shamrock*

. . . I arise today
Through the strength of heaven;
Light of the sun,
Splendor of fire,
Speed of lightning,
Swiftness of the wind,
Depth of the sea,
Stability of the earth,
Firmness of the rock.

THIS STAINED-GLASS WINDOW OF SAINT PATRICK IN FULL BISHOP'S REGALIA IS FOUND IN THE CATHEDRAL OF CHRIST THE LIGHT IN OAKLAND, CALIFORNIA.

Cyril of Jerusalem

Little is known of Cyril's early years except that he was born near Jerusalem in the fourth century and was well-read in theology and the Greek classics. He became Bishop of Jerusalem c.350, during a time of religious furor over various doctrines of the evolving church. As a forceful Christian theologian, he was against any form of Arianism and an enthusiastic supporter of the Nicene belief in the indivisible Trinity. He fell into disfavor with the Arian bishop, Acacius of Ceasarea, and was forced to flee to St. Silvanus, Bishop of Taraus. Eventually he returned to his see, but was again forced to flee the city several times afterward.

His works include a sermon on the Pool of Bethesda, a letter to the Emperor Constantius, three small fragments, and the famous "Catecheses." The letter describes a wonderful cross of light, extending from Calvary to the Mount of Olives, which appeared in May after Pentecost. His learned championship of what would become the orthodox Roman view was of enduring importance. He also advanced the notion of Jerusalem as a "holy city" and a pilgrimage center for Christians.

STATUS: *Bishop, Doctor of the Church*

BORN: *c. 313 AD, Caesarea, Jerusalem*

DIED: *c. 386 AD, Jerusalem*

VENERATED BY: *Roman Catholic Church, Eastern Orthodox Church, Oriental Orthodox Church, Anglican Communion*

CANONIZED: *Pre-Congregation*

SYMBOLS: *Shown holding a holy book or page of scripture; long white beard*

Father, through Cyril of Jerusalem you led your Church to a deeper understanding of the mysteries of salvation.

Let his prayers help us to know your Son better and to have eternal life in all its fullness.

Through our Lord Jesus Christ, your Son, who lives and reigns with you in the unity of the Holy Spirit, one God, for ever and ever.

Amen.

Joseph

The husband of Mary and Jesus' foster-father, Joseph appears in the Gospels of St. Luke, St. John, and St. Matthew. He is described as a descendant of the House of David and a carpenter by trade. The divine pregnancy of his betrothed was revealed in an angelic vision, and he humbly accepted his future role. After marrying Mary, they moved to Nazareth in Galilee, returning to Bethlehem a few months later to register for a tax census, where Mary gave birth. Warned by an angel to flee, he took his wife and son to Egypt to escape the wrath of Herod. Upon the latter's death, the family returned to Nazareth where, as a caring and nurturing father, Joseph raised Jesus and trained Him as a carpenter.

Joseph disappears from the New Testament before Christ's ministry. It is assumed he died of natural causes before Christ's crucifixion, probably at about 45, although he is frequently portrayed as an old man. Details of his biography were extended in the apocryphal Greek narrative The History of Joseph the Carpenter, written some 500 years later. This document appears to have sparked Joseph's cult status in the Egyptian Coptic and Eastern Orthodox churches, although a separate, and still thriving, cult became established in the West around the 10th century.

PATRON SAINT OF:
Carpenters, woodworkers, laborers, fatherhood, pregnant women, pioneers, doubters; Austria, Canada, China, South Korea, Mexico, Vietnam; the Universal Church

STATUS: *Foster father of Jesus*

BORN: *1st century BC, Bethlehem, modern Israel*

DIED: *1st century AD, Nazareth, modern Israel*

VENERATED BY: *Roman Catholic, Coptic, and Eastern Orthodox Churches, US Episcopal and US Evangelical Lutheran Churches*

CANONIZED:
Pre-Congregation

SYMBOLS: *Flowering rod with perched dove, symbol of his betrothal to Mary; carpenter's tools, ladder; shown as an old man with the Christ Child*

O God, you love your people and bless the ordinary lives we quietly live. As you blessed St. Joseph, bless what I do, however hidden and simple it may be, and let all I do be done with love. Amen.

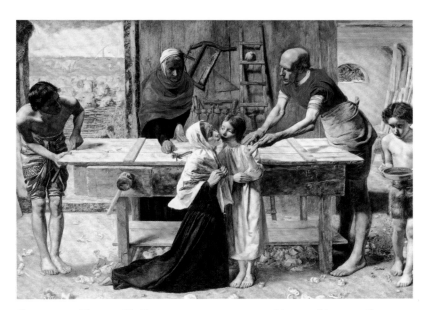

CHRIST IN THE HOUSE OF HIS PARENTS WAS PAINTED BETWEEN 1849 AND 1850 BY THE PRE-RAPHAELITE MASTER JOHN EVERETT MILLAIS, AND IS SOMETIMES CALLED SIMPLY THE CARPENTER'S SHOP. JOSEPH AND MARY ARE SHOWN TENDING HER SON, WHO HAS A SPLINTER IN HIS HAND, PRESAGING HIS CRUCIFIXION, WHICH IS ALSO ECHOED BY THE CRUCIFORM COMPOSITION, THE DROPS OF BLOOD ON HIS FOOT, AND THE LADDER, WOOD, NAILS, AND WOODWORKING TOOLS OF JOSEPH'S TRADE. TO THE RIGHT IS A YOUNG JOHN THE BAPTIST BEARING WATER, REMINDING US THAT HE WILL GO ON TO BAPTIZE JESUS SOME YEARS LATER.

Cuthbert

PATRON SAINT OF:
Northumbria

STATUS: *Bishop*

BORN: *c.634, Dunbar,
Northumbria*

DIED: *March 20, 687, Inner
Farne Island, Northumbria*

VENERATED BY: *Roman
Catholic Church, US Episcopal
Church*

CANONIZED:
Pre-Congregation

SYMBOLS: *Bishop holding a
second crowned head in his
hands; sometimes accompanied
by seabirds and animals*

*We would become
your Cuthbert people, O Christ,
shepherds of your sheep, peace
makers and hospitality givers open
to change and partnership, Spirit
led, in solitude and costly service.
. . . The grace of our Lord Jesus
Christ, the love of God and the
fellowship of the Holy Spirit be
with us all. Amen.*

Thanks to Bede, Cuthbert enjoys a reputation for sanctity and miracle working unmatched by any other early medieval British saint. Part mystic, part man of the world, he had a charismatic saintliness capable of inspiring immense devotion. Cuthbert was a product of the Irish Christian tradition exported to Scotland and thence to England, notably by St. Aidan. Appropriately, it was a vision of Aidan being carried to Heaven that inspired Cuthbert as a boy, tending sheep at night, to join the monastery at Melrose in Scotland. He was made prior in 664, a critical year for the development of early Christian Britain. The basic question was whether Irish Christian or Roman practices should have priority. At the Synod of Whitby in 664, Rome prevailed. It was a defeat Cuthbert took in excellent spirit.

In 676, Cuthbert left Lindisfarne to become a hermit, eventually settling on the tiny island of Farne, among the seabirds and gray waves of the North Sea. Numerous miracles were ascribed to Cuthbert during his life, and vastly more were ascribed to the tomb and relics of the "Wonder-Worker of England." He was buried first at Lindisfarne, but his relics were later relocated several times.

12TH-CENTURY FRESCO OF CUTHBERT, DURHAM CATHEDRAL. HIS TOMB WAS SECOND ONLY TO THAT OF THOMAS BECKETT AS A PILGRIMAGE SITE.

Nicholas von Flüe

A man of deep faith and lifelong integrity, "Brother Klaus" became the patron saint of Switzerland. He was the eldest son of wealthy peasants who, after a notable career as a farmer, member of the assembly, military leader, councillor, and judge, left his family of 10 children in 1467 to dwell as a hermit. This desire for a more contemplative life was prompted by a vision of a horse (his worldly existence) eating a lily (consuming his spiritualality.) It was said he subsisted only on Eucharist wafers for 19 years.

His reputation for sanctity grew to such an extent that, with the support of the pope, his cell at Ranft in central Switzerland became a recognized place of pilgrimage as well as a stop on one of the many roads to the shrine of Santiago de Compostela in Spain. But his chief claim to fame came in 1481, when he successfully brokered a compromise deal between rural Swiss cantons, which were determined that the Swiss Confederation should not be expanded, and the cities of Zürich and Lucerne, which were equally determined that it should. In doing so, he ended a dispute that posed a serious prospect of civil war.

PATRON SAINT OF: *Switzerland; Pontifical Swiss Guards*

STATUS: *Hermit, mystic.*

BORN: *March 21, 1417, Sachseln, Switzerland*

DIED: *March 21, 1487, Ranft, Switzerland*

VENERATED BY: *Roman Catholic Church, Swiss Protestants*

CANONIZED: *1947*

SYMBOLS: *Depicted as a bearded ascetic man in monk's robes*

My Lord and my God, take from me everything that distances me from you.
My Lord and my God, give me everything that brings me closer to you.
My Lord and my God, detach me from myself to give my all to you. Amen.

St. Nicholas is consulted by a priest, Heini am Grund. Illustration from Amtliche Luzerner Chronicle of 1513.

22

Clemens August Graf von Galen

STATUS: *Bishop, cardinal*

BORN: *16 March 1878, Dinklage, Germany*

DIED: *22 March 1946, Munster, Germany*

VENERATED BY: *Roman Catholic Church*

BEATIFIED: 2004

Almighty and everlasting God, as Bishop your servant Clemens August fearlessly defended your honor, the faith of the Church and the life of the weak; by his intercession grant that we will serve you always with all our heart and love all mankind as you love them. Through Jesus Christ. Amen.

Clemens August Graf von Galen was born into an aristocratic Catholic family. A student of theology, he was ordained as a priest in 1904 and appointed Bishop of Münster in 1933. Galen was regarded as nationalist and conservative, but this did not prevent him from opposing Hitler's National Socialist attacks on the Church, Catholic associations, and schools as early as 1934. He and Berlin Bishop Konrad Graf von Preysing became important spokesman for the opposition within the Church.

In 1941 Galen delivered three sermons that publicly attacked the Gestapo's terrorist methods, the murder of patients in psychiatric clinics, and the state confiscation of monasteries. The sermons were widely publicized both in Germany and abroad and gained much fame. Radio London broadcast them, they were scattered from Allied planes as leaflets, and even passed around by many Germans. In spite of his outcry, the National Socialists could not risk arresting the popular Bishop, the "Lion of Münster." Galen survived the war and was appointed a cardinal by Pius XII shortly before his death in 1946.

Toribio Alfonso de Mogrovejo

Born of a noble Spanish family, Toribio Alfonso de Mogrovejo was a pious child with a deep attachment to the Virgin Mary, fasting once a week in her honor. He studied humanities in college and became a law professor in Salamanca. Impressed by his abilities, King Phillip II appointed him Grand Inguisitor in Granada, and then in 1578 nominiated him for Archbishop of Lima.

Once in Peru, he made the 600-mile journey to Lima on foot, baptizing and teaching the residents along the way. In this remote new Spanish colony, he immediately brought order to the Church and proved himself a stern defender of native rights in the face of widespread Spanish oppression. In 1591, he established the New World's first seminary and oversaw the construction of chapels, schoolhouses, and hospitals. In 1604, he began the building of Lima Cathedral. He confirmed nearly half a million people, including Sts. Rose of Lima and Martin de Porres. He died at 67 of a fever after predicting the day and time of his death.

PATRON SAINT OF:
Lima, Peru; Valladolid, Spain; Native American rights; scouts

STATUS: *Bishop*

BORN: *November 16, 1538, Mayorga, Spain*

DIED: *March 23, 1606, Saña District, Peru*

VENERATED BY: *Roman Catholic Church, US Episcopal Church, Anglican Communion*

CANONIZED: *1726*

SYMBOLS: *Episcopal attire*

O God, who gave increase to Your Church through the apostolic labors and zeal for truth of the Bishop Saint Turibius, grant that the people consecrated to You may always receive new growth in faith and holiness.

Through our Lord Jesus Christ, Your Son, who lives and reigns with You in the unity of the Holy Spirit, one God, forever and ever. Amen.

Oscar Romero

O scar Romero, appointed archbishop of San Salvador in 1977, was the most high-profile victim of the struggle between left- and right-wing forces that destabilized Central America in the early 1980s. On March 24, 1980, while conducting Mass in San Salvador, he was shot and killed by a lone gunman. His death sparked a civil war that lasted 12 years and left an estimated 75,000 dead. Even at his funeral, attended by perhaps 250,000 mourners, as many as 50 people were killed as shots rang out from the roof of the National Palace.

It is not surprising the Church was drawn into so wide-ranging a conflict. During the three years when Romero was archbishop, six Catholic priests were murdered. Nine months after Romero's death, four American nuns were raped and murdered by a death squad (Dec. 2). Romero would prove himself a staunch opponent of oppression. His appeal in February 1980 to President Jimmy Carter to halt military aid to the government of El Salvador led directly to his death. In 1997, a campaign for his canonization was launched. Pope John Paul II declared him a Servant of God.

PATRON SAINT OF:
Caritas Internationalis

STATUS: *Bishop, martyr*

BORN: *1917, Ciudad Barrios, El Salvador*

DIED: *1980, San Salvador, El Salvador*

VENERATED BY: *Roman Catholic Church, in El Salvador*

CANONIZED: *2018*

. . . It may be incomplete, but it is a beginning, a step along the way, an opportunity for the Lord's grace to enter and do the rest.

We may never see the end results, but that is the difference between the master builder and the worker.

We are workers, not master builders; ministers, not messiahs.

We are prophets of a future not our own. Amen.

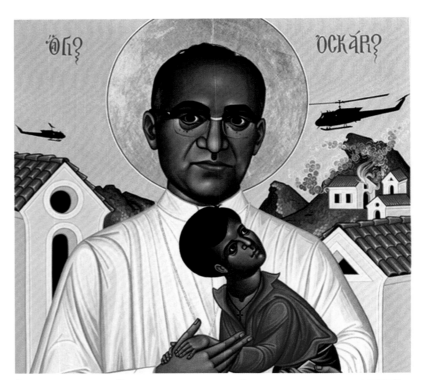

AMERICAN MILITARY AID, ROMERO CONTENDED, WOULD "UNDOUBTEDLY SHARPEN THE INJUSTICE AND THE REPRESSION INFLICTED ON THE PEOPLE, WHOSE STRUGGLE HAS OFTEN BEEN FOR THEIR MOST BASIC HUMAN RIGHTS."

Nicodemus of Mammola

Nicodemus's parents entrusted his edcation to a local priest. Soon known for his sanctity, the misspent lives of his male counterparts disgusted him. He was first turned away from the austere San Mercurius Abbey, where monks went barefoot and survived on chestnuts because the abbot, St. Fantinus, thought him too frail. Nicodemus persisted and was finally allowed to join.

He eventually sought more solitude and withdrew to live as a hermit on Monte Cellerano in Locri, Italy. But his reputation for piety soon brought him many spiritual students, whom he established in a separate community. Saracen incursions to the area eventually caused the monks and students to disperse to other monsteries. Nicodemus moved to a monastery near Mammola, Italy. When he died, his remains were buried there, and because he was already considered saintly it was renamed San Nicodemo in his honor. In 1580 his relics were eventually moved to a new, larger church in Mammola.

PATRON SAINT OF: *Mammola, Italy*

STATUS: *Hermit*

BORN: *c. 900 AD Cirò, Catanzaro, Italy*

DIED: *March 25, 990 AD, Mammola, Italy*

VENERATED BY: *Roman Catholic Church, Eastern Orthodox Church*

CANONIZED: *Pre-Congregation*

SYMBOLS: *Depicted as a thin, bearded, ascetic man*

Dearest St. Nicodemus, as you once turned away from your contemporaries for their dissipated lives, help us to draw back from the temptations of the world, the shining objects that lure us from the righteous path, and further aid us in devoting our lives to the worship of God the Father and his Son, Jesus Christ, in whose name we pray. Amen.

PORTRAIT OF SAN FANTINO AT THE SANCTUARY OF SAN NICODEMO, MAMMOLA (RC)

Ludger of Münster

L udger, or Liudger, was a missionary sent to Frisia and Saxony in northwest Germany, areas outside the Roman empire and, in the 8th century, still fiercely resistant to Christianity. In 753, he met Boniface (June 5) and, after studying under Gregory at Utrecht and Alcuin at York (May 20), he was ordained in 777 in Cologne. He then began an arduous seven-year missionary program in Frisia, which ended with only partial success. He visited Rome before retiring to Monte Cassino. In 787, he returned to Frisia, this time with more success.

In 793, Charlemagne charged him to perform missionary work in Saxony. It was now that Ludger began overseeing what would become Münster Cathedral (münster means monastery), as well as a number of other churches. In about 803, he was also instrumental in the establishment of an early convent in Westphalia, at Nottuln, headed by his sister, St. Gerburgis. By 805, he had also been made Bishop of Münster.

PATRON SAINT OF:
East Frisia, Münster

STATUS: *Bishop, missionary*

BORN: *c.744, Zuilen, Netherlands*

DIED: *809, Westphalia, Germany*

VENERATED BY: *Roman Catholic Church, Low Countries, Saxony*

CANONIZED:
Pre-Congregation

SYMBOLS: *Depicted flanked by swans; holding a book or cathedral*

O God, we seek the guidance of Ludger of Munster, he who never failed to make time to pray or meditate, even when his health was failing, because he knew it was the source of his strength. Let us learn from his example to express and celebrate our love and faith in an act of daily prayer. Amen.

Rupert of Salzburg

Known as the "apostle to the Bavarians," Rupert's early life remains largely a mystery. He was likely born in Gaul (modern France) and was possibly a member of the Merovingian royal family. By all accounts he lived a life of asceticism, spirituality, and charity. He was eventually consecrated Bishop of Worms in Germany, where he proved a devoted leader, but the pagan population eventually drove him from the city. In about 697 he was sent as a missionary to Regensburg in Bavaria to purge heretical pagan practices that had become mingled with Christian doctrines. There he won numerous converts, among them Duke Theodo of Bavaria, who in around 700 granted Rupert land in the ruined Roman city of Juvavum, which would become Salzburg. There he began the building of the church and abbey of St. Peter—today the site of Salzburg Cathedral—as well as a monastery at Mönchberg and Nonnburg Convent. He brought about many miracles, including healings. Today in Austria there are a number of churches and monasteries named for him.

PATRON SAINT OF:
Salzburg, Austria

STATUS: *Bishop, missionary*

BORN: *c. 660 AD*

DIED: *March 27, 710, Salzburg, Austria*

VENERATED BY: *Roman Catholic Church, Eastern Orthodox Church*

CANONIZED:
Pre-Congregation

SYMBOLS: *Depicted with a container of salt*

Dear Lord Jesus, Your holy bishop, Saint Rupert, built many sacred places and enabled many to learn about You and their faith through the nuns and monks that resided in these holy institutions. Through the intercession of Saint Rupert, we pray that we will build up the faith through our actions and love of others. Amen.

28

Sixtus III

STATUS: *Pope*

BORN: *4th century, Roman Empire*

DIED: *Augst 18, 440, Rome, Roman Empire*

VENERATED BY: *Roman Catholic Church*

CANONIZED: *Pre–Congregation*

Blessed St. Sixtus III, teach us to build our faith from day to day, as you once helped to rebuild Rome, your papal seat, brick by brick; reveal to us our many sins, and school us in the adoration of the Virgin Mary, in whose holy name we ask forgiveness for all our transgressions. Amen.

Sixtus was a prominent Roman clergyman who often corresponded with Augustine of Hippo, and was a patron of Pelagius, an advocate of free will and asceticism, who was later condemned as a heretic. He was named pope in 432, during a period when papal authority was under threat on a number of fronts. He succeeded in significantly strengthening the issue of Mary's rank, above all in Illyria in Greece, which the Eastern emperors had long sought to bring under their direct control. His acceptance of the Council of Ephesus of 431 made it clear that the Virgin was henceforth to be regarded as the Mother of God and not merely as the Mother of Christ. It was in commemoration of her new status that Sixtus III began the construction of Santa Maria Maggiore, one of the four papal basilicas.

Jonas and Barachisius

During the bloody persecutions of King Sapor of Persia, these two siblings from Beth-Asa left their monastery and interceded on behalf of nine Christians imprisoned in Hubaham. "Fear not, brothers," they proclaimed to the men, "but let us combat for the name of Jesus crucified, and like our predecessors we shall obtain the glorious crown promised to valiant soldiers of the Faith." As such, the nine went to their deaths; meanwhile Jonas and Barachisius were arrested for exhorting the martyrs to die. When ordered by the government to worship the sun, moon, fire, and water, they responded that it was more reasonable to obey the King of Heaven than an earthly prince. As punishment, Jonas was beaten with clubs, then was forced to spend the night in a freezing pond chained by one leg. Barachisius had red-hot iron plates and hammers placed under each arm and melted lead dropped into his eyes and nostrils. At the end, both brothers prayed for their tormenters.

PATRON SAINTS OF: *Monks, martyrs*

STATUS: *Martyrs*

BORN: *Late third century*

DIED: *c. 327 AD*

VENERATED BY: *Roman Catholic Church*

CANONIZED: *Pre-Congregation*

SYMBOLS: *Wine press for Jonas, boiling cauldron for Barachisius*

O heavenly Father, we ask that like Sts. Jonas and Barachisius we may give comfort to other Christians during times of tribulation, meanwhile maintaining our own faith and praying for the souls of those who are aligned against us. This we pray in the blessed name of Jesus Christ. Amen.

BROTHERS JONAS AND BARACHISIUS WERE MARTYRED WITH NINE COMPANIONS.

John Climacus

Known also as John of the Ladder, he was a 6th–7th century Christain monk, although there is little actual information about his life or origins. He joined St. Catherine's Monastery on Mt. Sinai—one of the two oldest monasteries in the world—at age 16 and was instructed about the spiritual life by the elder monk Martyrius. While in his fifties, he removed himself from the monastery, living instead at its foot as a hermit, in the process becoming one of the great scholars of the early Church. His reputation for sanctity was such that he was eventually persuaded to return to the monastery as abbot, or "igumen" as it is known in the Orthodox Church. There he functioned with such wisdom and devotion that Pope Gregory the Great wrote and asked to be in his prayers. John remained at the monastery for a further four years before resuming his life as a hermit and preparing himself for death.

STATUS: *Abbot, hermit*

BORN: *579, Syria*

DIED: *649, Jabal Mousa, Egypt*

VENERATED BY: *Roman Catholic Church, Eastern Orthodox Church, Eastern Catholic Church*

CANONIZED: *Pre-Congregation*

SYMBOLS: *Abbot's crozier, often shown climbing a ladder to heaven*

Dweller of the desert and angel in the body, you were shown to be a wonder-worker, our God-bearing Father John.

You received heavenly gifts through fasting, vigil, and prayer: healing the sick and the souls of those drawn to you by faith.

Glory to Him who gave you strength!

Glory to Him who granted you a crown!

Glory to Him who through you grants healing to all!

THE LADDER OF DIVINE ASCENT, DEPICTED IN A 12TH-CENTURY ICON, DESCRIBES THE ATTAINMENT OF SPIRITUALITY IN 30 STEPS, THE FINAL RUNG BEING UNION WITH CHRIST. AT ANY STAGE, DEVILS MAY PLUCK THE UNWORTHY FROM THE LADDER. JOHN CLIMACUS IS SHOWN WITH MONKS BEHIND HIM.

Benjamin the Deacon

This early deacon was an inspiring preacher of the Gospel and brought many converts, Persians and Greeks, into the fold. He was imprisoned for a year during the persecutions of Persian King Varanes V, but one of the nobles at court defended him. Benjamin was released with the proviso that he never preach again. Benjamin boldly proclaimed: "This I can never give up. For he who hides the talent given him will be given over to great suffering." He made good on these words, continuing his street ministry without thought to the consequences. The king had him seized again, and this time made sure he was tortured to death: sharp reeds were driven under his fingernails and toenails, and thrust into the tender parts of his body. A knotty stake was then driven into his bowels, at which time he finally expired.

His feast day is celebrated on October 13 by the Eastern Orthodox Church.

PATRON SAINT OF: *People named Benjamin*

STATUS: *Martyr*

BORN: *329, Persia*

DIED: *c. 424 AD, Persia*

VENERATED BY: *Roman Catholic Church, Eastern and Oriental Orthodox Churches*

CANONIZED: *Pre-Congregation*

SYMBOLS: *Depicted in jail maintaining his faith*

Dear Jesus, May we never fear voicing our love for You.

We pray that, like Saint Benjamin, we witness our faith always, even in the face of adversity. Amen.

APRIL

A month inaugurated by a spate of practical jokes on April Fools' Day, April derives its name from the Latin aperire, to open, reflecting the period when many plants burst into bloom. April is when Easter most frequently occurs; the most important event in the liturgical calendar, it commemorates the Passion and celebrates Christ's Resurrection.

The important weeklong Jewish festival of Passover, marking the Isrealites emancipation from Egyptian slavery, also usually occurs in April, starting on the first full moon after the vernal equinox in the Hebrew month of Nisan.

In England, April 23 commemorates the national patron, Saint George. Although it is not a public holiday, his distinctive flag of a red cross on a white background is flown from many churches and other buildings. The flag is also traditionally flown on English churches on other major religious feast days.

CHRIST'S AGONIZING DEATH ON THE CROSS ON GOOD FRIDAY IS PORTRAYED HERE ON THE SAYEN PANEL (1470) BY THE UNNAMED GERMAN MASTER OF THE STORY OF ST. GEORGE. THE ATTENDANTS AT THE SCENE ARE NEATLY DIVIDED, WITH SAINTS ON THE LEFT (THE BLESSED VIRGIN MARY, JOHN, AND MARY MAGDALENE), AND THE NOBLE PATRON OF THE PAINTING KNEELING IN PRAYER.

Hugh of Châteauneuf

Hugh was a pious young man from the Dauphine region who was made Canon of Valence while still a layman. In 1080 he became bishop of Grenoble and was escorted to Rome to be ordained by Pope Gregory VIII himself. A monumental task was then assigned to Hugh—restoring the See of Grenoble, which was corrupt and in a very poor spiritual state. After two years of reformation he had countered much abuse and fostered increased devotion, but still feeling frustrated, he asked to resign and join a Benedictine monastery. The pope refused his request and ordered him to go on with his work.

Hugh was also instrumental in the foundation of the Carthusian Order. He received Brune of Cologne, possibly his own teacher, and six of his companions in 1084, after dreaming of them beneath a banner of seven stars. Hugh gave St. Bruno the land on which the Grande Chartreuse was founded. Hugh died on April 1 and was canonized by Pope Innocent II.

PATRON SAINT OF:
Grenoble, France; invoked against headaches

STATUS: *Bishop, reformer*

BORN: *1053, Châteauneuf-sur-Isere*

DIED: *April 1, 1132, Grenoble, France*

VENERATED BY: *Roman Catholic Church*

CANONIZED: *1134*

SYMBOLS: *Lantern, three flowers*

In the midst of our confusing life these days, let us pray for the ability to rise above the fray and to see things in the light of faith as did Saint Hugh. Amen.

PAINTING OF ST. HUGH FROM THE CARTHUSIAN CLOISTER OF NUESTRA SEÑORA DE LAS CUEVAS A TRIANA BY FRANCISCO DE ZURBARÁN

Francis of Paola

2

PATRON SAINT OF:
Boatmen, mariners, naval officers; Calabria, Italy

STATUS: *Friar, founder*

BORN: *March 27, 1416, Paola, Italy*

DIED: *April 2, 1507, Plessis, France*

VENERATED BY: *Roman Catholic Church, Franciscans*

CANONIZED: *1519*

SYMBOLS: *Usually depicted with staff and cloak*

O God, exaltation of the lowly, who raised Saint Francis of Paola to the glory of your Saints, grant, we pray, that by his merits and example we may happily attain the rewards promised to the humble. Through our Lord Jesus Christ, your Son, who lives and reigns with you in the unity of the Holy Spirit, one God, for ever and ever. Amen.

FRANCIS OF PAOLA IN MANY WAYS REPRESENTS THE IDEAL OF THE MENDICANT FRANCISCAN FRIAR, HUMBLE, SELF-DENYING, AND DEVOUT, YET CAPABLE OF INSPIRING AWE AND REVERENCE AMONG THE UPPER ECHELONS OF SOCIETY. HE BECAME A POPULAR SUBJECT FOR CATHOLIC ARTISTS SUCH AS PROSPERO FONTANA (C.1512–97) DURING THE EARLY COUNTER-REFORMATION PERIOD.

Francis was born in Paola, in southern Italy. As an infant he suffered a condition that threatened the sight in one eye, and his frantic parents sought the intercession of Francis of Assisi (Oct. 4), vowing that their son would spend a year in a Franciscan convent—and the baby was immediately cured. And so at 13 Francis entered a Franciscan convent. Following pilgrimages to Assisi and Rome, he lived in seclusion, giving himself up to prayer and mortification. In 1464, one story goes, a boatman refused to ferry him across the Strait of Messina to Sicily. Francis laid his cloak on the water, tied one end to his staff for a sail, and navigated his own way across.

At 20 he had formed a movement that was to become the Hermits of St. Francis of Assisi, or the Minim Friars. They led a harsh life, espousing poverty and emphasizing penance, charity, chastity, and humility. Francis, famous for miraculous healings and prophecies, went on to found new monasteries throughout Calabria and Sicily.

Mary of Egypt

Mary of Egypt's history comes to us from a biography by the 6th-century Patriarch of Jerusalem, St. Sophronius. Mary's later piety was in sharp contrast to the dissolution of her early life. At age 12, Mary ran away to the cosmopolitan city of Alexandria, where it is believed she became a prostitute. After 17 years she joined a pilgrimage to Jerusalem for the Feast of the Exaltation of the Holy Cross. She saw the trip as an opportunity to exploit fellow pilgrims.

When she attempted to enter the Church of the Holy Sepulchre in Jerusalem, however, she felt held back by a mysterious force, and concluded that it was her impurity barring her entry. When she prayed for forgiveness and vowed to become an ascetic, she was able to enter. At the Monastery of St. John the Baptist on the banks of the River Jordan, she received absolution and Holy Communion. She crossed the river, carrying just three loaves of bread, and vowed to spend her life as a hermit in the wilderness. As an old women, naked and wild-haired, she met St. Zosimas of Palestine, who gave her a cloak. She asked to take communion from him at the Jordan, and he witnessed her cross the water on its suface. After death her body was found by him to be incorrupt. Her relics are venerated at Rome, Naples, Cremona, and Antwerp.

PATRON SAINT OF: *Chastity, fevers, skin diseases, deliverance from demons, temptations of the flesh*

STATUS: *Penitent, hermit*

BORN: *c.344, Egypt*

DIED: *c.421, Sinai Desert, Palestine*

VENERATED BY: *Roman Catholic Church, Eastern Orthodox Church*

CANONIZED: *Pre-Congregation*

SYMBOLS: *Depicted as naked, grey-haired, being handed a cloak by Zosimas; often shown with three loaves of bread*

In thee, O Mother, was exactly preserved what was according to the divine image. For thou didst take the cross and follow Christ, and by thy life, didst teach us to ignore the flesh, since it is transitory, but to care for the soul as an immortal thing. Therefore, thy spirit, St. Mary, rejoices with the Angels. Amen.

The starkness of Mary's 47 years of penitence in the desert attracted Counter-Reformation artists such as José de Ribera (1591–1652).

Isidore of Seville

A medieval scholar whose histories of the Iberian Peninsula were the primary source for later histories, Isidore was also a Catholic bulwark against the cultural depredations of the Visigoths. Born to an influential Catholic family in Cartagena, Spain, Isidore was educated in the cathedral school in Seville. He succeeded his brother St. Leander as bishop of Seville and presided over a period of major upheaval. The great institutions of the classical world were disintegrating under the pressure of the Visigoths—Eastern European invaders with a contempt for learning. Isidore set about creating a sense of national unity by assimilating the various foreign elements. The Visigothic kings had adopted the Arian heresy, which taught that Jesus was not one with God the Father. They were persuaded to abandon the heresy, and religious discipline was thus strengthened, becoming a formidable unifying force. From 619, Isidore presided over a series of councils at Seville and Toledo. At the Fourth Council of Toledo in 633, it was agreed that bishops would establish seminaries in their cathedral cities, ensuring that an enlightened education would counteract the dangers of barbarism.

PATRON SAINT OF:
Students, proposed patron saint of the internet and programmers

STATUS: *Bishop, Doctor of the Church*

BORN: *c.560, Cartagena, Spain*

DIED: *April 4, 636, Seville, Spain*

VENERATED BY: *Roman Catholic Church, Eastern Orthodox Church*

CANONIZED: *653*

SYMBOLS: *Bees, pen and book; associated with Sts. Leander, Fulgentius, Florentina*

O God, let me be inspired by St. Isidore, who stood firm against pagan invaders, stayed steady during an era of upheaval, and remained focused on creating national unity. As I go about the business of my daily life, let me maintain my determination, display an even temper, and encourage cooperation. These gifts I ask in the name of your Son, Jesus Christ. Amen.

SAN ISIDORO.

Vincent Ferrer

Dedicated as a missionary and preacher at a time when the Catholic Church was undermined by internal dissent, Vincent traveled all over western Europe, a tireless proponent Christianity. Legends about Vincent abound: It is said that his father learned in a dream that his son would be famous throughout the world, and his mother experienced no pain in childbirth. Vincent grew up a pious and charitable child. He entered the Dominican Order at age 18 and became a Master of Sacred Theology. Vincent refused all the dignities the Church sought to bestow on him, preferring to spread the Christian message throughout Spain, Switzerland, France, Italy, and the British Isles. He is also said to have converted many Jews to Catholicism in his homeland.

During the troubled period of the Avignon papacy from 1309–78, when seven popes resided in Avignon, reflecting the increasing dominance of the French kings over Rome, Vincent remained loyal to the Avignonese pope, Benedict XIII, encouraging him to end the division. He lived to see the end of the Great Schism, with the election of Pope Martin V in Rome in 1417.

PATRON SAINT OF:
Builders, construction workers, plumbers, prisoners, fisherman; Archdiocese of Valencia

STATUS: *Domincan friar, missionary*

BORN: *January 23, 1350, Valencia, Spain*

DIED: *April 4, 1419, Vannes, France*

VENERATED BY: *Roman Catholic Church, Anglican Church, Philippine Independent Church*

CANONIZED: *1455*

SYMBOLS: *Dominican habit, tongue of flame, pulpit, trumpet, wings, Bible*

O God, who didst vouchsafe to glorify Thy Church by the merits and preaching of Saint Vincent Ferrer, Thy Confessor: grant us Thy servants that we may be taught by his example, and be delivered by his patronage from all adversities. Amen.

Crescentia Höss

STATUS: *Contemplative nun*

BORN: *October 20, 1682, Kaufbeuren, Bavaria*

DIED: *April 5, 1744, Kaufbeuren, Bavaria*

VENERATED BY: *Roman Catholic Church*

CANONIZED: *2001*

SYMBOLS: *Dove*

Saint Crescentia, Your saintliness is something I hope to emulate today and in the future especially with your good financial acumen. May I use my financial blessings wisely and be generous with my money, time, talent, and treasures and aide those less fortunate in any way. Thank you Lord for another day to do your works. Amen.

K nown in her hometown of Augsburg as "the little angel," Anna Höss was the devout daughter of a poor weaver. She desired to enter the Tertiaries of Saint Francis but the convent was poor and because she had no dowry, the superior refused her admission. After the Protestant mayor pleaded her case, she was allowed to join, taking the name Maria Crescentia. But the mother superior resented her—calling her a parasite—and gave her the most menial tasks. Still, Crescentia's spirit shone through. A new mother superior recognized her true worth and made her mistress of novices. Eventually Crescentia herself was elected mother superior and was able to improve the finances of the convent. Her reputation as a spiritual counselor spread and she was soon being consulted by princes, bishops, and cardinals. She was sorely tried by her physical afflictions, suffering toothaches and headaches, and at one point she lost the ability to walk, while her hands and feet become so crippled that her body curled into fetal position. In spite of these trials she remained full of peace and joy until her death.

Jean Baptiste de la Salle

A notable scholar, Jean Baptiste became a canon of the cathedral at only 16. When his parents died he abandoned his education to care for his family and so was not ordained as a Dominican until age 27. He helped establish a school for the poor in Reims, and then founded the Institute of the Brothers of the Christian Schools (Christian Brothers). Moved by the plight of poor children with little hope of an education, he renounced his own wealth and formed a community of lay religious teachers, the first Catholic teaching order that did not include clergymen. The use of lay teachers brought him into conflict with the ecclesiastical authorities. Yet he succeeded in creating a network of excellent schools throughout France, noted for integrating religious instruction with secular subjects.

He pioneered training programs for lay teachers, founding a training seminary in Reims in 1685, and introduced Sunday courses for working men, secondary schools for modern languages, institutions dedicated to the care of delinquents, and schools specializing in arts, sciences, and technical skills. His work quickly spread around the globe, and led to the foundation of many other teaching orders throughout the 18th and 19th centuries that still flourish today.

PATRON SAINT OF: *Educators, school principles, Institute of the Brothers of the Christian Schools, Lasallian Educational Institutions*

STATUS: *Priest, educator, founder*

BORN: *April 30, 1651, Reims, France*

DIED: *April 7, 1719, Rouen, France*

VENERATED BY: *Roman Catholic Church*

CANONIZED: *1900*

SYMBOLS: *Stretched right arm with finger pointing up, instructing one or two children standing near him; books*

Father, You chose Saint John Baptist de la Salle to give young people a Christian education.

Give your Church teachers who will devote themselves to helping your children grow as Christian men and women.

Through our Lord Jesus Christ, your Son, who lives and reigns with you in the unity of the Holy Spirit, one God, for ever and ever. Amen.

Julie Billiart

Good and gracious God, just as Saint Julie followed Your light and Your call for her Sisters to carry Your light where ever they went; You invite us to follow Your light on our journey. Help us to continue to open our minds and hearts to Your light that we may truly have hearts as "wide as the universe." We ask this in Jesus' name, Amen.

Educated only at a village school, young Julie would recite the catechism to other children and explain it to them. She was confirmed at age nine and took a vow of chastity five years later. Known for her virtue and piety, she was called, "the saint of Cuvilly." At age twenty-two she suffered a nervous shock when a pistol was fired at her father by an unknown enemy. The resulting paralysis of the lower limbs confined her to bed for 30 years. She received Holy Communion daily and spent many hours in contemplation, devoloping an uncommon gift for prayer. During the French Revolution, Billiart took refuge in Amien and met Marie Louise Françoise Blin de Bourdon, a viscountess only recently released from imprisonment. Around this time Billiart had a vision of her crucified Lord surrounded by a group of religious women dressed in an unfamiliar habit. An inner voice proclaimed that she would begin an institute for the Christian education girls. She and de Bourdon founded the Sisters of Notre Dame de Namur, dedicated to the salvation of poor children and religious instruction of girls. Billiart went on to found 15 further convents.

Casilda of Toledo

Casilda of Toledo was likely the daughter of Moorish king Yahya ibn Ismail al-Mamun, who ruled the regions of northern Spain that were under Muslim control in the tenth and eleventh centuries. Casilda was known for her kindness to Christian prisoners, often bringing them bread in a basket hidden in her skirts. Often the prison guards stopped her and asked her what she was carrying; she told them "roses." When they insisted on seeing the basket, it was indeed full of roses.

When Casilda became ill with what was probably a female reproductive health issue, her father's Muslim doctors could not heal her. She embarked on a pilgrimage to the miraculous springs at San Vicente near the north coast of Spain, where many women, especially those suffering hemorrhages, went to be healed. Her father had to ask permission of the king of Burgos for his daughter to make the journey. Once Casilda bathed in the waters, however, her ailment disappeared. Afterward she converted to Christianity, was baptized in Burgos, and became a pious, prayerful hermit near the springs that cured her. She was said to have lived to be 100.

PATRON SAINT OF: *Infertile women and Muslim converts to Christianity; invoked against uterine hemorrhage and bad luck*

STATUS: *Hermitess*

BORN: *c. 950*

DIED: *c. 1050*

VENERATED BY: *Roman Catholic Church, Eastern Orthodox Church*

SYMBOLS: *Depicted carrying roses*

O St. Casilda, pray for us that we will find peace in our hearts helping all of God's children regardless of their culture, religion, or status. This we ask in the name of Jesus Christ, our Lord. Amen.

CASILDA OF TOLEDO BY FRANCISCO DE ZURBARÁN

Fulbert of Chartres

Fulbert was a scholarly young man who rose from humble stock. He studied at the Rheims Cathedral School under Gerbert of Aurillac, later Pope Sylvester II, and attended with the future king of France, Robert II. He eventually taught at the cathedral school at Chartres. At the turn of the millennium, when people feared the end of the world, he used the existing veneration of the Virgin Mary to calm them. He also promoted the Feast Day of Mary's Nativity, increasing her importance to Catholics, which in turn led to Chartres expanding its outreach as it became a center of Marian worship. (The cathedral already possessed her sacred tunic.) Fulbert, although not a priest, was made bishop of Chartres in 1006. He was a prolific letter writer and composer of hymns and reconstructed the iconic cathedral after a fire. Many of his ideas, especially those on maintaining the division between Church and State, were incorporated into the Gregorian church reforms of the 12th-century. Although never canonized, the Church gave permission for Fulbert to have his own feast day, which is celebrated in Chartres and Poitiers.

STATUS: *Bishop*

BORN: *c. 960 AD, France or Italy*

DIED: *April 10, 1028, Chartres, France*

VENERATED BY: *Roman Catholic Church*

SYMBOLS: *Shown with bishop's staff*

Lord Jesus, we pray that St. Fulbert will intercede for our clergy when they need strengthening to make the right decisions. May they always stay true to Church teachings and to You, we pray. Amen.

Stanislaus (Stanislaw) of Szczepanów

S tanislaus, the only son of a nobleman, was educated at the cathedral school at Gniezno (then Poland's capital). After travels to France and Belgium, he was ordained by the bishop of Kraków. In 1072, Stanislaus was elected as his successor, with strong papal support. Although Poland was only beginning to adopt Christianity, Stanislaus built firm relations with Rome. When Duke Boleslaw was crowned king in 1076, Stanislaus made it a condition that the metropolitan See of Gniezno would be reinstated and encouraged the new king to establish Benedictine monasteries throughout the country.

Stanislaus was forced to confront Boleslaw a number of times, even resurrectig Piotr, a dead man, to appeal to the king for him during a land dispute. Another time soldiers returning home from war found their estates and wives taken by overseers. Boleslaw ordered harsh punishment for the wives until Stanislaus intervened. At one point the bishop even excommunicated the king, who struck back by ordering his death for "treason." The bishop was hacked apart at the king's order during Mass, but the body was miraculously reintegrated. Boleslaw was dethroned and Stanislaus became the focus of a cult.

PATRON SAINT OF: *Moral order; Poland, Kraków*

STATUS: *Bishop, martyr*

BORN: *July 26, 1030, Szczepanów, Poland*

DIED: *April 11, 1079, Kraków, Poland*

VENERATED BY: *Roman Catholic Church*

CANONIZED: *1253*

SYMBOLS: *Episcopal insignia, sword, Piotr rising from the dead at his feet*

Dear Lord, we thank You for giving us Your martyr, St. Stanislaus, as an example of holiness. Help us to imitate the openness to Your will that he showed by answering Your call to serve You in the priesthood. St. Stanislaus, you began your life in the household of pious parents. From the foundation in the Faith that they gave you, you continued on the path of virtue and openness to God's will for you. Pray that all who are called to serve God in a religious vocation may respond generously to His call! Amen.

Sabbas the Goth

Bless me, heavenly Father, with the courage of St. Sabbas, who withstood the severe trials of persecution and refused to recant his faith, and who faced death still denouncing false beliefs. Let me walk in this martyr's shadow, Lord, and gain his conviction and faith. In Jesus' name I pray. Amen.

Born a Goth, Sabbas was raised a Christian and became a "cantor" (reader) to the Christian community in Romania. In 371, the Goths began the suppression of Christians in the Wallachian region of Romania, and Christians in Sabbas's village were forced to eat pagan sacrificial meat. Sabbas publicly proclaimed his Christian faith and refused to eat the meat. Because he was of little account, the Goth leader dismissed him.

The following year, Sabbas celebrated Easter with a priest, Sansala. Spies reported this defiance to the authorities, and three days later Athanaric, son of the Goth king, arrested Sansala. More punishment was meted out: Sabbas was dragged naked through thorn bushes, bound to a tree, and again forced to eat defiled meat. Once again Sabbas refused and was condemned to death by drowning. He staunchly declaimed his Christian faith and denounced Goth idolatry as he was bound to a wooden pole with a rock tied around his neck and thrown into the river. Christian advocates salvaged his relics and sent them to Thessalonica.

Saint Sabbas's martyrdom

Martin I

T he period between 537 and 752 is described as the Byzantine papacy, due to the attempted reconquest of the barbarian West, above all Italy, launched by Byzantine emperor Justinian. Though Justinian's conquests proved short-lived, they greatly strengthened Byzantium's hold over the papacy. Pope Martin I—Martin the Confessor—elected in 649, had been papal ambassador in Byzantium and was expected to favor Byzantium. The opposite proved to be the case. The definitive 11th century split between the Western and the Eastern Christian churches was prefigured during Martin's papacy. The issue was Monothelitism, enthusiastically embraced in the East, as energetically rejected in the West.

Martin almost immediately convened the Lateran Council to resolve the issue. It overwhelmingly dismissed Monothelitism as heresy. In revenge—and it took almost four years to arrange—Emperor Constans II subsequently had Martin seized. He was taken to the island of Naxos, where he was starved, and then brought in chains to Byzantium for trial as a "heretic, rebel, enemy of God, and of the state." Throughout the hearing, Martin was beaten, abused, and humiliated. He was then publicly flogged, but rather than executing him, Constans exiled Martin to Cherson in the Crimea, where he was starved to death.

STATUS: *Pope, martyr.*

BORN: *June 21, 598, Umbria, Italy*

DIED: *September 16, 655, Cherson, Crimea, Russia*

VENERATED BY: *Russian Orthodox Church*

CANONIZED: *Pre-Congregation*

Grant, almighty God, that we may withstand the trials of this world with invincible firmness of purpose, just as you did not allow your Martyr Pope Saint Martin the First to be daunted by threats of broken by suffering,

Through our Lord Jesus Christ, your Son, who lives and reigns with you in the unity of the Holy Spirit, one God, for ever and ever. Amen.

MARTIN I DEPICTED IN EXILE

Peter González

PATRON SAINT OF:
Spanish and Portuguese sailors

STATUS: *Priest*

BORN: *March 9, 1190,
Frómista, Spain*

DIED: *April 15, 1246, Tui,
Galicia, Castile and Leon*

VENERATED BY: *Roman
Catholic Church*

CANONIZED: *1741*

SYMBOLS: *Dominican garb;
holding blue candle or candle
with blue flame; lying on his
cloak spread over hot coals;
holding fire in his bare hands;
catching fish with his bare
hands; beside the ocean, holding
or protecting a ship*

*Almighty God, you bestowed the
singular help of Blessed Peter on
those in peril from the sea. By the
help of his prayers may the light
of your grace shine forth in all the
storms of this life and enable us
to find the harbor of everlasting
salvation. We ask this through
our Lord Jesus Christ, your Son,
who lives and reigns with you and
the Holy Spirit, one God, for ever
and ever.*

A nephew of the bishop of Astorga, Pedro González was an unlikely candidate for sainthood, energetically devoting himself to the pursuit of aristocratic pleasure as a youth. Appointed dean of Astorga Cathedral by his uncle in a fairly open act of nepotism, Pedro arrived in the city in splendor, cheered by the assembled crowds. His horse apparently threw him, however, and he landed either in a puddle or a dunghill. Humiliated, Pedro was made instantly aware of the fickleness of acclaim and the consequences of vanity. He renounced all worldly ambitions, joined the Dominicans, and gained fame as a preacher. Summoned to the court of Ferdinand III (May 30), in 1236, he accompanied the king to the siege of Córdoba, still a major Moorish stronghold. When the city fell to the Christians, Pedro is said to have urged compassion toward the defeated Muslim forces.

The rest of his life was spent in Galicia, in northwest Spain, preaching to fishermen and sailors.

16TH-CENTURY PAINTING OF THE BLESSED PETER GONZÁLEZ, BY
ALEJO FERNÁNDEZ, IN THE ALCÁZAR OF SEVILLE

César de Bus

L ike the pleasure-seeking St. Pedro González, César de Bus was affected by no less sudden a conversion. At eighteen the once-pious youth joined the French army and fought against the Protestant Huguenots, and when peace was restored occupied his time sailing and writing poetry. Upon the death of his brother, a canon (priest) of Salon, he succeeded in obtaining the vacated church stipend, which he sought for the gratification of worldly ambitions. Yet in 1582 he put aside his dissipations and was called to the priesthood.

He became the pre-eminent representative of the Counter-Reformation in France, a relentless and determined champion of Catholic belief in the face of the religious upheaval sparked by the Reformation. Inspired by Charles Borromeo (Nov. 4), he was seized by a "spirit of repentance," determined to "seek and love sacrifice." He became a leading champion of catechesis, a form of religious instruction aimed particularly at the young.

PATRON SAINT OF: *Christian Doctrine Fathers*

STATUS: *Priest, founder*

BORN: *1544, Cavaillon, France*

DIED: *1607, Avignon, France*

VENERATED BY: *Roman Catholic Church*

BEATIFIED: *1975*

Blessed Cesar de Bus, Pray for us that we will be able, as you did, to turn our back on temptation and worldly pursuits and remain on the right path and live a virtuous life. This we ask in Jesus' holy name. Amen.

Le Vénerable P. Cesar de BVS
Instituteur des Pères de la Doctrine Chretienne né a Cavaillon et mort a Avignon en Odeur de Sainteté en 1607 agé de 63 ans

CÉSAR WAS IN THE
VANGUARD OF THE
COUNTER-REFORMATION
IN FRANCE.

Bernadette Soubirous

Bernadette was an illiterate peasant girl, her father a miller, her mother a laundress. A sickly child who contracted cholera as a toddler and who suffered from asthma her whole life, she barely stood four and half feet tall. And yet it was to this simple child that, between February 11 and July 16, 1858, the Blessed Virgin Mary appeared 18 times at a spring at Lourdes in southwest France. Even before the visions had stopped, Bernadette had become one of the most famous figures in France, endlessly quizzed, relentlessly interrogated. For an illiterate 16-year-old, it was a distressing experience and at times she was variously dismissed as insane and hailed as a mystic. She was subsequently taken in by the Sisters of Charity in Nevers in central France. They taught her to read; she also became an accomplished seamstress. After a lifetime of medical issues, Bernadette died at only 35 years of age from tuberculosis, a scourge of the nineteenth century.

PATRON SAINT OF:
Lourdes, France; shepherds and shepherdesses, people ridiculed for their faith; invoked against bodily illness and poverty

STATUS: *Nun, mystic*

BORN: *January 7, 1844, Lourdes, France*

DIED: *April 16, 1879, Nevers, France*

VENERATED BY: *Roman Catholic Church*

CANONIZED: *1933*

SYMBOLS: *A rose with thorns*

Dear Saint Bernadette, Chosen by Almighty God as a channel of His Graces and Blessings, and through your humble obedience to the requests of Our Blessed Mother, Mary, you gained for us the Miraculous waters of Spiritual and physical healing. We implore you to listen to our pleading prayers that we may be healed of our Spiritual and physical imperfections. Amen.

BERNADETTE ENJOYS THE SINGULAR DISTINCTION OF BEING THE FIRST SAINT TO BE PHOTOGRAPHED.

Donnan of Eigg and Companions

Donnán was likely one of the wave of Christian Irish missionaries who sailed to Scotland in the last two decades of the 6th century. Donnan was a friend and disciple of St. Columba (June 9), the patron saint of Derry. Accompanied by a band of disciples, he began to preach among the pagan Picts of Galloway. An indefatigable apostle of the Christian faith, he founded churches as he moved through northern Scotland: at Colmonell, Carrick, Kintyre, Loch Garry, Sutherland, Loch Broom, Uist, and on the Isle of Arran. The headquarters of Donnan's "family" of monks and missionaries was eventually established on the island of Eigg (Inner Hebrides).

The arrival of the missionaries, however, provoked the resentment of a Pictish noblewoman who grazed her livestock on the island, and she determined to obliterate the monastic community. Lacking local support, she turned to the services of "pirates," perhaps early marauders from Jutland (Denmark), precursors of the Vikings. The assassins arrived as Donnan was celebrating Mass. At his request they allowed him to finish the service, and then shut the missionaries inside the refectory and set it alight. The entire community of 55 perished in the flames.

PATRON SAINT OF:
Eigg Island, Scotland

STATUS: *Missionary, martyr*

BORN: *Ireland*

DIED: *c. 617, Eigg, Scotland*

VENERATED BY: *Roman Catholic Church, Church of England*

CANONIZED:
Pre-Congregation

Saint Donnán, I pray that when challenged I may stand steadfast in my faith as you and your disciples, holy martyrs all, remained devout in the face of great peril. This I ask in the name of Jesus Christ, who protects and cherishes all those under his care. Amen.

Mary of the Incarnation (Carmelite)

Barbe Avrillot, a well-born child, studied with the nuns of the Order of Saint Clare near Paris. She was devout and unworldly, determined to enter a religious order, but at 16 her parents married her to Pierre Acarie, a wealthy nobleman. She bore six children, dedicating herself to their spiritual upbringing—her three daughters became Carmelites; her three sons entered the magistracy, the priesthood, and the military. Her husband supported the Catholic League against Henry IV, so faced political difficulties when Henry became king. His possessions were seized and he was exiled from Paris. Barbe wrote letters to people of influence with proof of his innocence. He was eventually acquitted and allowed to return to Paris.

A renaissance in religious piety was sweeping France, and Barbe became deeply involved in reforms of the religious orders and foundations of new congregations. Inspired by Teresa of Ávila, she founded the first Discalced Carmelite house in France in Paris,. After her husband died, she entered the order as Mary of the Incarnation.

PATRON SAINT OF:
Poor people, widows, orphans; invoked against poverty

STATUS: *Nun*

BORN: *February 1, 1566, Paris, France*

DIED: *April 18, 1518, Pontoise, France*

VENERATED BY: *Roman Catholic Church*

BEATIFIED: *1791*

Heavenly Father, You gave Blessed Mary of the Incarnation heroic strength in the face of the adversities she met along life's road and zeal for the extension of the Carmelite family. May we, Your children, courageously endure every trial and persevere to the end in Your love. Grant this through Christ our Lord. Amen.

A CONTEMPORARY PORTRAIT OF BARBE ACARIE WEARING THE DISTINCTIVE BLACK AND WHITE ROBES OF THE CARMELITE ORDER.

Leo IX

Bruno von Egisheim-Dagsburg was born to a noble family—his cousin became Holy Roman Emperor Conrad II—and was educated at Toul in the care of the bishop, and was made bishop himself in 1027. During his tenure he contended with famine and war, established a firm peace between France and the Holy Roman Empire, and built up a reputation as a reformer. In 1048, he was selected as successor to Pope Damasus II and arrived in Rome in humble pilgrim's clothing. He was consecrated in 1049, taking the name Leo IX. Leo reasserted the doctrine of celibacy at the Easter Synod of 1049 and stated his abhorrence of simony, the selling of church offices or possessions. He then embarked on the first his papal progresses through Italy, France, and Germany, where he presided over synods, met with higher clergy, and engaged in diplomatic initiatives.

In 1053, after diplomacy failed, Leo set out with an army of Italian and German volunteers to confront Norman invaders in the south of Italy. His forces suffered a terrible defeat, yet he immediately secured the loyalty of the enemy. Despite this, he was held in captivity in Benevento and did not long survive his return to Rome.

STATUS: *Pope*

BORN: *June 21, 1002, Edisheim, Upper Alsace, Holy Roman Empire*

DIED: *April 19, 1054, Rome, Italy*

VENERATED BY: *Roman Catholic Church*

CANONIZED: *1082*

SYMBOLS: *Depicted as bearded, wearing the papal pallium*

O God, who made blessed Leo IX the Vicar of Peter and committed to him the care of the universal Church, by his intercession keep your beloved flock ever safe, so that with integrity of faith and perfect charity your Church may journey to her heavenly homeland. Through our Lord Jesus Christ, your Son, who lives and reigns with you in the unity of the Holy Spirit, one God, for ever and ever. Amen.

Agnes of Montepulciano

Born to a noble family in southern Tuscany, at age nine the pious Agnes convinced her family to allow her to enter a Franciscan monastery. The nuns were called "the Sisters of the Sack" after the rough clothing they wore. In 1281 she was among the sisters sent to Proceno at the request of a local noble to found new convent. After serving as bursar, she was elected abbess when only 20. There she gained a reputation for performing miracles and was reported to have "multiplied loaves." Eventually she was recalled to Montepulciano to head that monastery, where her deep level of prayer led to many visions. Based on one such mysterical vision, she oversaw the building of a church in Florence, Santa Maria Novella, dedicated to the Blessed Mother. After another vision, this time of St. Dominc Guzman, she led the nuns in the monstary to embrace the Rule of St. Augustine as members of the Dominican Order. She was even instrumental in smoothing conflicts between warring families in the city. After her death, her body remained incorrupt, and her tomb became a site for pilgrimages.

STATUS: *Prioress, mystic*

BORN: *28 January 1268, Montepulciano, Papal States*

DIED: *20 April 1317, Montepulciano, Papal States*

VENERATED BY: *Roman Catholic Church, Dominican Order*

CANONIZED: *1726*

SYMBOLS: *Lily and lamb*

St. Agnes, you were devoted to the Blessed Sacrament and received communion with fervor and joy. Pray that we may also have recourse to Jesus truly present in the Host, and trust in His love and care for us . . . St. Agnes, you were the recipient of many mystical visions and graces, including being able to hold the Infant Jesus . . . Pray that we may hold Jesus first in our hearts and never lose Him by willful sin. Amen.

Anselm of Canturbury

Born to a noble family, in Alpine Italy. His father, a violent man, would not allow him to enter a monastery. At 23, Anselm escaped and crossed the Alps, traveling through Burgundy and Normandy. He submitted himself to the Rule of St. Benedict at Avranches, and in 1078 was consecrated abbot of Bec. The abbey became a center of learning famous throughout Europe as Anselm developed his reputation as a Christian philosopher. Anselm established links with Benedictines in England and, in 1089, was seen as the natural successor to the archbishop of Canterbury, Lafranc. King William II, however, saw a chance to seize the revenues of the see, and no appointment was made. In 1092, Anselm made his way to England and eventually, William agreed to return Canterbury's lands, and Anselm was consecrated.

Anselm continued to canvass for church reform, resisting William's desire to impose royal control over both church and state. William offered Anselm an ultimatum: exile or total submission. Anselm opted for exile in Normandy, and William promptly seized the revenues of the see. William's successor, Henry I, invited Anselm to return, but the two remained in conflict until the Concordat of London in 1107, a major step in establishing the rights of the Church over the king.

STATUS: *Archbishop, Doctor of the Church*

BORN: *Aosta, Italy*

DIED: *April 21, 1109, Canturbury, England*

VENERATED BY: *Roman Catholic Church, Anglican Communion, Lutheranisn*

CANONIZED: *1163*

SYMBOLS: *Shown with a ship; books; mitre, pallium, and crozier*

O my God, teach my heart where and how to seek You ... where and how to find You.

You are my God and You are my all and I have never seen You.

I cannot seek You unless You teach me or find You unless You show Yourself to me.

Let me seek You in my desire, let me desire You in my seeking.

Let me find You by loving You, let me love You when I find You.

Amen.

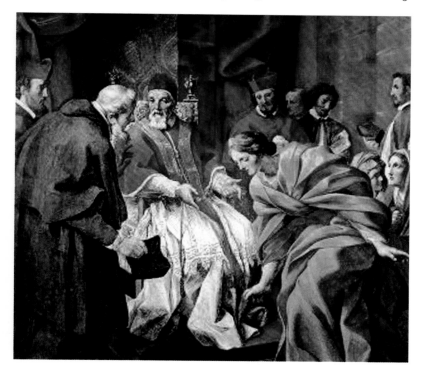

A FANCIFUL 16TH-CENTURY REPRESENTATION OF ANSELM (LEFT) GREETING MATILDA OF CANOSSA BEFORE POPE URBAN II.

Theodore of Sykeon

Born in the village of Sykeon, this noted ascetic was said to be the son of a local courtesan and an acrobat who performed in the Hippodrome for the emperor. When plague struck his village, Theodore lay near death until carried to the local shrine of St. John the Baptist to recover. He also frequented a shrine to St. George. At age 14 he went to live there, in a cave beneath the chapel, and soon became a noted healer and exorcist. Hearing of his exploits, a bishop named Theodosius ordained 17-year-old Theodore. When appointed bishop of Anastasiopolis, near the capital, Ankara, Theodore predicted the death of Emperor Maurice and "great tribulations, terrible scourges [that] threaten the world." This all came to pass when a 26-year war with Persia began, resulting in Maurice's death.

After rebel leader Heraclius became emperor, he asked the bishop for his blessing in an upcoming battle with the Persians, but refused the bishop's invitation to dine. Theodore remarked that not accepting his offer was "a sign of our defeat," and indeed Heraclius did lose the Battle of Antioch. Theodore was said to have cured a royal prince of leprosy among his many miracles and he especially favored neglected children.

PATRON SAINT OF:
Difficult marriages; invoked for or against rain

STATUS: *Hermit, bishop*

BORN: *Mid 7th century, Galatia*

DIED: *c. 623 AD, Turkey*

VENERATED BY: *Roman Catholic Church, Eastern Orthodox Church*

CANONIZED:
Pre-Congregation

O Lord, help us to trust that, like St. Theodore, when we are ailing in body and soul, we should turn to you in prayer. Even in this age of modern medicine, with your blessing upon us, our bodies will strive to be healed and our spirits lifted up in joy. For this we thank you. Amen.

George

George's background is hazy but he is believed to be a former Roman officer, a Christian of Greek descent. Much of what we know of this most venerated military saint is recorded in Jacobus de Voragine's *The Golden Legend*—a lengthy martyrology from the 13th century. The most popular legend tells of the pagan city of Silene in North Africa, which is beset by a dragon. The dragon's noxious breath forces the inhabitants to offer it two sheep a day. When they run out of sheep, they offer it their daughters. Finally, only one maiden is left, the king's daughter, who is led out to feed the beast. Fortunately for her, George appears on the scene and succeeds in stunning the dragon, and they take it to the city. George says he will slay it if the thousands of inhabitants convert to Christianity, to which they agree. While proclaiming his Christianity in Palestine, George was tortured, but miraculously survived; he then invoked God to destroy the local temple, after which he was dragged through the streets and beheaded.

PATRON SAINT OF:
Soldiers, knights, armorers, swordsmen, archers, farmers, England, Portugal, Catalonia, Genoa, Venice

STATUS: *Knight, martyr*

BORN: *Late 3rd century, Cappadocia (Turkey)*

DIED: *c.303, Palestine*

VENERATED BY: *Roman Catholic Church, Eastern Orthodox Church, Sunni Islam, Oriental Orthodoxy, Anglican Communion, Lutheranism*

CANONIZED:
Pre-Congregation

SYMBOLS: *Shown mounted, wearing armor, bearing a sword and a lance, and his colors, a white cross on a red field; occasionally shown trampling a dragon*

O GOD, who didst grant to Saint George strength and constancy in the various torments which he sustained for our holy faith; we beseech Thee to preserve, through his intercession, our faith from wavering and doubt, so that we may serve Thee with a sincere heart faithfully unto death. Through Christ our Lord. Amen.

THIS DEPICTION OF GEORGE'S COMBAT WITH THE DRAGON, BY LUCAS CRANACH THE ELDER (1472–1553), TAKES PLACE IN A WILD GERMANIC FOREST.

Fidelis of Sigmaringen

PATRON SAINT OF:
Lawyers and advocates; those who battle heresy

STATUS: *Priest, martyr*

BORN: *1577, Sigmaringen, Germany*

DIED: *April 24, 1622, Grüsch, Switzerland*

VENERATED BY: *Roman Catholic Church*

CANONIZED: *1746*

SYMBOLS: *Shown bearing a sword or spiked club; martyr's palm; lilies; head wound; trampling heretics; often paired with Joseph of Leonessa (Feb. 4)*

Fidelis, you predicted your coming martyrdom and went to your death with joy. Pray that we may overcome the fear of death and rejoice in being able to suffer for the Name. Amen.

Born Mark Rey or Roy, the young man read philosophy and civil and canon law at Freiburg University, where he then taught philosophy and earned a doctorate of law. He was known for his piety and chastity and even wore a hair shirt. For six years he traveled Europe with three Serbian men, visiting hospitals and churches to minister to the needy and praying at shrines. This was followed by a period as the "poor man's lawyer" in Alsace. Eventually he decided to follow his brother George into the Capuchin branch of the Franciscan Order, adopting the name Fidelis (faithful). A capable administrator, his career as superior of three successive houses was characterized by the intensity of his devotion and preaching, his skills as a confessor, and his compassion for the poor and sick. His tenure also spanned the turbulent and bloody Thirty Years' War, which saw much of his homeland decimated in the struggle between Catholic and Protestant forces. In 1622, Fidelis attempted to reconcile the heretical Zwinglians of Grisons canton, but after some initial success, he was assassinated, stabbed in church, after accusations of spying.

FIDELIS, HERE SHOWN TRAMPLING HERESY IN AN UNCHARACTERISTICALLY BRUTAL MANNER BY GIOVANNI TIEPOLO (1696–1770), IS ACCOMPANIED BY JOSEPH OF LEONISSA.

Mark the Evangelist

John Mark was born in Cyrene, Libya. The family moved to Palestine shortly after his birth, and his mother, Mary, became an admirer of Jesus of Nazareth. She even offered her house as a place where the first Apostles could meet. Mark is often identified as the young man who briefly accompanied Christ after His arrest in the Garden of Gethsemane, narrowly escaping his own arrest. He traveled with Paul and Barnabas (Mark's cousin) back to Antioch; Barnabas and Mark then both accompanied Paul on his first missionary journey, although Mark decided to return to Jerusalem when they reached Perga (Pamphylia) in Anatolia. This caused something of a rift with the senior Apostle, although Barnabas and Mark later went on to evangelize Cyprus under Paul's guidance.

MARK THE EVANGELIST BY IL PORDENONE (C. 1484 – 1539).

PATRON SAINT OF: *Barristers, motaries, glaziers, glassblowers, lions, the imprisoned; Venice, Egypt, Mainar*

STATUS: *Apostle, evangelist*

BORN: *5 AD, North Africa*

DIED: *April 25, 68 AD, Alexandria, Egypt*

VENERATED BY: *Roman Catholic Church, Eastern Orthodox Church*

CANONIZED: *Pre-Congregation*

SYMBOLS: *Winged lion, holding his Gospel, depicted with black hair and beard*

O Glorious St. Mark through the grace of God, our Father, you became a great Evangelist, preaching the Good News of Christ.

May you help us to know Him well so that we may faithfully live our lives as followers of Christ. Amen.

Pedro de San Jose Betancur

Born in the Spanish Canary Islands, Pedro grew up working as a shepherd and lived hermit-like in a cave (now a popular shrine). In 1649, he crossed the Atlantic, hoping to find work with a relative in Guatemala. After running out of money in Havana, Cuba, he served a priest there for a year before arriving in Guatemala. After laboring in a mill, he sought to enter the Society of Jesus, but failed to complete his studies and instead became a Franciscan tertiary at a convent in Antigua Guatemala. He worked tirelessly for the poor, the unemployed, and prisoners, raising enough money to found a pauper's hospital and several other charitable shelters and schools.

Pedro's selflessness attracted a following of other Franciscan tertiaries, and he went on to found the Order of the Bethlemites, which included female tertiaries.

PATRON SAINT OF:
Canary Islands, Guatemala, Central America; the homeless, those who serve the sick

STATUS: *Missionary, founder*

BORN: *March 21, 1626, Tenerife, Canary Islands*

DIED: *April 26, 1667, Guatemala City, Guatemala*

VENERATED BY: *Roman Catholic Churchm Canary Island, Guatemala*

CANONIZED: *2002*

SYMBOLS: *Holds a walking stick and bell*

Brother Pedro, pray for us—that we may always teach the love of Christ by the witness of our lives! Amen.

PEDRO DE SAN JOSE BETANCUR

Zita

Known also as Citha or Sitha, Zita a reminder that not all saints rise from noble, wealthy, or especially pious families. At the age of 12, Zita entered the service of the prosperous Fatinelli family, wool merchants in Lucca and worked there for the rest of her life. Her simple devotion was initially scorned by the family and servants, resulting in derision and beatings. But their torments could not disturb her serene inner peace, and her persistence, piety, abilities as a nursemaid to the Fatinelli children, and kindness to the poor and needy eventually transformed the household.

Zita gave her own food or that of her master to the poor. On one morning, Zita left her chore of baking bread to tend to someone in need outside the house. Several other servants made sure the Fatinellis were aware that she had abandoned her work. When they went to investigate, they claimed to have found angels in the Fatinelli kitchen, baking the bread for her. She died in the attic of the home where she had served and a star was said to have appeared above it.

PATRON SAINT OF:
Domestic workers, waiters, invoked to find lost keys

STATUS: *Virgin*

BORN: *c.1212, Monsagrati, Italy*

DIED: *April 27, 1272, Lucca, Italy*

VENERATED BY: *Roman Catholic Church, Italy*

CANONIZED: *1696*

SYMBOLS: *Shown tending children or the poor, barefoot, with rosary*

Dear Lord, we thank You for giving us Your servant, St. Zita, as an example of virtue. Help us to imitate the holiness she showed in offering her hard work to You throughout her many years as a domestic servant. St. Zita, you sent many years of your life serving others. Despite the difficult work of your daily life and the unpleasant attitudes of your coworkers, you faithfully persevered in virtue. Please present my petitions before God with such faithfulness! Amen.

Peter (Pierre) Chanel

C hanel was a pious youth born to a peasant family who was encouraged to enter the Church by his local priest. He was ordained in 1827 and joined a recently established missionary group, the Society of Mary (the Marists) in 1831. He was sent to French Polynesia in the Pacific in 1836 in the company of a number of other Marists. Chanel's destination was the island of Futuna, which he reached in November 1837. The practice of cannibalism had only recently been abolished by the local ruler, Niuliki.

Chanel, warmly greeted and endlessly enthusiastic, made striking headway. He learned the indigenous language, and his care for the sick earned him many converts. But his efforts fell afoul of Niuliki, who viewed Chanel as a direct threat to his authority—all the more so when Niuliki's son asked to be baptized. In April 1841, Niuliki had Chanel killed with an ax and his body chopped up.

PATRON SAINT OF: *Oceana*

STATUS: *Missionary, martyr*

BORN: *July 12, 1803, France*

DIED: *April 28, 1841, Futuna, French Polynesia*

VENERATED BY: *Roman Catholic Church, the Marists*

CANONIZED: *1954*

SYMBOLS: *Shown as gentle, kind, encouraging*

St Peter Chanel, you left your homeland to proclaim Jesus, Saviour of the world, to the peoples of Oceania.

Guided by the Spirit of God, who is the strength of the gentle, you bore witness to love, even laying down your life.

Grant that, like you, we may live our daily life in peace, in joy, and in fraternal love. Amen.

THIS STAINED-GLASS WINDOW FROM THE CHURCH OF ST. LOUIS, KING OF FRANCE IN ST. PAUL, MINNESOTA, SHOWS THE WARRIOR MUSUMUSU EXECUTING CHANEL, WHILE OTHERS LOOT HIS HUT.

Catherine of Siena

Catherine was said to be the 24th of 25 children of a wealthy Sienese dyer. She took a vow of chastity at seven after having a vision of Christ and became a Dominican tertiary at around 20. She lived at home as a virtual hermit, but after experiencing a mystic marriage with Christ she received the stigmata. She worked in a Sienese hospital and began to preach reform and repentance. Preaching proved to be her forte, despite being a laywoman. A group of followers, called the "Caterinati," formed around her. They attested to her persuasive powers and accompanied her on her travels.

By 1375, Catherine had broadened her canvas, preaching widely, campaigning for peace between the states of Italy, and traveling to Avignon to implore the pope, Gregory XI, to return to Rome. He did so, but died in 1378, whereupon his successor, Urban VI, was immediately opposed by a rival claimant. Catherine threw herself into supporting Urban, dictating numerous letters and becoming Urban's trusted advisor. She did not live to see a united Roman Church, however, dying of a stroke. Catherine was declared the first female Doctor of the Church in 1970.

PATRON SAINT OF: *Nurses, sick people, Diocese of Allentown, PA, USA; Europe; Italy; Bambang, Nueva Vizcaya, Samal, Bataan, Phillipines; invoked against fire, bodily ills, miscarriage, sexual temptation*

STATUS: *Mystic, activist, author, Doctor of the Church*

BORN: *March 25, 1347, Siena, Italy*

DIED: *April 29, 1380, Rome, Italy*

VENERATED BY: *Roman Catholic Church, Anglican Communion, Lutheranism*

CANONIZED: *1461*

SYMBOLS: *Always depicted wearing a white Carthusian habit*

Help us always to see in the Vicar of Christ an anchor in the storms of life, and a beacon of light to the harbor of your Love, in this dark night of your times and men's souls. Amen.

Pius V

30

O God, who in your providence raised up Pope Saint Pius the Fifth in your Church that the faith might be safeguarded and more fitting worship be offered to you, grant, through his intercession, that we may participate in your mysteries with lively faith and fruitful charity. Through our Lord Jesus Christ, your Son, who lives and reigns with you in the unity of the Holy Spirit, one God, for ever and ever. Amen.

B orn Antonio Ghislieri in northern Italy, Pius entered the Dominican Order at age 14 and was ordained in 1528, shortly after the Reformation began. He taught philosophy and theology, and then became an outstanding inquisitor at Bergamo. Under the patronage of Pope Paul IV he was appointed bishop, then cardinal, and finally head of the Roman Inquisition in 1558. Eight years later he was elected pope with the strong support of Charles Borromeo (Nov. 4).

It fell to Pius to implement the reforms of the Catholic Church announced at the Council of Trent in 1545, reforms inaugurated in response to the challenge of the Reformation. He also succeeded in creating a Christian coalition against the threat of Islam. In his personal life Pius was stringent and disciplined, and he expected this quality in others, introducing strictly supervised standards. To back these up he relied heavily upon the Inquisition, installing it in a new palace and strengthening its rules and powers.

POPE PIUS, DESPITE HIS PROMOTION OF THE NOTORIOUS INQUISITION, REGARDED HIMSELF AS RATHER TOO LENIENT IN HIS TREATMENT OF NON-CATHOLICS.

MAY

In the Catholic Church, the entire month of May is dedicated to the Blessed Virgin Mary. May Day, the first day of the month, has long been associated with Beltane, a European pagan festival of fertility and rising spirits. It is the custom to leave baskets of flowers on the porches of family and friends. The date is also now widely identified as Labor (or International Workers') Day. Mother's Day is celebrated on the second Sunday in May in many countries.

Ascension Thursday frequently falls in this month, occurring 40 days after Easter, and Pentecost (or Whitsunday) follows ten days later. Pentecost celebrates the sending of the Holy Spirit to the Blessed Virgin Mary and the assembled Apostles. It marks the end of the Easter season. Pentecost is regarded as the original foundation day of the Christian Church, and is celebrated in the Eastern Orthodox churches by a three-day festival.

HAVING BECOME AWARE OF CHRIST'S RESURRECTION, AND WITNESSING HIS ASCENSION, THE ELEVEN ORIGINAL APOSTLES AND JUDAS ISCARIOT'S REPLACEMENT, MATTHIAS, WERE INSPIRED BY THE HOLY SPIRIT TO FOLLOW THEIR OFTEN HAZARDOUS MISSIONARY JOURNEYS ON THE DAY OF PENTECOST. THIS RICHLY COLORED PANEL ILLUSTRATING THE EVENT, FROM THE 13TH-CENTURY UMBRIAN SCHOOL OF PAINTING, DOES NOT INCLUDE MATTHIAS.

Bertha of Kent

S aint Bertha, or Saint Aldeberge, was a queen of Kent whose influence supposedly led to the spread of Christianity throughout Anglo-Saxon England. One of history's enigmas, she is mentioned primarily in connection with her male family members. She was a Frankish princess born in the early 500s, the daughter of Charibert I, King of Paris. Bertha was married to to King Æthelberht of Kent while in her early teens. Bede records that a condition of her marriage was being allowed to "maintain inviolate the practice of the Christian faith." Bertha brought a Christian bishop named Leodheard with her to Kent as her confessor, and they used the ancient Roman church of St. Martin in Canterbury. This church was later taken over by Augustine and his companions as their base of operations. Augustine was a monk from Rome sent by Pope Gregory the Great to convert the Anglo-Saxons. King Æthelberht gave Augustine freedom to preach and did ultimately convert to Christianity. Modern retellings of Augustine's mission almost always include Bertha, suggesting that she played a role in Æthelberht's conversion.

STATUS: *Queen*

BORN: *539 AD, Neustria*

DIED: *612 AD, Canturbury*

VENERATED BY: *Roman Catholic Church, Eastern Orthodox Church, Anglican Communion*

CANONIZED:
Pre-Congregation

Thank you God for sending those ahead of us to prepare the way for us to do the work you have sent us to do. These soul preparers are a sacred and holy gift from the Spirit and we thank you. Amen.

A STATUE OF QUEEN BERTHA IN LADY
WOOTTON'S GREEN, CANTERBURY, KENT.

Athanasius

Known also as Athanasius the Great, Athanasius the Confessor or, primarily in the Coptic Orthodox Church, Athanasius the Apostolic, was the 20th bishop of Alexandria. At age 33 he was elected bishop of the powerful Eastern see of Alexandria and proved to be an energetically pastoral bishop and forceful promoter of the recently promulgated Nicene Creed in the face of the Arian tendency to deny the Trinity. As such, he created powerful enemies, who persuaded Emperor Constantine to banish Athanasius to Augusta Treverorum in northern Gaul.

In 346, Constantine's successor, Constantius II, allowed Athanasius to return to Alexandria following the death of a rival bishop, but he continued to be a target for his Arian detractors. In 356 he fled to the Libyan desert after being threatened by armed troops. There he continued to preach and write prolifically, including a Life of St. Antony (Jan. 17). He returned to Alexandria and died only eight years before Arianism was declared definitively heretical at the Council of Constantinople in 381.

PATRON SAINT OF:
Theologians, faithful Orthodox and Roman Catholic Christians

STATUS: *Bishop, Doctor of the Church.*

BORN: *c. 295, Alexandria, Egypt*

DIED: *373, Alexandria, Egypt*

VENERATED BY: *Roman Catholic Church, Eastern Orthodox Church*

CANONIZED:
Pre-Congregation

SYMBOLS: *Often shown as a bishop arguing with a pagan, a bishop holding an open book or a bishop standing over a defeated heretic*

ICON OF ST ATHANASIUS

My most loving Saint, behold me kneeling at thy feet, beseeching thee with all the affection of my heart to grant me thy special protection, particularly when in danger of offending God. O my dear and holy advocate, remember me before the throne of the most holy Trinity, and obtain for me from the infinite goodness of God, the virtues of humility, purity, obedience, and the grace to fulfill exactly the duties of my state.

MAY

Philip the Apostle (and James the Less)

Philip and James were among the original Twelve Apostles, although little is known about their backgrounds. According to John 1:43–44, Philip was one of the first to join Jesus, along with Peter (June 29) and Andrew (Nov. 30), and was from the same city, Bethsaida in Galilee. He is known to have distributed food among the throng in the Feeding of the Five Thousand. At the Last Supper, Philip asks Jesus to show God the Father to the assembled Apostles, wherein Jesus not only reveals His indivisibility from God the Father, but provides comfort for the Apostles in the future. Philip was also present at Pentecost, and received the Holy Spirit. He may have traveled to Asia Minor spreading the Gospel and is said to have been martyred there, possibly by stoning.

James the Less remains a more shadowy figure. He is described as the son of Alphaeus or sometimes called "James the Just," cited as the brother of Jesus. Unlike many of the Apostles, James likely remained in Jerusalem after Pentecost, and was apparently tried for sedition by the Jewish court, the Sanhedrin, and sentenced to death. He was cast from the parapets of the Temple and beaten to death.

PATRON SAINT OF:
Pastry chefs; Cape Verde, San Felipe Pueblo, Uruguay

STATUS: *Apostle, martyr*

BORN: *c. 3 AD, Galilee, Roman Empire*

DIED: *80 AD, Hieropolis, Turkey*

VENERATED BY: *Roman Catholic Church, Eastern Orthodox Church, Oriental Orthodox Church, Anglican Church, Lutheranism*

CANONIZED:
Pre-Congregation

SYMBOLS: *Red martyr, long-haired bearded man holding a book or basket of loaves and Tau cross*

O Glorious Saint Philip, at the Last Supper you said to Jesus, "Lord, show us the Father and it will be enough for us." Help us to make this our prayer also and to seek God in all things. Obtain for us the grace to know the Father and Jesus Christ whom he has sent—for in this does eternal life consist. Amen.

PHILIP'S FATE REMAINS VERY UNCLEAR, SOME SOURCES SAYING HE WAS CRUCIFIED, SOME THAT HE WAS STONED TO DEATH IN PHRYGIA.

Florian

Florian von Lorch was the Roman commander of the imperial forces in Noricum, modern-day Austria. Around 284 he converted to Christianity, but was rounded up by the governor of the province, Aquilinus, as part of a persecution ordered by the emperor Diocletian. Refusing to renounce his faith, he was whipped and flayed, then ordered to be burned at the stake. Standing by the pyre, he called out to the Roman soldiers, "If you wish to know that I am not afraid of your torture, light the fire, and in the name of the Lord I will climb onto it." Fearful of his words, the soldiers hurled him into the river Enns with a millstone tied to his neck. His body was later recovered and was interred in an Augustinian cemetary near Lorch. He later appear in a dream to a Christian woman, Valeria, asking to be reburied more appropriately. He was reinterred on the site of what from 1071 became the abbey of St. Florian, now a commanding Baroque structure, near Linz.

PATRON SAINT OF:
Chimney sweeps, firefighters, soapmakers; invoked against fire, floods, and drowning; Linz, Austria; Krakow, Poland

STATUS: *Military commander, martyr*

BORN: *c.250 AD, Aelium Cetium, Roman Empire (modern Austria)*

DIED: *May 4, 304 AD, Enns River*

VENERATED BY: *Roman Catholic Church, Eastern Orthodox Church*

CANONIZED: *Pre-Congregation*

SYMBOLS: *Depicted as a Roman officer or soldier; pitcher of water; pouring water over fire*

Florian, patron of firefighters I present to you all firefighters, especially (....). I ask that you pray for their protection. Ask the Lord to keep them safe from all harm and to bless them with courage and wisdom as they serve their communities. Amen.

THE MARTYRDOM OF ST. FLORIAN, ONE OF SEVEN PANELS DEPICTING THE LIFE OF THE SAINT PAINTED BY ALBRECHT ALTDORFER IN AROUND 1530.

Hilary of Arles

The history of Hilary, or Hillarius, is clouded. The child of an aristocratic family, he may have started out in Dijon, Belgica, or Provence and was possibly the son of another Hilary, prefect of Gaul in 396 and of Rome in 408. At any rate, at an early age Hilary joined the abbey of Lérins under his relation, St. Honoratus of Arles. Like Honoratus, he became bishop of Arles in 429 when only 29.

Hilary is perhaps most remembered for his protracted power struggle with Pope Leo I the Great. Hilary, contending he had the authority, embraced sees outside his own diocese. Specifically, he attempted to exercise primacy over the church of south Gaul, a right that seemed implied in the vicariate that had been granted to his predecessor, Patroclus of Arles. He even deposed the bishop of Besançon for challenging this primacy. The pope settled the dispute in 444 by extinguishing the the Gallican vicariate headed by Hilary, thus depriving him of his rights to consecrate bishops or oversee the church in the province.

STATUS: *Bishop, writer*

BORN: *403 AD, France*

DIED: *449 AD, France*

VENERATED BY: *Roman Catholic Church, Eastern Orthodox Church*

CANONIZED:
Pre-Congregation

SYMBOLS: *Depicted with a mitre and staff*

May God bless St. Hilary of Arles and us that provide the example to our children, and all youths, that we may seek His will and be blessed with the wisdom necessary to pass that on to them, and they to their friends. Thank You Abba, our Jesus, and His Holy Spirit. In Jesus name. Amen.

Marian and James

During the early spread of Christianity, Nero, among other Roman emperors, felt threatened by a religion that forbid the worship of pagan gods or "divine" leaders. No matter that Jesus had preached of a heavenly, not earthly, kingdom. By the third century a series of "rapid-turnover" emperors vowed to rid the world of Christians . . . and did so through savage acts of persecution. Known Christians were thus rounded up, tortured to renounce their faith, and if they refused, were put to death.

Two such martyrs were active Christians living in Numidia (modern Algeria) in the early third century. Marian was a lector, or reader, and James was a deacon. It was noted that two bishops visited them shortly before their arrest, encouraging them in their faith. Both men were imprisoned during the Valerian persecutions and unsuccessfully tortured on the rack to apostatize. Both experienced inspirational dreams of martyrdom before they were executed, which took place at Lambaesis during a mass decapitation. Their bodies and those of other Christians were thrown into a nearby river.

STATUS: *Martyrs*

BORN: *Early third century*

DIED: *c. 259 AD*

VENERATED BY: *Roman Catholic Church*

CANONIZED: *Pre-Congregation*

Saints Marian and James, Pray for us . . . that we will hold fast to our faith through our words and actions. We acknowledge that two faithful people facing the hardships of life during persecution in the third century may have a lot in common with those of us facing persecution for our faith today. Please inspire us to remain steadfast in our beliefs and courageous during times of oppression. This we ask in the name of Jesus Christ. Amen.

John of Beverley

John was educated in Canturbury, he was likely of noble parentage and was known personally to the great historian of the early Church, the Venerable Bede (May 25). He served as a priest first at Whitby before being made bishop of Hexham in 687. In 705 he was elevated to bishop of York, remaining in office until 717, when he retired to Beverley, where he founded a monastery.

He was associated with miracles both during his life and after his death, and a substantial cult grew up around him. His tomb developed into a major place of pilgrimage, a fact that largely accounts for Beverley's importance and prosperity in the Middle Ages. King Edward I visited it three times and helped to further the cult, actually carrying his banner north in 1300 on his way north to fight with the Scottish. Edward II, Edward III, and Henry IV also used the banner in military campaigns, while Henry V claimed his stunning victory at Agincourt against the French forces was the result of St. John's "miraculous intervention." Sadly, the sumptuous shrine containing his relics was destroyed in the Reformation.

STATUS: *Bishop, theologian*

BORN: *c. 7th century, Yorkshire, England*

DIED: *721, Beverley, Yorkshire*

VENERATED BY: *Roman Catholic Church, Anglican Communion, Orthodox Church*

CANONIZED: *1037*

Thou hast been given to the faithful, O most sacred John, as a beauteous tree of holiness, bearing all the virtues like most sacred blooms, filling all the land with the fragrance of miracles and the sweet fruit of healings. Wherefore, O namesake of grace, entreat Christ God, that He save us who honor thee. Amen.

John of Beverley in a 19th-century stained-glass window at Beverley Minster, commonly regarded as one of the most magnificent medieval churches in England.

Peter of Tarentaise

Born on a farm in Dauphine, France, Peter joined the Cistercian Order at Bonneveaux at age 20 along with his father and two brothers. Renowned for his piety, he was sent to serve as the founder and first abbot of Tamie Abbey in the Tarentaise Mountains between Geneva and Savoy, where he built a hospice for travelers. Against his protests, he was made archbishop of Tarentaise in 1142, and subsequently devoted his time to reforming the diocese and rooting out corrupt or immoral clergy, while aiding the poor and promoting education. He purportedly began the tradition of passing out bread and soup, called May Bread, just before harvest time, a custom that lasted until the French Revolution. After serving for thirteen years, Peter disappeared. He was eventually located working as a lay brother at a Cistercian abbey in Switzerland, but was prevailed upon to return to his shepherding duties in Tarantaise.

PATRON SAINT OF:
Tarentaise

STATUS: *Priest, founder*

BORN: *1102, France*

DIED: *September 14, 1175, Cirey, France*

VENERATED BY: *Roman Catholic Church*

CANONIZED: *1191*

SYMBOLS: *Depicted in Episcopal attire, Cistercian habit*

O Saint Peter of Tarentaise, thank you for your service to the poor. Please allow me to follow your example and do things with humility and not for glamor. Guide me to do the right deeds for the right reasons instead of wanting to make myself look good, which I am sometimes wrongly guilty of. Thank you, St Peter. Amen.

Pachomius the Great

Pachomius is considered the founder of Christian cenobitic monasticism. He was an Egyptian born in Thebes who converted to Christianity in 314, thereafter becoming a hermit in an attempt to imitate the example of Antony of Egypt (Jan. 17). Up to that time, holy men had almost always lived as hermits, in seclusion. But Pachomius envisioned another type of devotional experience, and conceived the idea of bringing these devout souls together in communities, in effect monasteries, dedicated to communal worship and communal work. He also set down a written rule of prayer that the monks were to repeat certain well-known prayers each day.

He established his first monastery around 320 in Tabennisi. Within a matter of years, it had attracted over 100 monks. Eight further monasteries followed. Pachomius subsequently spent most of his life at the monastery of Pabau. It has been estimated that 3,000 such monasteries were in existence in Egypt alone by the time of Pachomius's death. Within a further 20 years or so, the number had grown to 7,000.

STATUS: *Hermit, Abbot*

BORN: *c. 292, Thebes, Egypt*

DIED: *c. 346, Egypt*

VENERATED BY: *Roman Catholic Church, Eastern Orthodox Church, Coptic Church, Lutheran Church, Benedictines*

CANONIZED:
Pre-Congregation

SYMBOLS: *Black-garbed hermit; often crossing the Nile on a crocodile*

O God be merciful to me a sinner.

For in sacrifice you take no delight, burnt offering from me you Heavenly King, Comforter, spirit of truth, Who are everywhere present and fill all things, treasury of blessings, and give of life, come and dwell within us, cleanse us of all stain, and save our souls, O gracious One.

Holy God, holy and mighty, holy and immortal have mercy on us.

Glory be to the Father, and to the Son, and to the Holy Spirit, now and ever and forever. Amen.

A MEDIEVAL BYZANTINE MOSAIC OF PACHOMIUS.

John of Ávila

J ohn of Ávila was among the most charismatic and successful preachers of 16th-century Spain. Of Jewish converso descent, he trained first in law, then in philosophy and theology. Ordained in 1525, he had initially hoped to travel to Mexico, a Spanish colony only since 1521, as a missionary. Rather against his better judgment, John allowed himself to be persuaded by the archbishop of Seville, Don Alfonso Manrique, that his unusual sanctity could more usefully be employed buttressing the faithful in Spain itself. So began a 40-year career of ceaseless travel and preaching across Spain. John's sermons regularly attracted crowds in the thousands, who were drawn by his passion and mysticism. His pleas for reformation and his rejection of worldly goods were such that he was charged by the Inquisition of unreasonable criticism of the rich and of asserting that their wealth denied them any hope of going to heaven. The charges were rapidly dropped.

PATRON SAINT OF: *Spanish secular clergy; Andalusia, Spain*

STATUS: *Preacher, writer, mystic, Doctor of the Church*

BORN: *January 6, 1499, Almodóvar del Campo, Spain*

DIED: *May 10, 1569, Montilla, Spain*

VENERATED BY: *Roman Catholic Church*

CANONIZED: *1970*

Almighty and eternal God, who gave your holy Church blessed John of Avila as Doctor, grant that what he taught when moved by the divine Spirit may always stay firm in our hearts; and, as by your gift we embrace him as our patron, may we also have him as our defender to entreat your mercy. Through our Lord Jesus Christ, your Son . . . Amen.

TERESA OF ÁVILA (OCT. 15) WAS AMONG THOSE SWAYED BY JOHN OF ÁVILA'S FIERCE DENUNCIATIONS OF IMPIETY.

11

Odilo of Cluny

W hen Odilo, the offspring of French nobility, was made abbot of Cluny in Burgundy in 994, he became not merely one of the leading churchmen of his day but one of the greatest figures in Christendom. Cluny, founded in 910 by William I, Duke of Aquitaine, was the powerhouse of early medieval European monasticism. Under the generous terms of William's foundation, Cluny owed the monarch only prayer, meaning no temporal lord could assert any prior claim on the foundation. Cluny and its rapidly growing riches were answerable only to the pope. Overseen by a series of exceptional abbots, of whom Odilo was among the greatest, Cluny became not merely immensely wealthy, but exerted an influence, both theological and political, felt across Christendom. In a turbulent age Cluny offered order, stability, and certainty.

Odilo, once a crippled child, now consort of kings and princes, popes and bishops, took full advantage of his position. He was largely responsible for the introduction of All Souls' Day (Nov. 2) on the Christian calendar, and also attempted to impose a "Truce of God" on the brutally warlike rivalries of European kings jockeying for supremacy.

PATRON SAINT OF:
Souls in purgatory

STATUS: *Abbot*

BORN: *962, Auvergne, France*

DIED: *January 1, 1049, Souvigny, France*

VENERATED BY: *Roman Catholic Church, Eastern Orthodox Church, Benedictines*

CANONIZED:
Pre-Congregation

SYMBOLS: *Benedictine abbot with skull and crossbones at his feet*

O good Jesu! how sweet is Thy call! how sweet the inspiration of Thy Spirit, which as soon as Thou strikest on the heart, turns the fire of the Babylonish finance into love of the celestial country. So! as soon as thou strikest the heart of the youth, thou changest it. Amen.

WOOD CARVING OF ODILO OF CLUNY

Pancras of Rome

Pancras, said to have been converted to Christianity at only eight years old, traveled to Rome from Asia Minor with his uncle after the death of his parents. At age 14, during the Diocletian persecutions, the boy was brought before the emperor himself. He resolutely refused to renounce his faith and was ordered to be beheaded. He was buried in the catacombs on the Aurelian Way. His head was later removed to the basilica of St. Pancras, built over the site of his burial in about 500 (though since substantially remodeled). From an early stage, Saint Pancras was venerated together with Saints Nereus and Achilleus in a shared feast day and Mass formula on May 12. In 1595, Saint Domitilla was also added.

A particularly strong cult devoted to him developed in England. St. Pancras Old Church in London stands on what is thought to be one of the oldest sites of Christian worship in England, dating from hardly more than ten years after the martyr's death.

PATRON SAINT OF:
Children, headaches, perjury

STATUS: *Martyr*

BORN: *c. 290, Anatolia*

DIED: *May 12, 303 or 304, Rome, Italy*

VENERATED BY: *Roman Catholic Church*

CANONIZED:
Pre-Congregation

SYMBOLS: *Depicted as a young man in Roman legion armour; holding martyr's palm branch, book, quill, or sword*

O good Jesus, grant me the virtue of Hope in your promises in the same measure that St. Pancratius always trusted in your Providence, so that I may, through his intercession, obtain work and success in all my undertakings. Amen.

Julian of Norwich

Julian of Norwich—a woman, sometimes called Juliana—was among the most remarkable saints in medieval England. Dame Julian gained renown as an anchoress (female hermit), seer, and mystic whose writings exercised a striking influence on theological thought. Born in the commercial city of Norwich, she had firsthand knowledge of the effects of the Black Death, the Peasant's Uprising, and the suppression of the Lollards. It was here she chose the secluded life of a hermit, living in a cell beside St. Julian's Church, which may be responsible for her name.

At age 30, believing herself near death, she experienced a series of intense visions, or "showings," of the Passion of Christ. Though she wrote about them at the time, 20 years later she described these episodes in much greater detail in Revelations of Divine Love. Likely the first book written by a woman in English, it showed a remarkable knowledge of theology as well as exceptional psychological insight. Unusually for the era, she conceived of God as a "motherlike" fount of intense, universal love that would save all humanity at the Last Judgment, whatever humanity's many frailties and inevitable sinfulness.

PATRON SAINT OF:
Cats

STATUS: *Hermit, theologian, mystic*

BORN: *November 8, 1342, Norfolk, England*

DIED: *c.1416, Norwich, England*

VENERATED BY: *Roman Catholic Church, Anglican Communion, US Evangelical Lutheran Church*

CANONIZED: *Not formally*

SYMBOLS: *Depicted holding her book or writing, sometimes shown with a cat*

In you, Father all-mighty, we have our preservation and our bliss.

In you, Christ, we have our restoring and our saving.

You are our mother, brother, and Saviour. In you, our Lord the Holy Spirit, is marvellous and plenteous grace.

You are our clothing; for love you wrap us and embrace us.

You are our maker, our lover, our keeper.

Teach us to believe that by your grace all shall be well, and all shall be well, and all manner of things shall be well. Amen.

THE STATUE OF JULIAN OF NORWICH ON THE WEST FRONT OF NORWICH CATHEDRAL, MADE BY THE SCULPTOR DAVID HOLGATE IN 2014.

Matthias the Apostle

Matthias first appears in the Acts of the Apostles when he was chosen to replace the treacherous Judas Iscariot, who had hanged himself in shame. Unlike the other apostles Matthias was not chosen by Jesus, who had already ascended into Heaven, but was elected by lot—rather than Joseph (called Barsabbas or Justus)—by the remaining eleven to join their company.

Following the miracle of Pentecost, at which he was present, Matthias seems to have preached in Judea, and then went on a missionary journey to Cappadocia, in eastern Asia Minor, on the shores of the Caspian Sea. He apparently was stoned to death by pagans, but the exact site of his martyrdom is clouded: Colchis, in the mountainous Caucasus region of modern-day George (at the Georgian ruin of the Roman fortress Gonio, a marker indicates his burial spot); Sebastopol in the Crimea, or Jerusalem.

PATRON SAINT OF:
Carpenters, tailors, reforming alcoholics; invoked against smallpox

STATUS: *Apostle, martyr*

BORN: *Early 1st century AD*

DIED: *c. AD 64*

VENERATED BY: *Roman Catholic Church, Eastern Orthodox Church (Aug. 9)*

CANONIZED:
Pre-Congregation

SYMBOLS: *Shown in old age, carrying the supposed tools of his martyrdom, a halberd or an axe*

O Glorious Saint Matthias, in God's design it fell upon you to take the place of the unfortunate Judas who betrayed his Master. You were selected by the twofold sign of the uprightness of your life and the call of the Holy Spirit.

Obtain for us the grace to practice the same uprightness of life and to be called by that same Spirit to wholehearted service of the Church. Then after a life of zeal and good works let us be ushered into your company in heaven to sing forever the praises of Father, Son, and Holy Spirit. Amen.

MEDIEVAL ARTISTS TENDED TO SHOW MATTHIAS BEING MARTYRED USING AN AX OR HALBERD. HERE, FROM THE NUREMBERG CHRONICLE, THE APOSTLE HAS SUCCESSFULLY TOPPLED A DEMON FROM HIS SHRINE BEFORE MEETING HIS END.

Isidore the Laborer

Known also as Isidore the Farmer, his devout parents named him after their patron, St. Isidore of Seville. As an adult he toiled as a day laborer in the fields of wealthy landowner Juan de Vargas, but usually attended Mass before work. When the other farmhands complained that he was often late, Juan went to the fields and found Isidore at prayer while an angel was plowing in Isidore's stead. Juan eventually made Isidore bailiff of his entire estate. Isidore married his neighbor, a peasant girl, the pending saint Maria de la Cabeza, and they had one son. When the child fell into a deep well, witnesses said the water rose up and lifted the child to the top. Sadly the boy died young, and afterward the couple devoted themselves to God, living a life of celibacy, and helping the poor, though they had little themselves.

PATRON SAINT OF:
Farmers, laborers; Madrid, numerous cities worldwide

STATUS: *Lay visionary*

BORN: *1070, near Madrid, Spain*

DIED: *1130, Madrid, Spain*

VENERATED BY: *Roman Catholic Church*

CANONIZED: *1622*

SYMBOLS: *Sickle and sheaf of corn, spade, angel ploughing*

Grant, O Lord, that through the intercession of Blessed Isidore, the husbandman, we may follow his example of patience and humility, and so walk faithfully in his footsteps that in the evening of life we may be able to present to You an abundant harvest of merit and good works, Who lives and reigns world without end. Amen.

Brendan the Navigator

Brendan was an Irish monk and abbot, one of the Twelve Apostles of Ireland, 6th-century Irish monks said to have studied under St. Finian. In Ireland, he founded monasteries at Ardfert, Inishdadroum, Annadown, and most famously at Clonfert, where he is buried. His name "the Navigator" highlights the best-known aspect of his life: that he voyaged widely and regularly across the remote outposts of Christianity in northwest Europe. He certainly visited St. Columba (June 9) on the Scottish island of Iona; in Wales, he was likely the abbot of Llancarvon, where he taught Breton saint, Malo. Other reports have Brendan visiting Brittany in France, the Orkneys off the north coast of Scotland, the remote Shetland Islands, and possibly even the Faroes, deep in the North Atlantic. Most famously of all, legend claims that he and a group of monks (perhaps 17 to 60) also made a seven-year voyage in a leather-skinned curragh across to the Americas, the "Isle of the Blessed" or the "Promised Land of the Saints."

PATRON SAINT OF:
Sailors, whales; Clonfert, Kerry

STATUS: *Abbot*

BORN: *c. 489, Kerry, Ireland*

DIED: *c. 577, Galway, Ireland*

VENERATED BY: *Roman Catholic Church, Eastern Orthodox Church; in Ireland*

STATUE OF BRENDAN AT FENIT HARBOUR, KERRY, IRELAND.

Lord, I will trust You,

Help me to journey beyond the familiar and into the unknown.

Give me faith to leave the old ways and break fresh ground with you.

Christ of the mysteries,

Can I trust You to be stronger than each storm in me?

Do I still yearn for Your glory to lighten me?

I will show others the care You've given me.

I will determine amidst all uncertainty always to trust.

I choose to live beyond regret, and let You recreate my life. Amen.

Paschal of Baylón

Paschal was born to a poor but devout couple, the third of their sons. As a simple shepherd, he would bring a book with him each day as he tended his flocks, and he would ask passersby to identify the letters in the book. He believed that learning to read would further the exceptional spirituality he had displayed since early childhood. He was also very honest, even offering to pay for crops damaged when his livestock got loose. He joined the Reformed Franciscan Friars Minor of Peter of Alcántara as a lay brother in about 1564, and thereafter devoted his life to prayer and poverty. He possessed only one threadbare habit and often went barefoot in the rain and snow as he traveled about collecting alms for the monastery. Deeply contemplative, Paschal developed a reputation as a mystic with a particular veneration for the Eucharist, the miraculous transformation of the host and wine into the body and blood of Christ. On a mission to the Observant Franciscans in France to defend the Church against a Calvinist preacher, he was assaulted by Protestant Huguenots, and it was said he never fully recovered. His tomb in Villareal became a place of pilgrimage and soon the site of miracles.

PATRON SAINT OF:
Eucharistic confraternities and devotions, priests, cooks, shepherds; Torrehermosa, Alconchel de Ariza, Obando

STATUS: *Friar*

BORN: *May 16, 1540, Torrehermosa, Spain*

DIED: *May 17, 1592, Villareal, Spain*

VENERATED BY: *Roman Catholic Church*

CANONIZED: *1690*

SYMBOLS: *As a friar, with shepherd's crook; monstrance, Franciscan habit, before the Eucharist*

Saint Paschal, you were filled by the Holy Spirit with a wonderful love for the sacred mysteries of the Body and Blood of Christ. … The enduring fruit of love, generosity and kindness. Eliminating sadness from our lives. To the glory of God, our Father. Amen.

John I

Little is known about the background of this early pope. John first served as one of the seven deacons in Rome and for a time was a partisan of Antipope Laurentius. He later admitted his error in a letter to Pope Symmachus, begging his pardon. "Deacon John" was already frail when he was elected to the papacy and he protested against being sent by Theoderic the Great, Arian king of the Italian Ostrogoths, to Constantinople. There, John was to secure the moderation of a decree against the Arians, issued in 523 by Emperor Justin I of the Eastern Roman Empire. Theoderic, who intended this as a political rather than doctrinal maneuver—rebuffing Byzantine supremacy in his kingdom—threatened that if John should fail, there would be reprisals against the non-Arian Christians in Italy.

Fortunately, Emperor Justin received John honorably and promised to do everything the embassy asked of him, with the exception that those converting from Arianism to Catholicism would not be "restored," meaning they would not be allowed to retain their previous rank of deacon, priest, etc. This compromise enraged Theoderic, who arrested the returned pope and threw him into prison, where he died.

STATUS: *Pope, martyr*

BORN: *5th century, Tuscany*

DIED: *May 18, 526, Ravenna, Italy*

VENERATED BY: *Roman Catholic Church, Tuscany, Ravenna*

CANONIZED: *Pre-Congregation*

SYMBOLS: *Shown looking through prison bars*

O God, who reward faithful souls and who have consecrated this day by the martyrdom of Pope Saint John the First, graciously hear the prayers of your people and grant that we, who venerate his merits, may imitate his constancy in the faith. Through our Lord Jesus Christ, your Son, who lives and reigns with you in the unity of the Holy Spirit, one God, for ever and ever. Amen.

Dunstan

PATRON SAINT OF:
Blacksmiths, locksmiths, musicians, silversmiths

STATUS: *Archbishop*

BORN: *c. 909, Somerset*

DIED: *May 19, 988, Canturbury, England*

VENERATED BY: *Roman Catholic Church, Eastern Orthodox Church, Church of England*

CANONIZED: *1029*

SYMBOLS: *Holding a pair of tongs; with a dove*

Hail Dunstan, star and shining adornment of bishops, true light of the English nation and leader preceding it on its path to God.

You are the greatest hope of your people, and also an innermost sweetness, breathing the honey-sweet fragrance of life-giving balms.

In you, Father, we trust, we to whom nothing is more pleasing than you are. To you we stretch out our hands, to you we pour out our prayers.

Dunstan was among the most important reformers of the Anglo-Saxon church, not merely enlarging England's monasteries and imposing stricter adherence to the Rule of St. Benedict, but vigorously implementing improvements in education for the clergy. His goal was twofold: first, that better-administered monastic foundations and better-educated clergy would significantly increase the authority of the Church; second, that a more powerful Church would in turn reinforce the role of the state, i.e., monarch. Among Dunstan's most lasting achievements was to recast the English coronation ceremony, creating an explicitly Christian rite for the first time, and so underlining the idea that the monarch was divinely sanctioned. Similarly, the impartial application of "the king's justice" depended on there being a recognized and codified body of law. Much of it was Roman in origin and thereby tied the state yet more closely to the Roman Church.

Dunstan was ordained in 943 and became abbot of Glastonbury and bishop of Worcester before becoming archbishop of Canterbury under King Edgar. He spent his final years as a teacher in Canterbury. He was a skilled metalworker and craftsman as well as a noted musician.

DUNSTAN WAS BELIEVED TO HAVE CHASED AWAY THE DEVIL WITH A PAIR OF RED-HOT TONGS.

Bernardine of Siena

Born to the noble Albizzeschi family, but orphaned at six, Bernardine was was raised by a devout aunt. After a course in civil and canon law, he joined the Confraternity of Our Lady attached to the hospital of Santa Maria della Scala Church. During an attack of the plague, he ministered to the ailing, and, with ten companions, took charge of the entire hospital. After his ordination in 1404, he became perhaps the most famous preacher in Italy in the early 15th century. He not only drew huge crowds, he preached at prodigious length, sometimes for as much as four hours. From 1430, he wrote widely on theological matters and, recognizing the importance of educating the clergy, opened schools of theology at Perugia and Monteripido. He was not without his detractors: in Rome in 1427 he was charged with heresy, though acquitted. He subsequently preached in the city every day for 80 days. He turned down three bishoprics—Siena, Ferrara, and Urbino—and in 1436 was made vicar general of the Observant Franciscans and in 1438 vicar general of the Franciscans in Italy. In 1442, he resigned to return to preaching.

PATRON SAINT OF:
Advertisers, gambling addicts, those with chest problems; San Bernardino, California; Bernalda, Italy

STATUS: *Priest*

BORN: *September 8, 1380, Tuscany, Italy*

DIED: *May 20, 1444, Aquila, Italy*

VENERATED BY: *Roman Catholic Church, Franciscans*

CANONIZED: *1450*

SYMBOLS: *Tablet displaying the letters HIS; three miters for the three bishoprics he refused*

Father, You gave Saint Bernardine a special love for the holy name of Jesus.

By the help of his prayers, may we always be alive with the spirit of Your love.

We ask this through our Lord Jesus Christ, Your Son, who lives and reigns with You and the Holy Spirit, one God, for ever and ever. Amen.

SAINT BERNARDINO OF SIENA BY JACOPO BELLINI, C. 1450-55

Godric of Finchale

Godric of Finchale's life was set down by a contemporary, a monk named Reginald of Durham. Godric was born to a poor but virtuous Anglo-Saxon family and became a peddler, then a sailor, one who may have captained his own ship. By Reginald's account he was an adventurer and something of an entrepreneur. Following a revelatory visit to the shrine of St. Cuthbert (March 20) on the island of Lindisfarne, Godric discovered a religious calling that would make him one of the best-known holy men in England. After many pilgrimages that took him to Rome and Jerusalem and throughout the Mediterranean, he lived with a hermit named Aelric for two years, then for another 60 years he dwelled as a hermit at Finchale, near Durham, on the banks of the river Wear, praying in repentance for his former sins. He was especially known for his kindness to animals, protecting the wild creatures that lived near his home: hiding a deer from hunters and allowing snakes to warm up beside his fire.

STATUS: *Hermit, writer, hymnist*

BORN: *c.1065, Norfolk, England*

DIED: *May 21, 1170, Finchale Priory, England*

VENERATED BY: *Roman Catholic Church*

CANONIZED: *Pre-Congregation*

SYMBOLS: *Depicted as a hermit; snakes at his feet*

Dear Father, Saint Godric of Finchale enjoyed living in solitude with You, spending much time in prayer and meditation. He developed the gift of music without being educated in the field. He received his lyrics and melodies from the Blessed Mother, and shared the songs with the Church. I ask him to pray for all those in my family, friendships and parish who have been gifted with the call to lead the community in musical worship. Amen.

Rita of Cascia

Margherita Lotti ranks high among medieval saints whose lives inspired great devotion as well as providing an improbable number of miracles. At age 12, despite pleading to be allowed to enter a convent, she was married to a nobleman who combined cruelty and dissipation, and who was eventually murdered by a family enemy. Rita's two sons, who swore to avenge their father, died of dysentery after Rita asked God to prevent them from committing a mortal sin. At 36, she was admitted to the convent of St. Mary Magdalene at Cascia in Perugia. The nuns had been reluctant to accept her as she was not a virgin. Their doubts were swept aside when she was miraculously brought to the convent one night by St. John the Baptist, St. Augustine, and St. Nicholas of Tolentino.

Rita was known for performing mortifications of the flesh and for the efficacy of her prayers. Once when she was praying before an image of the crucified Christ, a small wound appeared on her forehead, like a puncture from the Crown of Thorns; it was believed to be a partial stigmata.

PATRON SAINT OF: *Lost causes, sickness, wounds, marital difficulties*

STATUS: *Nun, widow*

BORN: *c.1381, Perugia, Italy*

DIED: *May 22, 1457, Cascia, Italy*

VENERATED BY: *Roman Catholic Church, Aglipayan Church, Augustinians*

CANONIZED: *1900*

SYMBOLS: *Forehead wound, roses, bees, a thorn, grape vine, a palm leaf with three crowns*

Holy Patroness of those in need, Saint Rita, so humble, pure and patient, whose pleadings with thy Divine Spouse are irresistible, obtain for me from thy Crucified Christ my request (mention it here). Be kind to me, for the greater glory of God, and I promise to honor thee and to sing thy praises forever. Amen.

William of Perth

Born in Perth, William was wild as a youth but later devoted himself to the service of god. He became a baker and was said to offer every tenth loaf to the poor. Before Mass one morning, he found an abandoned child on the church steps, whom he adopted and taught to bake. After receiving the consecrated wallet and staff as a Palmer, William and his foster son, Cockermay Douci ("David the Foundling") set out to fulfill William's vow of visiting Holy Places. They stayed at Rochester, with plans to visit Canturbury, and, eventually, Jerusalem. But while in Rochester, David drew his benefactor into a false shortcut, and, intent on robbing him, felled him with a blow to his head and cut his throat.

The body was discovered by a mad woman, who plaited a garland of honeysuckle and placed it first on William's head and then her own, whereupon the madness left her. On learning her tale, the monks of Rochester carried the body to the cathedral and buried it. The shrine of St William of Perth became a site of pilgrimage second only to Canterbury's shrine of Saint Thomas Becket.

PATRON SAINT OF:
Adopted children

STATUS: *Martyr*

BORN: *12th century, Perth, Scotland*

DIED: *c. 1201, Rochester, England*

VENERATED BY: *Roman Catholic Church*

CANONIZED: *1256*

SYMBOLS: *Walking staff, Palmer's wallet, little dog*

Heavenly Father, Creator God, We thank You for the good example of St William of Perth. May we, like him, be generous to the poor, kind to those in need, and walk closely with you throughout our lives. Amen.

STAINED GLASS WINDOW IN ROCHESTER CATHEDRAL, LATE 19TH CENTURY

Simeon Stylites the Younger

Known also as St. Simeon of the Admirable Mountain, this saint was directly inspired by (although unrelated to) Simeon Stylites the Elder (Jan. 5), and devoted his life to similarly extreme religious asceticism. His mother, Martha, was also revered as a saint. The boy was, by the tender age of eight, already a member of a community of pillar dwellers, or stylites. They were centered around another pillar hermit, John, and Simeon had a pillar erected hear that of his mentor. Following John's death, Simeon, who spent a reported 68 years on a variety of pillars, embraced an even more extreme life, subsisting only on the branches of a nearby shrub. He was ordained by the Patriarch of Antioch, and thereafter numerous followers would ascend his pillar one by one to receive Holy Communion from him. He was also noted for converting many pagans. Later in life he was believed to be responsible for so many miracles that his final pillar near Antioch was referred to as the "Hill of Wonders." Some healings were effected simply by the faithful holding up pictures of Simeon.

STATUS: *Hermit*

BORN: *c.521, Antioch, Asia Minor*

DIED: *May 24, 597, Antioch, Asia Minor*

VENERATED BY: *Roman Catholic Church, Eastern Orthodox Church*

CANONIZED: *Pre-Congregation*

SYMBOLS: *Depicted on a pillar*

Dearest St. Simeon, you were born in Turkey to a sainted mother. You grew up with John, a stylite hermit, building a short stylite next to his. You lost your first tooth while living on a pillar, and you continued living in that way for sixty-eight years, sometimes eating only branches. You were ordained and heard confession from your followers, and were accounted to have performed many miracles. Let me, like you, never waiver in my faith regardless of what hardship I may face. Let me see my path clearly, as you did from your youth. This I pray in the name of Jesus Christ. Amen.

25

The Venerable Bede

B ede, known as "the Venerable Bede" starting in the 9th century, is the only English Doctor of the Church. Sent to the monastery at Monkwearmouth at the age of seven, he survived a major outbreak of the plague to became a Benedictine monk as well as an author and teacher. He is considered perhaps the foremost scholar of the early medieval church, producing as many as 60 books on subjects including spelling, natural history, astronomy, poetry, the lives of saints, biblical commentaries, and history. His five-volume *Ecclesiastical History of the English People* is the most complete and authoritative account of the Christian conversion of England.

Remarkably, this outpouring of knowledge was produced on the very margins of civilized, Christian Europe, in the twin monasteries of Monkwearmouth and Jarrow in remote and rugged Northumbria in the northeast of England. Uniting this lonely outpost with the wider Roman Church was Bede's constant goal. Among the many claims to fame of the man recognized as the "Father of English History" was his use of AD, or anno domini, "the year of our Lord," to indicate all dates after Christ's birth.

PATRON SAINT OF:
*English writers and historians;
Jarrow, England*

STATUS: *Monk, scholar,
Doctor of the Church*

BORN: *c. 673, Jarrow,
Northumbria, England*

DIED: *735, Jarrow,
Northumbria, England*

VENERATED BY: *Roman
Catholic Church, Eastern
Orthodox Church, Lutheran
Church*

CANONIZED: *1899*

SYMBOLS: *Shown bearing
writing implements*

*And I pray thee, loving Jesus, that
as Thou hast graciously given me to
drink in with delight the words of
Thy knowledge, so Thou wouldst
mercifully grant me to attain one
day to Thee, the fountain of all
wisdom, and to appear forever
before Thy face. Amen.*

No contemporary images of Bede exist. This portrait of the saintly monk dates from 1754.

Philip Neri

Philip Neri, born to an impoverished but noble family, was one of the towering figures of the Counter-Reformation, the Roman Church's response to the Reformation. He was educated by the Dominicans and much given to fasting and prayer. After devoting his early life to helping the poor, the sick, and the dispossessed of Rome, he went on to establish the Confraternity of the Most Holy Trinity in 1548. He was ordained in 1551 and considered missionaray work in India. But his brethren convinced him there were plenty to minister to in Rome.

His evening prayer meetings, which included scripture readings, songs, and a lecture, evolved into an institute known as the Congregation of the Oratory. The members also undertook missionary work and preached in a different church each evening, a radical notion for the era. Given papal sanction in 1575, the Oratorians would, with the Jesuits, become one of the keystones of the newly militant Catholic Church. They proved particularly successful in France, where by the mid-18th century there were 58 Oratorian communities. The Congregation of the Oratory closely reflected Neri's personality: informal, practical, and rather whimsically grand.

PATRON SAINT OF: *US Special Forces; Rome*

STATUS: *Founder, Oratorian*

BORN: *July 22, 1515, Florence, Italy*

DIED: *May 26, 1595, Rome, Italy*

VENERATED BY: *Roman Catholic Church, By Oratorians*

CANONIZED: *1622*

SYMBOLS: *Rosary, lily, angel holding a book*

Philip, my glorious patron, who didst count as dross the praise, and even the good esteem of men, obtain for me also, from my Lord and Saviour, this fair virtue by thy prayers. How haughty are my thoughts, how contemptuous are my words, how ambitious are my works. Gain for me that low esteem of self with which thou wast gifted; obtain for me a knowledge of my own nothingness, that I may rejoice when I am despised, and ever seek to be great only in the eyes of my God and Judge. Amen.

TIEPOLO'S DRAMATIC IMAGE OF THE VIRGIN AND CHILD APPEARING TO PHILIP NERI, PAINTED IN 1740.

MAY 27

Augustine of Canturbury

PATRON SAINT OF:
Canterbury, England

STATUS: *Bishop, missionary*

BORN: *Mid-6th century, Rome, Italy*

DIED: *c.604, Canterbury, England*

VENERATED BY: *Roman Catholic Church, Eastern Orthodox Church, Anglican Communion*

CANONIZED:
Pre-Congregation

SYMBOLS: *Benedictine robes, banner of the crucifixion, bishop baptizing a king, fountain, cross fitchée pastoral staff and book*

O Lord our God, who by your Son Jesus Christ called your Apostles and sent them forth to preach the Gospel to the nations: We bless your holy name for your servant Augustine, first Archbishop of Canterbury, whose labors in propagating your Church among the English people we commemorate today. Amen.

From an early age, Italian-born Augustine became prior of the Benedictine monastery of St. Andrew in Rome. Commissioned by his friend Pope Gregory the Great (Sept. 3) to evangelize the seven Anglo-Saxon kingdoms of southern and eastern England and to establish Roman liturgical rites among practicing Christians in the British Isles, Augustine set out with 40 monks. The expedition was temporarily halted in Gaul over a leadership dispute, which Gregory settled by appointing Augustine bishop. They arrived in Ebbsfleet in 597 and were met by King Ethelbert of Kent, who initially confined them to the marshy Isle of Thanet. Still, he was sympathetic, as his French-born wife Bertha was a Christian, and eventually the monks established a prayer house in Canterbury.

Augustine proceeded carefully, aware of the political fragility of the Anglo-Saxon English polity. His caution produced fruit when Augustine established his see at Canterbury, building the city's first cathedral, a cathedral school, and the monastery of SS. Peter and Paul, now called St. Augustine's. He also created sees at Rochester in Kent and London, and planned the archbishopric of York, which remains second in importance only to Canterbury in the Anglican Church.

THIS LATER BEARDED IMAGE OF THE PATRIARCH IS FAVORED BY THE VICTORIANS.

Bernard of Menthon

Born of a noble family in the County of Savoy, Kingdom of Arles, Bernard was educated in Paris. As an adult, he refused an arranged marriage and devoted himself to the service of the church, becoming ordained and working as a missionary in mountain villages. He was elevated to replace his religious mentor, Peter, the archdeacon of Aosta, and served in that capacity for 42 years.

For many centuries a pilgrim route across the Pennine Alps connected Aosta Valley to the Swiss canton of Valais. Bernard determined to protect travelers and pilgrims from bandits and extreme weather conditions in these treacherous passes. As a result, he has two passes named after him, the Great St. Bernard and the Little St. Bernard. At the summit of the first, Bernard built a monastery for Augustinian monks and then established a hospice at the highest point of each pass to provide shelter for travelers. The monks were also famed for rescuing stranded travelers, centuries later aided by large herding dogs, which took the name of the Alpine saint. These dogs are frequently depicted with a small cask of restorative brandy on their collars.

PATRON SAINT OF: *Mountain climbers, Alpine travelers, skiers, backpackers; the Alps, Aosta*

STATUS: *Priest*

BORN: *923, Menthon, Burgundy*

DIED: *June, 1001, Novara, Italy*

VENERATED BY: *Roman Catholic Church, Alpine regions*

CANONIZED: *1681*

SYMBOLS: *Shown in black habit, often leading a devil on a chain; with a dog*

St. Bernard, you are known as the saint of hospitality from your work in the Alps. Pray for the safety of all travelers this day. St. Bernard, you lived to the ripe old age of eighty; pray that we may live our lives in the service of God and our neighbor. Amen.

MONUMENTAL STATUES OF BERNARD PERCHED ON TALL CAIRNS GUARD THE APPROACHES TO BOTH PASSES THAT BEAR HIS NAME.

29

Bona of Pisa

This saint became a notable figure of faith and fortitude during the era of the Christian Crusades. From an early age, Bona was subject to religious visions—in one, the figure on the crucifix at the Holy Sepulchre church held out His hand to her. In another church, Jesus, James the Greater, and the Virgin Mary appeared to her. She dedicated herself as an Augustinian teritary at age 10, fasting on only bread and water. A few years later she made a pilgrimage to the Holy Land to visit her Crusader father. Captured and wounded by Muslim pirates on the return trip, she was imprisoned for months until her countrymen rescued her. In gratitude, she then led a large party of pilgrims a thousand miles to the Shrine of Santiago de Compostela in Spain, which honors James the Greater. After this, she was made one of the official guides along the dangerous pilgrimage route by the Knights of Saint James. She completed the arduous trip ten times, the last while ailing, and died soon after her return.

PATRON SAINT OF:
Travellers, specifically couriers, guides, pilgrims, flight attendants; Pisa

STATUS: *Nun*

BORN: *c. 1156, Pisa, Italy*

DIED: *c. 1207, Pisa Italy*

VENERATED BY: *Roman Catholic Church*

CANONIZED:
Pre-Congregation

St. Bona of Pisa, you traveled far and wide, making pilgrimages to holy places.

As I set out for my destination . . . I ask your protection as I journey there and back.

Through your intercession, may I be strengthened in my walk with Christ and fortified, as you were, to live a life of hope, faith, and love. May my journey be safe and my heart opened and converted. I ask this through Christ our Lord. Amen.

SANTA BONA, GIOVANNI LORENZETTI FUSARI, 2003

Joan of Arc

Born to a peasant farmer during the Hundred Years' War between France and an alliance of England and Burgundy, Joan was illiterate but intelligent. At age 13, heavenly voices—Archangel Michael, Catherine of Alexandria, and Margaret of Antioch—urged her to save France from its enemies. In 1429, Joan was received by Charles, Dauphin of France, who believed in her piety and appointed her to the army.

She led the French to victory over English forces besieging Orléans, gaining her the sobriquet, "Maid of Orléans." She then enjoyed victories at Patay and Troyes. She encouraged the Dauphin to be crowned Charles VII at Rheims. At the height of her success as an inspirational field commander, she led her forces to relieve Compiègne, which was surrounded by Burgundian troops. Captured by them she was sold to the English, imprisoned for nine months, then charged with heresy and witchcraft — accusations she refuted with common sense and good humor. Refusing to confess or recant, she was burned at the stake in Rouen.

Charles VII attempted to have the judgment overturned, and in 1456 Pope Callistus III quashed the verdict, proclaiming her innocence. Nevertheless, it would be almost 500 years before she was beatified by Pius X, and canonized by Benedict XV.

PATRON SAINT OF: *France; soldiers, martyrs, prisoners*

STATUS: *Virgin, visionary*

BORN: *c.1412, Domrémy, France*

DIED: *1431, Rouen, France*

VENERATED BY: *Roman Catholic Church, France*

CANONIZED: *1920*

SYMBOLS: *Shown in male armor, with cross, sword, Fleur de Lis*

In the face of your enemies,

in the face of harassment, ridicule, and doubt,

you held firm in your faith . . .

I pray that I may be as bold in my beliefs as you, St. Joan.

I ask that you ride alongside me in my own battles.

Help me be mindful that what is worthwhile

can be won when I persist.

Help me hold firm in my faith.

Help me believe in my ability to act well and wisely. Amen.

JOAN OF ARC AT THE CORONATION OF CHARLES VII, BY JEAN AUGUSTE DOMINIQUE INGRES, 1854

Petronilla

Petronilla's true history is clouded by a number of legends. She is represented as either the daughter of St. Peter or a devout convert, therefore his spiritual daughter. (In the Gnostic apocryphal Acts of St. Peter, dating from the 2nd century, a daughter of St. Peter is mentioned, but her name is not given.) Whatever their relationship, St. Peter cured her of palsy. She was said to be quite beautiful, and there are stories that St. Peter, in the role of father, locked her in a tower to keep suitors at bay. Another told of a pagan king named Flaccus who pursued her to such an extent that she went on a hunger strike and died. She was omitted from the fourth century Roman calendar of martyr's feasts, but after a basilica was raised over her remains and those of Sts. Nereus and Achilleus, her cult expanded widely and she gained inclusion in later martyrologies. It was during the 6th century that the story of her close relationship with the Apostle Peter solidified, possibly due to her name or perhaps due to the great antiquity of her tomb.

PATRON SAINT OF:
The dauphins of France, mountain travellers, treaties between Popes and Frankish emperors, invoked against fever

STATUS: *Virgin, martyr*

BORN: *Gallilee, Israel*

DIED: *1st or possibly 3rd century AD, Rome, Italy*

VENERATED BY: *Roman Catholic Church*

CANONIZED:
Pre-Congregation

SYMBOLS: *Depicted being healed by Saint Peter the Apostle, early Christian maiden with a broom, lying incorrupt in her coffin with flowers in her hair*

St. Petronilla, many legends circulated about you, including one about your being the biological daughter of St. Peter, but very few historical facts are known about you. You were certainly a martyr, venerated from the fourth century on. Please pray for the Church, that She may continue to grow and thrive in a world increasingly hostile to the Christian message.

Amen.

JUNE

With the ecclesiastical calendar entering its second period of Ordinary Time following Pentecost, June also sees the longest day of the year in the Northern Hemisphere, usually on the 22nd of the month.

Several major saints's days are observed during June, including the birth of Saint John the Baptist on June 24, and the shared feast of Saints Peter and Paul on June 29. On the following day, the heroic sacrifices of the First Holy Martyrs are collectively remembered, commemorating those early Christians who, in part due to their suffering and persecution, helped to establish the Church within the Roman empire.

THE BIRTH OF JOHN THE BAPTIST PREDATED THAT OF CHRIST THE REDEEMER BY ONLY A FEW MONTHS. IT REMAINS A FESTIVAL OF OUTSTANDING IMPORTANCE IN ALL CHURCHES, NOT LEAST IN THE ORTHODOX CHURCH. THIS PAINTING OF JOHN PREACHING BEFORE CHRIST BEGAN HIS MINISTRY IN EARNEST IS BY THE EARLY 15TH-CENTURY ITALIAN ARTISTS JACOPO AND LORENZO SALIMBENI.

Justin

Justin was born to Greek parents and studied philosophy at Antioch and Alexandria. Through his reading, particularly of Plato, Justin sought a vision of the supreme creator, and around 130 he converted to Christianity. He went on to become one of the most powerful and eloquent defenders of the early Church, using philosophical arguments rather than mysticism. He openly debated with Gnostics (who emphasized spiritual knowledge over orthodox teaching), Jews, and others.

Justin traveled to Rome in about 150, opening a philosophical school in the city and writing theological essays. His remaining principal works are the two Apologias, the first of which vigorously defends the Christian life and offered arguments to Emperor Antonius to abandon the persecution of the Church, and the Dialogue. He and several colleagues were arrested in Rome during the persecution under Marcus Aurelius, and were tried by prefect Rusticus (the account of their hearing is one of the few to survive). Invited to sacrifice to the Roman deities, Justin refused, saying "No right-minded man forsakes for falsehood . . . We are Christians, and we cannot sacrifice to idols." He and his companions were beheaded.

PATRON SAINT OF:
Philosophers

STATUS: *Martyr*

BORN: *c. 100 AD, Shechem (modern Nablus), Samaria*

DIED: *c.165, Rome*

VENERATED BY: *Roman Catholic Church, Eastern Orthodox Church, Oriental Orthodox Church, Anglican Church*

CANONIZED:
Pre-Congregation

SYMBOLS: *Sword, quill*

O God who revealed to Saint Justin in the sufferings of the Cross, the great wisdom of Jesus Christ, grant that through the pleadings of Your Martyr and our Patron we may overcome the many errors that surround us and that our faith may grow ever stronger. In deep humility we pray O Lord for the strength to imitate Saint Justin in his constant efforts to make known the riches of the Faith to his fellow men. Grant us the grace to be ever mindful of the many blessings we have received from You. Through Christ Our Lord. Amen.

A 16TH-CENTURY GREEK ICON OF JUSTIN IN PHILOSOPHER'S ROBES, PAINTED BY THEOPHANES THE CRETAN FOR THE WALLS OF STAVRONIKITA MONASTERY ON MOUNT ATHOS, GREECE.

Blandina and Companions

Blandina was a young Roman slave living in Lyon who, like her mistress, was a Christian convert. At the time, the Roman population of Lyon had been stirred to a fanatical hatred of Christians and they were harassed in the streets. Blandina was arrested and tried during the persecutions under Marcus Aurelius, along with her mistress, the bishop of Lyon, St. Pothinus, and a fellow slave, Ponticus. All were accused of barbaric acts such as incest and cannibalism. Because she was frail, her companions believed she would apostatize when pressed. But after undergoing extreme torture, she refused to recant. Furthermore, her accusers claimed they had never seen "a woman show such endurance." Roman citizens who converted to Christianity were allowed to be beheaded. But Blandina had no citizenship to ensure a swift death. She and her fellows were eventually led to the amphitheater where Blandina was wrapped in a net, thrown to wild bulls, and finally gored to death—a punishment particularly popular at the time.

STATUS: *Martyrs*

BORN: *c. 162 AD, Lyon, France*

DIED: *177, Lyon, France*

VENERATED BY: *Roman Catholic Church, Eastern Orthodox Church, Western Rite Orthodoxy, Eastern Catholic Churches, Angilcan Communion*

CANONIZED: *Pre–Congregation*

SYMBOLS: *Often shown with a bull*

Grant, O Lord, that we who keep the feast of the holy martyrs Blandina and her companions may be rooted and grounded in love of you, and may endure the sufferings of this life for the glory that shall be revealed in us; through Jesus Christ our Lord, who lives and reigns with you and the Holy Spirit, one God, now and for ever. Amen.

MARTYRDOM INVOLVING BULLS WAS PARTICULARLY POPULAR IN SOUTHWEST FRANCE AND IBERIA, AND MAY BE LINKED TO THE MODERN PRACTICE OF BULLFIGHTING.

John XXIII

J ohn was born Angelo Giuseppe Roncalli to a peasant family in northern Italy. He was ordained in 1904, and worked as secretary to the bishop of Bergamo and lectured in Church history. He served as a stretcher-bearer and chaplain in the Italian Army during World War I. In 1921, he was appointed director of the Council for the Propagation of the Faith by Pope Benedict XV. He served as a papal ambassador for Pope Pius XI, first to Bulgaria (1925–35), then as Apostolic Delegate to Turkey and Greece (1935–44); there, he worked with the Jewish underground, helping many to escape the Holocaust. In 1944 he was elevated to Cardinal and in 1953 became Patriarch of Venice.

His election to the papacy in 1958 was unexpected. A keen ecumenicist, his greatest achievement was convening the Second Vatican Council (1962–65), an opportunity to re-evaluate the role of the Catholic Church in the modern world, with a focus on social justice, human rights, and world peace. He also supported the World Council of Churches, opening dialogues across the Christian world. His unique and very active experience of two world wars undoubtedly drove his vision and sense of purpose. John died of cancer on June 3, 1963, after a brief but hugely significant pontificate, universally admired and loved.

PATRON SAINT OF:
Italian Army, Christian unity, Second Vatican Council; Bergamo

STATUS: *Pope*

BORN: *November 25, 1881, Sotto il Monte, Italy*

DIED: *June 3, 1963, Vatican City, Italy*

VENERATED BY: *Roman Catholic Church, US Evangelical Lutheran Church, Episcopal Church of America, Anglican Church of Canada*

BEATIFIED: *2000*

SYMBOLS: *Papal vestments, papal tiara, camauro*

Holy Immaculate Mary, help all who are in trouble. Give courage to the faint-hearted, console the sad, heal the infirm, pray for the people, intercede for the clergy, have a special care for nuns; may all feel, all enjoy your kind and powerful assistance, all who now and always render and will render, you honor, and will offer you their petitions. Hear all our prayers, O Mother, and grant them all. We are all your children: Grant the prayers of your children. Amen.

POPE JOHN XXIII MONUMENT AT ST. ANTHONY OF PADUA CHURCH, TURKEY, ISTANBUL

Petroc of Cornwall

Petroc, an important Celtic figure, was born in Wales, possibly the son of a Welsh king or chieftan. He and roughly 60 noble friends became monks and traveled to Ireland to study theology. Eventually he settled in Cornwall, England, carrying out his ministry from there. Decades later, Petroc made a pilgrimage to Rome and Jerusalem, then purportedly traveled to the Indian Ocean, where he lived as a hermit on an island and, famously, tamed a wolf. When he finally returned to Cornwall, he set up a monastic community and school at Little Petherick on the Camel River estuary. It came to be known as Petrocs-Stow (Place), later Padstow. When the hermit's life called to him again, he moved to nearby Bodmin Moor, where he was venerated by many followers and known for his miracles. He was noted for his humility: on one occasion when he predicted the cessation of a storm, and it continued to rain for many days, he went on pilgrimage as penance for his presumption in anticipating God's plans.

PATRON SAINT OF:
Cornwall

STATUS: *Abbot*

BORN: *6th century*

DIED: *c.564, Cornwall*

VENERATED BY: *Roman Catholic Church, Anglican Communion, Western Orthodoxy, in Cornwall, Brittany*

CANONIZED:
Pre-Congregation

SYMBOLS: *Wolf, stag, church*

Almighty God, by whose grace Petroc, kindled with the fire of your love, became a burning and shining light in our nation: inflame us with the same spirit of discipline and love, that we may ever walk before you as children of light; through Jesus Christ our Lord. Amen.

Boniface

St. Boniface, I ask that you intercede on my behalf. Help me to know and be strong in my vocation. Guide me on the path that leads to God. Likewise, help me to also encourage vocations in those around me. Help me to never stand in the way of someone's true calling from God. Give me the grace to help others discern God's will in their own lives. Help me to always be a positive encouragement to others. In Christ's name I pray. Amen.

Considered the founding father of Christianity in Germany, Boniface, first known as Wynfrith, was born to a prosperous family in Devon, England. He was educated there in a Benedictine monastery and ordained in 705. Choosing a missionary vocation, he was part of the Anglo-Saxon misson that preached to and converted the inhabitants of Frisia (northern Netherlands), before being directed by Pope Gregory II to evangelize in Hesse, Thuringia, and Bavaria. According to legend, he felled an oak tree near Fritzlar, Hesse, dedicated to the Nordic god Thor, to prove Christian superiority over local pagan superstition. He was often called "the apostle of the Germans."

Supported by the Frankish ruler Charles Martel, Boniface established many Benedictine foundations in Hesse and went on to become head of the Frankish church. At 80 he retired and returned to Frisia where, while preparing to confirm converts at Dokkum, his camp was attacked by local pagans. Forbidding any resistance from his armed guards, he was slain along with some 50 followers.

THE MARTYRDOM OF ST. BONIFACE WAS ONLY A TEMPORARY SETBACK FOR THE CHURCH IN THE LOW COUNTRIES.

Norbert of Xanten

Born to an aristocratic Rhineland family, Norbert was given various clerical benefices while living the life of a courtier. After a brush with death, he was ordained in 1115, and in 1120 established a reformist Augustinian community in the valley of Prémontré near Laon. Their mission included combating rampant heresies—particularly regarding the Blessed Sacrament, revitalizing those of the faithful who had grown indifferent and dissolute, plus effecting peace and reconciliation among enemies. Norbert entertained no pretensions that he or the men who joined his Order could be effective without God's power. Finding this help especially in devotion to the Blessed Sacrament, he and his Norbertines praised God for success in converting heretics, reconciling numerous enemies, and rebuilding faith in indifferent believers. Eventually, the Premonstratensian Order spread throughout France and the Holy Roman Empire.

In 1126 Norbert was appointed Archbishop of Magdeburg, a half-pagan, half-Christian territory, but his reformist zeal was not unopposed. Surviving several assassination attempts, he vigorously supported the exiled Pope Innocent II. During his final years, Holy Roman Emperor Lothair appointed Norbert Chancellor of Italy.

PATRON SAINT OF:
Invoked for safe childbirth;
Magdeburg, Germany;
Kingdom of Bohemia (Czech
Republic)

STATUS: *Bishop, founder*

BORN: *c.1075, Xanten,*
Germany

DIED: *June 6, 1134,*
Magdeburg, Germany

VENERATED BY: *Roman*
Catholic Church

CANONIZED: *2000*

SYMBOLS: *Monstrance,*
ciborium

Father, you made the bishop
Norbert an outstanding minister
of your Church, renowned for
his preaching and pastoral zeal.
Always grant to your Church
faithful shepherds to lead your
people to eternal salvation.
Through our Lord Jesus Christ,
your Son, who lives and reigns
with you in the unity of the Holy
Spirit, one God, for ever and ever.
Amen.

A STATUE ON THE CHARLES
BRIDGE IN PRAGUE SHOWING ST.
NORBERT (WITH A MONSTRANCE)
FLANKED BY ST. WENCESLAUS
(SEPT. 28) AND ST. SIGISMUND,
BOTH PATRON SAINTS OF THE
CZECH REPUBLIC.

JUNE 7

Robert of Newminster

Born in Gargrave, in the West Riding of Yorkshire, Robert studied at the University of Paris. He became a parish priest, and as such was regarded as devout, prayerful, merciful, and zealous over his vows of poverty. In 1132, he joined a group of pro-Benedictine monks, who were expelled from York, and helped them establish a monastery near Skeldale. After a difficult start, the monks gained fame for their holiness and this brought a new novice, Hugh, Dean of York, who donated his wealth to build the community a new facility. The presence of many natural springs in the region led to it being called Fountains Abbey. It became affiliated with the Cistercian reform, which had been introduced by Bernard of Clairvaux. In about 1138 Robert led a group of monks who had been sent out from Fountains to administer Newminster Abbey in Northumberland, built for them by Raymulph, Baron of Morpeth. Abbot Robert was said to be favored with the gifts of healing and prophecy.

STATUS: *Abbot, founder.*

BORN: *c. 1100, Gargreve, Yorkshire*

DIED: *June 7, 1159, Newminster Abbey, Northumberland*

VENERATED BY: *Roman Catholic Church*

CANONIZED:
Pre-Congregation

SYMBOLS: *Depicted as an abbot holding a church*

God our loving Father, you inspired Robert to establish a new monastery, and to preside as abbot with gentleness and justice.

As we honor today this man of prayer, may we also learn from his example.

We ask this through our Lord Jesus Christ, your Son, who lives and reigns with you and the Holy Spirit, one God, for ever and ever. Amen.

William of York

William FitzHerbert was born to a wealthy landowning Norman family, which ensured his progression into a profitable ecclesiastical office. However, William became involved in one of the intrigues that beset church and state at the time, most famously in the case of the slightly younger Thomas Becket (Dec. 29). Although William was patronized by the English king, Stephen (William had been his private chaplain), his first election to the office of archbishop of York in 1141 faced opposition by the powerful Cistercian Order, which owned extensive estates in Yorkshire. The Cistercians were supported by their founder, Bernard of Clairvaux (Aug. 20). Pope Eugenius III, himself a Cistercian, suspended and then deposed William following accusations of simony and incontinence. Despite powerful and violent supporters, William retired to Winchester. After the deaths of his successor at York, Henry Murdac (abbot of the Cistercian Fountains Abbey), Pope Eugenius, and St. Bernard, William was reinstated by Pope Anastasius IV in 1154. His triumphal re-entry to York was only marred by the bridge over the Ouse collapsing as he crossed it. Within weeks William was dead, possibly poisoned by the wine administered at Mass.

PATRON SAINT OF: *York, England*

STATUS: *Bishop*

BORN: *c.late 11th century, Yorkshire, England*

DIED: *June 8, 1154, York, England*

VENERATED BY: *Roman Catholic Church*

CANONIZED: *1227*

SYMBOLS: *Depicted crossing the Tweed River*

St. William, despite your positions being in constant flux you retained a marvelous equilibrium. Pray that we may exhibit such patience when we encounter various crosses throughout our lives. St. William, little is known about your personal life and yet you had the unwavering support of the people of your diocese. Pray for all bishops and archbishops, that they may fulfill their duties as shepherd of their flock. St. William, you now reign in heaven with Christ the Lord. Pray for us until we can thank you in person. Amen.

Columba of Iona

C olumba was born in Ireland and was said on his father's side to be descended from storied high king, Niall of the Nine Hostages. He studied theology and Latin at Clonard Abbey at a time when such learning flourished while, concurrently, the ancient Druidic foundations were collapsing as Christianity spread. Columba became a monk and was eventually ordained. He established monastic foundations at Derry (modern Londonderry), Durrow, and Kells, all of which later emerged as centers of learning and artistic endeavor. In 563 he and twelve companions settled on the island of Iona in the Inner Hebrides off the southwest Scottish coast. Under Columba's guidance, Iona became an influential center of missionary activity in Scotland and Northumbria, training monks, copying texts, and mediating in local affairs. He famously had an encounter with a ferocious "water beast" (possibly the Loch Ness monster?) that had killed a Pict and banished it to the depths of the River Ness. Columba eventually became known as the "apostle to the Picts"; he died in front of the altar of the abbey church.

PATRON SAINT OF:
Poets, bookbinders, relief from floods; Londonderry, Ireland; Scotland

STATUS: *Abbot, missionary*

BORN: *December 7, 521, Donegal, Ireland*

DIED: *June 9, 597, Iona, Scotland*

VENERATED BY: *Roman Catholic Church, Eastern Orthodox Church, Anglican Communion, Presbyterian Church, in Scotland*

CANONIZED:
Pre-Congregation

SYMBOLS: *Monk's robes, Celtic tonsure and crosier*

May the faith of Columba be ours in our watching and our waiting. May the peace of Columba be ours in our going and our returning. May angels watch over us through our waking and sleeping. May the God of Columba shield us and those we love and pray for on this day and always. Amen.

COLUMBA'S STORMY VOYAGE NORTH FROM IRELAND TO IONA, AND HIS FOUNDATION THERE OF A CENTER OF LEARNING AND MISSIONARY ACTIVITY, HAS BEEN CELEBRATED IN STAMPS AND STAINED GLASS.

Giovanni Dominici

The son of a Florentine silk merchant, Giovanni's father died before he was born. As a child he spent his free time in the Dominican Santa Maria Novella church, so it was not surprising he chose that order for his vocation. But due to his lack of formal education and a severe speech impediment, he was refused admission again and again. In 1372 he was finally accepted and began his studies in Pisa and Florence. His sharp mind and grasp of theological intricacies surprised his superiors, who sent him to Paris for further study. In order to preach effectively, he begged the intercession of Saint Catherine of Siena—and was cured of his speech defect. After twelve years teaching and preaching reform in Venice, he established a number of Dominican convents of strict observance in Venice and Fiesole. He was sent as envoy of Venice to the conclave of 1406 in which Gregory XII was elected. The following year, the pope appointed him archbishop of Ragusa, and later named him cardinal in 1408. It was Dominici who persuaded the resignation of Gregory XII in an attempt to end the Western Schism.

STATUS: *Cardinal*

BORN: *c. 1355, Florence*

DIED: *June 10, 1419, Buda, Kingdom of Hungary*

VENERATED BY: *Roman Catholic Church*

BEATIFIED: *1832*

Blessed Giovanni Dominici, we pray that you instill in us the same faith that kept you seeking acceptance by the Dominicans, the same courage with which you faced your physical affliction, and the same wisdom you provided to counsel your flock in Venice as well as guide the pope. This we ask in the name of Christ our Lord. Amen.

JUNE

Barnabas the Apostle

Barnabas, originally named Joseph, was a Jew ("Levite") from Cyprus. He was not listed among the original Twelve Apostles, but was added by Luke (Oct. 18), and features prominently in Acts of the Apostles. The name Barnabas, meaning "son of consolation," was given to him by the other Apostles, and he emerges as a good-natured man of persuasive powers. In Acts he is described as disposing of property and donating the proceeds to the Apostles (Acts 4:36–37), and then is sent to Antioch to consolidate the Christian community there. Barnabas calls on the support of St. Paul (Jan. 25), then travels with Paul to Jerusalem, and supports Paul during the debate with St. Peter concerning the admission of Gentiles to the Faith. His association with Paul continues when he accompanies Paul to Jerusalem, and then travels with Paul on his first missionary journey to Cyprus and Asia Minor.

PATRON SAINT OF:
Peacemakers, invoked against hailstorms; Cyprus

STATUS: *Apostle, Martyr*

BORN: *1st century AD, Cyprus*

DIED: *c. 61 AD, Salamis, Cyprus*

VENERATED BY: *Roman Catholic Church, Eastern Orthodox Church*

CANONIZED:
Pre-Congregation

SYMBOLS: *Often holding a book and olive branch; often with St. Paul*

With the Apostles, Barnabas the levite

Shines in the glory won by many labors,

Through love of Jesus, he despised as nothing

All that he suffered....

Lord God Almighty, through the intercession

Of your great servant, give us strength to labor

For our salvation, that we may in heaven

Praise you for ever. Amen.

THE MARTYRDOM OF BARNABAS IS NOT MENTIONED IN THE NEW TESTAMENT, BUT LEGENDS TELL OF HIM BEING STONED THEN BURNED, EITHER AT THE CYPRIOT PORT OF SALAMIS, OR IN GREECE.

Onouphrios (Onofrio)

When Christianity was first emerging as the dominant faith of the Roman Empire, a group of hermits, ascetics, and monks drew apart from their fellows, leading lives of great deprivation as a testament to their piety. Called the "Desert Fathers," they left a deep impression on Eastern spirituality. Drawn by the devotion of these men, many of the faithful were motivated to go out into the desert, or other harsh environment, risking encounters with wild animals or robbers, forsaking all but the basic necessities, and living only for prayer.

Onouphrios was said to be an Egyptian monk who forsook the collective monastic life at Thebes to wander the desert. His history was recorded by Paphnoutios the Ascetic, who was studying the hermit life, wondering if it was his calling, when he encountered the elderly, naked, bearded, unkempt hermit. Onouprhios invited him into his cave and they spoke all night, but by morning the hermit lay near death. Paphnoutios covered him with his cloak, and the cave immediately disappeared. He became a popular mythical figure in the early Middle Ages, with a basilica, Sant Onofrio, dedicated to him on the Janiculum Hill in Rome.

PATRON SAINT OF:
Weavers, jurists; Centrache, Italy

STATUS: *Hermit*

BORN: *Unknown*

DIED: *c. fourth or fifth century AD*

VENERATED BY: *Roman Catholic, Eastern Orthodox, Oriental Orthodox, Eastern Catholic Churches*

CANONIZED:
Pre-Congregation

SYMBOLS: *Depicted as old hermit with long hair and a loincloth of leaves; an angel bringing him the Eucharist or bread*

I beg you, St. Onouphrios, to allow me to find my own home. I have lived for a long time under a roof that is not mine, and although I have four walls to protect me, I need a house that is mine alone, where I can make my own decisions. Grant me the miracle of having a decent home to live in and where I can raise a family . . . Let me find a place where I can be comfortable, protected, and loved—a place to worship God. Amen.

ICON OF ONUPHRIUS. PROVENANCE AND DATE UNKNOWN.

Anthony of Padua

PATRON SAINT OF:
Animals, fishermen, horses, lost objects, the poor; Portugal, the Philippines, Lisbon, Padua

STATUS: *Monk, preacher, Doctor of the Church*

BORN: *Augsut 15, 1195, Lisbon, Portugal*

DIED: *June 13, 1231, Arcella, Padua, Italy*

VENERATED BY: *Roman Catholic Church*

CANONIZED: *1232*

SYMBOLS: *Book, bread, Infant Christ, lilies*

O Saint Anthony, come to the rescue of my weakness, taking away the diseases and dangers of soul and body; help me to always put my trust in God, especially in times of trial and suffering. Bless my work, my family, your devotees around the world or spiritually present here: obtain for all benevolence of heart towards the poor and the suffering. Amen.

Born to a family of Portuguese nobles, Anthony was famed for his sanctity, gentleness, preaching, and vast profusion of miracles. At 15, he joined the Augustinians, first in Lisbon, then at the remote northern convent of Santa Croce. It was to Santa Croce in 1220 that the headless corpses of St. Berard and his companions, Franciscan monks martyred in Morocco, were brought. Anthony, determined to emulate them and fired by a zeal for martyrdom, joined the Franciscans.

His desire was thwarted when he fell ill and he was forced to set sail for home. His ship was blown to Sicily, and he made his way to Assisi. There the Franciscans, unsure what to make of the sickly, waif-like Anthony, sent him to a rural hospice in Romagna. It was there that he discovered his gift for preaching. In 1224, St. Francis himself sent Anthony, now a fierce opponant of heresy, to Lombardy and France. The remaining years of his life were spent mostly in Padua, where he established a convent and where his fame as a preacher as well as a peacemaker reached its height. Wracked with dropsy, he spent his last days as a hermit, living under a walnut tree, near Venice.

BOTH ST. FRANCIS AND THE INFANT CHRIST ARE SAID TO HAVE APPEARED TO ST. ANTHONY. REPRESENTATIONS OF THE SAINT COMMONLY SHOW HIM WITH THE INFANT CHRIST, SUCH AS THIS 17TH-CENTURY PAINTING BY THE SPANISH PAINTER ANTONIO DE PEREDA.

Methodius of Constantinople

The child of wealthy and distinguished Sicilian parents, Methodius I (sometimes Methodios) played a key part in the final resolution of the violent split in the Eastern Church over iconoclasm, the bitter dispute as to whether the veneration of icons—images of God, Christ, Mary, and his saints—was heretical. This had begun around 730, when the Byzantine emperor, Gregory III, sided with those who regarded icons as sinful: the iconoclasts, or image-breakers. In 821, Methodius, a staunch opponent of iconoclasm, already an abbot and returning from a mission to Rome, was arrested and exiled by Emperor Michael II. Michael's successor, Theophilos, an even more determined iconoclast, initially released Methodius, before in turn re-arresting, torturing, and imprisoning him. On Theophilos's death in 842, Methodius was released on the orders of the Empress Theodora, who, like Methodius, was a fervent iconodule. Methodius was almost at once made patriarch. On March 11, 843, he symbolically restored the icons to the great church of Hagia Sophia in Constantinople. This, the "Triumph of Orthodoxy," has ever since been marked on the First Sunday of Great Lent, one of the holiest days in the Orthodox calendar.

STATUS: *Patriarch*

BORN: *c.790, Syracuse, Sicily*

DIED: *847, Constantinople, modern Turkey*

VENERATED BY: *Eastern Orthodox Church, Roman Catholic Church*

CANONIZED: *Pre-Congregation*

SYMBOLS: *Depicted with a long beard, holding a Bible or page of scripture*

God, Light and Shepherd of souls, You established St. Methodius as Bishop in Your Church to feed Your flock by his word and form it by his example. Help us through his intercession to keep the faith he taught by his word and follow the way he showed by his example. Amen.

Vitus and Companions

The child martyr St. Vitus has always been widely venerated, above all in Central Europe. There are a variety of legends about him, the most popular claiming that at the age of seven, already a devout Christian, he was tortured and forced to recant by his father, a senator in Lucania in southern Italy. Instead, he fled with his Christian tutor and nanny—Modestus and his wife, Crescentia. They eventually arrived in Rome, where Vitus expelled a demon from the son of the Roman emperor, Diocletian. Still refusing to renounce their Christianity, Vitus and his companions were tortured until an angel miraculously returned them to Lucania, where they died.

The cult of St. Vitus became more important than his actual life. His remains were said to have been transferred to St.-Denis in France in 756 and from there to Corvey in western Germany. In 925, the king of East Francia, Henry I, presented one of the saint's hands to Wenceslas, the duke of Bohemia. The church he built to house it, St. Vitus's Cathedral, is today the largest Gothic church in the Czech region.

PATRON SAINT OF:
Dancers, actors, dogs, epileptics, comedians, oversleeping, snake bites, storms; Rijeka, Croatia; Czechoslovakia; Prague; Serbia

STATUS: *Martyr*

BORN: *c. 290 AD, Sicily*

DIED: *c. 303 AD, Lucania, Italy*

VENERATED BY: *Roman Catholic Church*

CANONIZED:
Pre-Congregation

SYMBOLS: *In a cauldron, with rooster or lion*

Grant us, O God, through the intercession of St. Vitus, a true appreciation of the value of our soul and its redemption by the Precious Blood of Your Son Jesus Christ, so that, for the sake of the salvation of our soul, we will bear all trials with fortitude. Give this Your youthful servant and heroic martyr as a guide and protector to Catholic youths, that following his example they may after a victorious combat receive the crown of justice in Heaven. Through Christ our Lord. Amen.

SAINT VITUS
MONUMENT

Lutgardis

Lutgardis was born in Belgium, in what was called the Low Countries. She was forced at age 12 to join a Benedictine convent after her family lost its money, meaning she could expect no dowry and hence make a suitable marriage. At first she lived in the convent without any religious vocation, coming and going at will. But one day she had a vision of Christ showing her the wound in his side, and she was so moved that at age 20 she made her solemn profession as a Benedictine nun. The other nuns predicted this conversion would not last, but over the course of the next decade she began to experience extreme states of religious ecstasy, including reported levitations and blood emanating from her forehead in a form of stigmata said to have been acquired from Christ's Crown of Thorns. Lutgardis consistently refused to become abbess but in 1205 she was elected prioress of her community. In 1216, seeking stricter religious discipline, she joined a Cistercian convent at Aywières (Awirs). Unable to master the French spoken there, she grew increasingly isolated. Still, she managed to contribute to the Christocentric mysticism of the time. She was blind for the last 11 years of her life.

PATRON SAINT OF: *Blindness, childbirth, the disabled; Flanders; Flemish National Movement*

STATUS: *Nun, mystic*

BORN: *1182, Tongeren, Belgium*

DIED: *June 16, 1246, Aywières, Belgium*

VENERATED BY: *Roman Catholic Church, By Cistercians, in Belgium*

CANONIZED: *2012*

SYMBOLS: *Christ extending his hand from the cross; witnesses Christ showing his Heart to the Father*

Dear Jesus, help me to embrace my lot in life and accept it, as Lutgardis did, with grace and view it as an opportunity to grow in knowledge of and dedication to you. Amen.

SANTA LUTGARDA BY GOYA, 1787.

Rainerius

17

PATRON SAINT OF:
Travelers; Pisa, Italy

STATUS: *Hermit, monk*

BORN: *c.1115–1117, Pisa, Italy*

DIED: *c.1160, Pisa, Italy*

VENERATED BY: *Roman Catholic Church*

CANONIZED: *Before 1181*

SYMBOLS: *Bearded hermit in hair shirt*

Grant me, O Lord, the strength to turn away from material things and to place my trust in the gifts that enrich the spirit. With pious St. Rainerius as my guide, let me supply aid and comfort to the needy and offer greater devotion to You, Lord. In Jesus' name. Amen.

ST RAINERIUS BY CECCO DI PIETRO

Rainerius, the son of a prosperous merchant and ship owner, spent a dissolute youth, mostly as a minstrel and man of the world. In his travels he met Alberto, a holy man, once a noble from Corsica, who wore a cloak made of animal fur, like a goat. Alberto had joined the monastery of St. Vitus and was known for his good works aiding the poor. Rainerius was so impressed by his new friend, he converted to Christianity. In order to journey to the Holy Land, he set himself up as a merchant, where his trips to many countries trading with sailors made him wealthy. Eventually he did visit the Holy Land, where he had a vision warning him that his wealth was interfering with his devotion to God. He gave away his money and lived like a beggar for seven years, visiting many holy places and shrines. He returned to Pisa in 1153, living at the monastery of Saint Andrew and then St. Vitus. His fame as a preacher grew, and his followers began treating him like a saint, even in his lifetime, supposedly for performing miracles and expelling demons.

Gregoria Barbarigo

Gregorio Giovanni Gaspare Barbarigo was born to a wealthy, influential Italian family. Under the guidance of his father, a Venetian senator, he studied the natural sciences and completed a course of diplomacy. In 1643 he accompanied the Venetian ambassador to Münster for negotiations in preparation for the Peace of Westphalia, which ended the Thirty Years War. He remained in Münster, where he met the archbishop Fabio Chigi and future pope Alexander VII. After three years, he resumed his studies in Padua, with courses in Greek, mathematics, history, philosophy. In seeking a religious vocation, he was advised by his spiritual advisor to become a diocesan priest. Pope Alexander VII called him to Rome in 1656, conferring on him a number of duties including the leadership of the Tribunal of the Apostolic Signatura. When the plague epidemic broke out that same year, the pope gave him the task of bringing relief to the victims. Barbarigo personally visited the sick, organized burials, and especially aided the widows and the orphans. In 1657 he was made bishop of Bergamo and elevated to cardinal in 1660. Four years later he was made bishop of Padua, where he served for 33 years.

PATRON SAINT OF:
Diocese of Bergamo, Diocese of Padua

STATUS: *Cardinal*

BORN: *September 16, 1625, Venice*

DIED: *June 18, 1697, Padua*

VENERATED BY: *Roman Catholic Church*

CANONIZED: *1960*

SYMBOLS: *Cardinal's attire, crucifix*

O God, You were pleased to have blessed Gregory,

Your Confessor and Bishop,

renowned as one who cherished his flock

and loved the poor:

in Your mercy see that we extol his merits

and imitate his charity.

Through our Lord Jesus Christ. Amen.

GREGORIO BARBARIGO BY ERMANNO STROIFFI

Romauld

Romauld Onesti was born to an aristocratic Italian family, but when, as a youth, he witnessed his father kill a relative in a duel over property, he fled to a monastery near Ravenna. He eventually became a monk there, but, ironically, some other monks found him to be "uncomfortably holy" and they eased him out of their community. The young man determined to become a martyr and set out as a missionary to Hungary, but illness forestalled him. It recurred each time he tried to proceed.

Romauld spent 30 years traveling Europe and founding monsteries and hermitages. Although a Benedictine, he reversed the general trend in medieval Europe toward the integration of monastic communities with the wider world. Instead he established the Camaldolese Order, which demanded an almost hermit-like observance on the part of its members. The order's name comes from the monastery of Camaldoli in Tuscany, founded by Romauld. He admonished his monks to follow an extreme form of contemplation and a strict rule of prayer while shut away from the distractions of the world. Later his father became a monk, and when he lapsed, his son kept him on course.

PATRON SAINT OF: *Discovery of thieves; haymakers; Milan, Italy*

STATUS: *Abbot, hermit, founder*

BORN: *c.951, Ravenna, Italy*

DIED: *June 19, 1027, Val di Castro, Italy*

VENERATED BY: *Roman Catholic Church, Eastern Orthodox Church*

CANONIZED: *1582*

SYMBOLS: *Crutch, ladder*

St. Romuald, you composed your own Rule for the monasteries you founded and gave very sound advice for the religious within these writings. Pray that we may obedient to God's will in whatever state of life He has called us, and that we please Him in all we do. St. Romuald, you were the victim of calumny, which . . . even your fellow monks believed to be true and caused you to be excommunicated; yet you bore this with extreme patience and humility. Help us to be as humble when we are denounced and ridiculed and to stay strong in our beliefs. Amen.

ROMUALD IN AN ALTARPIECE OF 1641 IN THE CHURCH OF SAN ROMUALDO IN RAVENNA. BEYOND THE GAUNT FIGURE OF THE SAINT, AN ANGEL FIGHTS OFF A DEMON.

17 Irish Catholic Martyrs

While a number of those English and Welsh Catholics killed during and after the Reformation were recognized as martyrs by Rome without any great delay, the same was not so true of Ireland's Catholic martyrs. This was not the result of discrimination on the part of the Roman authorities, but because almost no reliable information existed on the estimated 260 Irish men and women believed to have been killed for their faith by the English Crown. It was only in the second half of the 19th century that systematic efforts were made to investigate those known or thought to have died. In 1992, 17 of these martyrs were beatified. None have yet been canonized. They were chosen as representative of those who died: the list is in no sense definitive. Some, such as Bishop Dermot O'Hurley, tortured and hanged in Dublin in 1584, are relatively well documented. Of others, such as the Wexford sailors—three seamen executed in 1581 after a failed attempt to arrange the escape of the Catholic Viscount Baltinglass and his Jesuit chaplain—their names and the fact of their deaths are all that is known.

STATUS: *Martyrs*

BORN: *Ireland*

DIED: *From 1537–1714, Ireland, England, Wales*

VENERATED BY: *Roman Catholic Church*

BEATIFIED: *1992*

Lord, so great is our love for you

That even though we walk in a world where speaking your name can mean certain death

Your faithful still speak it

And speak it all the louder.

Help us work for a world where all may speak their creeds

And pray their prayers without fear of violence.

Hear the prayers of those who abide with you in dangerous times and in dark valleys,

And who die with your name on their lips.

Draw them quickly to your side

Where they might know eternal peace. Amen.

IRELAND REMAINED A STRONGHOLD OF CATHOLIC RESISTANCE TO THE REFORMATION IN THE BRITISH ISLES. APPALLINGLY BLOODY EVENTS, SUCH AS THE SIEGE OF DROGHEDA BY CROMWELL'S PARLIAMENTARY FORCES IN 1649 (ABOVE), DID MUCH TO PROMOTE THE ANTAGONISM BETWEEN CATHOLICS AND PROTESTANTS THAT CONTINUES TO THIS DAY.

Aloysius Gonzaga

PATRON SAINT OF:
AIDS victims, Jesuit novices, the young

STATUS: *Religious*

BORN: *March 9, 1568, Castiglione delle Stiviere, Italy*

DIED: *June 21, 1591, Rome, Italy*

VENERATED BY:
Roman Catholic Church, By Jesuits

CANONIZED: *1726*

SYMBOLS: *Rosary, lily, crown, cross, skull*

O Saint Aloysius, adorned with angelical manners, although I am thy unworthy servant, I recommend to thee in an especial manner the chastity of my soul and body; I conjure thee, by thy angelical purity, to commend me to Jesus Christ, the spotless Lamb, and to His most holy Mother, the Virgin of virgins. Preserve me from every grievous sin; never suffer me to sully my soul with any impurity, imprint deeply in my heart the sentiment of the fear of God. Amen.

B orn to an aristocratic family, Aloysius was a sickly child, but one who enjoyed a remarkable vocation from an early age. In spite of his fledgling faith and his frail health, his father sent his first-born son and heir to military camp at the age five and often came to watch him marching around the camp. At eight Aloysius went with one of his brothers to serve in the court of Grand Duke Francesco I de' Medici. It was here he developed the kidney disease that troubled him the rest of his life. After reading a book about the Jesuits—and, to the fury of his father—he joined that order in Rome in 1585 (though his death at 23 meant that he was never ordained). This desire for a religious life was in part due to his growing up amid the violence and turmoil of Rennaissance Italy . . . as well as having witnessed the murder of two brothers.

In 1590, he claimed a vision of the Archangel Gabriel informed him that he would die in less than a year, which he did, after caring for plague victims in Rome.

AN 18TH-CENTURY GERMAN IMAGE OF ALOYSIUS. HE WAS BURIED IN THE CHURCH OF ST. IGNATIUS IN ROME, THOUGH HIS HEAD WAS LATER TRANSFERRED TO THE BASILICA IN THE TOWN OF HIS BIRTH.

ST. ALOISIUS

Sir Thomas More

Thomas More, lord chancellor under Henry VIII, is perhaps most noted for opposing the king's separation from the Catholic Church. More enjoyed a reputation as a martyr for freedom of conscience, a staunch defender of Catholicism as well as Humanist values. Yet the truth is murkier: He was a fearsome opponent of Reform movements, calling Lutheranism "the most pestiferous and pernicious poison." He not only oversaw the interrogation and torture of reformers, but had a number burned at the stake. His essential view that the Catholic Church was a central prop of England itself never wavered. To attack the Church was akin to declaring war against the fundamental fabric of the state. Therefore, any such assaults, even if instituted by Henry himself, had to be resisted.

More, imprisoned in April 1534 and tried on a charge of treason, was a lawyer to the last. He never explicitly denied the king's self-asserted role as head of the Church, he simply refused to be drawn on the subject. It did him little good. He was found guilty and beheaded.

PATRON SAINT OF: *Statesmen, Catholic lawyers*

STATUS: *Lord chancellor, scholar, martyr*

BORN: *1478, London, England*

DIED: *1535, London, England*

VENERATED BY: *Roman Catholic Church, Anglican Communion*

CANONIZED: *1935*

SYMBOLS: *Axe*

Give me the grace, Good Lord: To set the world at naught. To set the mind firmly on You and not to hang upon the words of men's mouths. To be content to be solitary. Not to long for worldly pleasures. Little by little utterly to cast off the world and rid my mind of all its business. Not to long to hear of earthly things, but that the hearing of worldly fancies may be displeasing to me. Amen.

THOMAS MORE, CAPTURED HERE IN ONE OF THE MOST PENETRATING TUDOR PORTRAITS, PAINTED BY HANS HOLBEIN IN 1527, MAY HAVE BEEN UNFORGIVING IN MATTERS OF STATE. BUT THAT HE WAS A MAN OF HIGH INTELLIGENCE, EXCEPTIONALLY WELL READ, AND NO LESS EXCEPTIONALLY WELL CONNECTED, WAS ALWAYS CLEAR.

Ethelreda (Aethelthryth)

Etheldreda was one of the four pious daughters of the Anglo-Saxon king Anna of East Anglia, who all eventually retired from secular life and went on to found abbeys. At around age 16 Etheldreda was given in marriage to a local fenland prince, Tondbert. As she had already taken a vow of "perpetual virginity," the marriage was never consummated. On Tondbert's death, Etheldreda secluded herself in Ely in the Fens. Her father married her off again, however, this time to the king of Northumbria, Ecgfrith. Not only did she again refuse to consummate this marriage, she actually became a nun. Escaping her husband's lust-filled wrath, she again fled to Ely, where she founded an abbey. Following her death, her sister Sexburga (July 6) succeeded her as abbess, as would her niece and great-niece. Etheldreda is also commemorated by the 13th-century church of St. Etheldreda in London, once part of the palace of the bishop of Ely.

PATRON SAINT OF:
Cambridge University, widows, invoked against throat and neck ailments

STATUS: *Princess, queen, abbess*

BORN: *c.636, Suffolk, England*

DIED: *June 23, 679, Ely, England*

VENERATED BY: *Roman Catholic Church, Eastern Orthodox Church, Western Orthodox Church, Anglican Communion*

CANONIZED:
Pre-Congregation

SYMBOLS: *Abbess holding a model of Ely Cathedral*

O St. Etheldreda, I pray for you to hear my plea. Teach me to put away the desire for material things as you put away the privileged life of a princess when you pledged yourself to Christ. Even through two forced marriages, you kept your vows of chastity and remained faithful to our Lord. These are the qualities of true devotion I seek to emulate. This I ask in the name of Jesus Christ. Amen.

ST. ETHELDREDA IS SEEN HERE IN A STAINED-GLASS WINDOW IN THE CHURCH OF ST. ETHELDREDA IN LONDON. THE CROSIER IN HER LEFT HAND INDICATES HER STATUS AS AN ABBESS, THE CHURCH IN HER RIGHT IS EVIDENCE OF HER FOUNDATION OF THE ABBEY AT ELY.

John the Baptist

Johhn the Baptist is among the few saints who enjoy two main feast days. This day celebrates his birth and ministry; the other (Aug. 29) celebrates his martyrdom. John was the son of Zechariah and Elizabeth (Nov. 5) and the cousin of Jesus. Little is known of his early years, but Jesus acknowledged him as an important forebear of His ministry. For a time John withdrew into the wilderness, wearing camel skins and subsisting on locusts and honey. He re-emerged as an itinerant preacher in the Jordan River valley around 27 AD, proclaiming the imminent coming of the Messiah and offering baptism in repentance of sins.

Among John's followers were several who would become Christ's Apostles; crucially, he also baptized Jesus. Yet his function as a herald of Jesus is ambiguous: Something of a fire-and-brimstone preacher, he was impatient, irascible, and inspired—and not afraid to use shock and awe to capture his audience. He called the Jewish Pharisees and Sadducees who came to hear him "Ye offspring of vipers". Still, he was humble enough to insist his followers transfer their allegiance to Jesus once His ministry began. John's career ended when he was imprisoned and executed on a whim by Herod the Tetrarch.

PATRON SAINT OF:
Knights Hospitaller, summer solstice; Jordan; Penzance, Cornwall; Puerto Rico and its capital San Juan

STATUS: *Prophet, martyr*

BORN: *Late 1st century BC*

DIED: *c. 29 AD*

VENERATED BY: *All Christian denominations that venerate saints, Islam, Druze*

CANONIZED:
Pre-Congregation

SYMBOLS: *Depicted with lamb, with cross, in animal skins, bearded and often unkempt, platter with his head, pouring water from hands or scallop shell*

Holy Father, let me offer up to Thee the prayer of St. John the Baptist: Consecrate me through your strength and make known the glory of your excellence and show me your son and fill me with your spirit which has received light through your knowledge. Amen.

IN ST. JOHN IN THE WILDERNESS (C.1500), BY THE DUTCH MYSTIC PAINTER HIERONYMOUS BOSCH, THE PROPHET IS SHOWN TRANSFIXED BY THE LAMB (SYMBOLIC OF CHRIST), APPARENTLY UNAWARE OF THE BIZARRE, SULTRY, AND VAGUELY MALEVOLENT LANDSCAPE THAT SURROUNDS HIM.

Prosper of Aquitaine

STATUS: *Theologian*

BORN: *c.390, Roman province of Aquitaine*

DIED: *c.455, Rome*

VENERATED BY: *Roman Catholic Church, Eastern Orthodox Church, Anglican Communion, Reformed Episcopal Church, Lutheranism*

CANONIZED: *Pre-Congregation*

SYMBOLS: *Depicted holding a scroll defending orthodoxy*

Heavenly Father, Just as St. Prosper of Aquitaine saw with clear eyes the heresy of others, let me have similar clarity of vision when it comes to any falsehoods, deceit, or slanders offered by those around me. Let me not judge without cause, but let me speak out against all untruths. Amen.

Prosper was born in what is now southwest France and was possibly educated in Bordeaux. Even though he was a layman, he involved himself in the religious controversies of the day, especially defending Augustine of Hippo (Aug. 28), with whom he corresponded, and supporting orthodoxy, the adherence to the Church's accepted creeds. St. Photios called him the "Eradicator of Heresies." Around 417 Prosper arrived in the seaport of Marseilles, a refugee from the Gothic invasions of Gaul, and lived there as a monk. He played a vital role in the Pelagian controversy in southern Gaul in the 420s, helping to put down a revolution of the Pelagian Christians with the help of Augustine and Pope Celestine I. In 431 he appeared before Celestine to request support of Augustine's teachings; the pope responded with a letter of praise. Around 440 Prosper was attached to Pope Leo I in a secretarial or notary capacity.

Josemaría Escrivá de Balaguer

E scrivá was born to a middle-class family in northeast Spain; his father was a merchant and partner in a textile company. Josemaria felt he was "meant for something special" after seeing the footprints of a barefoot monk in the snow. After being ordained in 1925 and studying in Madrid and Rome, he became an enormously influential Aragonese doctor of law and theology. He was forced into hiding during the Spanish Civil War (1936–39) due to the anti-clerical tendencies of the Popular Front government, and he supported Franco's Nationalists. He first developed the idea of Opus Dei (literally "Work of God") in 1928. His vision was to fully incorporate the laity into the activities of the Church through the sanctification of their secular work.

He formally founded the Priestly Society of the Holy Cross, linked to Opus Dei, in 1943 and moved to Rome in 1946, where the movement was given papal approval in 1950. Much criticized, but supported by the highest ranks of the Catholic Church, Escrivá pursued his vision unswervingly, organizing conferences and workshops, encouraging vocations to the priesthood, and writing.

PATRON SAINT OF: *Opus Dei, sufferers of diabetes*

STATUS: *Priest, founder*

BORN: *January 9, 1902, Barbastro, Spain*

DIED: *June 26, 1975, Rome, Italy*

VENERATED BY: *Roman Catholic Church, by Opus Dei*

CANONIZED: *2002*

SYMBOLS: *Priest attire, rosary*

O God, through the mediation of Mary our Mother, you granted your priest Saint Josemaria countless graces, choosing him as a most faithful instrument to found Opus Dei, a way of sanctification in daily work and in the fulfillment of the Christian's ordinary duties.

Grant that I too may learn to turn all the circumstances and events of my life into occasions of loving you and serving the Church, the Pope and all souls with joy and simplicity, lighting up the pathways of this earth with faith and love . . . Amen.

Cyril of Alexandria

STATUS: *Bishop, Doctor of the Church*

BORN: *c.376, Alexandria, Egypt*

DIED: *444, Alexandria, Egypt*

VENERATED BY: *Roman Catholic, Eastern Rite Catholic, Eastern Orthodox, Oriental Orthodoxy, Anglican Communion, Lutheranism, Nestorian Churches*

CANONIZED: *Pre-Congregation*

SYMBOLS: *Bishop's miter, book*

Hail, Mother and virgin, eternal temple of the Godhead, venerable treasure of creation, crown of virginity, support of the true faith, on which the Church is founded throughout the world.

Through you the human race, held captive in the bonds of idolatry, arrives at the knowledge of Truth. What more shall I say of you? Hail, through whom kings rule, through whom the Only-Begotten Son of God has become the Star of Light to those sitting in darkness and in the shadow of death. Amen.

C yril is known as one of the outstanding theologians of the 5th century. He was the nephew of Theophilus, who rose to the powerful position of patriarch of Alexandria. Cyril was raised and well educated under his guidance, studying theology and the Christian writers of the day in addition to rhetoric and humanities. When Theophilus died in 412, Cyril succeeded him, but only after a riot between his supporters and those of his rivel Archdeacon Timotheus. Cyril became a highly partisan defender of the supremacy of the see of Alexandria in the Eastern Church, a position bolstered by his argument against the doctrine that Christ existed in two forms—one divine and one human—as promulgated by Nestorius, the patriarch of Constantinople.

The Nestorian position implied that the Blessed Virgin Mary could only be the mother of Christ, not the mother of God. Presiding over the Council of Ephesus in 431, Cyril defeated Nestorius, and as a result the Nestorian Church split away from Eastern Orthodoxy. Cyril emphasized the presence of God in each and every human being. He was proclaimed a Doctor of the Church in 1882.

A MID-13TH CENTURY WALL PAINTING OF CYRIL FROM THE CHURCH OF THE HOLY APOSTLES IN PEC, SERBIA.

Irenaeus

I renaeus was a second-century bishop noted for his invaluable role in guiding and expanding Christian communities in the south of France and, more widely, for the development of Christian theology by combating heresy and supporting orthodoxy. Probably of Greek origin, he was raised as a Christian by his family rather than converting as an adult, like many others of his time. He actually witnessed the preaching of Polycarp, the last known living connection with the Apostles, who in turn had heard the words of John the Baptist. When Lyon required someone to minister to their needs, Polycarp supposedly sent Iranaeus. He acted as a negotiator during the Christian persecutions under Marcus Aurelius, and succeeded the bishop of Lyon, St. Pothinus, one of the victims of that persecution.

It was not until the early 20th century that his writings came to light. They revealed a thoughtful analysis of the apostolic succession that embraced all of human history, and particularly that of the Hebrew and Christian traditions, which came to a zenith in the life of Christ.

PATRON SAINT OF:
Apologists and catechists

STATUS: *Bishop, martyr*

BORN: *c. 130 AD, Smyrna, Asia Minor*

DIED: *c. 202 AD, Lyon, France*

VENERATED BY: *Roman Catholic, Eastern Catholic, Assyrian Church of the East, Eastern Orthodox, Oriental Orthodox, Anglican Communion, Lutheranism*

CANONIZED:
Pre-Congregation

SYMBOLS: *Lighted torch, book, the color red*

It is not thou that shapest God it is God that shapest thee.

If thou art the work of God await the hand of the artist who does all things in due season.

Offer Him thy heart, soft and tractable, and keep the form in which the artist has fashioned thee.

Let thy clay be moist, lest thou grow hard and lose the imprint of his fingers. Amen.

AMONG THE WRITINGS OF ST. IRENAEUS WAS A FORCEFUL CONDEMNATION OF GNOSTICISM IN HIS ADVERSUS HAERESES (AGAINST HERESIES).

Peter

PATRON SAINT OF:
Fishermen, shipwrights,
stonemasons; the Papacy, Rome

STATUS: *Apostle*

BORN: *c. 1 AD, Bethsaida,*
modern Israel

DIED: *c. 64 AD, Rome, Italy*

VENERATED BY: *Roman*
Catholic Church, Eastern
Orthodox Church, Evangelical
Lutheran Church, most Christian
churches that venerate saints

CANONIZED:
Pre-Congregation

SYMBOLS: *Two crossed keys,*
book, inverted cross, depicted at
the gates of Heaven

O God, who has given unto Thy
blessed Apostle Peter the keys to
the kingdom of heaven, and the
power to bind and loose: grant that
we may be delivered, through the
help of this intercession, from the
slavery of all our sins:

Who lives and reigns world without
end. Amen.

T he "First Apostle" doesn't have his own day in most calendars, but shares this day with St. Paul (Jan. 29). Born near the Sea of Galilee, to a family of fishermen, Simon and his brother Andrew witnessed Christ walking on water. Jesus said that Simon would become a "fisher of men" and calling him the "rock of the Church," renamed him Cephas (Peter in English, which means rock).

Peter remains the most important of the original disciples, emerging from the Gospels as strong but impetuous and fallible: Immediately after Christ's crucifixion Peter denied knowledge of Him three times. Yet Peter was the first Apostle to whom Christ appeared after His resurrection, and he became the leader of the Christian community in Jerusalem; even St. Paul deferred to his judgment. Briefly imprisoned by Herod Agrippa, he was freed by an angel. He seems to have made missionary journeys to Samaria and Antioch. Archaeological evidence increasingly suggests that he traveled to Rome. The apocryphal Acts of Peter describes him fleeing from the persecutions of Nero, but encountering Christ and returning to face martyrdom—being crucified upside down.

THE HISTORIAN EUSEBIUS DESCRIBES PETER BEING CRUCIFIED UPSIDE DOWN, AT HIS OWN REQUEST, TO AVOID IMITATION OF CHRIST.

Theobald of Provins

Theobald was the son of a French nobleman, Arnoul, Count of Champagne. As a pious youth he was intrigued by hermits like John the Baptist and even visited a nearby hermit, Burchard, who lived on an island in the Seine. As a young man he refused to get married or fight as a soldier, as his father had trained him to do. When a war broke out between his cousin, Odo II, and Conrad the Salic over the crown of Burgundy, Theobald would not lead troops in aid of his cousin. He finally convinced his father to let him follow his vocation.

He left home with a friend, Walter, to become a hermit in Sussy; they then travelled to Pettingen and found work as day laborers. They took up the pilgrim route, the Way of St. James, and afterward embarked on another pilgrimage to Rome, planning to visit the Holy Land by way of Venice. After Walter fell ill and died near Vicenza, Theobald found a group of Camoldolese hermits in the area under the guidance of St. Romauld. The bishop of Vicenza eventually ordained Theobald. His mother gained permission from his father to stay with him and became a hermit herself. Numerous miracles, both before and after his death, are attributed to Theobald.

PATRON SAINT OF: *Farmers, winegrowers, shoemakers, beltmakers, charcoal-burners, bachelors, invoked against fever, afflictions associated with the eyes, dry cough, infertility, panic attack; Provins*

STATUS: *Knight, hermit*

BORN: *1033, Provins, County of Champagne*

DIED: *June 30, 1066, Sajenega, County of Sossano*

VENERATED BY: *Roman Catholic Church*

CANONIZED: *1073*

SYMBOLS: *Depicted as a hermit or knight*

O Theobald, just as you embarked on many journeys throughout your youth seeking a true vocation— with pilgrimages to holy sites and encounters with hermits—allow me to follow your example, letting my faith bolster me and keeping my feet upon the path to salvation. This I pray in the name of Jesus Christ. Amen.

JULY

The seventh month of the Gregorian calendar, July, was originally named by Mark Antony in honor of another celebrated calendrical reformer, the Roman leader Julius Caesar. In terms of agriculture, July is traditionally a time of waiting while crops come to fruition. Ripening may well be severely delayed if it rains on Saint Swithun's Day, July 15, in which case tradition holds it will continue to rain for a further 40 days. The celebrations for two great early modern theologians fall in late July: author and monk Thomas à Kempis (who, oddly, is not recognized as a saint) on July 24 and Ignatius of Loyola on July 31.

ONE OF THE TOWERING FIGURES OF THE CATHOLIC COUNTER-REFORMATION, IGNATIUS OF LOYOLA WAS A SPANISH NOBLEMAN AND SOLDIER WHO WENT ON TO FOUND THE MISSIONARY ORDER OF THE SOCIETY OF JESUS, OR THE JESUITS. THE CASTING OUT OF DEVILS FROM A POSSESSED COUPLE IS THE ONE MIRACLE ATTRIBUTED TO HIM, AN ACT REPRESENTED HERE BY PETER PAUL RUBENS (1577–1640).

Junipero Serra

Born Miquel Josep Serra i Ferrer (Junípero was to honor St. Juniper), Serra entered the Franciscan Order in 1730. Academically gifted, he became a professor of theology at age 24. After joining the Missionary College of San Fernando in 1749, he journeyed to North America. He arrived in Veracruz and, despite a crippling riding accident, then walked 200 arduous miles to Mexico City. For 15 years he took on missionary work to be near the Native Americans, learning their languages. A passionate and volatile preacher, during his dramatic sermons he was said to scourge himself.

In 1768, the Spanish emperor expelled the Jesuits from Spain's colonies, and Serra, with a group of Franciscans, took over the Jesuit missions in Baja California. Under his presidency, nine California missions were established, stretching 600 miles from San Diego to San Francisco. When he fell afoul of the military commander in California, he returned to Mexico City to argue successfully that the authority of the Franciscans over the army and baptized Native Americans should be increased. With their large populations of Native Americans, the missions kept the region within the Spanish political sphere. He was the first saint canonized in America, by Pope Francis.

PATRON SAINT OF: *Vocations, Hispanic Americans; California*

STATUS: *Friar, founder*

BORN: *November 24, 1713, Majorca, Spain*

DIED: *August 28, 1784, Carmel, California*

VENERATED BY: *Roman Catholic Church*

CANONIZED: *2015*

SYMBOLS: *Usually shown in Franciscan robes, brandishing a cross, sometimes with Native American companions*

O God, in Your ineffable mercy, You chose Saint Junípero Serra as a means of gathering many peoples of the Americas into Your Church. Grant that through his intercession our hearts may be united in You in ever greater love, so that at all times and in all places we may show forth the image of Your Only-Begotten Son, our Lord Jesus Christ, who lives and reigns with You in the unity of the Holy Spirit, one God, forever and ever. Amen.

Bernardino Realino

PATRON SAINT OF:
Lecci

STATUS: *Priest*

BORN: *December 1, 1530,
Carpi, Italy*

DIED: *July 2, 1616, Lecci,
Province of Naples*

VENERATED BY: *Roman
Catholic Church*

CANONIZED: *1947*

SYMBOLS: *Priest's attire*

*Dear St Bernardino, just as
you ministered to young people,
help me to be an example and
encouragement to youthful faith.
Let me put aside any judgement
and open my heart to those who
are seeking a safe haven, a respite
from family troubles, or guidance
to a surer, more stable path. This I
ask in the name of Jesus Christ, our
Lord. Amen.*

B ernardino was born into a noble family—his father was a collaborator of Cardinal
Cristoforo Madruzzo. He studied philosophy and medicine in Bologna, but
switched to law when the woman he loved urged him to study something that offered
wealth and position. He graduated with a degree in both civil and canon law and served
as a tax collector, civil administrator, judge, and fief superintendent to the Marquis of
Pescara. Once, during confession, the Jesuit priest noted Bernadino's inclination for
a religious life. After a weeklong spiritual retreat with the Jesuits in 1564, Bernardino
joined the order. Ordained in 1567, he chose the life of a humble parish priest.
In 1583 he encouraged other diocesan priests to improve their moral-theological
education, making them better confessors and preachers. In 1610, he suffered a fall
that left him with two wounds that never healed. Some of his blood was collected
in vials shortly before he died. After his death, the blood was said to have liquified.
Today, his remains are preserved in Lecci in the Chiesa del Ges.

Thomas the Apostle

The Apostle Thomas, or Didymus ("the twin"), has three key functions in the Gospels . . . and in the proof of Christian belief in the face of skepticism. He is remembered for doubting the reports of Christ's Resurrection, until confronted by Jesus in the flesh (John 20:24–29); Jesus rebukes him, pointing out that Thomas now believes only because he has seen the evidence, but "blessed are they that have not seen, and yet have believed." Earlier, and by way of balance, Thomas's second important act was to confirm, during the raising of Lazarus, that he was ready to die alongside Jesus for his faith, thus providing a justification for innumerable subsequent martyrdoms. Thirdly, at the Last Supper, Thomas indicates that he doesn't understand where Christ is going, or how the Apostles can continue to follow Him, provoking the response "I am the way, and the truth, and the life: no man cometh unto the Father, but by me." (John 14:6).

PATRON SAINT OF:
Surveyors, architects, construction workers, geometricians, theologians; India, Sri Lanka, Pakistan, the East Indies

STATUS: *Apostle, martyr*

BORN: *Early 1st century AD*

DIED: *December 21, 72 AD*

VENERATED BY: *Roman Catholic Church, Eastern Orthodox Church, all other churches that venerate Christian saints*

CANONIZED:
Pre-Congregation

SYMBOLS: *Depicted as a young man placing his finger in Christ's wounded side; bearing a carpenter's square or spear*

Almighty and ever living God, who didst strengthen thine apostle Thomas with sure and certain faith in thy Son's resurrection: Grant us so perfectly and without doubt to believe in Jesus Christ, our Lord and our God, that our faith may never be found wanting in thy sight; through him who liveth and reigneth with thee and the Holy Spirit, one God, now and for ever. Amen.

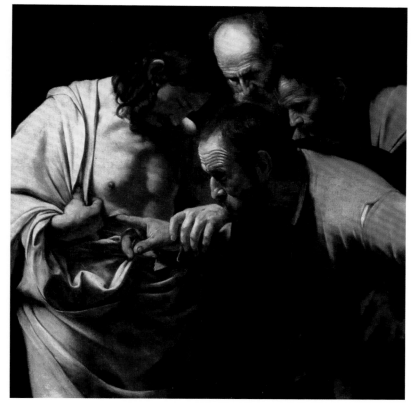

"DOUBTING" THOMAS EXAMINING THE SPEAR WOUND IN THE RESURRECTED CHRIST'S SIDE, PORTRAYED WITH UNFLINCHING REALISM BY CARAVAGGIO c.1602.

Elizabeth of Portugal

E lizabeth, called the "Peacemaker" and known as Isabella in Spain, was the daughter of the king of Aragon. At 17 she became queen of Portugal by marriage to King Denis (Diniz). She bore him a son and a daughter, but the union was not happy; Elizabeth turned her energies to prayer and the care of the unfortunate, continuing the benevolent practices of her youth. Asked by the king not to the feed the poor, one time he acosted as she carried bread in her apron . . . and the bread turned to roses.

She was an active conciliator with her husband in the negotiations for the Treaty of Alcanices, and they also arbitrated between Fernando IV of Castile and James II of Aragon, Elizabeth's brother. By riding a mule onto the field of battle, it was said she prevented her son from killing his father over the latter's loyalty to his illegitimate son, Afonso Sanches. After Denis died, Elizabeth withdrew from public life to become a Franciscan tertiary with the Poor Clares. As mother of the current king of Portugal, however, she was called upon to prevent a war between her son and the king of Castile, for his mistreatment of his wife—her granddaughter—which exertions exhausted her to the point of death.

PATRON SAINT OF:
Brides, charity workers, victims of adultery; Coimbra, Portugal

STATUS: *Queen*

BORN: *January 4, 1271, Saragossa, Spain*

DIED: *July 4, 1336, Estremoz, Portugal*

VENERATED BY: *Roman Catholic Church*

CANONIZED: *1625*

SYMBOLS: *Depicted in royal garb with a dove or olive branch, carrying roses in her apron*

Saint Elizabeth, whom I have chosen as my special patron, pray for me that I, too, may one day glorify the Blessed Trinity in heaven. Obtain for me your lively faith, that I may consider all persons, things, and events in the light of almighty God. Amen.

ELIZABETH AT HER DEVOTIONS, ACCOMPANIED BY AN ATTENDANT NUN, PAINTED BY THE FLEMISH ARTIST PETRUS CHRISTUS APPROXIMATELY 120 YEARS AFTER ELIZABETH'S DEATH.

Anthony Mary Zaccaria

Born of noble parents, Anthony lost his father at age two. His mother, in order to teach him compassion for the poor, made him her almoner, the person who distributes aid from a wealthy patron to the needy. Initially trained as a doctor in Padua, Anthony began studying for the priesthood in 1527 and was ordained in 1529. He became the spiritual advisor to Countess Ludovica Torelli of Guastalla in 1530, and followed her to Milan. After recruiting two Milanese noblemen as sponsors, he established the Clerics Regular of St. Paul. This reformist order was dedicated to intense, open-air preaching and the correct administering of the sacraments based on the writings of St. Paul, while also attending the sick. The order received papal approval in 1533, and Anthony made its headquarters the church of St. Barnabas in Milan, hence the order's popular name of "Barnabites." He also laid the foundations of two other religious orders: a group of uncloistered nuns, the Angelic Sisters of St. Paul, and a lay congregation for married people, the Laity of St. Paul, sometimes referred to as the Oblates of St. Paul.

PATRON SAINT OF:
The Barnabite order, Angelic Sisters of St. Paul, Laity of St. Paul, physicians

STATUS: *Priest, founder*

BORN: *1502, Cremona, Italy*

DIED: *July 5, 1539, Cremona, Italy*

VENERATED BY: *Roman Catholic Church, Barnabites*

CANONIZED: *1897*

SYMBOLS: *Black cassock, lily, cross, chalice, host*

St. Anthony Mary Zaccaria, continue your work as doctor and priest by obtaining from God healing from my physical and moral sickness, so that free from all evil and sin, I may love the Lord with joy, fulfill with fidelity my duties, work generously for the good of my brothers and sisters, and for my sanctification. Amen.

Maria Goretti

Saint Mary Goretti who, strengthened by God's grace, did not hesitate, even at a young age, to shed your blood and sacrifice life itself to defend your virginal purity, look graciously on the unhappy human race, which has strayed far from the path of eternal salvation. Teach us all, and especially youth, with what courage and promptitude we should flee for the love of Jesus, anything that could offend Him or stain our souls with sin. Amen.

Born to a peasant farming family in the Marche in central Italy, Maria Teresa Goretti is one of the youngest saints ever to be canonized. After the death of her father, her family became so poor that they were forced to give up their own farm and work as hired laborers. While in Le Ferriere, near Latina, they even shared their home with another family, the Serenellis. Maria was left to tend the house while her mother and other family members toiled in the fields. One day Alessandro, the Serenelli's 20-year-old son, threatened her with an awl and tried to rape her. When she fiercely resisted, protesting that "it is a sin," he tried to choke her and then stabbed her 11 times. She ran for the door, but he caught her and delivered three more wounds. Her loud cries alerted her mother, who rushed her to the hospital in Nettuno, but she died the following day, having forgiven her attacker. Alessandro was convicted of murder, sentenced to 30 years imprisonment, and later repented of his actions, asking her mother for forgiveness, which she offered. After his release, he became a lay brother in a monastery and lived to see Maria's canonization almost half a century after her murder.

Willibald

One of the most widely traveled of all Anglo-Saxons, Willibald is considered the first Englishman to visit the Holy Land. Willibald was brother to both St. Winnebald and St. Walburga (Feb. 25). The son of a chieftan, he entered a Benedictine abbey in Hampshire at age five. In 722 he set off on a pilgrimage to Rome, where he was laid low by the plague. After a miraculous recovery he traveled to Naples, Ephesus, and Cyprus. He set out for the Holy Land, arriving in Jerusalem in 725, and then traveled to Tyre, Constantinople, and back to Rome via Monte Cassino, where he stayed at the monastery for ten years, working as a sacristan, dean, and porter.

In 740, Pope Gregory III sent him to Germany. He was ordained by his cousin Boniface on July 22, 741, and assigned to missionary work at Eichstätt. Along with his brother, Winnebald, he founded the monastery at Heidenheim in southern Germany in 752. Winnebald was appointed the abbot, and his sister Walburga governed the female community. Willibald served as a bishop in Eichstätt for four decades. After his death, Willibald's body was found to be incorrupt.

PATRON SAINT OF: *Grid makers, diocese of Eichstatt*

STATUS: *Bishop, missionary*

BORN: *c. 700 AD, Wessex, England*

DIED: *787 AD, Eichstätt, Germany*

VENERATED BY: *Roman Catholic Church, Eastern Orthodox Church*

CANONIZED: *Pre-Congregation*

SYMBOLS: *Bishop overseeing building of a church*

Dearest Lord, Let me, like St. Willibald, find in prayer a closer contact with You and with your Son, Jesus Christ. Disperse any wayward thoughts so that my prayers may bring me deeper and deeper into a truly spiritual life. Amen.

WILLIBALD IS SHOWN HERE SUPERVISING THE CONSTRUCTION OF THE MONASTERY AT HEIDENHEIM, IN A 15TH-CENTURY ENGRAVING.

Kilian

*St. Kilian, devoted carrier of God's
message and martyr for your piety,
I pray that you will relieve the
pain of my rheumatism and gout.
In return I will promise to renew
my faith daily and also carry the
message of redemption into the
world. This I ask in the name of
Jesus Christ. Amen.*

Kilian was a native of Ireland who, as an ordained "traveling' bishop," journeyed to the pagan regions of Franconia and Thuringia with eleven companions, intent on missionary work. From 686 he adopted Würzburg as the base of his mission and succeeded in converting the local lord, Duke Gozbert, and much of the local population to Christianity.

Kilian came into conflict with Gozbert, however, because the duke had married his brother's widow, Geilana, in violation of the sacred scriptures. Kilian persuaded Gozbert to separate from his wife. Geilana had not converted to Christianity, and when she heard of Kilian's admonitions, she was so enraged that she arranged for Kilian and his companions, Colman and Totnan, to be murdered. The story has it that she concealed the murder from Gozbert, but subsequently went insane. In 743, the first bishop of Würzburg, St. Burchard, transferred the relics of the three martyrs—after wonderful cures had brought fame to their burial place—to the Church of Our Lady. The skulls of the saints, inlaid with precious stones, were transferred to the newly finished Cathedral of the Savior in 752.

STATUE OF SAINT KILIAN (WITH FORTRESS MARIENBERG IN THE BACKGROUND)

Augustine Zhao Rong and Companions

July 9 celebrates the martyrdom of 33 Western missionaries and 87 Chinese Catholics killed during periods of persecution in China from the Manchu (Qing) dynasty (c. 1648) up to 1930. The persecutions before the Boxer Rebellion of 1900 were against Catholics and Protestants both and largely due to imperial edicts, especially after Christianity increased in many areas beyond the control of the government. Officials granted clemency if the accused apostatized, but few did so. Ultimately many converts fled to the port cities in Gunagdong or in Indonesia. This feast was inaugurated by Pope John Paul II in 2000.

Augustine Zhao Rong was the most notable of many Chinese converts who were turned upon by their fellow citizens. Augustine Zhao was a soldier who had escorted the Franciscan priest Gabriel John Tauin du-Fresse to Beijing, and he became so impressed by his ward's pacific saintliness that he asked to be baptized. He was ordained as a priest and went on to continue missionary work, but was arrested in Chengdu in central China, and tortured, then starved to death in prison.

STATUS: *Martyr*

BORN: *c.1746, Wuchuan, China*

DIED: *1815, Chengdu, China*

VENERATED BY: *Roman Catholic Church*

CANONIZED: *2000*

O God, who in your wonderful providence have strengthened your Church through the confession of the Martyrs Saint Augustine Zhao and companions, grant that your people, faithful to the mission entrusted to it, may enjoy ever greater freedom and witness to the truth before the world. Through our Lord Jesus Christ, your Son, who lives and reigns with you in the unity of the Holy Spirit, one God, for ever and ever. Amen.

MEMORIAL PLAQUE AT SAINT FRANCIS XAVIER CHURCH

10

Emmanuel Ruiz and Companions

STATUS: *Priest, martyr*

BORN: *May 5, 1804*

DIED: *July 10, 1860*

VENERATED BY: *Roman Catholic Church*

CANONIZED: *1926*

SYMBOLS: *Depicted ascending to heaven with his co-martyrs*

O God, let me understand and share the faith of the Holy Martyrs, pious men like Emmanual Ruiz, who suffered great tortures yet never betrayed or turned away from You. Let me go forth armed with devotion and courage, holding fast to my beliefs, even in the face of tribulation or doubt. This I ask in the name of Jesus Christ, your Son. Amen.

Emmanuel Ruiz was a Spanish Franciscan missionary to Syria. During the Druse uprising, he and other Franciscan missionaries, plus three young Maronites, were tortured and then executed after refusing to apostatize and convert to Islam. From the time of St. Stephen the Church has had its martyrs, but the nineteenth century is distinguished by a great number. The brutality of these martyrdoms harks back to a distant era, but many of the victims lived in recent centuries. Such modern martyrs were those in Damascus during the massacre by the Druse in 1860. A quarrel between a Maronite and a Druse was the occasion for the opening attack. The Druse were armed, but the Christians allowed themselves to be disarmed by the Turkish authorities with the intent of preserving order. Within three weeks every Maronite village in main and southern Lebanon was pillaged or burned, six thousand Maronites were murdered or maimed. The massacre broke out in Damascus on July ninth, and in three days there were three thousand adult male victims.

Benedict of Nursia

Benedict of Nursia remains one of the towering figures of the Christian world; it was he who established the practical means of organizing Western monastic communities. Today, his influence is substantial—in the Middle Ages, it was immense. His designation by Pope Paul VI in 1964 as patron saint of Europe was a precise reflection of this eminence.

Much of what is known of Benedict's life was written by Pope Gregory I in the 6th century. He was likely the son of a Roman noble. As a young man, he spent three years as a hermit, attracting wide renown, before establishing 12 monasteries at Subiaco, each with 12 monks and a superior, with Benedict as abbot. The monastery at Monte Cassino is said to have been founded by him in 529. It was here that he wrote the Rule of St. Benedict. Written in 73 short chapters, Benedict's Rule stresses pax (peace), ora (prayer), and labora (work). It details how the monks' days should be divided regarding time spent at prayer, working, eating and drinking, and sleeping and waking, how best to serve their communities, and how to treat recalcitrant members. The tone throughout is moderate, encouraging, and wise.

PATRON SAINT OF: *Agricultural workers, the dying, monks, cavers, schoolchildren, sufferers from gallstones, nettle rash, and temptation; Europe*

STATUS: *Abbot, Founder*

BORN: *March 2, 480, Nursia, Italy*

DIED: *March 21, 547, Monte Cassino, Italy*

VENERATED BY: *Roman Catholic Church, Eastern Orthodox Church (March 14), Anglican Communion*

CANONIZED: *1220*

SYMBOLS: *Broken cup, broken plate, crosier, raven*

Gracious and Holy Father, give us the wisdom to discover You, the intelligence to understand You, the diligence to seek after You, the patience to wait for You, eyes to behold You, a heart to meditate upon You, and a life to proclaim You. Amen.

An early Renaissance painting of St. Benedict, by Fra Angelico, c.1440, in the Dominican Convent of St. Mark in Florence.

Veronica

V eronica, also known as Berenike, most likely lived in first century Jerusalem. Although she is not mentioned in the canonical gospels, she is a celebrated saint in many Christian countries. The closest similar story is that of the unnamed woman who touched the hem of Jesus' robe and was healed (Luke 8:43–48). Tradition insists that Veronica was moved by pity at sight of Jesus carrying His cross to Calvary, and gave Him her veil so that He could wipe His forehead and that an image of His face was miraculously impressed upon the cloth. This relic became known as the Veil of Veronica. Her charitable act was eventually commemorated as the sixth Station of the Cross in many Catholic, Anglican, Lutheran, Methodist, and Western Orthodox churches.

PATRON SAINT OF:
Linen weavers, laundry workers, images, Santa Veronica, San Pablo City, Laguna

STATUS: *Disciple*

BORN: *c. 1st century AD*

DIED: *c. 1st century AD*

VENERATED BY: *Roman Catholic Church, Eastern Orthodox Church, Anglican Communion*

CANONIZED:
Pre-Congregation

SYMBOLS: *Cloth that bears the image of Christ's face*

O My Jesus, Saint Veronica served You on the way to Calvary by wiping Your beloved face with a towel on which Your sacred image then appeared. She protected this treasure, and whenever people touched it, they were miraculously healed. I ask her to pray for the growth of my ability to see Your sacred image in others, to recognize their hurts, and to feel the same compassion for them as she did for You. Show me how to wipe their faces, serve their needs, and heal their wounds, reminding me that as I do this for them, I also do this for You. Amen.

SAINT VERONICA, BY HANS MEMLING, C. 1470.

Henry II

Henry was a Holy Roman Emperor who staunchly defended the Catholic Church at the dawn of a new millennium. The priveleged son of Duke Henry of Bavaria and Princess Gisela of Burgundy, Henry received both his education and spiritual guidance from bishop and future saint, Wolfgang of Regensberg. An intelligent and devout student, he was even considered a candidate for the priesthood. Nevertheless, upon his father's death, he was made Duke of Bavaria and in 1002 became King of Germany. He encouraged reforms in Church practices and also peacefully ended a revolt, then mercifully pardoned the rebel forces. In 1014 Pope Benedict VIII crowned him head of the Holy Roman Empire in Rome.

Henry donated much of his wealth to churches and monasteries and was a great patron of the poor as was his wife, St. Cunigunde of Luxembourg. Because they remained childless it was said they had both taken vows of chastity. Henry suffered from illness and a crippling condition late in life, but did not abdicate his responsibilities.

PATRON SAINT OF: *Benedictines Oblates*

STATUS: *Holy Roman Emperor*

BORN: *May 6, 973, Bad Abbach, Germany*

DIED: *July 13, 1924, Göttingen, Germany*

VENERATED BY: *Roman Catholic Church*

CANONIZED: 1145

SYMBOLS: *Crown, scepter, globus cruciger, imperial regalia*

Lord, you filled Saint Henry with your love and raised him from the cares of an earthly kingdom to eternal happiness in heaven.

In the midst of the changes of this world, may his prayers keep us free from sin and help us on our way toward you. Amen.

HENRY II IN A SACRAMENTARY C. 1002–1014

Kateri Tekakwitha

PATRON SAINT OF:
Ecologists, environmentalists, exiles

STATUS: *Mohawk convert, virgin*

BORN: *1656, Ossernenon, New York (modern Auriesville)*

DIED: *1680, Kahnawake, Canada*

VENERATED BY: *Roman Catholic Church*

BEATIFIED: 1980

SYMBOLS: *Lily, turtle*

O God, who among the many marvels of your grace in the New World, did cause to blossom on the banks of the Mohawk and St. Lawrence, the pure and tender Lily, Kateri Tekakwitha, grant, we beseech You, the favor we beg through her intercession—that our hearts may be enkindled with a stronger desire to imitate her innocence and faith. Through Christ our Lord. Amen.

The daughter of a Mohawk chief, Kateri lost her entire family to a smallpox epidemic when she was only four, and she was left with unsightly facial scars and poor eyesight. She was adopted by an uncle, chief of the Turtle Clan, and began to show an interest in Christianity—not surprising, since her mother had been an Algonquin who had converted to Catholicism. At age 20, she was baptized by a Jesuit priest.

Kateri was a zealous convert, who consequently alienated fellow members of her tribe. Mistrust turned to persecution, and she was threatened with torture and death if she refused to renounce her newfound religion. Kateri was forced to flee to an established community of Native American Christians in Kahnawake, Quebec. She dedicated the rest of her life to prayer, penance, care of the elderly, and chastity. The self-imposed austerity of her life broke down her already fragile health and she died at only 24. Eyewitnesses reported that her disfiguring smallpox scars disappeared at the time of her death. Kateri was the first Native American to be beatified and is especially revered by Native American Catholics.

Bonaventure

An outstanding theologian and philosopher of the 13th century, Bonaventure was also an able minister general of the Franciscan Order. John of Fidanza acquired his name (meaning "good fortune") when he was miraculously cured of a childhood illness through Francis of Assisi (Oct. 4). He entered the Franciscan Order in 1243 and, after studying in Paris, became a master of theology in 1255. At age 35, Bonaventure was appointed Franciscan minister general and was instrumental in restoring harmony to an order bitterly divided order over the nature of their ministry—should they adhere to the traditional Rule, with emphasis on self-denial and poverty or embrace a more worldly ideal, playing a leading role in universities and in political life? Bonaventure strove to heal the rift with a rational treatise on the nature of the Franciscan Rule, which the order adopted.

He was instrumental in procuring the election of Pope Gregory X and was rewarded with the titles of cardinal and bishop of Albano in 1273. Along with Thomas Aquinas, Bonaventure is regarded as one of the greatest thinkers of the 13th century.

PATRON SAINT OF: *Lyon, Canary Islands*

STATUS: *Bishop, confessor, Doctor of the Church*

BORN: *1221, Bagnoregio, Italy*

DIED: *July 15, 1274, Lyon, France*

VENERATED BY: *Roman Catholic Church*

CANONIZED: **1482**

SYMBOLS: *Cardinal's hat on a bush, ciborium, Franciscan robes, reading or writing*

St. Bonaventure Cardinal, Bishop and Doctor of the Church, you chose a life that embraced mortification and great humiliation. You served those who were rejected and sick, you risked illness for yourself. You made your life a continuous prayer and spent hours meditating on the wounds of Christ.

St. Bonaventure, please pray for me that I may have a sincere and humble heart.

Pray that I may not lose sight of Jesus' wounds and thus walk on the straight path to eternal salvation. Pray that I may take a great many souls with me to Our Heavenly Father. Amen.

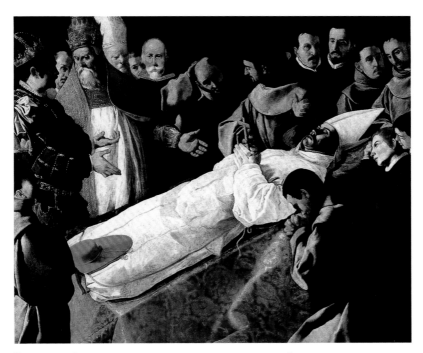

BONAVENTURE'S DEATH AT AGE 52 CUT SHORT A BRILLIANT CAREER. IT WAS ALSO SHROUDED IN MYSTERY—IT HAS BEEN SUGGESTED THAT HE WAS POISONED. HIS ROLE IN SEEKING A RESOLUTION OF THE SCHISM BETWEEN THE EASTERN AND WESTERN CHURCHES WAS OFTEN HOTLY DEBATED AND EARNED HIM ENEMIES AMONG THE CURIA.

Osmund

O smund, a nobleman who was ordained as a priest, served as counselor to William the Conqueror, whom he accompanied during the invasion of England. Made Chancellor in 1070, he oversaw many civil transactions and was a Chief Commissioner responsible for drawing up the Domesday Book, a manuscript record of the "Great Survey" of much of England and parts of Wales completed in 1086. Some sources maintain he was made Earl of Dorset at this time. Osmund was consecrated as bishop of Old Sarum Cathedral (Salisbury) by the authority of Gregory VII in 1078 and developed "Sarum Use," which regulated the Divine Office, Mass, and Calendar in his diocese, and was soon adopted throughout the British Isles. Henry I's biography suggests that Osmund may have overseen the youth's education; the future king was consistently in the bishop's company during his formative years.

PATRON SAINT OF:
Mentally ill people, paralysed people; invoked against insanity, mental illness, paralysis, ruptures, toothache

STATUS: *Bishop*

BORN: *c. early 11th century*

DIED: *December 3 or 4, 1099*

VENERATED BY: *Roman Catholic Church, Church of England*

CANONIZED: 1457

O God, our heavenly Father, who raised up your faithful servant Osmund to be a bishop and pastor in your Church and to feed your flock: Give abundantly to all pastors the gifts of your Holy Spirit, that they may minister in your household as true servants of Christ and stewards of your divine mysteries; through Jesus Christ our Lord, who lives and reigns with you and the Holy Spirit, one God, for ever and ever. Amen.

ST OSMUND STATUE IN SALISBURY CATHEDRAL

Hedwig of Poland

The well-educated and pious daughter of King Louis I of Hungary, Hedwig (Jadwiga in Polish) became one of Poland's great monarchs. The Poles had agreed to accept a daughter of Louis as their ruler, and so she was crowned "king" at around age 10. Hedwig had been promised in marriage to William of Austria, but after much prayer agreed to marry Jogaila of Lithuania. A pagan, he promised to convert to Catholicism. Hedwig and her newly styled husand, King Władysław Jagiełło, worked together on affairs of state. When rebellious nobles of the Kingdom of Hungary-Croatia imprisoned her mother and sister, she marched into the Kingdom of Galicia–Volhynia, formerly under Hungarian rule, and persuaded most of the inhabitants to become subjects of the Polish Crown. She mediated between her husband's quarreling kin, and between Poland and the Teutonic Knights. She died at age 25 after giving birth to a daughter, who, sadly, also died. Hedwig represented the virtues of holy women, benevolence and mercy.

PATRON SAINT OF: *Queens, a united Europe*

STATUS: *Queen*

BORN: *1373/4, Buda, Hungary*

DIED: *July 17, 1399, Kraków, Poland*

VENERATED BY: *Roman Catholic Church*

CANONIZED: *1997*

SYMBOLS: *Depicted with scepter and crown*

O Lord, I pray to thank you for blessed saint Hedwig of Poland, who so wisely supported the use of common speech in prayer, advocated for the translation of scripture into the national language, and further believed in the singing of hymns, that all of her people might hear your Word and praise your name. Amen.

QUEEN JADWIGA'S OATH, BY JÓZEF SIMMLER, 1867

Elizabeth of Russia

PATRON SAINT OF:
Russia

STATUS: *Grand duchess, abbess, martyr*

BORN: *November 1, 1864, Hesse, Darmstatt, Germany*

DIED: *July 18, 1918, Alapaevsk, Russia*

VENERATED BY: *Russian Orthodox Church*

CANONIZED: *1981 (Russian Orthodox Church Outside Russia); 1992 (in Russia)*

SYMBOLS: *Holding a Russian cross*

Emulating the Lord's self-abasement on earth, you gave up royal mansions to serve the poor, overflowing with compassion for the suffering.

And taking up a martyr's cross in your meekness,

You perfected the Savior's image within yourself,

Therefore entreat Him to save us all, O wise Elizabeth. Amen.

The child of royalty, Elizabeth was born to Duke Ludwig IV of Hesse and Princess Alice, a daughter of Queen Victoria. The beauteous Elizabeth drew many suitors, but wed a Russian grand duke, Sergei, son of Elizabeth's great-aunt, the Empress Maria Alexandrovna, and Tsar Alexander II of Russia. Like Elizabeth, Sergei was sensitive, artistic, and intensely religious. Brought up as a German Lutheran, she converted to Russian Orthodoxy. Sadly, in 1905, Sergei was assassinated by an anarchist.

After Sergei's death Elizabeth wore mourning clothes, sold her most valued possessions, and founded the Convent of SS. Martha and Mary in Moscow, becoming its abbess and dedicating herself to charitable works. After the Russian Revolution, Bolshevik leader Lenin ordered the Cheka (secret police) to arrest Elizabeth, a reminder of the old order. In exile in Yekaterinburg, she was joined by family members and a convent sister. On July 17, Cheka men drove the prisoners to a remote village. They were beaten and thrown into a mineshaft, then hand grenades and a burning brand were hurled into the mine. The White Army later discovered the bodies of Elizabeth and her companions. Her remains lie today in the Church of Mary Magdalene in Jerusalem.

A PASTEL PORTRAIT OF ELIZABETH AROUND THE TIME OF HER WEDDING, BY FRIEDRICH AUGUST VON KAULBACH (1850–1920).

Macrina the Younger

Born into a leading religious family in Cappadocia, Macrina's parents were Basil the Elder and Emmelia, and her grandmother became St. Macrina the Elder. She had nine younger siblings, including brothers who went on to become Basil the Great (Jan. 2) and St. Gregory of Nyssa (Jan. 10).

Her father arranged a marriage for her at age 12, but when her fiancé died, she dedicated herself to a religious life, becoming a nun. A leading holy woman, scholar, and religious instructress, she is regarded as one of the most prominent nuns in the Eastern Church. Her brother Gregory's biography of his sister records that she had a major influence on her family after her mother died. Not only was her devout life an outstanding example to her younger siblings, she also provided a rigorous critique of their ideas and a willingness to engage with them in penetrating philosophical discussions. It was probably Macrina's example that inspired Basil to pursue the monastic ideal, and three of her brothers—Basil, Gregory, and Peter—went on to become bishops.

STATUS: *Virgin, teacher*

BORN: *c. 327 AD, Caesarea, modern Turkey*

DIED: *July 19, 379 AD, Pontus, modern Turkey*

VENERATED BY: *Roman Catholic Church, Eastern Catholic Church, Eastern Orthodox Church*

CANONIZED: *Pre-Congregation*

SYMBOLS: *Depicted as a monastic with the schema*

St. Macrina, your purity and chastity became the standard for holy women throughout the Dark and Middle Ages. Pray that all Christian women today embrace the virtues of modesty, chastity, and courage and become an example that is desperately needed in our society. In Jesus' name I pray. Amen.

Margaret of Antioch

Although most likely a legendary martyr, Margaret remains a popular saint. According to Voragine's Golden Legend, she was the beautiful daughter of a pagan priest of Antiochia in central Turkey. Though her father derided her belief in Christianity, he attempted to protect from the Diocletian persecutions by secreting her on his rural estate as a shepherdess. Another legend says her father drove her from his home, and she became the servant of her own nursemaid.

At age 15 Margaret refused of an offer of marriage from the Roman prefect, her faith was revealed, and she was summarily tortured, including being beaten and raked with combs, and having her flesh torn with pincers. Miraculous interventions prevented her death, notably when she was swallowed by a dragon. The cross she was holding forced the beast to regurgitate her. As with so many of her martyred contemporaries, she was eventually beheaded. Margaret's cult was enormously popular in medieval Europe, and she was numbered as one of the Fourteen Holy Helpers.

PATRON SAINT OF:
Childbirth, pregnant women, exiles, the falsely accused, the dying

STATUS: *Virgin, martyr*

BORN: *c. 289 AD, Antiochia, modern Turkey*

DIED: *c. 304 AD, Antiochia, modern Turkey*

VENERATED BY: *Roman Catholic Church, Eastern Orthodox Church, Western Rite Orthodoxy, Anglican Communion, Coptic Orthodox Church of Alexandria*

CANONIZED:
Pre-Congregation

SYMBOLS: *Usually shown with a vanquished dragon, often holding a cross with a halo of seven stars*

O God, grant us through the intercession of Thy holy Virgin and Martyr Margaret, undauntedly to confess the Faith, carefully to observe the chastity of our state of life, and to overcome the temptations of the world, the flesh, and the devil, and thereby escape the punishments of eternal damnation. Amen.

SAINT MARGARET OF ANTIOCH

Lawrence of Brindisi

Lawrence was born to a wealthy Venetian merchant family trading in Brindisi, in the Spanish Kingdom of Naples. After studying in Venice, he entered the Capuchin Order and was ordained in 1582. As an effective administrator and preacher he rose swiftly through the ranks, by 1596 becoming definitor-general of the Franciscan Order, with a special brief for converting Jews. An arch example of a vigorous, career-building, Counter-Reformation priest, Lawrence was responsible for successfully establishing many Capuchin houses across central Europe during the wars of religion; he notoriously led a German Catholic army into battle against the Ottoman Turks in 1601, armed only with a crucifix.

In 1602, Lawrence was elected vicar-general of the Capuchins, but refused to renew the post three years later, preferring to perform ambassadorial tasks and writing. He is noted for an important essay he produced condemning Lutheranism. After being recalled as a special envoy to the King of Spain regarding the actions of the Viceroy of Naples in 1619, he completed his mission, then died on his birthday.

PATRON SAINT OF: *Brindisi*

STATUS: *Priest, Doctor of the Church*

BORN: *July 22, 1559, Brindisi, Italy*

DIED: *July 22, 1619, Lisbon, Portugal*

VENERATED BY: *Roman Catholic Church*

CANONIZED: *1881*

SYMBOLS: *Shown leading army against Turks, with infant Jesus, cross*

O God, who for the glory of your name and the salvation of souls bestowed on the Priest Saint Lawrence of Brindisi a spirit of counsel and fortitude, grant, we pray, that in the same spirit, we may know what must be done and, through his intercession, bring it to completion. Through our Lord Jesus Christ, your Son. Amen.

JULY

Mary Magdelene

Mary Magdalene remains a difficult figure to pin down historically. Most Gospels agree that she attended Christ during his ministry, prayed by the Cross at the Crucifixion, went to anoint Christ's body at the tomb and was the first person to whom the resurrected Christ appeared. But her earlier life, and exactly which biblical "Mary" she is, remains problematic. Her name derives from Magdala, a town in northern Galilee. She has sometimes been identified as Mary the sister of Martha and Lazarus of Bethany (July 29), who is described anointing Christ's feet with expensive perfumed oil (John 12:2–8). A similar scene occurs when an unnamed fallen woman anoints Christ's feet at the house of Simon the Pharisee (Luke 7:37–38). Luke and Mark refer to Mary Magdalene as someone whom Jesus had cured of possession by seven demons, which would suggest she was a repentant sinner. Gregory the Great propounded that all these references were to the same woman, a proposal rejected during the revision of the General Roman Calendar in 1969, where she was acknowledged as the uncontentious sister of Martha and Lazarus.

PATRON SAINT OF: *Women, apothecaries, converts, glovemakers, hairdresser, perfumeries, tanners;*

STATUS: *Apostle to the Apostles*

BORN: *1st century BC, Magadala, Israel*

DIED: *1st century AD*

VENERATED BY: *Roman Catholic, Eastern Catholic, and Eastern Orthodox Churches, Oriental Orthodoxy, Anglican Communion, Lutheranism, Baha'i Faith*

CANONIZED: *Pre-Congregation*

SYMBOLS: *Western: alabaster box of ointments; Eastern: myrrhbearer or holding red egg*

Mary Magdalene, woman of many sins, who by conversion became the beloved of Jesus, thank you for your witness that Jesus forgives through the miracle of love. You, who already possess eternal happiness in His glorious presence, please intercede for me, so that some day I may share in the same everlasting joy. Amen.

The Victorian obsession with "fallen women" made Mary Magdalene a very popular subject in art. Pre-Raphaelite painters and others, such as George Frederic Watts (1817–1904, above), often rendered her in a sacred manner that nevertheless suggested a more profane interest on the part of the artist — and viewer.

Bridget (Birgitta) of Sweden

Bridget, mother of St. Catherine of Sweden (March 24) and founder in 1350 of the Brigittine Order of nuns, is Sweden's best-known saint. Though married at age 13 and the mother of eight children, religion dominated her life. Following a pilgrimage to Santiago de Compostela, in 1349 the widowed Bridget traveled to Rome with her daughter, Catherine, to seek papal permission for her proposed order. Other than a pilgrimage to the Holy Land, she remained in Rome until her death, her sanctity and gentle nature making a deep impression. She had a series of visions, chiefly of the Nativity and of Purgatory. Anxious to know the precise number of blows Christ had received during the Passion, she claimed that Christ himself appeared to tell her that the number was 5,475. To honor his wounds, He instructed Bridget to say 15 Our Fathers, 15 Hail Marys, and 15 other prayers, which He then revealed to her every day for a year. Though Bridget died in Rome, her body was brought back to Vadstena, headquarters of her order.

PATRON SAINT OF: *Widows; Europe, Sweden*

STATUS: *Abbess, mystic, founder*

BORN: *1303, Uppland, Sweden*

DIED: *July 23, 1373, Rome, Italy*

VENERATED BY: *Roman Catholic Church, Anglican Communion, Lutheranism*

CANONIZED: *1391*

SYMBOLS: *Book, pilgrim's staff*

O Jesus, now I wish to pray the Lord's Prayer seven times in unity with the love with which You sanctified this prayer in Your Heart. Take it from my lips into Your Divine Heart. Improve and complete it so much that it brings as much honor and joy to the Trinity as You granted it on earth with this prayer. May these pour upon Your Holy Humanity in Glorification to Your Painful Wounds and the Precious Blood that You spilled from them. Amen.

An image of St. Bridget produced in 1476 in a breviary intended for use by Brigittine nuns.

Euphrasia of Constantinople

T he daughter of a Euphrasia was the daughter of a nobleman and was related to Roman emperor Theodosius I. Although betrothed at age seven, she went with her mother to Egypt after the death of her father, where both of them became nuns. After her mother died, the emperor ordered her back home, hoping to marry her to a promising young senator. She pleaded with Theodosius by letter to be excused from her marriage contract, requesting he give her inheritance to charity. The emperor eventually approved her petition.

She was renowned for her humility, meekness, and charity, and whenever she felt temptation, her mother superior suggested she perform manual labor, such as carrying heavy stones from place to place. It is said she once carried stones for 30 days straight. She is reported to have healed a crippled, deaf child, and exorcised a woman possessed by devils; after her death, her abbess had visions of Euphrasia being transported to God's throne.

PATRON SAINT OF:
Nursemaids, nursing mothers

STATUS: *Virgin*

BORN: *380, Constantinople, Eastern Roman Empire*

DIED: *March 13, 410, Egypt*

VENERATED BY: *Roman Catholic Church, Eastern Orthodox Church*

CANONIZED:
Pre-Congregation

SYMBOLS: *Often depicted holding portraits of her three saintly brothers*

Hear us, O God, our Saviour: that as we rejoice in the feast of blessed Euphrasia, Thy Virgin: so we may be taught by its devotion towards Thee. Through Jesus Christ, Thy Son who lives and reigns with Thee in they unity of the Holy Ghost God world without end. Amen.

EUPHRASIA CARRIED HEAVY ROCKS AS A PENITENTIAL LABOR

James the Greater

J ames, the English form of the Hebrew Jacob, was a Galilean fisherman who
became one of the Twelve Apostles. Possibly the cousin of Jesus, he is referred to
as "the Greater" to distinguish him from younger apostle James "the Less" (May 3).
The Gospel of St. Mark describes Jesus naming James and John "the Sons of Thunder"
for their evangelizing zeal. He was among the three Apostles closest to Jesus (along with
his brother John, and Peter) and was chosen to witness both Christ's Transfiguration
and the Agony in the Garden. James's physical similarity to Jesus was one reason Judas
Iscariot had to identify Jesus to the Roman guards in Gethsemane. James was the first
Apostle to be martyred, beheaded at the order of Herod Agrippa I to appease Jewish
critics of Christianity; his accuser repented at the last moment . . . and was executed
alongside him.

James possibly remained in Jerusalem after the Crucifixion to preach, although some
legends have him evangelizing in Iberia. Spanish tradition insists that his remains,
either transported by the Apostles or miraculously floating in a stone sarcophagus,
landed near Compostela in Galicia, where his cult took root.

PATRON SAINT OF:
*Pilgrims, horsemen, laborers,
hatmakers, veterinarians,
apothecaries, sufferers from
rheumatism and arthritis; Spain*

STATUS: *Apostle, martyr*

BORN: *1st century AD,
Galilee*

DIED: *c. 44 AD, Judaea,
modern Israel*

VENERATED BY: *Roman
Catholic Church, Eastern
Orthodox Church (April 30)*

CANONIZED:
Pre-Congregation

SYMBOLS: *Scallop shell,
pilgrim's cloak and broad-
brimmed hat, a staff, black
beard, sword*

*Hear us, O God, our Saviour: that
as we rejoice in the feast of blessed
Euphrasia, Thy Virgin: so we may
be taught by its devotion towards
Thee. Through Jesus Christ, Thy
Son who lives and reigns with Thee
in they unity of the Holy Ghost
God world without end. Amen.*

SAINT JAMES THE GREAT BY GUIDO RENI

JULY

Anne and Joachim

The parents of the Blessed Virgin Mary do not appear in the Bible, but feature in the apocryphal Protoevangelium of James. Anne was born in Bethlehem in Judea. The couple are described as being well-off and devout, enjoying their life in Nazareth, although they were also quite old and childless. Joachim, who was reproached in the Temple for his sterility when his sacrifice was rejected, retreated to the desert to pray for offspring. While he was away both he and Anne were informed by angels that indeed they could expect a wondrous child, and in due course Mary was born. In thanks for this gift from God, Anne and Joachim gave their three-year-old daughter to the Temple, where she would be raised. This story parallels that of elderly, barren Hannah, in the Old Testament, who bore Samuel and dedicated him to the service of God, and John the Baptist's aged parents in the New Testament. Veneration for St. Anne began in the East (the Orthodox churches celebrate this feast on July 25), but she had become a popular saint in the West, especially in Germany, by the 15th century.

PATRON SAINT OF:
Anne and Joachim:
Grandparents Anne:
Housewives, women in labor,
the childless

STATUS: *Parents of the*
Virgin Mary

BORN: *c. 50 BC*

DIED: *1101, P Calabria, Italy*

VENERATED BY: *Roman*
Catholic Church, Eastern
Catholic Church, Eastern
Orthodox Church, Oriental
Orthodoxy, Anglican
Communion, Lutheranism,
Islam

CANONIZED:
Pre-Congregation

SYMBOLS: *Anne wears red*
and green robes, often carries a
book; Joachim depicted with
lamb or doves

Good parents of the Blessed Virgin
Mary, grandparents of our Savior,
Jesus Christ,

When life seems barren, help us to
trust in God's mercy. When we are
confused, help us to find the way to
God. Amen.

St. Anne and her husband Joachim with Mary

Pantaleon

Pantaleon was born to a wealthy pagan father and a Christian mother, St. Eubula, in the Christian region of Nicomedia located in western Asia Minor. He studied medicine and became personal physician to the future Roman Emperor Galerius Maximianus. During this period he abandoned his faith, but later reclaimed it under the influence of St. Hermolaus. There are numerous accounts of Pantaleon's miraculous healing powers. One legend sees Pantaleon confronted by pagan doctors, with whom he competed to cure a victim of paralysis; simply by mentioning Jesus's name, Pantaleon cured the man. He supposedly converted his own father by returning sight to a blind man.

During the persecutions of Diocletian, Pantaleon was denounced, tried, nailed to a tree in a mock crucifixion, and then beheaded. Pantaleon's relics, mainly phials of his dried blood, can be found in Istanbul, Madrid, Lyon, and Ravello in Italy. His blood in Ravello is said to miraculously liquefy on his feast day. During the plague outbreak in mid-14th century Europe, Pantaleon, the patron saint of doctors, became known as one of the guardian martyrs, the Fourteen Holy Helpers.

PATRON SAINT OF: *Physicians, midwives, lottery winners, torture victims*

STATUS: *Martyr*

BORN: *c. 275 AD, Nicomedia, modern Turkey*

DIED: *c. 303 AD, possibly Constantinople*

VENERATED BY: *Roman Catholic Church, Eastern Orthodox Church, Oriental Orthodoxy, Anglicanism*

CANONIZED: *Pre-Congregation*

SYMBOLS: *Box with medicines, spatula or long handled spoon, martyr's cross*

St. Pantaleon who during your life had great pity for the sick and with the help of God often relieved and cured them, I invoke your intercession with God, that I may obtain the grace to serve Him in good health by cheerfully fulfilling the duties of my state of life.

Amen.

THIS DETAIL IS OF AN ILLUSIONISTIC CEILING FRESCO BY GIAN ANTONIO FUMIANI IN THE CHURCH OF SAN PANTALEON, VENICE. PAINTED BETWEEN 1684 AND 1704, IT SHOWS A NUMBER OF EVENTS FROM PANTALEON'S STORY.

28

Prochorus, Nicanor, Timon and Parmenas

STATUS: *Deacons, martyrs*

BORN: *Early 1st century AD, Jerusalem*

DIED: *Late 1st century AD*

VENERATED BY: *Roman Catholic Church, Eastern Orthodox Church, Oriental Orthodoxy*

CANONIZED: *Pre-Congregation*

SYMBOLS: *Prochorus is depicted as the scribe of St. John the Baptist*

O God, let me display the faith, valor, and piety shown by the Seven Deacons when they faced martyrdom during the early days of the Church. Allow me to face my own trials with the sure knowledge that You are beside me, supporting me and encouraging me at all times. This I pray in the name of your Son, Jesus Christ, our Lord. Amen.

These are four of the seven men named in Acts 6:1–6 as the early Church's first deacons. The others were Stephen (Dec. 26), Philip (June 6), and Nicolas of Antioch. They were appointed during the period after Christ's Resurrection and Ascension, during the time when St. Peter was organizing the early Church. Their function was to serve the Twelve Disciples, and to minister to the needs of Greek Christians, much as the Disciples did for Jewish Christians.

Various traditions recount their activities. Prochorus had been a companion of St. John the Baptist (June 24, Aug. 29) and was possibly the nephew of Stephen the Protomartyr. He became bishop of Nicomedia and was eventually martyred at Antioch in Syria. Nicanor traveled to Cyprus, but was martyred during the persecutions of Vespasian. Timon turned east and was appointed bishop of Bostra in Arabia, but was burned to death by the Persians at Basra. Parmenas went on missionary journeys in Asia Minor, and then sailed to Cyprus where he became bishop of Soli. Later he retired to mainland Greece and was martyred at Philippi during the persecutions under Trajan, sometime around 98 AD.

FRA ANGELICO'S FRESCO FROM THE NICCOLINE CHAPEL (C.1448) IN THE VATICAN SHOWS ST. PETER BLESSING THE SEVEN DEACONS. STEPHEN IS KNEELING, PHILIP IS CLAD IN BLUE.

Martha, Mary, and Lazarus

The sisters Martha and Mary and their brother Lazarus feature three times in the New Testament as friends of Jesus Christ. In the Gospel of Luke (10:38–42) Martha invites Jesus to their home in Bethany. While she prepares a meal, her sister Mary (possibly Mary Magdalene, July 22) kneels listening to Jesus; Martha rebukes her for not helping, but Jesus points out that Mary "has chosen the better part" by listening to Him.

In John, 11:1–44 Martha seeks out Jesus to tell him her brother Lazarus has died, a calamity that Mary claims would not have happened if Jesus had been present. In His most dramatic and controversial miracle, Jesus restores Lazarus to life, despite the body having been entombed for four days. Finally, with the events of the Passion gathering momentum, Martha and Mary again provide Christ with a meal at Bethany (John 12:1–18), where Lazarus joins them. Once again Martha cooks, and Mary anoints Christ's feet before His final return to Jerusalem.

PATRON SAINT OF:
Martha: Butlers, cooks, domestic workers, maids; Tarascon; Villajoyosa; Pateros Lazarus: those suffering leprosy

STATUS: *Companions of Jesus*

BORN: *Early 1st century AD, Bethany, modern Israel*

DIED: *c. mid-1st century AD, possibly Cyprus*

VENERATED BY: *Roman Catholic and Eastern Orthodox Churches, Oriental Orthodoxy, Anglican Communion, Lutheranism, Islam*

CANONIZED:
Pre-Congregation

SYMBOLS: *Mary: holding a myhrr jar and handkerchief; Lazarus: emerging from tomb wrapped for burial*

O God, heavenly Father, your Son Jesus Christ enjoyed rest and refreshment in the home of Mary and Martha of Bethany: Give us the will to love you, open our hearts to hear you, and strengthen our hands to serve you in others for his sake; who lives and reigns with you, now and for ever. Amen.

LAZARUS, IN AN UNATTRIBUTED SPANISH PAINTING FROM THE 15TH CENTURY, FLANKED BY MARY (LEFT) AND MARTHA (RIGHT).

Peter Chrysologus

O God, who made the Bishop Saint Peter Chrysologus an outstanding preacher of your incarnate Word, grant, through his intercession, that we may constantly ponder in our hearts the mysteries of your salvation and faithfully express them in what we do. We ask this through our Lord Jesus Christ, your Son. Amen.

As a child, Peter was given into the care of Cornelius, bishop of Imola, who baptized him, educated him, and ordained him a deacon. He became known for his sermons, which reveal common sense, warmth, and tolerance, especially toward Jews and pagans, which was unusual for the era. In his extant homilies, he explained Biblical texts briefly and concisely. He also condemned Arianism and Monophysitism as heretical and further explained the Apostles' Creed, the mystery of Incarnation, and other topics in clear, simple language. He dedicated a series of homilies to Saint John the Baptist and the Blessed Virgin Mary and advocated daily reception of Eucharist.

Peter was appointed archbishop of Ravenna, then the capital of the western Roman Empire, by Valentinian III in around 435. Peter was named Chrysologus—meaning "golden-worded" in Greek—in the 9th century, providing the Western Church with a counter-balance to the Orthodox Church's famous John Chrysostom ("golden-tongued," Sept. 13). He was also known as the "Doctor of Homilies" for the concise but theologically deep reflections he delivered while serving as bishop of Ravenna.

SAINT PETER CHRYSOLOGUS, DIOCESAN MUSEUM, IMOLA

Ignatious of Loyala

31

A towering figure of the revitalization of the Catholic Church during the Counter-Reformation, Loyola's martial background prepared him well for the battle to extend the faith in Europe and overseas. Like his forceful contemporaries, his origins lay in Spain, where he was born to a noble family in the Basque country. He served in the Spanish army and was severely wounded during the Siege of Pamplona. It was during his convalescence that he discovered his vocation. He undertook a pilgrimage to Jerusalem, then studied in Paris.

It was in the French capital, in 1534, that he formed a group of enthusiasts (including Francis Xavier, Dec. 3) dedicated to converting Muslims to Christianity. Although that venture never really developed, it became the essential seed that would grow into the foundation of the Society of Jesus—or Jesuits—a group dedicated to missionary activity under the direct authority of Pope Paul III. Ignatius devoted the last 15 years of his life to the missionary order, expanding its membership to over 1,000, and establishing schools and seminaries throughout Europe and the colonial world.

PATRON SAINT OF: *Society of Jesus (Jesuits), soldiers, educators; Basque country*

STATUS: *Priest, founder*

BORN: *October 23, 1491, Guipúzcoa, Spain*

DIED: *July 31, 1556, Rome, Italy*

VENERATED BY: *Roman Catholic Church, Anglican Communion, Jesuits*

CANONIZED: *1622*

SYMBOLS: *Eucharist, book, cross, rosary, chasuble*

Take, Lord, receive all my liberty, my memory, my understanding, my whole will, all that I have and all that I possess. You gave it all to me, Lord; I give it all back to you. Do with it as you will, according to your good pleasure. Give me your love and your grace; for with this I have all that I need. Amen.

IGNATIUS'S LEG WOUND WHILE DEFENDING PAMPLONA WAS A TURNING POINT IN HIS CAREER.

AUGUST

Named by Roman emperor Augustus after himself, the month of August is associated with vacations and holidays. However, some gruesome martyrdoms are also tied to August: Saint Lawrence's ordeal on the gridiron on August 10, the flaying of Saint Bartholomew the Apostle on August 24, and the beheading of Saint John the Baptist on August 29. From more recent times, the Nazis execution of Teresa Benedicta of the Cross (Edith Stein), a Jewish convert to Roman Catholicism, is commemorated on August 9.

On a brighter note, the dedication of the great early medieval basilica of Santa Maria Maggiore in Rome occurs on August 5, the day before the feast of the Transfiguration, while the Blessed Virgin Mary's ascendance to the throne as Queen of Heaven is marked on August 22.

THE ASCENT OF THE BLESSED VIRGIN MARY TO BECOME THE QUEEN OF HEAVEN IS HERE ENVISAGED IN AN EXTRAORDINARY MANNER BY THE UNNAMED GERMAN PAINTER, THE MASTER OF AACHEN, IN AROUND 1485.

Alphonsus Liguori

O ne of the most significant and important churchmen in 18th-century Italy,
Alphonsus was a tireless missionary to the poor in Naples and the surrounding
areas. The high-spirited young man trained as a lawyer but abandoned his career
in 1723 to become a priest, and was ordained in 1726. In Naples, he opened
what eventually grew to become 72 "Evening Chapels" to minister to the young
dispossessed of the city. When he discovered that conditions among the poor in
rural areas were even worse, he was greatly troubled. In 1732, he founded the
Congregation of the Most Holy Redeemer, or the Redemptorists, when Sister Maria
Celeste Crostarosa told him that it had been revealed to her that God had chosen
him to found it. It is still active today. Initially, their success was limited by local laws
and customs and, although Alphonsus sold all he owned to help feed the rural poor
during the famine of 1763, it was not until after his death that the Redemptorists
had a major impact. He became bishop of Sant'Agata dei Goti in 1762. He was also a
noted theologian, the author of 111 works.

PATRON SAINT OF:
*Suffers with arthritis,
confessors, moralists,
theologians, vocations; Naples,
Pagani, Cancello*

STATUS: *Bishop, founder,
Doctor of the Church*

BORN: *September 27, 1696,
Campania, Italy*

DIED: *August 1, 1787,
Campania, Italy*

VENERATED BY: *Roman
Catholic Church*

CANONIZED: *1839*

SYMBOLS: *Sometimes a
crosier with an image of the
Crucifixion*

*I love you, most dear Lady; and
for the love I bear you, I promise
to serve you willingly for ever and
to do what I can to make you loved
by others also. I place in you all my
hopes for salvation; accept me as
your servant and shelter me under
your mantle, you who are the
Mother of mercy. Amen.*

ALPHONSUS GIVING THANKS TO THE BLESSED SACRAMENT, FROM A MID-19TH-CENTURY
STAINED-GLASS WINDOW IN CARLOW CATHEDRAL, IRELAND.

Eusebius of Verceilli

PATRON SAINT OF:
Vercelli, Italy

STATUS: *Bishop*

BORN: *March 2, 283,
Sardinia, Italy*

DIED: *August 1, 371, Vercelli,
Italy*

VENERATED BY: *Roman
Catholic Church, Eastern
Orthodox Church*

CANONIZED:
Pre-Congregation

SYMBOLS: *Gray-bearded
figure in bishop's miter and staff*

*Lead us, Lord God, to imitate
the constancy of Saint Eusebius in
affirming the divinity of your Son,
so that, by preserving the faith he
taught as your Bishop, we may
merit a share in the very life of your
Son, who lives and reigns with you
in the unity of the Holy Spirit, one
God, for ever and ever. Amen.*

When his father was martyred in Sardinia, Eusebius's mother took him to Rome, where he later became a lector. Made bishop of Vercelli in Lombardy in 340, he was to become one of the most energetic defenders of the orthodox Christian belief in the divinity of Christ. This doctrine was officially affirmed at the Council of Nicaea in 325, in the face of the Arian heresy, a doctrine that held that Jesus Christ is the Son of God, and was begotten by God the Father, but is distinct from God the Father. Following the Council of Milan in 355, which was called by the Arian-supporting Roman emperor, Constantius II, to rebuke those opposing Arianism, Eusebius was exiled, first to Syria, then to Asia Minor, and finally to Egypt. Freed in 362 by the new emperor, Julian, Eusebius remained in the East, cooperating with another great champion of orthodoxy, St. Athanasius of Alexandria (May 2), before returning to Vercelli the following year. There he worked closely with St. Hilary of Poitiers (Jan. 13) in the continuing struggle against Arianism.

Lydia Purpuraria

Lydia was a successful merchant in the city of Thyatira in Greece. She made her living selling purple cloth and dye, which was highly valued at the time as the color of royalty. Little is known of St. Lydia's origins, and even her name is uncertain. She has commonly been referred to as "Lydia of Thyatira," "Lydia of Philippi," and "The Woman of Purple," all of which are likely descriptors of her place of origin and occupation as a dyer. Many believe that Lydia was a widow, as she was described as the sole head of her household.

Lydia is believed to be the apostle Paul's first known convert to Christianity. As Paul, Silas, and Timothy were traveling through the city of Philippi, they met a female merchant of purple dye who was willing to listen to Paul's words. After Lydia and her household were baptized, she insisted on allowing Paul and his companions to stay in her home for the duration of their stay in Philippi.

The Orthodox Church places great significance on St. Lydia, granting her the title of "equal to the apostles."

PATRON SAINT OF: *Dyers*

STATUS: *Early convert and apostle*

BORN: *1st century, Greece*

DIED: *Unknown*

VENERATED BY: *Roman Catholic Church, Episcopal Church, Eastern Orthodox Church, Lutheranism*

SYMBOLS: *Purple cloth, purple veil/shawl*

Pour out upon us, Lord, the spirit of knowledge and love of you, with which you filled your handmaid blessed Lydia, so that, serving you sincerely in imitation of her, we may be pleasing to you by our faith and our works. Through our Lord Jesus Christ, your Son, who lives and reigns with you in the unity of the Holy Spirit, one God, for ever and ever. Amen.

Jean-Baptiste Vianney

PATRON SAINT OF:
Confessors, parish priests, Archidiocese of Dubuque and Kansas City

STATUS: *Priest*

BORN: *May 8, 1786, Dadilly, France*

DIED: *August 4, 1859, Ars, France*

VENERATED BY: *Roman Catholic Church, Anglican Communion*

CANONIZED: *1925*

SYMBOLS: *Cassock, suplice, preaching bands, stole, rosary, crucifix, Bible*

I love You, O my God, and my only desire is to love You until the last breath of my life. I love You, O my infinitely lovable God, and I would rather die loving You, than live without loving You. Amen.

Despite being no more than the parish priest of one of the smallest parishes in France, Jean-Baptiste Vianney became one of the most celebrated Catholic priests in Europe. While struggling as a theology student (he found Latin difficult) at age 20, which was the earliest his father would free him from the family farm, he found himself drafted into Napoleon's army. Illness prevented him from reporting at first, and, after he received a second notice, a stranger led him into the forest, where he joined a group of deserters. When the amnesty for deserters was declared in 1810, he resumed his studies and was eventually ordained in 1815. As a parish priest in Ars, he became known not just for his sanctity and piety, but as a confessor. By the 1850s, upward of 20,000 people per year were descending on the town in order for Vianney to hear their confessions. Vianney, who generally rose at one in the morning and spent as many as 18 hours a day taking confession, asked frequently if he could leave Ars to live a quieter, more contemplative life, but was as frequently rebuffed by his bishop. He disapproved of frivolities like music and dancing and was known for his "fire and brimstone" sermons.

SAINT JOHN VIANNEY DEPICTED IN A STAINED GLASS WINDOW IN THE SAINT FELIX CHURCH IN LAISSAC, AVEYRON, FRANCE

Oswald of Northumbria

Oswald, king of Northumbria from 634 to 642, the most powerful of the kingdoms emerging in Dark Ages Britain, played a crucial role in the spread of Christianity in England. Exiled in 616 to Iona after his father, Athelfrith, had been killed in battle by Welsh prince Cadwallon, Oswald converted to Christianity. When, in turn, Oswald fought to regain his kingdom in 634 in what was called the Battle of Heavenfield, he claims to have been visited the night before by St. Columba (June 9). Before the battle, he had a wooden cross erected; his nobles swore to convert to Christianity if they were victorious. Oswald subsequently recruited an Irish monk from Iona, Aidan (Aug. 31), to convert the Northumbrians.

Oswald was killed at the Battle of Maserfield in 1642, fighting the pagan Mercians under their king, Penda. Almost at once, miracles were ascribed to the place of his death. When Oswald's body was later taken for burial at Bardney Abbey in Lincolnshire, the monks agreed to accept it only after a column of light shone from it.

PATRON SAINT OF:
Soldiers

STATUS: *King, martyr*

BORN: *c.604, Northumbria, England*

DIED: *August 5, 642, Shropshire, England*

VENERATED BY: *Roman Catholic Church, Eastern Orthodox Church, Anglican Communion*

CANONIZED:
Pre-Congregation

SYMBOLS: *King in crown, carrying sceptre and orb, ciborium, sword, palm-branch, and/or with his raven*

Oswald, you were known for your love of your people, your piety, and your zealousness in evangelizing. Pray that we may further the cause of Christianity in our own times and help save souls. St. Oswald of Northumbria, pray for us! Amen.

OSWALD OF NORTHUMBRIA ICON

Francesca Maria Rubatto

6

PATRON SAINT OF:
*Capuchin Sisters of Mother
Rubatto*

STATUS: *Nun, foundress*

BORN: *14 February 14,
1844, Italy*

DIED: *August 6, 1904,
Montevideo, Uruguay*

VENERATED BY: *Roman
Catholic Church, Eastern
Orthodox Church*

CANONIZED: *1993*

SYMBOLS: *Nun's habit*

*Mother Francisca, Kingdom
wanderer, tireless educator, grant
us the power of Jesus' spirit that
encouraged and held you in your
life path. Show us the horizon that
charmed your steps; spread your
deep conviction and your cheerful
hope in the possibility that you
discovered exists in each brother,
each sister, to grow and to explore
into dignifying freedom. Walk
with us with your tender and firm
wisdom, so that we can respond
with generosity to the commitment
of favoring—with our being and
doing—a world of brothers and
sisters, where we can all be happy.
Amen.*

Formerly Anna María Rubatto, later St. Maria Francesca Rubatto, was known for her charitable work, having devoted her life to caring for children, the sick, and the abandoned. After losing both parents by the age of 19, she served under noblewoman Mariana Scoffone from 1864 to 1882, teaching catechism to children and providing aid to the needy. After Scoffone's death in 1882, Francesca Maria began to work in a church in Loano. After leaving church one day, she encountered a young construction worker who had been injured by a falling stone. She cleaned his wound and offered him two days' wages so he could recover at home. The sisters of the convent currently under construction had been searching for a spiritual guide, and—seeing Rubatto's act of kindness—asked that she become their director. Accepting their offer, Rubatto became a nun and took the name Francesca Maria. After the establishment of "Mother Rubatto's Capuchin Sisters' Institute," she traveled the world, founding homes in Montevideo, Uruguay, Argentina, and Brazil. Rubatto travelled to Montevideo one last time before her death in 1904. She remains the only Uruguayan to have been beatified.

Cajetan

Born to a noble family in Vincenza, part of the Republic of Venice, Cajetan studied in Padua and received degrees in both civil and canon law. He worked as a diplomat for Pope Julius II, and after the pope's death he left the papal court and returned to Vincenza, where he founded a hospital for incurables. He was ordained as a priest in 1516. During the Sack of Rome in 1527 Cajetan was caught by the anti-catholic forces and scourged to make him confess the whereabouts of "his riches" which the mob mistakenly presumed him to have. Afterward he fled to Venice, where around this time he became the principal founder of the Theatines, more properly the Congregation of Clerks Regular of the Divine Providence. Overall, he was a crucial early figure in the Catholic Church's attempts to counter Protestant teachings by means of spiritual rebirth among clergy and laity alike. His own piety had earlier been underlined by his joining the Oratory of Divine Love, an order intended to alleviate poverty. Cajetan died, exhausted, suffering at the end what has been called "a mystical crucifixion."

PATRON SAINT OF: *Gamblers, bankers, the unemployed, good fortune; Albania, Argentina, Brazil, El Salvador, Guatemala*

STATUS: *Priest, founder*

BORN: *October 1, 1480, Vicenza, Italy*

DIED: *August 7, 1547, Naples, Italy*

VENERATED BY: *Roman Catholic Church*

CANONIZED: *1671*

SYMBOLS: *Usually shown in Theatine robes*

O glorious St. Cajetan, you studied to be a lawyer, but when you felt that the Lord was calling you to his service, you abandoned everything and became a priest. You excelled in virtues, shunning all material rewards for your labor, helping the many unemployed people of your time. You provided loans without interest and you attracted a lot of benefactors who donated to your resources . . . . Look on us with mercy. We wish to find employment that could help us and our families live with dignity. Amen.

Dominic

God of Truth you gave your church a new light in the life and preaching of our Father Dominic. Give us the help we need to support our preaching by holy and simple lives. We ask this through our Lord Jesus Christ, your Son, who lives and reigns with you and the Holy Spirit, God, forever and ever. Amen.

S t. Dominic, founder in 1216 of the Dominicans (Friars Preachers, or Black Friars), was among the most significant figures of the medieval church. His insistence on intellectual rigor, on preaching, on unquestioned faith, and on good works, helped revive a Church that was increasingly complacent and corrupt, but still faced a heretical movement—Catharism—that threatened its very foundations. Born to a noble family with an early reputation for sanctity and good works, Dominic was highly educated and, at the age of only 25, was made a canon of the cathedral of Osma in Burgos. In 1201, he was appointed its superior. It was in this capacity that he accompanied a Spanish diplomatic mission to Denmark.

Having reached France en route to Denmark, Dominic was now brought face to face with the reality of the Cathars. He was as impressed by their evident sincerity and the effectiveness of their organization as he was appalled by their heresy, to say nothing of the feebleness of Rome's response. The Cathars, Dominic understood, could only be directly confronted. "Zeal must be met by zeal, humility by humility . . . preaching falsehood by preaching truth," he asserted. Though from 1218 the Dominicans were based in Bologna in northern Italy, Dominic continued to travel widely, generally barefoot, preaching, organizing, and cajoling with remarkable intensity.

SANTO DOMINGO DE GUZMÁN, PORTRAIT BY THE SPANISH PAINTER CLAUDIO COELLO IN 1670

Teresa Benedicta of the Cross

Teresa Benedicta was born Edith Stein, to a Jewish family in what is now Poland and what was then part of the German Empire. She was an exceptionally bright child, academically very gifted, who at 13 declared herself an atheist. She gained a doctorate in philosophy from Göttingen University in 1916. A latent spirituality, inspired by reading the life of Teresa of Ávila (Oct. 15), subsequently developed within her. In 1922, she responded to that calling and converted to Catholicism. In 1933, despite a brilliant career as a teacher and philosopher, she became a Discalced Carmelite nun in Cologne, the order founded by Teresa of Ávila, appropriately taking the name Teresa. In 1938, recognizing that, Catholic convert or not, Teresa was still a Jew in the eyes of the persecuting Nazis, the Carmelites arranged for her to be smuggled to Holland and apparent safety. However, she and her sister were taken to Auschwitz on August 2, 1992, and were killed one week later. A colleague, Professor Jan Nota, memorably called her "a witness to God's presence in a world where God is absent."

PATRON SAINT OF: *Martyrs, orphans; Europe*

STATUS: *Nun, martyr*

BORN: *1891, Breslau (Wroclaw), Poland*

DIED: *1942, Auschwitz, Poland*

VENERATED BY: *Roman Catholic Church, Carmelites*

CANONIZED: *1998*

SYMBOLS: *Book, flames, Star of David.*

O my God, fill my soul with holy joy, courage and strength to serve You. Enkindle Your love in me and then walk with me along the next stretch of road before me. I do not see very far ahead, but when I have arrived where the horizon now closes down, a new prospect will open before me and I shall met with peace. Amen.

Lawrence

Little is known about Lawrence other than that he was one of seven deacons of Rome—in Lawrence's case charged with guarding the treasures of the Church, reputedly including the Holy Grail—under Pope Sixtus II. Lawrence had met the future pope, a higly esteemed teacher, in his home country of Spain and both men eventually left that country for Rome. When Sixtus was martyred, the prefect of Rome demanded the Church's treasures from Lawrence. He distributed as much as he could to the poor before facing the prefect. When ordered to produce the treasure, he called in the indigent, ailing, and crippled, saying "these are the Church's treasures." Like the other six deacons before him, Lawrence was condemned to death on the orders of the emperor Valerian. According to legend, Lawrence was slowly roasted to death, at one point asking to be turned over, complaining, "This side is done . . . Have a bite."

PATRON SAINT OF:
Chefs, roasters, comedians, librarians, students, tanners; Rome, Rotterdam

STATUS: *Deacon, martyr*

BORN: *December 1, 225, Valencia, Spain*

DIED: *August 10, 258, Rome, Italy*

VENERATED BY: *Roman Caholic Church, Eastern Orthodox Church, Anglican Communion, Lutheranism*

CANONIZED:
Pre-Congregation

SYMBOLS: *Gridiron, dalmatic (priest's tunic)*

O Generous patron of the Church's poor, St. Lawrence, pray to the One God, Father, Son and Holy Spirit that all the poor of the Church in need in every corner of the world may feel the effect of the love of their brothers and sisters who seek to help them.

Deliver the Church from the greed and envy of the powerful and protect her rights and property so that she may serve the needy in freedom, giving them good things for soul and body. Amen.

ST. LAWRENCE IN STAINED GLASS WINDOW BY FRANZ MAYER & CO.. HE IS HOLDING A PALM BRANCH, A SYMBOL FOR MARTYRDOM.

Clare of Assisi

C lare Offreduccio was daughter to the wealthy Count of Sasso-Rosso. After hearing St. Francis preach in the city, this pious young woman asked him to help her lead a life devoted to God. Francis placed her in the Benedictine convent of San Paulo, where she traded her fine gown for a modest habit. When her father tried to force her to return home, ostensibly for an arranged marriage, she clung to the altar and showed him her shorn hair, vowing to have no husband but Christ. Francis sent her to another monastery, where she was joined by her sister. A small dwelling was built for them next to the church of San Damiano. As more women joined them, they became known as the Poor Ladies of San Damiano, later the Order of St. Clare or Poor Clares. Her followers went barefoot, slept on the ground, ate no meat, and observed almost complete silence. When Pope Gregory IX offered Clare a dispensation from the vow of strict poverty in 1228, she declined. The Pope then granted the order the Privilegium Pauperitatis—meaning nobody could oblige them to accept any possession.

PATRON SAINT OF: *Goldsmiths, television, needleworkers, ESP, invoked against eye disease; Santa Clara, California*

STATUS: *Abbess, foundress*

BORN: *July 16, 1194, Assisi, Italy*

DIED: *August 11, 1253, Assisi, Italy*

VENERATED BY: *Roman Catholic Church, Anglican Communion, Lutheranism*

CANONIZED: *1255*

SYMBOLS: *Monstance, pyx, lamp, habit of the Poor Clares*

Blessed Saint Clare, whose very name means light, illumine the darkness of our minds and hearts so that we might see what God wishes us to do and perform it with a willing and joyful heart. Before your birth, a Heavenly voice foretold that you would be a light illuminating the world. Amen.

CLARE, PAINTED C.1320 BY SIMONE MARTINI, BASILICA OF ST. FRANCIS, ASSISI. "THEY SAY THAT WE ARE TOO POOR," WROTE ST. CLARE, "BUT CAN A HEART WHICH POSSESSES THE INFINITE GOD BE TRULY CALLED POOR?"

Jane Frances de Chantal

PATRON SAINT OF:
Forgotten people, widows, loss of parents, parents separated from children

STATUS: *Baroness, foundress*

BORN: *January 28, 1572, Burgundy, France*

DIED: *December 13, 1641, Moulins, France*

VENERATED BY: *Roman Catholic Church*

CANONIZED: *1767*

SYMBOLS: *Nun's habit, Sacred Heart*

Saint Jane, you forgave the man who killed your husband. Help me learn to forgive a particular person in my life who has caused me harm. You know how difficult it is to forgive. Help me to take the steps you took to welcome this person back into my life. Amen.

Jane Frances de Chantal's life was shaped by tragedy. By the age of 27, her mother, sister, husband, stepmother, and two of her children had died, leaving only a controlling father-in-law to support her. Although Jane was a pious woman, this last loss was more than she could bear, and she suffered a long period of deep depression. She found it impossible to forgive the man who had killed her husband in a hunting accident and struggled with this for months. Then she heard a sermon by Saint Francis de Sales that helped her finally forgive her husband's killer and move on. With Francis' support, Jane founded the Congregation of the Visitation in 1610. The order was uncommon for its acceptance of women who were old, sick, or unable to adhere to the strict guidelines of other orders. Often criticized for accepting such women, she steadfastly defended this practice. By her death in 1641, the Congregation of the Visitation had established 86 houses, with the help of donations from likeminded noblewomen.

Pontian and Hippolytus

Pontian, the pope from 230–35, and Hippolytus, the so-called anti-pope, embody both the doctrinal differences that bedeviled the early Christian church and the almost constant threat of persecution its members faced within the Roman empire. Hippolytus, presumed to have been born in Rome, was among the most important writers of the early Christian Church, though only fragments of his works survive. His opposition to a series of popes—Callixtus (r.217–222), Urban I (r.222–230), and then Pontian himself—was based partly on a dispute, not unlike Arianism (see page 12), concerning the divinity of Christ and His exact relationship to His father. Hippolytus also rejected Callixtus's ruling that sinners should be allowed back into the Church if they were genuinely repentant, a judgment that in fact did much to broaden the appeal of the Church. As a result, around 220 he declared himself a rival bishop of Rome, or "anti-pope." Nonetheless, Hippolytus seems to have reconciled to the pope when he and Pontian were arrested on the orders of the emperor Maximinus Thrax, who exiled them to Sardinia, where both died in the island's mines.

STATUS: *Pontian: Pope, Martyr; Hippolytus: Priest, Anti-pope, Martyr*

BORN: *Late 2nd century, Italy*

DIED: *236, Sardinia, Italy GRC*

VENERATED BY: *Roman Catholic Church*

CANONIZED: *Pre-Congregation*

SYMBOLS: *Horses, prison guards (Hippolytus)*

O God, let us honor the memory of fallen martyrs like Pontian and Hippolytus, who, though opposed in life, found themselves reconciled when facing death at the hands of a pagan ruler. Give us the courage and strength to defend our faith and the wisdom to find common ground with our enemies. In Christ's name we pray. Amen.

Maximilian Kolbe

PATRON SAINT OF:
*Recovering drug addicts,
families, journalists, political
prisoners, pro-life movement*

STATUS: *Priest, founder,
martyr*

BORN: *January 8, 1894,
Zdunska Wola, Poland*

DIED: *August 14, 1941,
Auschwitz, Poland*

VENERATED BY: *Roman
Catholic Church, Anglican
Communion, Lutheranism*

CANONIZED: *1982*

SYMBOLS: *Franciscan habit,
the Rycerz Niepokalanej, Nazi
concentration camp uniform,
crucifix, rosary, palm of
martyrdom.*

*Grant O Lord Jesus, that I too may
give myself entirely without reserve
to the love and service of my
Heavenly Queen in order to better
love and serve my fellow man in
imitation of Your humble servant,
St. Maximilian Kolbe. Help me to
learn by this example and grow in
sanctity, knowing you call us all to
Sainthood. Amen.*

Kolbe was born in Poland, at the time part of the Russian Empire. Inspired by a childhood vision of the Virgin Mary, in 1907 he escaped to Austria and joined the Franciscans. He was ordained in 1918, returning to what was then a newly independent Poland. He was a remarkably active priest, having already already established the Militia Immaculata, (the "Army of Mary"), which vigorously promoted Catholicism through veneration of the Virgin. He was no less energetic in Poland, founding Catholic newspapers and a radio station as well as the monastery of Niepokalanów. Between 1930 and 1936, he also established a monastery in Japan outside Nagasaki.

When the Germans invaded Poland in 1939, Kolbe instantly provided a rallying point for resistance, using his radio station to broadcast anti-Nazi messages. He sheltered huge numbers of refugees at the monastery in Niepokalanów, among them 2,000 Jews. Catholic priest or not, in February 1941 he was rounded up by the Gestapo. By May he had been sent to Auschwitz. There, he volunteered to replace of one of ten men arbitrarily selected by the commandant to be starved to death after one of the prisoners disappeared. Kolbe survived with no food or drink for three weeks before he was given a lethal injection of carbolic acid.

FATHER KOLBE IN 1936

Alypius of Thagaste

St. Alypius of Thagaste served as a Roman magistrate in his youth, but left that profession to follow his close friend Augustine of Hippo into service to the Church. Much of what we know of Alypius comes from Saint Augustine's Confessions, in which Augustine calls Alypius "the brother of my heart." He held deep-rooted beliefs in morality and chastity, believing that marriage would only distract him from his attempts to seek greater wisdom. One mention of Alypius describes the internal turmoil he felt when, despite his strong sense of morality, he was taken to watch the violent gladiatorial battles of the Roman arena. Although he tried at first to keep his eyes shut, Alypius eventually found himself drawn to the violent games, even returning later to see the spectacle again with his friends. In time, however, he repented for this lapse in moral judgement. Alypius was present in the garden in Milan at Augustine's conversion, and he and Augustine were baptized by St. Ambrose at the Easter vigil in April 387. Afterward they returned to Thagaste, where Alypius helped Augustine found North Africa's first monastery; he himself was made bishop of Thagaste in 394. He died around 430, shortly after Saint Augustine.

PATRON SAINT OF: *Morality*

STATUS: *Bishop*

BORN: *360 AD, Thagaste, Africa Preconsularis*

DIED: *430 AD*

VENERATED BY: *Roman Catholic Church, Eastern Orthodox Church*

CANONIZED: *1584*

SYMBOLS: *Mitre/bishop's hat.*

Lord God, you raised up Your bishops Alypius and Possidius to be, with Saint Augustine, apostles of truth and promoters of religious life. May we find freedom in truth and bondage in love, so that we may remain responsible to your call and consecrated to your service. Grant this through our Lord Jesus Christ who lives and reigns with You in the unity of the Holy Spirit, One God, for ever and ever. Amen.

THE CONVERSION OF ST. AUGUSTINE (GOZZOLI) THE FIGURE AT RIGHT IS THOUGHT TO BE ALYPIUS

Roch (Rocco)

Although he was one of the most popular saints of the Middle Ages, especially as the patron saint of plague sufferers—whose intercession against the devastating ravages of the disease was consistently invoked—it seems unlikely that Roch ever existed. Traditionally, Roch—also called Rock, Rocco, or Rollox—was the son of the noble governor of Montpellier and a noble-but-barren mother, who conceived him only after she prayed to the Virgin. Roch himself claimed to have had a been born with a red cross on his chest. At the age of 20, he embarked on a pilgrimage to Rome. Encountering the inevitable plague sufferers along his journey, he miraculously cured them by making the sign of the cross. When Roch himself contracted the plague, he took himself off to a forest where a spring miraculously gushed, and a dog brought him bread and cured him by licking his wounds. He died either in his native Montpellier, imprisoned by his own uncle, or in Voghera in Italy.

PATRON SAINT OF:
Sufferers from plague, invalids, apothecaries, bachelors, dogs, pilgrims, those falsely accused; Istanbul

STATUS: *Pilgrim*

BORN: *c.1295, Montpellier, France*

DIED: *August 16, 1327, Montpellier, France/Voghera, Italy*

VENERATED BY: *Roman Catholic Church, Episcopal Church*

CANONIZED: *1591*

SYMBOLS: *Thigh plague wound, dog offering bread, pilgrim's hat and staff*

O Blessed St Roch, Patron of the sick, have pity on those who lie upon a bed of suffering. Your power was so great when you were in this world, that by the sign of the Cross, many were healed of their diseases. Now that you are in heaven, your power is no less. Offer then to God our sighs and tears and obtain for us that health we seek. Through Christ our Lord. Amen.

SAINT ROCH BY FRANCESCO FRANCIA

Jeanne Delanoue
(Saint Joan of the Cross)

Despite a reputation in her youth for being selfish and self-involved, Jeanne Delanoue dedicated much of her later life to the protection of the poor, sick, and abandoned. Her father was a draper, and her mother ran a store selling religious goods to pilgrims of a nearby shrine. When her mother died, Jeanne took over her store at the age of 25 and ran it efficiently, even keeping it open on Sundays when other businesses were closed. Two years later, however, Jeanne met a poor widow named Francoise Fouchet, who prophesied that Delanoue would spend the rest of her life caring for those in need. Jeanne, although devout, remained skeptical. But before long. Jeanne changed her ways entirely, shutting down her business and devoting her life to providing for the poor, healing the sick, and caring for orphans. Jeanne Delanoue established three orphanages using the money her business had earned, and later founded the Sisters of Saint Anne of Providence of Saumur to help further provide for the needy. By the time of her death in 1736, her congregation had established twelve communities throughout France.

PATRON SAINT OF: *The poor, orphans*

STATUS: *Merchant, philanthropist, foundress*

BORN: *June 18, 1666, Saumur, France*

DIED: *August 17, 1736, Fencet, France*

VENERATED BY: *Roman Catholic Church*

CANONIZED: *October 31, 1982*

SYMBOLS: *Nun's habit, cross*

O God, who have taught your Church to keep all the heavenly commandments by love of you as God and love of neighbor; grant that, practicing the works of charity after the example of blessed Jeanne, we may be worthy to be numbered among the blessed in your Kingdom. Through our Lord Jesus Christ, your Son, who lives and reigns with you in the unity of the Holy Spirit, one God, for ever and ever. Amen.

Helena, Mother of Constantine

H elena was the mother of Constantine, the East Roman emperor whose reign began in 306 and who, in 313, by the Edict of Milan, made Christianity the official religion of the empire. Helen was likely born of Greek parentage in Drepanum, Asia Minor, which her son renamed Helenapolis in her honor after her death. Though not a member of the noble classes, she was wife to Flavius Constantius, an Illyrian army officer. Later, he became one of the four emperors of the Tetrarchy and divorced Helena as his stature rose.

Helena was an exceptionally devout Christian and was known for establishing a series of lavish religious foundations in the Holy Land. In 325, in Jerusalem, on the site of what was said to have been Calvary, the place of Christ's crucifixion, Helena apparently discovered the remains of the Cross on which Christ had died as well as the nails that had held Him to it. These almost instantly became the most prized relics in Christendom, brought back to Rome by Helena and housed in what today is the church of Santa Croce in Gerusalemme.

PATRON SAINT OF:
New discoveries

STATUS: *Empress*

BORN: *c.248, Drepanum, modernTurkey*

DIED: *c.328, Constantinople, Turkey/Rome, Italy*

VENERATED BY: *Roman Catholic Church, Eastern Orthodox Church, Oriental Orthodox Church, Anglican Communion, Lutheranism*

CANONIZED:
Pre-Congregation

SYMBOLS: *Often represented in her quest to find the "True Cross"*

Blessed Helena, How fortunate is the world that you raised your son Constantine to be open-minded and that he later chose the path of Christianity, not just for himself, but for all his domain as emperor. We thank you for all you did to spread the love of Christ and his holy Word. Amen.

ST. HELENA'S SEARCH FOR THE 'TRUE CROSS' WAS CELEBRATED BY THE ARTIST PIERO DELLA FRANCESCA (C.1460).

Jean Eudes

Jean—or John—Eudes was a revered French priest, orator, and writer. He grew up on a farm and became a priest around the age of 24, but fell ill shortly after being ordained. Upon his recovery, he chose to care for the sick during outbreaks of plague in 1627 and 1631 despite the risk to his own health. He isolated himself during these times to avoid infecting his peers, living in a large cask in a field for weeks at a time. Known as the "prodigy of his age," he preached over a hundred missions in his region and further afield and was a tireless evangelist and confessor.

Eudes founded the Order of Our Lady of Charity in 1641 as a means to provide refuge for prostitutes who wished to change their way of life. He then established the Congregation of Jesus and Mary, also known as the Eudists, in 1643, with the aim of providing education to priests and offering missions.

PATRON SAINT OF:
Eudists, missionaries, Diocese of Baie-Comeau, Order of Our Lady of Charity

STATUS: *Priest, mystic*

BORN: *November 14, 1601, Normandy, France*

DIED: *August 19, 1680, Normandy, France*

VENERATED BY: *Roman Catholic Church*

CANONIZED: *1925*

SYMBOLS: *Priest's attire, Sacred Heart.*

O Heart all loveable and all loving of my Saviour, be the Heart of my heart, the Soul of my soul, the Spirit of my spirit, the Life of my life and the sole principle of all my thoughts, words and actions, of all the faculties of my soul and of all my senses, both interior and exterior. Amen.

Bernard of Clairvaux

One of the most active and influential churchmen of his day, Bernard was born to a wealthy Burgundian landowning family. At 23 he joined the monastery at Cîteaux, accompanied by four of his brothers and 27 friends. The Rule of Benedict, which guided monastic communities for around 500 years, was falling into misuse, yet Bernard did much to restore and reform it. Ordered to found a new monastery at Clairvaux, he became its abbot for the rest of his life—refusing three offers of bishoprics. From Clairvaux emanated a new monastic vigor, carried by the Cistercians, who by the time of Bernard's death had founded more than 300 monastic communities throughout Europe and the Britain.

In spite of preferring a life of contemplation, Bernard was very active in public affairs, mediating between the Cluniac and Cistercian monks, and in the controversial papal election of 1130. He argued vigorously against the teachings of Peter Abelard and promoting the Second Crusade. He also helped secure papal approval for founding the Knights Templar.

PATRON SAINT OF:
Beekeepers, wax-makers

STATUS: *Abbot, founder, Doctor of the Church*

BORN: *1090, Fontaines, France*

DIED: *1153, Clairvaux, France*

VENERATED BY: *Roman Catholic Church*

CANONIZED: *1174*

SYMBOLS: *White Cistercian habit, often shown carrying three miters, or bearing book and pen, trampling a demon*

I desire to communicate spiritually, that Your Blood may purify, Your Flesh strengthen, and Your Spirit sanctify me. May I never forget that You, my divine Redeemer, died for me; may I die to all that is not You, that hereafter I may live eternally with You. Amen.

A STAINED-GLASS WINDOW SHOWING BERNARD AT PRAYER.

Pius X

Giuseppe Melchiorre Sarto was born to a poor family in the northern Veneto, at a time when entering the church provided a good option for those without means. He was ordained in 1858 and served as a rural pastor until he was appointed chancellor to the bishop of Mantua in 1875, succeeding to the see nine years later, and reviving the city's fortunes. In 1893 he was appointed patriarch of Venice, often an indication of a future papacy, and indeed he was elected pope in 1903.

His principal concerns involved reform of the Church to combat modernist tendencies, which he vigorously opposed. He is seen as an extreme conservative, weeding out dissent and disobedience within the clergy. He also instituted more positive changes: he reorganized the Roman curia, developed a revised Code of Canon Law, and encouraged greater cooperation between the Church and the laity. Pius was also known for regularly gaving homily sermons in the pulpit, which was a rare practice at the time.

PATRON SAINT OF: *Ardiocese of Atalanta and Des Moines, first communicants, pilgrims, Patriarchy of Venice*

STATUS: *Pope*

BORN: *June 2, 1835, Riese, Italy*

DIED: *August 20, 1914, Rome, Italy*

VENERATED BY: *Roman Catholic Church*

CANONIZED: *1954*

SYMBOLS: *Winged lion, symbolizing St. Mark, patron saint of Venice*

Glorious Pontiff, Saint Pius, devoted servant of our Lord and loving child of Mary, I invoke you as a Saint in Heaven. I give myself to you that you may always be my father, My protector, and my guide in the way of holiness and salvation. Aid me in observing the duties of my state of life. Obtain for me great purity of heart and a fervent Love of the interior life after your own example. Amen.

22

PATRON SAINT OF:
Children, students, eyesight, sufferers of syphilis; Autun

STATUS: *Martyrs*

BORN: *2nd century*

DIED: *Symphorian: August 22, 178; Timotheus: 311*

VENERATED BY: *Roman Catholic Church, Eastern Orthodox Church*

CANONIZED:
Pre-Congregation

SYMBOLS: *Young man being dragged to martyrdom, mother looking on*

O God, we pray that you may instill in us the faith that was shown by the many martyrs who chose death rather than sacrificing to or worshipping false idols. Let us go forth in the world armed with such devotion that any challenges to our own faith will be met with calm certainty. This we ask in the name of your Son, Jesus Christ. Amen.

Symphorian and Timotheus

Symphorian and Timotheus were two Christian martyrs who share a common feast day, although they died at different times and in different places. Symphorian was a young nobleman who was studying in Autun after his conversion to Christianity. When he encountered a statue of the pagan goddess Cybele, Symphorian failed to show reverence. As a result he was brought before the provincial governor and ordered to choose between worshiping Cybele and death. Symphorian was martyred after requesting tools with which he could destroy the statue, and is often depicted with his mother looking on and offering him encouragement.

Timotheus was a Syrian priest who traveled from Antioch to Rome. He became a respected preacher during his time in Rome, briefly befriending and living with Pope Sylvester I. After spending 15 months in Rome, Timotheus was martyred by Tarquinus Perpenna during the persecutions of Diocletian. After being imprisoned, tortured, and eventually beheaded, Timotheus was buried in the garden of a Christian woman named Theon.

THE MARTYRDOM OF SAINT SYMPHORIAN, BY JEAN AUGUSTE DOMINIQUE INGRES

Rose of Lima

Born to a middle-class but impoverished Spanish colonial family, Rose was baptized Isabel de Flores, but an Indian servant remarked that as a baby Isabel was "como una rosa," (like a rose) and the nickname was adopted. As a girl she worked hard to help support her family, taking in needlework and selling dried flowers. At the same time, she chose Catherine of Siena (April 29) as a spiritual mentor, undertaking severe penances such as self-flagellation and extreme fasting, which induced visions. Like Catherine's, her penances also provoked vomiting, and it is thought that she was probably bulimic. Rose became a Dominican tertiary at age 20 and retreated to a hermitage in her parents' garden, where she slept on broken tiles. She took over several rooms in the family home to create an infirmary for the destitute, as well as children, Indians, slaves, and the elderly, which boosted her cult in Lima. She died at age 31, having prophesied the date of her death. Rose of Lima was the first canonized saint of the Americas.

PATRON SAINT OF: *Florists, embroiderers, gardeners, those ridiculed for their piety*

STATUS: *Virgin*

BORN: *April 20, 1586, Lima, Peru*

DIED: *August 24, 1617, Lima, Peru*

VENERATED BY: *Roman Catholic Church, Anglican Communion*

CANONIZED: *1671*

SYMBOLS: *Roses, anchor, infant Jesus*

Gracious God, You filled the heart of St Rose with charity and missionary zeal, and gave her the desire to make You known among all peoples.

Fill us who honour her memory today, with that same love and zeal to extend your kingdom to the ends of the earth.

We ask this through our Lord Jesus Christ, your Son, who lives and reigns with You and the Holy Spirit, one God forever and ever. Amen.

ST. LUCIA AND ST. ROSE OF LIMA BY ENRICO REFFO (1910).

Bartholomew

PATRON SAINT OF:
Tanners and leatherworkers

STATUS: *Apostle*

BORN: *1st century AD, Cana*

DIED: *1st century AD,
Albanopolis, Caucasia*

VENERATED BY: *Roman
Catholic Church, Eastern
Orthodox Church*

CANONIZED:
Pre-Congregation

SYMBOLS: *Being flayed,
bearing a flaying knife,
sometimes shown flayed and
carrying his skin*

*God and loving father, You
have given us the glorious
Apostle Bartholomew as our
beloved Patron Saint and powerful
advocate in heaven. . . . Teach us
to cherish, proclaim, and practice
the Gospel message of Christ,
which Saint Bartholomew so
eloquently preached and finally
sealed with his heroic martyrdom.
We ask this in Christ's name.
Amen.*

In truth, there are few historical details about the early life of Bartholomew, except that he is mentioned in all the lists of the Twelve Apostles that appear in the New Testament. Some Biblical scholars identify him as the man called Nathaniel, who is introduced to Jesus by the Apostle Philip. He is mentioned as a witness to the Ascension in Acts. Bartholomew is later thought to have preached in Mesopotamia, Persia, and possibly India, although accounts of his particularly gruesome martyrdom—being flayed alive, or having his skin peeled from his body, before decapitation—place the event at Derbend (Albanopolis) in upper Armenia, on the shores of the Caspian Sea.

His relics were translated eventually to Rome, and are claimed by the church of St. Bartholomew on the Tiber. King Canute's wife apparently donated one of Bartholomew's arms to the see of Canterbury in the 11th century, which explains the enormous popularity of his cult in medieval England, where over 160 churches were dedicated to him.

BARTHOLOMEW IS OFTEN REPRESENTED AFTER BEING FLAYED, AND SOMETIMES BEARING HIS OWN SKIN.

Louis IX of France

Louis succeeded to the French throne at age eleven in 1226 upon the death of his father Louis VIII, although his mother acted as regent for the next nine years. Renowned as a just and fair Christian ruler, his reign saw the flowering of French Gothic culture and the creation of hospitals and institutions of learning such as the Sorbonne. Louis also founded the exquisite Sainte-Chapelle on the Ile de la Cité to house the relic of Christ's Crown of Thorns, donated by the crusader Baldwin. Louis was not free from the prejudices of the age, however, and in 1269 he decreed that Jews should wear a red badge on their clothing to distinguish them.

In 1244, Louis embarked on a Crusade, capturing the city of Damietta in the Nile delta, but was himself captured, and then freed only after returning the city to Muslim hands and paying a huge ransom. Undeterred, he launched a further Crusade in 1270 against the Muslims of Tunisia. The venture turned disastrous after an outbreak of typhoid, from which Louis himself died.

TRIUMPHANT MARTIAL ATTITUDES.

PATRON SAINT OF: *Barbers, printers, stonemasons; France*

STATUS: *King*

BORN: *April 25, 1214, Poissy, France*

DIED: *August 25, 1270, Tunis, North Africa*

VENERATED BY: *Roman Catholic Church, Anglican Communion*

CANONIZED: *1297*

SYMBOLS: *Depicted as a regal knight, crowned, with fleur-de-lis*

O holy King St. Louis, worthy son of our Holy Father. Be my guide and protector, so that I may never stray from the path of virtue but increase daily in holiness and perfection, and finally merit to be numbered among the chosen ones of our Seraphic Father in Heaven. Amen.

Elizabeth Bichier des Ages

STATUS: *Noblewoman, foundress*

BORN: *July 5, 1773, Poitou, France*

DIED: *August 26, 1838*

VENERATED BY: *Roman Catholic Church*

CANONIZED: *1947*

SYMBOLS: *Paper and quill, habit*

Lord, our God, grant that Your faithful spouse, St. Elizabeth, may enkindle in us the flame of Divine love that she enkindled in other virgins for the everlasting glory of Your Church. Amen.

Jean Elizabeth Bichier was born into French nobility in 1773, and was directly impacted by the events of the French Revolution when she was only 16. Her father's death and her oldest brother's emigration left Bichier and her mother more vulnerable to attacks and harassment from members of the revolution, leading to her eventual (if brief) imprisonment in Châteauroux. After her release, she was still unable to practice her religion fully and frequently gathered others to form prayer groups. When she and a former servant attended a secret Mass held by Andrew Fournet, she and Fournet bonded and conspired to use Bichier's home to provide religious education for the local children. In 1807, When the Catholic church was once again able to hold services in public, Bichier and Fournet gathered a small congregation of women and founded the Sisters of the Cross, Sisters of St. Andrew. The members of this new order professed public vows of chastity, poverty, and obedience while following the evangelical way of life.

Monica

Monica is important as the mother of St. Augustine of Hippo (Aug. 28), and it is largely from his Confessions that we know of her. Raised as a Christian, she married Patricius, a wealthy but dissolute pagan, and they had three children. Her patience eventually led Patricius to convert shortly before his death in 371. She had less immediate success with her oldest son Augustine, who took after his father, and despite her entreaties refused to be baptized. Argument failing, she set an example of piety through fasts, prayer, and vigils. Augustine left for Rome, and Monica set off after him, catching up with her son in Milan, where she also met St. Ambrose (Dec. 7). Together, through logic and enlightenment, they convinced Augustine to convert, and he was baptized in 387. On the return journey to Africa, Monica died at Ostia, where her relics remain in the church of Sant'Agostino.

PATRON OF: *Mothers, wives, various mothers' associations*

STATUS: *Widow*

BORN: *331, Tagaste, North Africa*

DIED: *387, Ostia, Italy*

VENERATED: *Roman Catholic Church, Eastern Orthodox Church*

CANONIZED: *Pre-Congregation*

SYMBOLS: *Widows' clothes or black nun's habit*

Dear Saint Monica, you were once the mournful mother of a prodigal son. Your faithfulness to prayer brought you and your son so close to God that you are now with him in eternity. By your intercession and God's grace, your son St. Augustine became a great and venerable Saint of the Church. Please take my request to God with the same fervor and persistence with which you prayed for your own son. Amen.

MONICA IS NORMALLY SHOWN WEARING A BLACK NUN'S HABIT, REFLECTING HER ROLE AS A WIDOW.

Augustine of Hippo

28

PATRON SAINT OF:
Theologians, printers, brewers;
invoked against sore eyes

STATUS: *Bishop, Doctor of*
the Church

BORN: *354, Tagaste, North*
Africa

DIED: *430, Hippo Regius*
(Bône), modern Annaba,
Algeria

VENERATED BY: *Roman*
Catholic Church, Eastern
Orthodox Church, US
Episcopal and Evangelical
Lutheran churches

CANONIZED:
Pre-Congregation

SYMBOLS: *Usually as a*
bearded bishop, with book,
often accompanied by a flaming
heart pierced by arrows

Act in me O Holy Spirit, that my
work, too, may be holy. Draw my
heart O Holy Spirit, that I love
but what is holy. Strengthen me
O Holy Spirit, to defend all that
is holy. Guard me, then, O Holy
Spirit, that I always may be holy.
Amen.

Despite a late conversion—he was baptized at 33, largely due to his Christian mother Monica (Aug. 27)—Augustine became one of the towering thinkers and theologians of the early medieval church. He studied law and rhetoric at Carthage and delved deeply into Platonic philosophy. He also joined the heretical Manichaean sect, which renounced the scriptures of the Old Testament. In 383 he left North Africa to teach rhetoric in Rome, and a year later was appointed professor of rhetoric in Milan. Here he met St. Ambrose (Dec. 7) who demonstrated it was possible to resolve the Bible's teachings with Platonic ideas. In 386, Augustine retired to live a communal contemplative life near Milan. After rejecting Manichaeism, and under Ambrose's guidance, he prepared for baptism. Returning to Tagaste, he set up a monastic community of laymen on his family's estate.

Augustine was appointed bishop of Hippo in 395 and over the next 34 years developed the model of an episcopal ministry, one actively involved in pastoral, ecclesiastical, and lay legal matters. He is ranked as one of the four original western Doctors of the Church.

THE TRIUMPH OF SAINT AUGUSTINE PAINTED BY CLAUDIO COELLO, C. 1664

Sabina

S aint Sabina was a Roman noblewoman and martyr, the daughter of Herod Metallarius and widow to Senator Valentinus. Little else is known of Sabina's life beyond the circumstances of her death, as is the case for her slave, Saint Serapia. Serapia, who had abandoned her possessions and sold herself into voluntary slavery to Sabina, was responsible for converting Sabina to Christianity. When Serapia refused to revere the gods of Rome, she was tortured and beheaded. Sabina rescued Serapia's remains and had them placed in her own family's mausoleum so that they would be buried together, before she herself was executed for her faith. In 430 her relics were carried to a specially built basilica, Santa Sabina, on the Aventine Hill. It had been constructed on the site of her house, which was originally situated near a temple of Juno. Originally dedicated to both Sabina and Serapia, the church is now limited to Sabina—and is her major shrine.

PATRON SAINT OF: *Diocese of Avezzano, Italy*

STATUS: *Noblewoman, martyr*

BORN: *1st century, Rome*

DIED: *c. 126, Rome*

VENERATED BY: *Roman Catholic Church, Eastern Orthodox Church*

CANONIZED: *Pre-Congregation*

SYMBOLS: *Palm frond*

God our Father, every year you give us joy on this feast of Saint Sabina. As we honor her memory by this celebration, may we follow the example of her holy life. We ask this through Christ our Lord. Amen.

THE RELICS OF ST. SABINA

Jeanne Jugan

PATRON SAINT OF:
Destitute elderly

STATUS: *Foundress*

BORN: *October 25, 1792*

DIED: *August 29, 1879*

VENERATED BY: *Roman Catholic Church*

CANONIZED: *2009*

SYMBOLS: *Black hooded cloak with white coif, shown aiding the elderly*

Jesus, you rejoiced and praised your Father for having revealed to little ones the mysteries of the Kingdom of Heaven. We thank you for the graces granted to your humble servant, Jeanne Jugan, to whom we confide our petitions and needs. Father of the poor, you have never refused the prayer of the lowly. We ask you, therefore, to hear the petitions that she presents to you on our behalf. Jesus, through Mary, your Mother and ours, we ask this of you. Amen.

Known also as Mary of the Cross, Jeanne grew up during the political upheavals of the French Revolution. After her fisherman father was lost at sea, her mother struggled to provide for her eight children and was forced to offer them religious instruction in secret during the anti-Catholic persecutions. Jeanne worked as a shepherdess while still a child and later toiled as a hospital nurse until her own health problems intruded. At 25, she became an associate of the Congregation of Jesus and Mary founded by St. John Eudes. For 12 years she was a servant to another member of the order. One day she encountered Anne Chauvin, an elderly woman who was blind, partially paralyzed, and had no one to care for her. Jeanne took her in and even gave up her bed. She eventually gathered more destitute women together, and by 1841 had rented a room to house them. This was the beginning of the congregation of the Little Sisters of the Poor. This became Jugan's life work, caring for these women and even going door to door to support the order.

JEANNE JUGAN, SISTER AND SERVANT OF THE POOR

Aidan of Lindisfarne

S aint Aidan of Lindisfarne was an Irish monk, missionary, and the first Bishop of the monastary on the Holy Island of Lindisfarne. In addition to being credited with converting the Anglo-Saxons of Northumbria to Christianity, he was well known for his kindness to animals, his strict ascetic lifestyle, and his willingness to travel great distances to carry out missions and evangelize. According to Bede, he was originally a monk at the monastery founded by St. Columba on the island of Iona. Sent forth as a missionary at the request of King Oswald, Aidan established many churches, schools, and monasteries throughout Northumbria, and became famous for his patience and humility as he traveled on foot from village to village. On one occasion, Aidan is said to have saved a stag from hunters by making it invisible; on another, it was said that his prayers saved the city of Bamburgh from being burned by a pagan army by turning the flames back toward the attackers.

PATRON SAINT OF: *Firefighters; Northumbria*

STATUS: *Bishop*

BORN: *c. 590, Ireland*

DIED: *August 31, 651, Northumberland*

VENERATED BY: *Roman Catholic Church, Eastern Orthodox Church, Anglican Communion, Lutheranism*

CANONIZED: *Pre-Congregation*

SYMBOLS: *Monk holding a flaming torch; stag*

Leave me alone with God as much as may be. As the tide draws the waters close in upon the shore, Make me an island, set apart, alone with you, God, holy to you. Then with the turning of the tide prepare me to carry your presence to the busy world beyond, the world that rushes in on me till the waters come again and fold me back to you. Amen.

AIDAN OF LINDISFARNE, STAINED GLASS AT HOLY CROSS MONASTERY

SEPTEMBER

With the gathering of the harvest and the autumnal equinox occurring in the Northern Hemisphere, September also marks the Indiction, the beginning of the Eastern Orthodox Church year. The Nativity of the Blessed Virgin Mary (or the Theotokos —meaning God-bearer—as she is named by the Orthodox churches) is celebrated by most denominations on September 8. The Exaltation of the Holy Cross is observed on September 14, and the following day is devoted to Our Lady of Sorrows.

September 29, known as Michaelmas, is a day of recognition for the actions and achievements of the archangels Michael, Raphael, and Gabriel, the principal messengers of God in the earthly realm. The day was traditionally associated with the payment of agricultural rents and church tithes.

ALTHOUGH ANGELS RATHER THAN SAINTS, MICHAEL, RAPHAEL, AND GABRIEL ARE CELEBRATED IN MUCH THE SAME WAY. THEIR LIVELY REPRESENTATION BY FRANCESCO BOTTICINI (C.1446–98) INCLUDES THE FIGURE OF TOBIAS, WITH HIS DOG AND FISH, WHOSE ENCOUNTER WITH RAPHAEL IS RELATED IN ONE OF THE BOOKS OF THE APOCRYPHAL BOOK OF TOBIT.

Giles of Provence

Giles was a Greek hermit, probably legendary, whom some stories name the son of King Theodore of Athens. He eventually settled in a forest near Nîmes in the south of France, his only companion a deer that fed him with milk. Hunted one day by a local king, known as Wamba, the deer took shelter with Giles, who was then wounded by an arrow intended for the animal. Wamba was so impressed by the hermit's humility and sanctity that he built him a monastery, St.-Gilles-du-Gard, where the saint eventually died.

Giles was one of the most venerated of saints in the Middle Ages, the spread of his cult throughout Europe witnessed by churches dedicated to him in France, Spain, Germany, Poland, Hungary, Slovakia, and Great Britain and the numerous manuscripts commemorating his virtues and miracles. St.-Gilles-du-Gard itself became a major place of pilgrimage, not least as a stop on one of the many pilgrimage routes to Santiago de Compostela in northern Spain. Numerous miracles were ascribed to his shrine. He is also traditionally one of the Fourteen Holy Helpers, those saints invoked for aid against a variety of illnesses.

PATRON SAINT OF:
Forests, horses, rams, hermits, beggars; cancer victims, the disabled, the mentally ill, sufferers from epilepsy; Edinburgh

STATUS: *Hermit*

BORN: *c. 650, Athens, Greece*

DIED: *c. 710, Languedoc, France*

VENERATED BY: *Roman Catholic Church, Eastern Orthodox Church, Anglican Communion, Church of Scotland*

CANONIZED:
Pre-Congregation

SYMBOLS: *Arrow, hermitage, hind (deer)*

Almighty God,

By whose grace Giles, kindled with the fire of your love,

Became a burning and shining light in the Church;

Inflame us with the same spirit of discipline and love,

That we may ever walk before You as children of light.

Amen.

St. Giles and the Hind from an altarpiece (c.1500) by a Flemish painter known only as the Master of St. Giles. Here the king, Wamba, has been elevated to the king of France. St. Giles, an arrow in his right hand, comforts the deer after the king has chased it.

SEPTEMBER

Blessed Martyrs of September

The convulsions of the French Revolution included the legal murder of from 16,000 to 40,000 aristocratic members of the Ancien Régime between June 1793 and July 1794. This bloodbath was presaged in September 1792 by the murder of 191 Catholic priests in an outbreak of extraordinary and improbable violence in Paris. Those killed in the "September Massacres" were already prisoners of the state, arrested after refusing to swear a 1790 oath of loyalty that effectively stripped the pope of his authority in France. That the Church in France was a natural target of the Revolution was understandable. It enjoyed privileges that placed it at the center of the Ancien Régime. It was believed to be immensely wealthy. For the new apostles of the Age of Reason, it was also a bastion of superstition. Those arrested were held in three main locations in Paris: the Carmelite monastery in the rue de Rennes, the seminary of St. Fermin, and the abbey of St.-Germain-des-Prés. Those killed, among them the archbishop of Arles and the bishops of Beauvais and Saintes, 127 secular priests, 45 monks, and 5 laypeople, were collectively beatified by Pope Pius XI in 1926.

STATUS: *Martyrs*

BORN: *Early-to-mid 18th century*

DIED: *1792, Paris, France*

VENERATED BY: *Roman Catholic Church, France*

BEATIFIED: *1926*

Grant a joyful outcome to our prayers, O Lord, so that we, who each year devoutly honor the day of the passion of the holy Martyrs of September, may also imitate the constancy of their faith. Through our Lord Jesus Christ, your Son, who lives and reigns with you in the unity of the Holy Spirit, one God, for ever and ever. Amen.

AN ILLUSTRATION, PUBLISHED IN 1862 IN FRANCE, OF THE SEPTEMBER MASSACRES. THE CATHOLIC PRIESTHOOD WAS NOT THE EXCLUSIVE TARGET OF THE MOB; MANY ARISTOCRATS WERE ALSO KILLED.

Gregory the Great

The medieval Catholic Church, based in Rome and presided over by the pope, was the most powerful institution in Europe. Every Christian emperor, king, and prince owed allegiance to it. This was ancient Rome recast, but where once Rome's emperors directed the fate of Europe, it was now the city's popes. The man responsible for this extraordinary transformation was Gregory the Great.

Gregory, appointed pope in 590, was an exceptionally able administrator but he became pope after Italy had suffered over a century of barbarian incursions that imperiled the remnants of Roman imperial control. Such rule as did exist was based in Constantinople, a court not merely distant, but only vaguely concerned over the fate of Rome. It was also home to an Orthodox Christian Church presided over by a patriarch proclaimed the "universal" head of the Church.

Gregory's response to Constantinople's authority was devastatingly effective. He ignored it. He cast himself as the direct heir of St. Peter, the first bishop of Rome. On his own authority, he negotiated peace treaties and appointed rulers. Gregory, himself a Benedictine monk, presided over an enormous surge in monastic communities in many parts of Europe.

PATRON SAINT OF: *Teachers, students, musicians, singers*

STATUS: *Pope, Doctor of the Church*

BORN: *c.540, Rome, Italy*

DIED: *March 12, 604, Rome, Italy*

VENERATED BY: *Roman Catholic Church, Eastern Orthodox Church*

CANONIZED: *Pre-Congregation*

SYMBOLS: *Usually shown writing, or with quill and scroll, Holy Spirit in form of dove, double or triple cross*

St. Gregory, you were born as a Roman Senator's son and became a prefect yourself. Pray that we may continue to grow in our faith, reveling in the beautiful traditions of our Church, and passing down these traditions to future generations. Amen.

GREGORY'S FAME RESTS SIGNIFICANTLY ON THE SUBSTANTIAL NUMBER OF HIS WRITINGS THAT HAVE BEEN PRESERVED, INCLUDING 850 OF HIS LETTERS. THIS 10TH-CENTURY ANGLO-SAXON MANUSCRIPT ILLUSTRATION IS A PRECISE EXAMPLE OF A CULT THAT REINFORCED THE NOTION OF GREGORY AS AN INDEFATIGABLE MAN OF LETTERS.

Birinus

Birinus was a Frankish Benedictine monk who was made bishop by Asterius in Genoa. Sent to England in 634 by Pope Honorius I, he played a key role in spreading Christianity across Wessex in the southwest of England, after St. Augustine's initial Christianizing mission to Kent in 596.

Birinus's most notable convert was Cynegils, the king of Wessex, whose baptism into the Church facilitated an alliance with King Oswald, who was already a Christian, against the Mercians. Birinus later baptised the king's son and grandson, to whom he also stood as godfather. Cynegils subsequently awarded Birinus the settlement of Dorchester-on-Thames as the seat of his diocese. Birinus established a series of churches, particularly at Dorchester itself, where he was buried, and later at Winchester, the capital of Wessex and the new seat of the diocese of the kingdom. He supposedly laid the foundations for St. Mary's Church in Reading and built the first church in Ipsden, a small chapel.

PATRON SAINT OF:
Berkshire, Dorchester

STATUS: *Bishop, missionary*

BORN: *c.600 AD, France*

DIED: *December 3, 649/650, Dorchester, England*

VENERATED BY: *Roman Catholic Church, Eastern Orthodox Church, Anglican Communion*

CANONIZED:
Pre-Congregation

SYMBOLS: *Shown baptizing a king*

Let us pray that we may be true heralds of the Gospel like St Birinus, praying for all those who do not know Christ that they may encounter him, and that we may be instruments in making Him known in word and deed to all. Amen.

A 19TH-CENTURY STAINED-GLASS WINDOW OF ST. BIRINUS IN DORCHESTER ABBEY.

Mother Teresa

The Blessed Teresa of Calcutta, Mother Teresa to the rest of the world, became one of the best-known humanitarians of the 20th century. Born to Catholic Albanian parents in what today is Macedonia, Teresa's vocation was evident from age 12. When she was 18, she joined the Sisters of Loreto and, as a teacher in India, took her vows in 1931. She adopted the name Teresa after St. Thérèse of Lisieux (Oct. 1). Her move to Calcutta (modern Kolkata) was a brutal introduction to the horrors of Indian urban poverty during the great Bengal famine of 1943, when millions died. She worked there for the rest of her long life.

The Missionaries of Charity, established by Teresa in 1950 in the Calcutta slums, is one of the world's foremost charitable foundations, boasting more than 600 missions in 123 countries and over one million volunteer workers. As recognition of the diminutive Teresa, dressed in a white sari with blue bands, spread, she was increasingly showered with honors, including the 1979 Nobel Peace Prize. Yet she remains a controversial figure; her insistence that suffering was "a gift of God" and her absolute opposition to abortion were troubling, and many of her hospitals were criticized for their poor levels of medical care.

PATRON SAINT OF:
World Youth Day

STATUS: *Nun, missionary*

BORN: *August 26, 1910, Skopje, Macedonia*

DIED: *Spetember 5, 1997, Calcutta, India*

VENERATED BY: *Roman Catholic Church, Missionaries of Charity, India, Macedonia*

BEATIFIED: *2003*

SYMBOLS: *White sari, with blue bands*

Give us a heart as beautiful, pure, and spotless as yours.

A heart like yours, so full of love and humility.

May we be able to receive Jesus as the Bread of Life, to love Him as You loved Him, to serve Him under the mistreated face of the poor.

We ask this through Jesus Christ our Lord. Amen.

MOTHER TERESA WAS A FAMILIAR AND POPULAR FIGURE ON THE STREETS OF CALCUTTA, WEARING HER DISTINCTIVE WHITE SARI WITH BLUE BANDS AND HEAD COVERING, ADAPTING LOCAL CLOTHING TO A NUN'S HABIT.

Bertrand de Garrigues

STATUS: *Priest*

BORN: *. 1195, Garrigue, diocese of Nimes, France*

DIED: *April 18 1230, Garrigue, diocese of Nimes, France*

VENERATED BY: *Roman Catholic Church*

BEATIFIED: *July 1881*

SYMBOLS: *Bertrand holding a church*

Almighty, eternal God, You dedicated the joy of this day to the glorification of Blessed Bertrand. Mercifully grant that we may always strive to retain and complete by our works that faith which he continually proclaimed. Amen.

Blessed Bertrand of Garrigue was a priest and evangelizer well-known for his close friendship with Saint Dominic de Guzman. He was one of the first of Saint Dominic's followers, and later served as his second in command whenever Dominic was absent. Bertrand, who worked with the Cistercians and joined the Dominicans in 1216, helped the Domincans survive and thrive in their early years. He governed the first Dominican foundation in Paris, and was instrumental in establishing their tradition of scholarship. He was an austere man, deeply dedicated to his order, who spent the whole of his life traveling and giving sermons. It is said that, after a night of prayer at Notre Dame with Dominic, both men were granted the gift of tongues in order to preach to German pilgrims in their own language. Bertrand grew sick and died when he was only 35 years old, but continued his work after death: many miraculous cures were attributed to his grave, which soon became a site for pilgrimage.

Antoine-Frédéric Ozanam

Ozanam, a lawyer and then a professor of literature at the Sorbonne in Paris, was one of the most important influences on the Catholic Church in mid-19th-century France. While the Church struggled to reassert itself in the face of the bitter anti-clericalism fostered by the French Revolution, Ozanam argued that, whatever its shortcomings, the institution had been an overwhelming force for good in the shaping of medieval and modern Europe. A staunch advocate of papal authority, he also recognized that the Church had to adapt if it was to have meaning in an increasingly industrialized world.

Born in Milan, but raised in Lyon, he fell in with prominent liberal Catholics while studying law in Paris. In May of 1833, at only 20 years of age, he and a group of other young men co-founded he charitable Society of St. Vincent de Paul, dedicated to tackling poverty. The founders developed their method of service under the guidance of Sister Rosalie Rendu, of the Congregation of the Daughter of Charity of Saint Vincent de Paul, who was known for attending the poor in the Paris slums.

PATRON SAINT OF: *Politicians, economists, social workers, teachers, journalists, criminologists, anthropologists, historians, geographers, environmentalists*

STATUS: *Lawyer, founder*

BORN: *April 23, 1813, Milan, Italy*

DIED: *September 8, 1853, Marseille, France*

VENERATED BY: *Roman Catholic Church*

BEATIFIED: *1997*

SYMBOLS: *Pointing to Christ in a sphere of glory on his chest*

Mary, Blessed Patron of the Society of Saint Vincent de Paul, we beseech you to intercede with your Son, our Lord Jesus Christ, for the world today . . . we entrust especially to you the most vulnerable and distressed of our brothers and sisters; all those who do not have the Faith; those who are afraid or overwhelmed by trouble; the whole Church, our priests, our bishops, our seminarians and our deacons; all healthcare professionals; and our families, friends, and work colleagues. Amen.

BLESSED

FREDERIC OZANAM

OZANAM'S HEALTH WAS FRAIL THROUGHOUT HIS LIFE. HE DIED OF CONSUMPTION AT AGE 40 ON HIS RETURN FROM ITALY, WHICH HE HAD VISITED IN THE HOPE THAT ITS CLIMATE WOULD HELP HIM COUNTERACT THE ILLNESS.

Corbinian

PATRON SAINT OF:
Archdiocese of Munich and Freising, Germany

STATUS: *Bishop*

BORN: *c. 670, Châtres, France*

DIED: *September 8 c. 730, Freising, Germany*

VENERATED BY: *Roman Catholic Church, Eastern Orthodox Church*

CANONIZED:
Pre-Congregation

SYMBOLS: *Saddled bear; bear carrying luggage; bishop with a bear and mule; bishop with Duke Grimoald at his feet*

O Saint Corbinian, who remained steadfast in your determination to complete your journey to Rome, I pray that I may follow your blessed example, that my faith in the the Lord may remain equally steadfast and that the occasional doubts I may feel will flee away. This I ask in the name of Christ, our Lord. Amen.

Corbinian's earliest years are a mystery. Born in Frankish territory, he was named Waldesigo at birth, but his mother Corbiniana renamed him Corbinian shortly after the death of his father. He spent fourteen years living as a hermit on the road to Orleans, until he was eventually compelled to make a pilgrimage to Rome. On his way there, Corbinian's mule was killed by a bear; Corbinian then commanded the bear to carry his luggage to Rome in the mule's stead. Upon his arrival in Rome, Corbinian was tasked by Pope Gregory II to travel to Bavaria to evangelize and act as a minister to Duke Grimoald. Grimoald had married his own brother's widow, a practice frowned upon by the Church, and Corbinian's vocal disapproval of this infuriated Grimoald's wife, who called him a foreign interloper. She arranged to have Corbinian killed, forcing him to flee the country until Grimoald and his wife were no longer in power. At that point the new ruler, Huebert, invited him to return. He spent the rest of his life in Bavaria, carrying out his original mission.

SAINT CORBINIAN DEPICTED IN THE MIRACLE OF THE BEAR (1489) BY JAN POLACK. DIOCESAN MUSEUM IN FREISING, GERMANY.

Peter Claver

Peter Claver was born to a poor but distinguished family in Catalonia, Spain, but aspired to a university education in Barcelona, where he encountered the Society of Jesus. He joined the order in 1602 and moved to the Jesuit college in Majorca. There he was advised to seek his vocation in the New World. He agreed to be sent to Cartagena, on the Caribbean coast of Colombia in 1610. He began working under his mentor and inspiration, the Jesuit Father Alfonso de Sandoval, and was ordained in 1616.

Cartagena was one of the principal slave ports in Spanish America, with some 10,000 souls passing through its markets each year. Peter undertook to minister to the slaves as the ships from Africa arrived—their human cargo often enduring terrible, crowded conditions—feeding them and treating any wounds or sickness before they were sold. Peter is estimated to have baptized over 300,000 African-Americans and heard the confession of more than 5,000 slaves a year. He traveled inland to visit his converts on the plantations where they worked, lodging in the slaves' quarters. Peter also visited British and French prisoners of war and ministered to condemned criminals.

PATRON SAINT OF:
Slaves, African-Americans, seafarers; Colombia

STATUS: *Priest, missionary*

BORN: *June 1580/1, Verdú, Spain*

DIED: *September 8, 1654, Cartagena, Colombia*

VENERATED BY: *Roman Catholic Church, US Evangelical Lutheran Church*

CANONIZED: *1888*

SYMBOLS: *Shown in Jesuit robes ministering to African-American slaves*

O God, who made Saint Peter Claver a slave of slaves and strengthened him with wonder, charity, and patience as he came to their aid, grant, through his intercession, that, seeking the things of Jesus Christ, we may love our neighbor in deeds and in truth. Through our Lord Jesus Christ, your Son, who lives and reigns with you in the unity of the Holy Spirit, one God, for ever and ever. Amen.

John Francis Regis

SEPTEMBER

10

PATRON SAINT OF:
Lacemakers, social workers, marriage; Regis University, Regis High School, New York City

STATUS: *Confessor, missionary*

BORN: *January 31, 1597, Fontcouverte, France*

DIED: *December 31, 1640, La Louvesc, France*

VENERATED BY: *Roman Catholic Church, Jesuits*

CANONIZED: *1737*

SYMBOLS: *Often shown cradling a crucifix*

O God, whose priest, Saint John Francis Regis, a friend of the poor, the sick, and the wayward, eagerly desired to evangelize the peoples of North America; grant, we ask, that we who serve You in his place may be filled with his same spirit of zeal. Amen.

The child of noble parents, John Francis was educated at the Jesuit college of Béziers. At age 19 he entered the Jesuit novitiate at Toulouse and took his vows two years later. His life as a newly ordained priest began in Toulouse, where he worked with victims of bubonic plague. He then moved to the Jesuit college at Montpellier, where he preached Catholic doctrine, ministered to poor and fallen women, visited hospitals, and worked for the conversion of the Huguenots.

He organized collections of donations from the wealthy and established hostels for prostitutes, setting up destitute girls as lacemakers. John Francis's reputation for moral integrity and zealous good works began to spread, and the local bishop invited him to the diocese of Viviers in the Ardèche, where he continued his missionary work. Toward the end of his life he alternated periods when he pursued his good works in the city with long stretches when he undertook missionary journeys for the Society. These arduous treks finally impacted his health and he died of pneumonia at age 43. The place where he died was turned into a mortuary chapel, and waters of a nearby stream were attributed with miraculous cures.

SAINT FRANCIS REGIS, SJ PREACHING BY MICHEL ANGE HOUASSE; BEGINNING OF THE 18TH-CENTURY, MUSEO DEL PRADO, MADRID, SPAIN

Theodora of Alexandria

Theodora of Alexandria was a saint and Desert Mother who enjoyed a happy marriage to a prefect of Egypt. But a rich man, captivated by her beauty, eventually lured her into adultery. She felt such a need for penance afterward, that she disguised herself as a man (fearing her husband would find her in a convent) and joined a monastery in Thebaid. The other monks did not discover her true gender until after her death. At one point, she was accused of fathering a child while away buying provisions and was cast out to raise the child for seven years… until the monks received a message from God that "Theodore" was forgiven. After her death, her husband became tonsured at the same monastery and her foster child later became its head.

The Desert Mothers was the name given to female Christian ascetics who lived in the deserts of Egypt, Palestine, and Syria during the 4th and 5th centuries. Although some lived as hermits, the majority dwelled in monastic communities. Other pious women from that time who influenced the early ascetic or monastic tradition but lived outside the desert are also described as Desert Mothers.

STATUS: *"Monk," Desert Mother*

BORN: *c. 491 AD*

DIED: *Unknown*

VENERATED BY: *Roman Catholic Church, Eastern Orthodox Church, Oriental Orthodox Church*

CANONIZED: *Pre-Congregation*

SYMBOLS: *Attire of a male monk*

With fasting didst thou consume thy body utterly; with vigilant prayer didst thou entreat thy Fashioner, that thou shouldst receive the complete forgiveness of the sin thou hadst wrought; which receiving in truth, thou didst mark out the path of repentance for us all. Amen.

THEODORA OF ALEXANDRIA ICON

Ailbhe of Emly

12

PATRON SAINT OF:
Wolves; Munster, the Archdiocese of Cashel and Emly

STATUS: *Bishop*

BORN: *5th century*

DIED: *528*

VENERATED BY: *Roman Catholic Church, Eastern Orthodox Church*

CANONIZED:
Pre-Congregation

SYMBOLS: *Wolf, pack of wolves, Bishop holding cathedral of Cashel*

O, Saint Ailbhe, I pray that you will nourish my faith the same way the she-wolf nourished you as an infant, and that you will inspire me to offer spiritual comfort to others, as you received comfort in the forest in your time of need. This I ask in the name of our Lord, Jesus Christ. Amen.

S aint Ailbhe, also known as St. Elvis or Eilfyw, is venerated as one of Irelands foremost patrons. He is said to predate St. Patrick. Much of his life is recorded only in legends, and there is some thought that they have their roots in pre-christian mythology. In one of these legends, he was the son of a slave and a king of Munster, Cronan, who ordered that the infant Ailbhe be executed. He was left in the woods instead, where he was nursed to health by a she-wolf, like Romulus and Remus the founders of Rome. The wolf protected him until he was discovered and adopted by visiting Britons. It is said that, later in life, Ailbhe encountered that same wolf and protected her and her cubs from a hunting party. He later traveled to Rome where he was ordained a bishop by the pope. He is also said to have baptized and fostered the patron saint of Wales, Saint David, and to have founded the monastery and diocese of Emly, Ireland. When he died, his body was carried off on a ghostly ship.

John Chrysostom

J ohn was a towering figure of the early Church, a dynamic preacher, a tireless campaigner against paganism, and a vehement, if controversial, critic of abuses inside and outside the Eastern Church. His name Chrysostom, apparently bestowed after his death, means "golden-mouthed." His influence—and popularity—rested not merely on the potency of his preaching but on its straightforwardness.

In 398, he was made archbishop and patriarch of Constantinople, but he accepted the position with reluctance. The position not only obliged him to live amid the splendors of the imperial court, bu also brought him into immediate contact with those who opposed him. Theophilus, the patriarch of Alexandria, for example, had long schemed to gain religious authority over Constantinople. John also clashed with the empress Eudoxia, whose extravagances and high-living John openly deplored. In 403, Theophilus and Eudoxia succeeded in having John briefly banished. In 404, he was banished again, despite the best efforts of Pope Innocent I to have him reinstated. Eventually exiled to a remote outpost of the Eastern Empire, he died en route.

PATRON SAINT OF:
Educators, preachers, invoked against epilepsy; Constantinople/ Istanbul

STATUS: *Bishop, Doctor of the Church*

BORN: *c. 347, Antioch, modern Turkey*

DIED: *September 14, 407, Pontus, modern Turkey*

VENERATED BY: *Roman Catholic Church, Eastern Orthodox Church, Oriental Orthodox Church, Assyrian Church of the East, Ancient Church of the East, Anglican Communion, Lutheranism*

CANONIZED:
Pre-Congregation

SYMBOLS: *Bishop's robes, beehive, white dove*

Lord, God of inconceivable power, incomprehensible glory, immeasurable mercy, unspeakable kindness, look on us in your tender love and show your rich mercy and compassion to us and those who pray with us. Amen.

A Byzantine mosaic of John Chrysostom from the Hagia Sophia

Notburga

Notburga worked as a cook in the household of Tyrolian Count Henry of Rattenburg. Her generous heart compelled her to give leftover food to the poor, but her mistress, Ottilia, ordered her to give it to the pigs instead. Notburga then set aside some of her own food, especially on Fridays, and brought it to the poor. Her legend says that that once Henry met her and demanded to know what she was carrying. She showed him, but instead of food, he saw wood shavings. Still, Ottilia dismissed her . . . and soon fell ill. Notburga remained with her and nursed her in preparation for death.

Notburga's then took a position with a farmer in Eben am Achensee, but only if she could attend church the evenings before Sundays and festivals. One evening her master insisted she continue toiling in his fields, and she threw her sickle into the air. "Let my sickle be judge between me and you," she cried. The sickle remained suspended in mid air. Count Henry eventually rehired her; shortly before she died she told him to place her in a cart drawn by oxen and to bury her where they came to rest.

PATRON SAINT OF:
Servants, peasants

STATUS: *Almsgiver*

BORN: *c. 1265, Rattenberg, Austria*

DIED: *September 13, 1313, Buch, Austria*

VENERATED BY: *Roman Catholic Church*

CANONIZED: *1862*

SYMBOLS: *Ear of corn, or flowers and a sickle in her hand; sickle may be suspended in the air*

Heavenly Lord, Saint Notburga served as a maid for a nobleman and then went to work for a peasant family. She discovered that she preferred working for the poor and devoted the rest of her life to this. I ask her to pray for me when I have opportunities to work for those who cannot afford my services. Help me, O God, to consider people as a higher priority than money, not basing my services on what they can pay, but on whether or not I can supply what they're needing. When I am the one who cannot afford others' services, be generous with me, too, dear Lord. Amen.

THE BAROQUE PAINTING OF SAINT NOTBURGA IN THE CHURCH ON BLED ISLAND, NORTHWESTERN SLOVENIA

Leobinus of Chartres

The son of peasants, Leobinus was a field worker and shepherd in his youth. His thirst for education led him to the monastery at Noailles, France, where he worked for the monks by day and was taught by them at night. His late night studying by candlelight annoyed the monks who had to wake for early prayers, so Leobinus put a screen around the candle and pressed on. He was a friend of St. Carilef and a student of St. Avitus of Perche, who suggested that Leobinus join his monastery. During the war between the Franks and Burgundians, Leobinus was captured by raiders and tortured for the location of the monstery's treasure. When he would not answer, they threw him into the water and left him for dead, thinking they had drowned him. He eventually recovered. A noted reformer, he was made bishop of Chartres with the consent of King Childebert I. He possessed the gift of healing, in particular dropsy (edema).

PATRON SAINT OF: *Innkeepers/wine merchants of Chartres*

STATUS: *Priest, bishop, hermit*

BORN: *Unknown*

DIED: *556 AD*

VENERATED BY: *Roman Catholic Church*

CANONIZED: *Pre-Congregation*

SYMBOLS: *Shown on deathbed receiving last rites from St. Caletric*

Dear Jesus, thank you for the opportunity to receive a good education. Please help me to always do my best at my schoolwork, even when I may get frustrated and want to give up. Please help me to use my time and talents to help my classmates who may be struggling with their schoolwork. Amen.

Cornelius

PATRON SAINT OF:
Invoked against hearing ailments, epilepsy

STATUS: *Pope, martyr*

BORN: *Rome*

DIED: *June 253 AD, Civitavecchia, Italy*

VENERATED BY: *Roman Catholic Church*

CANONIZED:
Pre-Congregation

SYMBOLS: *Cow's horn or portrayed with a cow nearby.*

St. Cornelius, you did not wish to be pope, but the Holy Spirit guided the Church to elect you. Pray for our current pontiff, that he may follow the will of God in everything he does. . . . Cornelius, you now reign in heaven with Christ forever; pray that we may see Him face to face. Amen.

Cornelius, a Roman priest whose name meant "battle horn," succeeded Pope Fabian (Jan. 20), who was martyred in 250 during the Decian persecutions. These trials required all citizens to offer a (pagan) religious sacrifice in front of commissioners or face death. The election of a new pope was postponed until the persecutions subsided, and in the meantime the Church was administered by a council whose spokesman was a presbyter called Novatian. Although Cornelius ruled for little more than two years, he had to contend not merely with a further round of persecutions of the infant Church, but a potentially damaging schism led by Novatian. The split centered on whether those who had renounced their faith—or offered pagan sacrifice—when threatened with execution could be received back into the Church. Novatian, who declared himself antipope in opposition to Cornelius, maintained they could not; Cornelius argued that true repentance was sufficient. Cornelius was able to muster ample support for his position and thereafter had Novatian excommunicated. His triumph proved short-lived, however. In 252, Cornelius was exiled by the new emperor, Trebonianus Gallus. He died the following year from mistreatment during his exile, although other reports claim he was beheaded.

Hildegard of Bingen

German abbess Hildegard, also known as the "Sibyl of the Rhine," was among the most remarkable figures of the medieval church: a mystic, herbalist, composer, and author. Born of a noble family, she was educated at a Benedictine convent at Disibodenberg and began to wear their habit by age 15. From childhood on she regularly experienced series of visions, which lasted throughout an unusually long life. In 1136, she became abbess of the convent. In 1150, after a lengthy dispute with the abbot at Disibodenberg, she founded a new convent at Rupertsberg. She opened another such convent at Eibingen in 1165.

In 1141, she claimed she had been ordered by God to record her visions, though they caused her great physical and emotional torment. The result was the Scivias ("Know the Way"), an immensely long and vividly illustrated account of 26 such religious visions, both prophetic and apocalyptic in nature. She subsequently wrote two further such works. Hildegard is famed, too, as a poetess and composer: almost 80 of her musical works have survived.

PATRON SAINT OF:
Musicians, writers

STATUS: *Abbess, mystic, philosopher, composer*

BORN: *c.1098, Böckelheim, Germany*

DIED: *September 17, 1179, Bingen, Germany*

VENERATED BY: *Roman Catholic Church*

CANONIZED: *2012*

SYMBOLS: *Wild rose sprinkling water as a blessing*

God is the foundation for everything.

This God undertakes, God gives.

Such that nothing that is necessary for life is lacking.

Now humankind needs a body that at all times honors and praises God.

This body is supported in every way through the earth.

Thus the earth glorifies the power of God. Amen.

HILDEGARD UNDERGOING A VISION AND DICTATING TO A SCRIBE, IN AN ILLUSTRATION FROM THE SCIVIAS. HILDEGARD DESCRIBED HER VISIONS AS THE "SHADE OF THE LIVING LIGHT." HER EMPHASIS ON THIS LIGHT HAS LED TO THE SUGGESTION THAT HER VISIONS MAY HAVE BEEN A FORM OF MIGRAINE.

Joseph of Cupertino

Born in the Kingdom of Naples, Joseph was slow to learn as a child and considered a nuisance by his mother. From all accounts, he was scarcely capable of even the most basic of tasks, but was nonetheless possessed a profoundly mystical streak that manifested itself most memorably by bouts of uncontrollable levitation. It is said that even the sound of church bells was enough to send him into religious raptures from which it was almost impossible to bring him down to earth. It was this sanctity that led to his being ordained a Franciscan in spite of his disability.

As news of the "Flying Friar" spread, he became an object of fascination, drawing ever-larger crowds to view him defy gravity. The Church, increasingly embarrassed that Joseph was rapidly becoming the focus of a cult, did its best to hide him in remote and obscure monastic foundations. For the last 30 years of his life, Joseph was treated like a virtual prisoner. In addition to levitation, he was much given to self-mortification, fasting, and prayer.

PATRON SAINT OF:
Astronauts, aviators, the mentally handicapped, students; Copertino, Osimo

STATUS: *Priest, mystic*

BORN: *1603, Cupertino, Italy*

DIED: *1663, Osimo, Italy*

VENERATED BY: *Roman Catholic Church, Franciscans*

CANONIZED: *1767*

SYMBOLS: *Crucifix, Franciscan habit, levitating*

Dear St. Joseph of Cupertino, who while on earth did obtain from God the grace to be asked at your examination only the questions you knew, obtain for me a like favour in the examinations for which I am now preparing. In return I promise to make you known and cause you to be invoked. Through Christ our Lord I pray. Amen.

St. Joseph of Copertino is lifted in flight at the site of the Basilica of Loreto, by Ludovico Mazzanti (18th century)

Januarius

There are few contemporary texts detailing the life of Januarius; much of what we know of the patron saint of Naples comes to us from legends. He was born in Benevento to a wealthy noble family, and began his life as a priest when he was just 15 years old. He became a bishop by the age of 20 and showed great bravery by concealing and protecting other Christians during the persecutions of Diocletian. Januarius became close friends with St. Sossius and even predicted Sossius's martyrdom. When Sossius was arrested for his faith, Januarius visited him in prison and was arrested in turn, and the two were later executed together by beheading. Januarius is perhaps best known, however, for the repeated miracle of his blood's liquefaction: there have been countless reports over the centuries of a vial of Januarius' blood spontaneously liquifying, solidifying, and liquefying again, often during papal visits to the city of Naples, where the faithful gather three times a year to witness the miracle.

PATRON SAINT OF:
Blood banks, volcanic eruptions; Naples, Tilbury

STATUS: *Bishop, martyr*

BORN: *April 21, 272, Benevento or Naples*

DIED: *c. 305, Pozzuoli, Campania*

VENERATED BY: *Catholic Church, Eastern Orthodox Church (April 21)*

CANONIZED:
Pre-Congregation

SYMBOLS: *Vials of blood, palms, Mount Vesuvius*

God, You enable us to celebrate the memorial of Your Martyr, St. Januarius. Grant that we may also enjoy his company in eternal beatitude. Amen.

TRADITIONAL PORTRAIT OF SAINT JANUARIUS

John Coleridge Patteson and Pacific Martyrs

STATUS: *Martyr*

BORN: *April 1, 1827*

DIED: *September 20, 1871*

VENERATED BY: *Roman Catholic Church, Anglican Church of England, Anglican Church of Melanesia*

CANONIZED: *Anglican Church of England, Anglican Church of Melanesia*

Almighty God, you called your faithful servant John Coleridge Patteson and his companions to be witnesses and martyrs in the islands of Melanesia, and by their labors and sufferings raised up a people for your own possession: Pour out your Holy Spirit upon your Church in every land, that by the service and sacrifice of many, your holy Name may be glorified and your kingdom enlarged; through Jesus Christ our Lord. Amen.

The South Pacific was home to various island cultures that worshipped a number of different gods. As early as 1794, a missionary attempt was launched in Tahiti, followed by similar efforts in New Zealand in 1814, Hawaii in 1820, and Tonga in 1822. It was a daunting undertaking: the attempted imposition of a wholly alien doctrine over a vast, little-known area, the greater majority of whose peoples had had no contact with the West in any form. A number of organizations, chiefly British and French, Protestant and Catholic alike, spearheaded the attempt. Several figures stand out in this epic endeavor. One is the ill-fated Marist Peter Chanel (April 28), clubbed to death in Futuna in 1841. Another was John Coleridge Patteson, a high-born Anglican parson, was persuaded in 1855 to join the Melanesian Mission. Patteson, who arrived at Auckland in 1855, proved an inspired choice, a cheerful and resourceful figure who embraced his calling with zeal. In 1861, he was appointed bishop of Melanesia. Sadly, in 1871, natives in the Solomon Islands murdered Patteson as a protest against the abduction and enslavement of islanders by white men.

THE DEATH OF PATTESON SPARKED A RENEWED MISSIONARY EFFORT IN THE SOUTH PACIFIC. IN 1881, A CHURCH IN MELANESIA WAS CONSECRATED IN HIS MEMORY, SHOWN HERE IN A CONTEMPORARY ILLUSTRATION FROM THE LONDON ILLUSTRATED NEWS.

Matthew the Apostle

Matthew was a Jewish tax collector at Capernaum employed by the Romans when he was called to become an Apostle by Christ. In his own Gospel, Matthew describes the event pithily: " . . . [Jesus] saw a man, named Matthew, sitting at a receipt of custom: and he saith unto him, Follow me. And he arose, and followed him." Matthew is referred to as Levi in the Gospels of Mark and Luke, and possibly as the brother of James the Less (May 3). Although he appears in all lists of the Twelve Disciples, and it is assumed he witnessed Christ's story, he is not associated with any particular event. He likely continued to spread the word in the Holy Land after the Resurrection until the persecutions of Herod Agrippa (42 AD), and then evangelized in either Parthia, Persia, or Ethiopia. Little early evidence supports his martyrdom, yet most Roman martyrologies attest to it with varying details and locations.

PATRON SAINT OF:
Tax collectors, accountants, bankers, customs officials, stockbrokers, security guards; Ethiopia

STATUS: *Apostle, evangelist*

BORN: *Early 1st century AD, Galilee, modern Israel*

DIED: *Late 1st century AD*

VENERATED BY: *Roman Catholic Church, Eastern Orthodox Church, all churches that honor saints*

CANONIZED:
Pre-Congregation

SYMBOLS: *A winged man; with money bags or box; sometimes wearing spectacles or with a quill or pen, book or manuscript; with tools of martyrdom*

Matthew, you left everything to follow Christ. Pray that we may have the courage to deny ourselves, take up our crosses, and follow Him as you did. St. Matthew, you shed your blood for the sake of the Name; pray that we may be loyal to God until death. Amen.

THE LACK OF ANY RELIABLE DETAIL CONCERNING THE ALLEGED MARTYRDOM OF ST. MATTHEW ALLOWED CARAVAGGIO FREE SCOPE TO CREATE A MOVING YET VIOLENT COMPOSITION. IT IS THOUGHT THAT THE FACE IN THE BACKGROUND, EMERGING FROM THE SHADOWS BEHIND THE EXECUTIONER, IS A SELF-PORTRAIT OF THE ARTIST.

Thomas of Villanova

22

PATRON SAINT OF:
*The poor; Santolan, Alimodian,
Miag-ao, Villanova University*

STATUS: *Archbishop of
Valencia*

BORN: *November 1486,
Ciudad Real, Spain*

DIED: *September 8, 1555,
Valencia, Spain*

VENERATED BY: *Roman
Catholic Church*

CANONIZED: *1658*

SYMBOLS: *A bishop
distributing alms to the poor*

*I will love you, Lord, in every way
and without setting limits to my
love. You set no limits to what you
have done for me, you have not
measured out your gifts. I will not
measure out my love. I will love
you, Lord, with all my strength,
with all my powers, as much as I
am able. Amen.*

Even though Thomas of Villanova rose to the position of archbishop, he never abandoned his deep devotion to the care and protection of the poor. Born Tomás García y Martínez, his father was a prosperous miller, who, with his wife, regularly distributed food to the poor. The boy himself often went without food and clothes so that he could give as much as he could to those in need. At the age of sixteen, Thomas entered the University of Alcala de Henares to study the arts and theology and later became a professor there, teaching the arts, logic, and philosophy. In 1516, he decided to join the Augustinian friars in Salamanca and was ordained in 1518. Thomas was known for his ascetic lifestyle, his passionate writing, and his dedication to charity and philanthropy. Even as archbishop, he wore only the habit he received as a novice and even sold his own bed to donate more money. He also offered work, education, and housing to the poor, which gave them the opportunity to help themselves and become self-sufficient. For his unceasing dedication to charitable work, Thomas was commonly known as the "father of the poor."

THOMAS OF VILANUEVA HEALS THE SICK, MURILLO

Padre Pio of Pietrelcina

Padre Pio was an Italian priest, mystic, and stigmatist. Born Francesco Forgione to peasant farmers, Pio declared at the age of five that he would devote his life to God. In 1903 he joined the Capuchins as a novitiate, taking the name Fra Pio in honor of Pope Pius I, and was ordained a priest in 1910. His health was always precarious, but from 1918 on he bore the marks of the stigmata, wounds that emulate those of Christ at the Crucifixion, for the rest of his life. Despite this, Pio remained unbelievably active, and he became famous for exhibiting the stigmata, thereby generating much interest and controversy. He was said to have heard some 25,000 confessions a year, and his humble but approachable, indeed amicable, attitude made him one of the most popular figures in the Italian Catholic Church in the 20th century. To some extent he reveled in his popularity—no bad thing in a century of turbulence—and in 1956 Pio established the Casa Sollievo della Sofferenza, a center for biomedical research, in the town where he lived and died.

PATRON SAINT OF: *Civil defense volunteers, adolescents; Pietrelcina*

STATUS: *Friar*

BORN: *1887, Pietrelcina, Italy*

DIED: *1968, San Giovanni Rotondo, Italy*

VENERATED BY: *Roman Catholic Church, By Capuchins*

CANONIZED: *2002*

SYMBOLS: *A bearded Capuchin, usually smiling, stigmata*

Stay with me, Lord, for it is necessary to have

You present so that I do not forget You.

You know how easily I abandon You.

Stay with me, Lord, because I am weak and I need Your strength, that I may not fall so often . . .

Stay with me, Lord, for You are my light,

and without You, I am in darkness. Amen.

A YOUNG PADRE PIO CLEARLY SHOWING THE MARKS OF THE STIGMATA ON HIS HANDS. HE OFTEN WORE MITTENS TO PROTECT THEM.

Gerard Sagredo

24

*O God, who were pleased to give
light to your Church by adorning
blessed Gerard with the victory
of martyrdom, graciously grant
that, as he imitated the Lord's
Passion, so we may, by following
in his footsteps, be worthy to attain
eternal joys. Through our Lord
Jesus Christ, your Son. Amen.*

Much of what is known of this saint comes from *The Long Life of St. Gerard*, a compilation from the 13th or 14th century. As a child, Gerard suffered a serious illness, and his parents credited his recovery to the prayers of the Benedictine monks of San Giorgio in Venice. As a result, they sent the boy to them to experience a spiritual life. Gerard emerged a learned Benedictine monk. When he determined to make a pilgrimage to the Holy Land, he traveled east overland via Hungary. The king, Stephen (Aug. 16), convinced him to remain there, as tutor to Stephen's son, later St. Emeric. Gerard then entered a hermitage until Stephen established the see of Csanad, with Gerard (Gellért to the Hungarians) as its bishop. Gerard energetically set about evangelizing the divided kingdom, but on Stephen's death he became a target for anti-Christian factions. He was captured in Buda, and cast from the cliffs into the Danube, possibly in a barrel lined with nails. Gerard was canonized on the same day as King Stephen and Emeric, and with them is a patron saint of Hungary.

S<small>TATUE OF</small> S<small>T.</small> G<small>ERARD IN</small> S<small>AN</small> R<small>OCCO,</small> V<small>ENICE.</small>

Sergius of Radonezh

One of Russia's leading saints and an early mystic, Sergius's greatest achievement was the revival and reform of the monastic (cenobite) tradition. Baptized Bartholomew, as a youth his wealthy family fled Rostov when threatened by the Tatars, becoming farmers at Radonezh, north of Moscow. Upon their parents' deaths, Sergius and his brother Stefan became forest hermits in the Makovets Hill, but soon developed a community of disciples, building a chapel and, in 1345, a monastery of wooden shelters where they reconstituted the Rule of Theodore the Studite. It was around this time that Sergius was ordained as a priest.

He went on to found around 40 more monasteries, and his original foundation became the heart of northern Russian Orthodoxy and missionary activity. Sergius has been called the Francis of Assisi of Russia, as his love of nature, sympathy for peasants, apparently mystical visions, and overwhelming humanity draw strong parallels with the founder of the Franciscan Order. Sergius died in 1392, but in 1422 his incorrupt relics were discovered and placed in the new cathedral of Troitse-Sergiyeva Lavra, which he founded.

PATRON SAINT OF:
Students; Russia

STATUS: *Abbot*

BORN: *May 14, 1314, Rostov, Russia*

DIED: *September 25, 1392, Sergiyev Posad, Russia*

VENERATED BY: *Roman Catholic Church, Eastern Orthodox Church, Anglican Communion, Lutheranism, US Episcopal Church*

CANONIZED: *1452*

SYMBOLS: *White bearded monk with abbot's staff, hplding scroll*

Grant us, O Lord, that amid the uncertainties of this world we may cling with all our heart to the things of heaven, for through the Abbot blessed Sergius you have given us a model of evangelical perfection. Through our Lord Jesus Christ, your Son. Amen.

SERGIUS BLESSING THE CRUSADE AGAINST THE TARTARS BY THE PRINCE OF MOSCOW, DMITRI DONSKOI, IN 1380.

Cosmas and Damian

Little is known for certain about Cosmas and Damian. They were brothers, possibly twins, probably born in Arabia, who practiced medicine and refused to accept fees for their services. They are thus seen as the patron saints of doctors, alongside Luke the Evangelist (Oct. 18) and Pantaleon (July 27). They were apparently arrested for their Christian beliefs under Diocletian, and managed to survive execution by drowning, burning, and stoning, but were eventually beheaded. One of the demonstrations of the medical skills of Cosmas and Damian involved Justinian, suffering from a withering leg ailment, who had his leg amputated by them. They miraculously attached a replacement from a black corpse, fortunately assisted by angels.

PATRON SAINT OF:
Physicians, nurses, surgeons, dentists, apothecaries, barbers, the blind; against hernias and pestilence; the Medici family

STATUS: *Martyrs*

BORN: *Mid third century, Arabia*

DIED: *c. 287, Syria*

VENERATED BY: *Roman Catholic Church, Eastern Orthodox Church*

CANONIZED:
Pre-Congregation

SYMBOLS: *Surgical implements*

Assist us we pray, Cosmas and Damian, in every distress. We do not ask for ourselves only, but for all our relatives, families, friends, and enemies, so that, restored to health of soul and body, we can give glory to God, and honor to you, our saintly protectors. Amen.

Vincent de Paul

Vincent was known for his complete dedication to the poor. He was born to a farming family in southwest France and remained an essentially humble man among his Counter-Reformation contemporaries. He studied at Dax and then at the Univesity of Toulouse—his education paid for by the sale of his father's oxen—and was ordained as a priest in 1600. While traveling by sea from Marseille on family business, he is said to have been kidnapped by Barbary pirates and enslaved, finally escaping with his master, a former Christian priest, in 1607.

He traveled to Rome, then served as chaplain to Marguerite de Valois, and briefly worked as a parish priest at Clichy near Paris before entering the service of the Gondi family, under whom his vocation for caring for the poor was fostered. In 1622, his experience of enslavement led him to be created chaplain to the galley slaves, and he went on to found the Congregation of the Mission (the Vincentians or Lazarists) and, with Louise de Marillac (March 15), the Daughters of Charity.

PATRON SAINT OF:
Charity, lost things, hospitals, prisoners, volunteers, horses, leprosy; Madagascar

STATUS: *Priest, founder*

BORN: *April 24, 1581, Pouy, France*

DIED: *September 23, 1660, Paris, France*

VENERATED BY: *Roman Catholic Church, Anglican Communion, France*

CANONIZED: *1737*

SYMBOLS: *Shown helping the poor*

Obtain from Our Lord, help for the poor, relief for the infirm, consolation for the afflicted, protection for the abandoned, a spirit of generosity for the rich, grace of conversion for sinners, zeal for priests, peace for the Church, tranquility and order for all nations, and salvation for them all. Amen.

SEVENTEENTH-CENTURY PORTRAIT OF VINCENT BY SIMON FRANÇOIS DE TOURS

Wenceslaus

PATRON SAINT OF:
*Czech Republic, Prague,
Slovakia, Bohemia, Moravia*

STATUS: *Martyr*

BORN: *c. 903, Prague,
modern Czech Republic*

DIED: *September 28, 935,
Stara Boleslav, modern Czech
Republic*

VENERATED BY: *Roman
Catholic Church, Eastern
Orthodox Church, in the Czech
Republic*

CANONIZED:
Pre-Congregation

SYMBOLS: *In armor, with
black eagle on his arms or
banner, crown, dagger*

*St. Wenceslaus, you were
an intelligent and peaceable
ruler, pious and forgiving
of wrongs. Pray for all our
leaders today, that they may be
compassionate and kind, shrewd
but noble, and that they may
follow the morality of the Christian
religion. Wenceslas, pray for us!
Amen.*

Wenceslaus I, Duke of Bohemia, ascended to the title at only 15 during a time of religious and civil unrest and soon became a figurehead for Bohemian (Czech) independence. He had been raised a Christian by his grandmother, St. Ludmilla, and was said to have been protected in battle by angels. As a result, he ended the persecution of Christians and built churches. His younger brother Boleslav (a non-Christian) was eager for control, however, and, supported by their mother, was also keen to forge a relationship with the Bavarians who threatened the duchy from the south. Once Wenceslaus had produced an heir, his mother lured him to Boleslav's castle, where he was cut down in front of the altar by Boleslav.

Among his legends are claims that an army of knights sleeps under Blaník, a mountain in the Czech Republic, who will awaken and, under the command of Wenceslaus, bring aid to the Czech people. A similar legend in Prague says that when the Motherland is in danger, the equestrian statue of Wenceslaus will come to life, raise the army sleeping in Blaník, and upon crossing the Charles Bridge his horse will trip over a stone, revealing the legendary sword of Bruncvík, allowing Wenceslaus to slay all their enemies.

STATUE OF SAINT WENCESLAUS IN ST. VITUS CATHEDRAL, PRAGUE.

Luigi Monza

This Roman Catholic priest was the founder of the Secular Institute of the Little Apostles of Charity. His mission was defined by answering the needs of the poor and the ailing, and he further used his congregation as a means of spreading his mission.

Born in Varese to a poor farm family, Luigi began studying for the priesthood at eighteen. He was appointed prefect at the Collegio Villoresi San Giuseppe di Monza in 1916, and in 1925 he was ordained as a priest for the Milan archdiocese. He was accused and jailed by the Facists for planning an attack on a magistrate, but he was eventually aquitted. In 1929 he was transferred to Saronno, where he worked as a youth minister, and later, in Lecco, he saw to the needs of the sick and the poor. He believed that the modern world was "paganized," and during World War II tended to the victims, while trying to shield his parishioners from the horrors of war. The model of a parish priest, he founded his order, The Secular Institute of the Little Fathers of Charity, in 1937 to promote his pastoral mission and to tend to the poor.

PATRON SAINT OF: *Secular Institute of the Little Apostles of Charity*

STATUS: *Priest, founder*

BORN: *June 22, 1898, Cislago, Italy*

DIED: *September 29, 1954, Lecco, Italy*

VENERATED BY: *Roman Catholic Church*

CANONIZED: *2006*

SYMBOLS: *Cassock*

Blessed Luigi Monza, good shepherd always waking in prayers in the nights,

looking for the lost sheep during the day, you have given us the vivid and fertile image of the mystery of the grain rotting to produce the ear.

Intercedes for us, that we may obtain prayer and charity, saints to flourish among us, endless hope to the weak and for our families and communities to live in the happiness of being one in heart and soul. Amen.

SEPTEMBER

Jerome

Possibly the most famous theologian in Church history, Jerome is one of the Four Western Fathers; the others being Augustine of Hippo (Aug. 28), Ambrose of Milan (Dec. 7), and Gregory the Great (Sept. 3). He was born Eusebius Hieronymus Sophronius to wealthy parents in modern Slovenia. He enjoyed an adventurous youth before studying the classics and rhetoric in Rome under Donatus, and then traveled in Gaul and Germany. He was baptized in around 365, and became a monk in Aquileia. In 373 he traveled with three companions to Antioch, visiting Athens and many cities in Anatolia on the way. It was here that he reputedly extracted a thorn from a lion's paw, and the beast is said to have remained his faithful companion.

While in Syria, Jerome learned Hebrew, and was ordained in Antioch. He went to Constantinople and studied under Gregory Nazianzen (Jan. 2), where he began to translate Eusebius's Chronicle from Greek to Latin. He returned to Rome and was retained as secretary by Pope Damasus I, who instructed him to produce a new Latin translation of the Bible. The resulting manuscript became the Vulgate Bible, the canonical Catholic text still in use today.

PATRON SAINT OF:
Archaeologists, archivists, librarians, students

STATUS: *Priest, Doctor of the Church*

BORN: *c. 342, Stridon, Dalmatia*

DIED: *420, Bethlehem, modern Israel*

VENERATED BY: *Roman Catholic Church, US Episcopal Church, US Evangelical Lutheran Church*

CANONIZED:
Pre-Congregation

SYMBOLS: *Shown in the desert or in his study, accompanied by a lion; red cardinal's robes and cardinal's hat, usually writing*

O Lord, show Your mercy to me and gladden my heart. I am like the man on the way to Jericho who was overtaken by robbers, wounded and left for dead. O Good Samaritan, come to my aid. I am like the sheep that went astray. O Good Shepherd, seek me out and bring me home in accord with Your will. Let me dwell in Your house all the days of my life and praise You for ever and ever with those who are there. Amen.

JEROME IS FREQUENTLY REPRESENTED WEARING A CARDINAL'S ROBES AND BROAD-BRIMMED HAT.

OCTOBER

In October the longer nights draw close in northern climes, and although the weather can still be clement, the year begins to wane as leaves turn gold and night frosts begin to cover lawns and gardens. Despite this, some glorious achievements come forward for celebration during the month, including those of the humble St. Francis of Assisi on October 4, founder of the Franciscan Order and patron saint of all living things, and those of St. Luke on October 18. The most gentle and contemplative of the Evangelists, Luke was a doctor and the companion of St. Paul on some of his missionary journeys. The Gospel of St. Luke provides one of the best-loved accounts of the Nativity, and Luke went on to write the Acts of the Apostles. The lesser-known Apostles Simon and Jude are celebrated on October 28.

GIOVANNI BELLINI'S PAINTING SAINT FRANCIS IN ECSTASY (C.1480) CAPTURES THE SAINT DURING HIS RETREAT IN THE WILDERNESS IN THE UMBRIAN LANDSCAPE. THE ASS, BEARING THE MARK OF THE CROSS ON HIS BACK, REMINDS US OF CHRIST AND THE CONSTANT PRESENCE OF GOD IN THE NATURAL WORLD.

OCTOBER

Therese of Lisieux

Marie-Françoise-Thérèse Martin, or Thérèse of the Child Jesus, was one of four daughters of a Norman watchmaker who all became nuns. Thérèse, however, was exceptional in her devotion and was given special permission to enter the Carmelite Order at age 15. She did not undertake the traditional penance regime of self-mortification, did not claim ecstasies or visions, but trod a simple path to faith. Her life was cut tragically short by tuberculosis, and she died after a long, bravely borne illness at only 24.

The key to Thérèse's fame rests upon her short but moving autobiography, The Story of a Soul, subtitled The Little Flower, which became a widely translated bestseller after her death. It was first published in a heavily edited and rewritten form. Nevertheless, the book provided a simple and approachable path to faith and spirituality that appealed to modern sensibilities. Its impact was enormous: miraculous cures were attributed due to her intercession, and her cult grew rapidly. A revised version of her book, based on her original manuscript, was published in 1952, which proved even more successful.

PATRON SAINT OF:
Missionaries, HIV and tuberculosis sufferers, florists, gardeners; France, Russia

STATUS: *Nun, virgin, Doctor of the Church*

BORN: *January 2, 1873, Alençon, France*

DIED: *September 30, 1897, Lisieux, France*

VENERATED BY: *Roman Catholic Church, by Carmelites*

CANONIZED: *1925*

SYMBOLS: *Shown in Carmelite habit holding roses, crucifix*

O Little Therese of the Child Jesus, please pick for me a rose from the heavenly gardens and send it to me as a message of love.

O Little Flower of Jesus, ask God to grant the favors I now place with confidence in your hands . . .

St. Therese, help me to always believe as you did in God's great love for me, so that I might imitate your "Little Way" each day. Amen

STATUE OF SAINT THERESE OF LISIEUX AT THE CHURCH OF OUR LADY VICTORIOUS, PRAGUE

Leodegar

Leodegar was the son of a high-ranking Burgundian nobleman, Bodilon, Count of Poitiers and Paris ahd his wife Sigrada of Alsace, who later became a nun in the convent of Saite-Marie. His brother was Warinus. After a childhood spent at the court of Clotaire II, king of the Franks, where he attended the palace school, he was sent to study with his uncle, Dido, the Archbishop of Poitiers. At 20, Dido made him an archdeacon. After being ordained, he lived at the monastery of St. Maxentius in Poitou. Elevated to abbot, he became known for the introduction of the Benedictine rule, and for his reformation of the secular clergy.

In 656 he was called to the court of Neustria by the widowed Queen Bathilde, the regent to Prince Childeric, to aid with the government and school her children. Under the queen's influence he became bishop of Autun in Burgundy in 663. When Autun was attacked in 675, Leodegar was captured by the allies of his long-standing enemy, Ebroin of Neustria. Leodegar was blinded and his tongue was cut out. Yet he lived on until he was again captured in 679, falsely blamed for the death of Childeric. After a mock trial, he was beheaded.

PATRON SAINT OF: *Millers, the blind, against blindness*

STATUS: *Bishop, martyr*

BORN: *c. 615 AD, Autun, France*

DIED: *October 2, 679, Somme, France*

VENERATED BY: *Roman Catholic Church, Eastern Orthodox Church*

CANONIZED: *Pre-Congregation*

SYMBOLS: *Man having his eyes gouged out with a gimlet, bishop holding a hook with two prongs, gimlet*

Lord, I do not look to the world for strength or encouragement, but I look to Your Word where I am convinced that You will protect and guard that which You have entrusted to me until the day when Christ will come to judge all people and take us to live in heaven. . . It is in Your strength and through Your power that I remain faithful though tested by fire. May the purifying of my faith, worth more than gold, bring praise, glory, and honor to Jesus my Lord and Savior. Amen.

DETAIL OF ONE OF THE STAINED-GLASS WINDOWS IN THE CHOIR OF ST-LÉGER D'ORVAULT CHURCH

Théodore (Theodora) Guérin

Saint Theodora, Born Anne-Thérèse Guérin, was pious from an early age, and was already vocal about her desire to devote her life to the church by the age of 10. She cared for her mother and sister for ten years after her father's death 1813, before entering the congregation of the Sisters of Providence of Ruillé-sur-loir. In 1841, she and five other sisters established the Academy of Saint Mary-of-the-woods, the first Catholic women's liberal arts college in the US. Theodora went on to personally oversee the founding of eleven more schools, two orphanages, and several free pharmacies. Although Theodora herself suffered from poor health all her adult life, the miracles attributed to her after her death both involved miraculous cures. One sister who prayed at Theodora's crypt was cured of both nerve damage and a cancerous tumor, and a man who prayed to Guerin in 2001 found that his deteriorating eyesight began to improve.

PATRON SAINT OF:
Diocese of Lafayette in Indiana

STATUS: *Superior general, founder*

BORN: *October 2, 1798, Étables-sur-Mer, France*

DIED: *May 14, Saint Mary-of-the-Woods, Indiana, U.S.*

VENERATED BY: *Roman Catholic Church*

CANONIZED: *October 15, 2006*

SYMBOLS: *Nun's habit, rosary*

Saint Mother Theodore Guerin, valiant woman of God, intercede for us in our needs. Implore for us through Jesus, the Christ, the gifts of a living faith, abiding hope and steadfast charity, so that through a life of prayer and service with others we may aid in promoting the Providence of God among all peoples. Saint Mother Theodore Guerin, pray for us. Amen.

Francis of Assisi

One of the most widely recognized saints in the Church due to both his renowned love for all living beings and the influential mendicant order of friars he founded, Francis was born to a wealthy Umbrian cloth merchant's family. He enjoyed a privileged upbringing and even fought in various local wars, until his health broke down in 1203. Recovering from a fever, he experienced a revelation: "There is God in everything, but in my heart there is no God." He turned his attention to the poor and underprivileged, living as a beggar, and retreating as a hermit to a ruined chapel. This habit of retreat into the countryside cemented his reputation as a lover of all living beings as manifestations of God's all-embracing creation.

In 1208, Francis adopted a hooded brown robe and rope belt, based on a shepherd's outfit, and began preaching on the road. Francis called his group of 12 followers the Friars Minor. By the time papal consent for the new order was granted in 1223, the band had expanded into a successful, effective, yet humble missionary order. In 1224, with his strength ebbing, Francis received the miracle of the stigmata—the first on record.

PATRON SAINT OF:
Animals, animal welfare societies, the environment; Italy, Assisi

STATUS: *Friar, founder*

BORN: *c.1181, Assisi, Italy*

DIED: *October 3, 1226, Portiuncula, Italy*

VENERATED BY: *Roman Catholic Church, US Episcopal Church, Evangelical Lutheran Church, Anglican Communion, Old Catholic Church*

CANONIZED: *1228*

SYMBOLS: *Bearded, tonsured, in Franciscan hooded robes, with stigmata, often surrounded by birds or animals, book and skull*

Lord make Me an instrument of Your peace
Where there is hatred let me sow love.
Where there is injury, pardon.
Where there is doubt, faith.
Where there is despair, hope.
Where there is darkness, light.
Where there is sadness joy. Amen.

ONE OF THE SCENES FROM BENOZZO GOZZOLI'S CYCLE OF EPISODES FROM THE LIFE OF ST. FRANCIS, DATING FROM AROUND 1450, CAPTURES THE SAINT'S FAMOUS SERMON TO THE BIRDS, AND THE DEDICATION OF HIS BASILICA AT ASSISI, SET AMONG THE UMBRIAN HILLS.

Bruno of Cologne

Born into the prominent Hartenfaust family, Bruno studied in Reims before his ordination in Cologne in 1055. He returned to Reims as professor of theology and head of the episcopal school, eventually becoming chancellor of the church of Reims in 1075. A highly respected and influential teacher, he was celebrated for his eloquence. In 1080 when Manasses was deposed. Bruno was encouraged to become bishop, but refused, deciding instead to pursue the life of a hermit.

Bruno moved to the Grenoble region with six companions in 1084, under the protection of St. Hugh (April 1), bishop of Grenoble. With his help they sought out a place for their hermitage at Chartreuse in the bleak terrain of the lower Alps, where lived an austere life of prayer and study. This was the foundation of the Carthusian Order. Despite his wish for obscurity, the fame of Bruno's new order spread. In 1090, he was summoned to Rome by Pope Urban II, a former pupil, to discuss the reformation of the clergy. Bruno persuaded the pope to allow him to continue his hermit's life. He founded the hermitage of St. Mary of La Torre in Calabria, where he is buried.

PATRON SAINT OF:
Calabria

STATUS: *Hermit, founder*

BORN: *c. 1030, Cologne, Germany*

DIED: *October 5, 1101, Calabria, Italy*

VENERATED BY: *Roman Catholic Church, by Carthusians*

CANONIZED: *1623*

SYMBOLS: *Contemplating a skull, with a book and cross; sometimes crowned with a halo of seven stars; always depicted wearing a white Carthusian habit*

Thy life, O Father Bruno was resplendent with many monastic virtues.

As thou was unwavering in thy faith to thy last breath, O Saint, pray that we emulate thy virtues and thereby be found worthy of eternal salvation. Amen.

THE VISION OF ST. BRUNO BY JUSEPE DE RIBERA (1643). BRUNO WAS AN INFLUENTIAL WRITER AND SCHOLAR, WHOSE COMMENTARIES ON THE PSALMS AND THE EPISTLES OF ST. PAUL DEMONSTRATE HIS ELOQUENCE AND LEARNING. THE CARTHUSIAN ORDER WAS INNOVATIVE IN PROMOTING THE IDEALS OF CONTEMPLATIVE SOLITUDE, WITHOUT COMPLETELY EXCLUDING THE COMMUNAL MONASTIC LIFE.

Marie Rose Durocher

Marie Rose Durocher was the tenth of eleven siblings born to a prosperous farming family. At the age of 16, she attempted to follow in her older sister and join the Congregation of Notre Dame, but was forced to leave after two years due to poor health. At home again she served as housekeeper and secretary to her brother, Theophile, a curate. It was only after she met with Bishop Ignace Bourget at the age of 32 that she left this position to found, with his encouragement, a congregation for the education of Christian youth. She took the name Sister Marie-Rose in 1844, and called her new congregation the Sisters of the Holy Names of Jesus and Mary. The sisters began teaching out of a schoolhouse, but due to demand for their services they were forced to move to larger premises. The number of prospective pupils continued to rise and the sisters eventually established four convents (in Longueuil, Belœil, Saint-Lin and Saint Timothée) employing 30 teachers and enrolling 448 pupils.

PATRON SAINT OF: *Longueuil, Quebec*

STATUS: *Founder*

BORN: *October 6, 1811, Saint-Antoine-sur-Richelieu, Lower Canada, British Empire*

DIED: *October 6, 1849, Longueuil, Province of Canada, British Empire*

VENERATED BY: *Roman Catholic Church*

BEATIFIED: *1982*

SYMBOLS: *Nun's habit, nun with glasses, nun teaching children*

Blessed Marie-Rose, you who have found grace before God, intercede for us. Obtain for us the audacity of Faith, the simplicity of Hope, and the power of Love. We ask this in the name of Jesus Christ, our Lord. Amen.

A PAINTING OF CANADIAN NUN EULALIE DUROCHER, ALSO KNOWN BY HER RELIGIOUS NAME MARIE-ROSE DUROCHER.

Artaldus

STATUS: *Bishop*

BORN: *1101, Saxony*

DIED: *September 7, 1206, Lochieu, France*

VENERATED BY: *Roman Catholic Church*

CANONIZED: *1834*

Blessed St. Artaldus, please pray to God for me that I be physically cured of my illness and that my body will once again begin to function properly, healthy and strong and full of energy. This I ask in the name of Jesus Christ, our Lord. Amen.

Artaldus (also called Arthaud) was born in the castle of Sothonod in Savoy. At the age of 18, he went to serve in the court of Duke Amadeus III, but a year or two after, he became a Carthusian at Portes Charterhouse in Bénonces. After gaining years of experience as a priest, he was sent by the prior of the Grande Chartreuse to found a charterhouse near his home, in a valley in the Valromey called "the Cemetery." Here Artaldus established himself with six of his fellow Carthusians from Portes. The community was no sooner settled in when the buildings were destroyed by a fire. Artaldus was forced to start over from scratch, on a new site on the Avieres River. It was dedicated to Our Lady in 1132. The new charterhouse, however, could not contain the spreading fame of Artaldus. Like his master St. Bruno he was consulted by the pope, and when well over 80—and despite his protests—he was called to become bishop of Belley. After two years he resigned and returned to Aviere, where he lived out his life.

Thaïs

The story of Thaïs is most likely a legend, a cautionary tale invented for edification. This Thaïs shares her name with another Thaïs, who lived hundreds of years earler and was of of wide notoriety in the Hellenistic world. Hailing from ancient Athens, she had traveled the world with the campaign of Alexander. Even if the later Thaïs's story is apocraphyl, she remains on the Catholic calendar with a feast day on October 8.

Also known as Thaïs the Penitent, she was a beautiful courtesan living in 4th-century Alexandria, a cosmopolitan cultural crossroads. It was said learned about this new faith from one of three teachers: St. Paphnutius of Heracleopolis, an Egyptian bishop; St. Bessarion, a disciple of St. Anthony in the Egyptian desert; or St. Serapion, a bishop in the Nile delta. Although she had succeeded in becoming wealthy, she realized that she was living a life of sin. After her conversion, she spent three years in prayer, performing penance and isolating herself to avoid further temptation. At this time, she spoke only with her spiritual advisors. When she finally emerged from isolation, she joined a group of desert nuns, where she lived for only fifteen days before her death.

PATRON SAINT OF:
Sinners

STATUS: *Repentant courtesan*

BORN: *c. 4th century*

DIED: *c. 4th century*

VENERATED BY: *Roman Catholic Church, Eastern Orthodox Church*

CANONIZED:
Pre-Congregation

SYMBOLS: *Woman in red robe*

Lord God, you kept the penitent, Saint Thaïs faithful to Christ's pattern of poverty and humility. May her prayers help us to live in fidelity to our calling and bring us to the perfection you have shown us in your Son, who lives and reigns with you and the Holy Spirit, one God, for ever and ever. Amen.

Denis and Companions

*O God, who sent Saint Denis
and his companions to preach
your glory to the nations and
strengthened them for their mission
with the virtue of constancy in
suffering, grant, we pray, that we
may imitate them in disdaining
prosperity in this world and
in being undaunted by any
trial. Amen.*

In the 3rd century Denis was sent as a Christian missionary from Italy to Gaul. He set out with his companions, Rusticus and Eleutherius, for Roman Paris and settled on the Île de la Cité, an island in the Seine, some distance from the Romans on the Left Bank. Denis, known as the first bishop of Paris, made many conversions among the Gauls, but the pagan priests were alarmed by his success. The three Italians were taken to the highest hill in Paris, now Montmartre, and beheaded. It is believed that the name—Mount of Martyrs—derives from this event. Legend declares that Denis picked up his severed head and walked two miles, preaching all the way. In fact, the bodies were thrown in the Seine and recovered and buried by converts, who constructed a chapel over the tomb. Dagobert I, king of the Franks, founded the abbey of St.-Denis and a Benedictine monastery at the site. In the 12th century, Abbot Suger rebuilt the church, which became the burial place of French kings and the first northern Gothic building in Europe. Veneration of St. Denis and his companions began soon after their deaths. In time, the phrase "Montjoie! Saint Denis!" became the war cry of the French armies. Denis, a patron saint of France, is one of the Fourteen Holy Helpers.

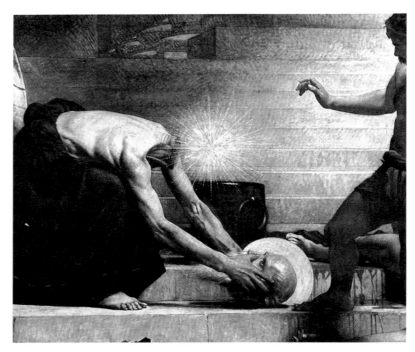

THIS PAINTING FROM THE PANTHÉON IN PARIS DATES FROM THE 19TH CENTURY, A PERIOD WHEN THE CATHOLIC CHURCH WAS CONCERNED WITH RE-ESTABLISHING ITS PRESENCE WITHIN A NOW SECULAR REPUBLIC. THE VIOLENT METHOD OF DENIS'S MARTYRDOM HAD GREAT RESONANCE FOR THOSE WHO HAD WITNESSED DECAPITATIONS UNDER THE GUILLOTINE.

Francis Borgia

Francis was the son of the duke of Gandía in Valencia, great-grandson of Rodrigo Borgia—the notorious Pope Alexander VI, and great-grandson of King Ferdinand of Aragon. Although he wished to become a monk, his family sent him to the court of Holy Roman Emperor Charles V. Francis accompanied Charles on military campaigns, was appointed equerry to Empress Isabella, and married a Portuguese noblewoman, with whom he had eight children. In 1539, while accompanying the empress's remains back to Spain he began to contemplate the vanity of worldly success and was determined to reform his life. When he succeeded to the dukedom of Gandía, he put aside worldly success and dedicated himself to the Church. In 1546, then widowed, he spent time in Rome as the disciple of Ignatius of Loyola, founder of the Jesuit Order. Francis finally renounced his dukedom in favor of his eldest son and was ordained a priest. In 1554 he became the Jesuits' commissary general in Spain and, in 1565, the third father general of the Society of Jesus.

PATRON SAINT OF:
Invoked against earthquakes; Portugal

STATUS: *Priest*

BORN: *October 28, 1510, Valencia, Spain*

DIED: *September 20, 1572, Rome, Italy*

VENERATED BY: *Roman Catholic Church*

CANONIZED:
Pre-Congregation

SYMBOLS: *Skull, often crowned with an emperor's diadem*

O Lord Jesus Christ, the pattern and reward of true humility, we beseech Thee, that as Thou didst make blessed Francis a glorious follower of Thee in the contempt of worldly honour, so thou wouldst grant us to be partakers of the same imitation and glory. Amen.

FRANCIS BORGIA IS FREQUENTLY PORTRAYED WITH EITHER A SKULL OR AN EMPEROR'S CROWN, A REMINDER OF HIS REJECTION OF WORLDLY POWER.

Maria Soledad

PATRON SAINT OF:
The Servants of Mary

STATUS: *Founder*

BORN: *December 2, 1826, Madrid, Kingdom of Spain*

DIED: *October 11, 1887, Madrid, Kingdom of Spain*

VENERATED BY: *Roman Catholic Church*

CANONIZED: *1970*

SYMBOLS: *Nun's habit, nun praying over map*

O most loving heart of Jesus, I commend to you this night my loving heart and soul that they may rest peacefully in you. Since I cannot praise you while I sleep, may my guardian angel replace me that all my heart's beats may be so many acts of praise and thanksgiving offered to your loving heart and that of your eternal Father. Amen.

Maria Soledad, born Manuela, was the child of a couple who ran a small business in Madrid. She devoted her life to serving the sick and the poor. Even in her childhood, she was known to visit sick people and worked at a school that provided free education to the poor. Guided by this desire for the religious life she managed to join a priest's fledgling religious cluster of women after the Dominicans refused to admit her due to her frail constitution. But a series of struggles saw her in a conflicted position of leadership that ended with her being removed and reinstated twice. When she heard that Miguel Martínez Sanz, a Third Order Servite, was forming a group of seven women to minister to the needy in their homes, she offered herself . . . and became the seventh. The congregation that she helped found in 1851—The Servants of Mary, Ministers to the Sick—has provided aid to those in need since its inception. Although several instances of slander resulted in her removal from her position on more than one occasion, she was reinstated each time, serving as superior until her death in 1887.

RELIGIOUS PRINT WITH SAINT SOLEDAD TORRES ACOSTA, 1890-1900

Wilfred of York

Wilfrid left his family at age 14 for the court of King Oswy of Northumbria, and went on to study at Lindisfarne. He traveled to Rome, studied under the archdeacon Boniface (June 5), and joined a monastery in Lyon, before returning to England and becoming abbot of the monastery at Ripon, which he placed under Benedictine rule. Familiar with Roman liturgical practice after his journey to Italy and advocating its adoption in the English Church, Wilfrid's was a powerful and persuasive voice at the Synod of Whitby in 664, and he was subsequently appointed bishop of York.

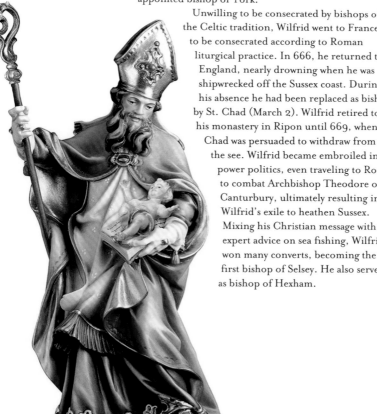

Unwilling to be consecrated by bishops of the Celtic tradition, Wilfrid went to France to be consecrated according to Roman liturgical practice. In 666, he returned to England, nearly drowning when he was shipwrecked off the Sussex coast. During his absence he had been replaced as bishop by St. Chad (March 2). Wilfrid retired to his monastery in Ripon until 669, when Chad was persuaded to withdraw from the see. Wilfrid became embroiled in power politics, even traveling to Rome to combat Archbishop Theodore of Canturbury, ultimately resulting in Wilfrid's exile to heathen Sussex. Mixing his Christian message with expert advice on sea fishing, Wilfrid won many converts, becoming the first bishop of Selsey. He also served as bishop of Hexham.

PATRON SAINT OF: *Ripon, Middlesbrough*

STATUS: *Bishop, missionary*

BORN: *c.633, Northumbria, England*

DIED: *c.709, Oundle, England*

VENERATED BY: *Roman Catholic Church, Eastern Orthodox Church, Anglican Communion*

CANONIZED: *Pre-Congregation*

SYMBOLS: *Fishing net; baptizing, preaching, engaged in theological disputes, landing from a ship*

Almighty God, who called our forebears to the light of the gospel by the preaching of your servant Wilfrid: help us who keep his life and labor in remembrance, to glorify your name by following the example of his zeal and perseverance, through Jesus Christ your son, our Lord. Amen.

WILFRID WAS A PROLIFIC BUILDER OF CHURCHES AND FOUNDER OF MONASTERIES, AND INITIATED THE REBUILDING OF YORK MINSTER.

Edward the Confessor

The son of King Ethelred II "the Unready" and Emma of Normandy, Edward was one of the last Anglo-Saxon rulers of England. He spent much of his early life in exile in Normandy following the Danish invasion of England. Returning to England in 1041, he became king the following year. Edward brought with him a retinue of Norman nobles, who were much resented by the English court.

His early reign was dominated by his father-in-law, Godwin, Earl of Wessex, who became the effective king. Edward's attempts to assert his regal authority came to a head when he appointed the Norman bishop of London, Robert of Jumièges, archbishop of Canterbury, rejecting Godwin's candidate. In 1051, Edward outlawed Godwin and his family, including Edward's own wife, Edith. Two years later the exiled earl and his sons returned, and Godwin's son Harold (Godwinson) continued to expand the power of the Godwins, securing the succession to the English throne when Edward—who was childless—died in 1066.

PATRON SAINT OF:
Kings, separated spouses, difficult marriages, the British royal family

STATUS: *King*

BORN: *c. 1006, Islip, England*

DIED: *January 5, 1066, London, England*

VENERATED BY: *Roman Catholic Church, Anglican Church*

CANONIZED:
Pre-Congregation

SYMBOLS: *Arms contain a golden cross flory and five gold doves on a blue shield; ermine robes*

Most glorious St. Edward, you showed your devotion to God with patience, gentleness and generosity. Like you, may I serve to strengthen the Kingdom of God through patient prayer and charity. Amen.

WHEN HENRY II CAME TO THE THRONE IN 1154, THE CULT OF EDWARD WAS PROMOTED IN ASSOCIATION WITH THE ENGLISH ROYAL FAMILY. EDWARD WAS REPRESENTED AS A HOLY MAN, WHO PERFORMED MIRACLES, AND HEALED PEOPLE BY TOUCH. HERE HE IS SEEN, FLANKED BY STS. EDMUND AND JOHN THE BAPTIST, ACCOMPANYING THE KNEELING RICHARD II IN THE LEFT PANEL OF THE FAMOUS WILTON DIPTYCH (C.1395).

Callixtus I

Callixtus I, also known as Callistus I, lived as a slave in 3rd century Rome. His early life was not especially noble, by most accounts. He was arrested once for fleeing the city after losing the alms that his master had collected for local orphans and widows; he was later arrested again for fighting in a synagogue while trying to borrow money from some Jewish worshippers. He was sentenced to work in the mines of Sardinia, resulting in a period where he suffered very frail health after his eventual release. Once he recovered, he became a deacon and served as the superintendent to the Christian cemetery that is now known as the Catacombs of St. Callixtus. He was named Bishop of Rome some eighteen years later, quickly becoming a controversial figure for his practice of offering absolution of any and all sins. Hippolytus of Rome was so opposed to these practices that he led a movement against Callixtus within the church, becoming the first antipope. Callixtus was martyred in 222.

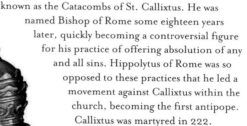

PATRON SAINT OF: *Cemetery workers*

STATUS: *Pope*

BORN: *c. 2nd century*

DIED: *c. 222, Rome*

VENERATED BY: *Roman Catholic Church*

CANONIZED: *Pre-Congregation*

SYMBOLS: *Well, grindstone*

O God, who raised up Pope Saint Callixtus the First to serve the Church and attend devoutly to Christ's faithful departed, strengthen us, we pray, by his witness to the faith, so that, rescued from the slavery of corruption, we may merit an incorruptible inheritance. Through our Lord Jesus Christ, your Son, who lives and reigns with you in the unity of the Holy Spirit, one God, for ever and ever. Amen.

Teresa of Avila

Teresa of Ávila was one of the most remarkable saints of the 16th century, a Spanish Carmelite nun and mystic who raised devotion and poverty, centered on absolute obedience to God, to a new extreme. She not only founded the Discalced (or barefoot) Carmelites, but also established 17 convents across Spain. In addition, she wrote widely on mystical theology.

Though Teresa entered the Carmelite convent in castellated hilltop Ávila in 1535, at 20, it was many years before she had her first visions of Christ. They continued for six years and led directly to her establishing a reformed Carmelite order to duplicate the sufferings of Christ. Between 1557 and 1582, she founded numerous convents. In 1568, with St. John of the Cross (March 5), she also established a monastery for the Discalced Carmelite Brethren. Piety on this scale, however, did not make Teresa popular. Her ruthless insistence on extreme poverty and flagellation alienated many Carmelites, and for a time she was forbidden from opening new convents. In 1970 she was made a Doctor of the Church, at the time sharing the honor with one other woman, Catherine of Siena (April 29).

PATRON SAINT OF:
Headaches, the sick; Spain, Croatia

STATUS: *Mystic, founder, Doctor of the Church*

BORN: *March 28, 1515, Ávila, Spain*

DIED: *October 4, 1582, Alba de Tormes, Spain*

VENERATED BY: *Roman Catholic Church, Anglican Communion, Lutheranism*

CANONIZED: *1622*

SYMBOLS: *Book and quill, pierced heart*

Let nothing disturb you,
let nothing frighten you,
all things will pass away.
God never changes;
patience obtains all things,
whoever has God lacks nothing.
God alone suffices. Amen.

Margaret Mary Alacoque

Margaret Mary Alacoque was a distinctly pious child, eschewing normal play for prayer and silent reflection. She took her first Communion at the age of nine, and secretly practiced the mortification of the flesh until she became bedridden with rheumatic fever for four years. During this time, she received a vision from the Virgin Mary and vowed to devote her life to God . . . and found herself instantly returned to health. She continued to experience visions throughout her life, believing that this was a normal part of every person's life.

After some financial resersals her family recovered their wealth and Margaret found herself attending social events with her brothers. One night, while returning from a Carnival ball in her finery, she experience a visitation of a scourged Christ; He reminded her of her vow but also of His love for her. So at the age of 24 she joined the Visitation Convent at Paray-le-Monial. Few around her believed her when she spoke of her visions, an exception being the Jesuit Claude de la Colombiere, who supported her. She was later named novice mistress of the monastery, serving from 1686 until her death in 1690.

PATRON SAINT OF:
Polio patients, devotees of the Sacred Heart, invoked against the death of parents

STATUS: *Nun, mystic*

BORN: *July 22, 1647, France*

DIED: *October 17, 1690, France*

VENERATED BY: *Roman Catholic Church*

CANONIZED: *1920*

SYMBOLS: *Nun's habit, Sacred Heart, nun kneeling before Jesus*

Pour out on us, we pray, O Lord, the spirit with which you so remarkably endowed Saint Margaret Mary, so that we may come to know that love of Christ which surpasses all understanding and be utterly filled with your fullness. Through our Lord Jesus Christ, your Son. Amen.

OCTOBER

17

PATRON SAINT OF:
Churches in Eastern Mediterranean, churches in North Africa

STATUS: *Bishop, martyr*

BORN: *c. 50 AD, Roman Syria*

DIED: *July 6, 108 AD, Rome, Italy*

VENERATED BY: *Roman Catholic Church, Eastern Orthodox Church, Oriental Orthodoxy, Nestorianism, Anglican Communion, Lutheranism*

CANONIZED:
Pre-Congregation

SYMBOLS: *Lions, chains; holding his writing*

Receive in tranquility and peace, O Lord, the souls of your servants who have departed this present life to come to you. Grant them rest and place them in the habitations of light, the abodes of blessed spirits. Give them the life that will not age, good things that will not pass away, delights that have no end, through Jesus Christ our Lord. Amen.

Ignatious of Antioch

Ignatius was not merely one of the earliest Christian martyrs—said to have been devoured by lions in the Colosseum in Rome during the persecutions of Trajan—but also one of the Apostolic Fathers, those early Christians presumed to have had personal contact with Christ's own Apostles. Having converted to Christianity at a young age, it is said that Ignatius was appointed bishop of Antioch in Syria by St. Peter himself (June 29) and was a follower, along with his friend Polycarp, of John the Apostle (Dec. 27). But his importance lies also in his surviving writings, produced during his arduous overland journey from Antioch to Rome following his arrest as a Christian, when he was escorted by 10 Roman soldiers. His writings deal not only with spiritual matters and forms of worship, but, just as importantly, with the organization and hierarchy of the Church. He was the first person to use the term "catholic," meaning universal, to describe the infant Christian Church.

IMAGES OF ST. IGNATIUS CONVENTIONALLY DEPICT HIM EITHER WITH CHAINS, A SYMBOL OF HIS IMPRISONMENT, OR, AS HERE, WITH LIONS, THE BEASTS THAT ENSURED HIS END — AND MARTYRDOM — IN ROME.

Luke the Evangelist

Like St. Paul the Apostle (Jan. 25), Luke was born a Greek Gentile, probably in Antioch, and was trained to practice medicine. After St. Paul's return to Antioch from his first missionary journey, Luke traveled with him to Rome, and was shipwrecked with him at Malta. Luke is the author of the third Gospel, and of the Acts of the Apostles, yet at no point does he claim to have witnessed any of the events; it is likely he converted as a result of meeting Paul. Luke probably wrote the third Gospel and the Acts of the Apostles after Paul's death. Still, Luke appears to have benefited from the companionship of St. Paul, as both his Gospel and Acts reveal a lively storyteller, with close attention to detail and a concern with linking sacred history to the events of the profane world. Women feature more prominently in Luke, and he provides insights about the early church and Eastern Mediterranean culture. In Acts, Luke describes Christ's work in the 40 days between His Resurrection and His Ascension and birth of the new church under the leadership of Peter. A 2nd-century writer described Luke as dying unmarried at age 84.

PATRON SAINT OF: *Physicians, surgeons, painters, picturemakers*

STATUS: *Evangelist*

BORN: *Early 1st century AD, Antioch, Syria*

DIED: *March 84 AD, Thiva, Greece*

VENERATED BY: *Roman Catholic Church, Eastern Orthodox Church, all other Christian churches that venerate saints*

CANONIZED: *Pre-Congregation*

SYMBOLS: *Winged ox, physician, a book or pen, paint brush or palette, man painting Virgin Mary*

Most wonderful St. Luke, you are animated by the Heavenly Spirit of Love . . .

May the Holy Spirit, instructor of the faithful, help me to understand Christ's words and faithfully apply them in my life. Amen.

IN ORTHODOX ART, LUKE IS OFTEN DEPICTED BEARDED AND WRITING, AS IN THIS ICON FROM THE LATE 16TH-CENTURY MOSCOW SCHOOL.

North American Martyrs

saac Jogues became a Jesuit in 1624, and in 1636 he was sent to New France (Canada) as a missionary to the Hurons and Algonquins, allies of the French. In 1642, Mohawk Iroquois captured Jogues and his companions, a lay brother, René Goupil, and Guillaume Couture. They took them back to their village, Ossernenon (Auriesville, New York), where Goupil was hacked to death for blessing a native child, while several of Jogues's fingers were cut off. Forced to live as a slave, Jogues taught them the rudiments of Christianity. He was ransomed after 13 months and sailed for Europe. Undeterred, Jogues returned to Canada where a tentative peace had been forged between the Native Americans and their French allies. In 1646, Jogues entered Mohawk country, accompanied by layman, Jean de Lalande. When sickness and crop failure hit the Mohawks, Jogues became the scapegoat—he and Lalande were clubbed to death and beheaded.

Another French Jesuit missionary, Jean de Brébeuf, and his companion Gabriel Lalemant, had achieved hundreds of conversions among the Hurons, but they fell afoul of the Huron war with the Iroquois. Captured by the latter, they were scalped, tortured with boiling water and fire, and finally beheaded and partly eaten. The other Jesuit martyrs commemorated on this day are Charles Garnier, Antoine Daniel, and Noel Chabanel.

PATRON SAINTS OF:
Canada

STATUS: *Priests, lay brothers, martyrs*

BORN: *Early 17th century, France*

DIED: *Mid-17th Century, New France (Canada)*

VENERATED BY: *Roman Catholic Church*

CANONIZED: *1930*

O God, who did inflame the hearts of your sainted Martyrs with an admirable zeal for the salvation of souls, grant us, we beseech You, what we now ask for this blessing, so that the favors obtained through their intercession may make manifest before men the power and glory of Your name. Amen.

A MOSAIC IN THE CATHEDRAL BASILICA OF ST. LOUIS, IN ST. LOUIS, MISSOURI, SHOWING ISAAC JOGUES, RENÉ GOUPIL, AND THE HURON SAINT KATERI TEKAKWITHA (JULY 14).

Mary Bertilla Boscardin

Born Anna Francesca, Saint Mary Bertilla Boscardin experienced a great deal of suffering in her childhood. She was abused often by her violent alcoholic father, and received little in the way of education. Those around her considered her slow, referring to her as a "goose," and she was regularly mocked by other children. She worked as a servant until she was twelve, then labored as a kitchen maid and laundress at the Teachers of Saint Dorothy, Daughters of the Sacred Heart convent for three years. She was later sent to study nursing at a hospital in Treviso, Italy, and after completing her studies began providing aid to victims of diphtheria in the children's ward. It was here that Mary became renowned for her selfless and diligent sense of duty to her patients; even when Treviso was bombarded by air raids, she steadfastly provided care for patients who were too ill to be evacuated. Her superior, however, disliked Maria's newfound recognition, and reassigned her to work in the laundry room instead. She was reinstated to the children's ward four months later, but died shortly afterward during a surgical operation intended to remove a tumor. Her tomb in Vicenza became a pilgrimage site, and several miraculous healings are attributed to her resting place.

PATRON SAINT OF:
The sick

STATUS: *Nun, nurse*

BORN: *October 6, 1888, Italy*

DIED: *October 20, 1922, Treviso, Italy*

VENERATED BY: *Roman Catholic Church*

CANONIZED: *1961*

SYMBOLS: *Nun holding crucifix and white lilies*

Lord, we are often ignorant when it comes to your blessed ways. Like your servant, Saint Maria Bertilla, teach us so that we, too, may hopefully become saints. Amen.

21

PATRON SAINT OF:
Students

STATUS: *Martyrs*

BORN: *Southwest England*

DIED: *c. 383 AD, Cologne, Germany*

VENERATED BY: *Roman Catholic Church*

CANONIZED:
Pre-Congregation

SYMBOLS: *Ursula clutching arrows*

O ye glorious virgins, fulfil now my desire, and when the hour of death arrives, hasten to my assistance:

be present at that terrible moment, and defend me from the assault of the demons.

Let not one of you be then absent; come with the Virgin Mother at your head.

If any remnant of sin still cling to me and soil me with its stain, remove it by your prayer.

Let the foe be aware of your presence, and bewail his own confusion. Amen.

Ursula and the 11,000 Virgins

Legend has it, Ursula was a Romano-British princess who lived around 300 AD. She was the daughter of King Dionotus of Dumnonia, the region known today as Dorset, Devon, and Somerset. She apparently set sail with 11,000 virginal handmaids for the coast of Brittany, to meet her future husband, the pagan governor Conan Meriadoc of Armorica. A miraculous storm brought them to a Gaulish port, where Ursula swore she would undertake a pilgrimage to Rome. There, she convinced the Pope, Cyriacus and Sulpicius, Bishop of Ravenna, to join her. Unfortunately, when Ursula and her virgin followers arrived in Cologne, Germany, they were massacred by the beseiging Huns because they refused to copulate with them. The virgins were beheaded, while Ursula, their leader, was shot with an arrow. This is said to have happened around 383 AD. The legend of St. Ursula was embellished and elaborated by medieval historians and has been remarkably persistent. The basilica of St. Ursula in Cologne contains the alleged relics of the saint and her virgin companions.

Peter of Alcantara

Peter's father was the governor of Alcántara, in central-western Spain, and his mother was from a noble family. At age 14 he was sent to the University of Salamanca and two years later become a Franciscan of the Stricter Observance in Extremadura. Ordained as a priest in 1524, he was soon intent on reforming the Constitution of the Stricter Observants. His severe and ascetic ideas met with opposition, so he retired to the mountains of Portugal where he intended to live an eremitic life. Soon other friars came to join him, and several small religious communities were established.

In 1555, he started the Alcantarine Reform, an order that went completely barefoot; the extreme austerity of his interpretation of Franciscan rule was influential throughout Iberia and the Spanish colonies. Peter was a devout mystic, who frequently entered an ecstatic state. He existed on bread and water, wore no more than a sackcloth habit and cloak, and only traveled on foot. He was the confessor of the fiercely pious Teresa of Ávila (Oct. 15) and was said to have aided her in her foundation of the Carmelite Order of nuns.

PATRON SAINT OF:
Nightwatchmen, Eucharistic adoration; Brazil, Extremadura, Spain

STATUS: *Monk, mystic, founder*

BORN: *1499, Alcántara, Extremadura, Spain*

DIED: *1562, Ávila, Spain*

VENERATED BY: *Roman Catholic Church, by Franciscans*

CANONIZED: *1669*

SYMBOLS: *Franciscan friar's habit*

Loving God, with your help,

St Peter of Alcantara persevered in imitation of Christ's humility, patience and poverty: through his prayers may we continue faithfully our journey through life and come, one day, to the new life of heaven.

We ask this through Christ our Lord. Amen.

SAINT PETER OF ALCÁNTARA, PAINTED WOOD SCULPTURE BY PEDRO DE MENA (1628)

23

John of Capistrano

PATRON SAINT OF:
*Jurists, military chaplains;
Belgrade, Hungary*

STATUS: *Priest*

BORN: *June 24, 1386,
Capestrano, Italy*

DIED: *October 23, 1456,
Ilok, Croatia*

VENERATED BY: *Roman
Catholic Church, by
Franciscans*

CANONIZED: *1690 or
1724*

SYMBOLS: *Shown in
Franciscan robes*

*Lord, you raised up Saint John
of Capistrano to give your people
comfort in their trials. May your
Church enjoy unending peace
and be secure in your protection.
Through our Lord Jesus Christ,
your Son, who lives and reigns with
you for ever and ever. Amen.*

John was an Italian Catholic priest from Abruzzo who gained fame as a preacher, theologian, and inquisitor. In 1456 he earned the nickname the "soldier saint" when at age 70 he helped lead a crusade against the invading Ottoman Empire at the seige of Belgrade.

The son of a courtier who had come to Italy with Louis I of Anjou, titular King of Naples, John became a lawyer and in 1412 was appointed governor of Perugia. When war broke out between Perugia and Sigismondo Malatesta in 1416, John was dispatched as an ambassador of Perugia, but was betrayed and thrown into prison. On his release he entered the Franciscan Order, dedicated himself to a life of extreme asceticism, and became an eloquent preacher. He was a passionate opponent of heresy of all kinds, and was especially zealous in his pursuit of the Hussites. After the fall of Constantinople, Pope Callixtus III sent John to preach a crusade against the invading Turks. His rhetoric inspired a huge gathering of troops, who marched on the city of Belgrade in the summer of 1456 and turned the Turkish troops away. For his inciting of antisemitic violence, he was called "the scourge of the Jews."

Anthony Mary Claret

The son of a woolens manufacturer from Catalonia province, Anthony enjoyed childhood pilgrimages to the local shrine of Our Lady of Fussimanya. He started out as a Jacquard loom programmer, but soon found his vocation and was ordained as a Carthusian priest in 1835. Drawn to missionary work, he entered the Jesuit novitiate in Rome but had to leave due to illness. Returning to Spain, he began a pastoral ministry on behalf of the poor, including the application of rustic medicine. His superiors eventually sent him as an Apostolic Missionary throughout Catalonia, where he traveled on foot from mission to mission and drew such crowds he often had to preach in town plazas. After giving retreats in the Canary Islands, he returned to Spain and founded the Missionary Sons of the Immaculate Heart of Mary (the Claretians) in 1849. This resulted in his immediate assignment to the archbishopric of Cuba. At the time the vigorous demands for independence in the Spanish colony, combined with strong religious factionalism arising from local African-American cults such as Voodoun and Santeria, made Anthony's residence in Cuba a difficult one. He resigned in 1857, returning to Spain to become confessor to Queen Isabella II.

PATRON SAINT OF: *Weavers, textile merchants, Catholic press, Claretians; Diocese of Canary Islands*

STATUS: *Bishop, missionary, founder*

BORN: *December 23, 1807, Sallent, Spain*

DIED: *October 24, 1870, Narbonne, France*

VENERATED BY: *Roman Catholic Church*

CANONIZED: *1950*

SYMBOLS: *Bishop's robe, crozier, an open book, cathechism, two students at his side, his bent arm pointing to the sky*

St Anthony, make my troubles your own. Speak a word for me to the Immaculate Heart of Mary. Ask her to obtain for me, through her powerful intercession, the graces I yearn for so ardently: a blessing to strengthen me during life and Her assistance at the hour of my death leading me to a happy eternity. Amen.

PORTRAIT OF THE SPANISH ECCLESIASTIC ANTONIO MARÍA CLARET (1807-1870)

Crispin and Crispinian

PATRON SAINT OF:
Cobblers, glove makers, lacemakers; leather workers, tanners, saddlers, shoemakers, weavers

STATUS: *Missionaries, martyrs*

BORN: *3rd century AD*

DIED: *285/286 AD, Rome*

VENERATED BY: *Roman Catholic Church, Eastern Orthodox Church*

CANONIZED:
Pre-Congregation

SYMBOLS: *Depicted holding shoes*

Almighty ever-living God, who gave Saints Crispin and Crispinian the grace of suffering for Christ, come, in your divine mercy, we pray, to the help of our own weakness, that, as your Saints did not hesitate to die for your sake, we, too, may live bravely in confessing you. Through our Lord Jesus Christ, your Son. Amen.

The offspring of a noble Roman family in the 3rd century AD, twin brothers Crispin and Crispinian were both devoted Christians. During the reign of Roman emperor Diocletian they were forced to flee persecution for their faith, ending up at Soissons, preaching Christianity to the Gauls while making shoes by night. They not only earned enough to support their mission, they were even able to give aid to the poor.

Their success, however, gained the ire of Rictus Varus, the governor of Belgic Gaul. He had them apprehended, tortured, and thrown into a river with millstones around their necks. Yet they somehow survived . . . until they were beheaded at the order of Emperor Maximian. In the sixth century a basilica was erected at Soissons over their graves, and St. Eligius, a noted goldsmith, made a costly shrine for the head of St. Crispinian.

Alfred the Great

K ing Alfred, called "the Great," reigned from 871 to 899 and is perhaps the best known of all Anglo-Saxon rulers. He remains an important figure in English history, not only as the first sovereign of a unified Wessex and steadfast opponent of Danish incursions from the east, but as a fortifier of the Christian Church in England. Like many near contemporaries (such as Charlemagne in France and Stephen in Hungary) Alfred used Christianity to weld together a robust body politic in his nation state. His support for Church reform, learning, and monastic communities in particular, provided a solid footing for the healthy growth of both church and state in Anglo-Saxon England.

The fifth son of Aethelwulf, King of Wessex, the boy was received by Pope Leo IV during a visit to Rome with his father in 855. A great scholar, Alfred translated the classics for his father's subjects and seemed destined for a life in the church. He eventually became king, though forced to spend much of his reign fighting off the marauding Danes who threatened England (or bribing them for peace).

PATRON SAINT OF:
British royal family

STATUS: *King, scholar*

BORN: *849, Wantage, England*

DIED: *October 26, 899, Winchester, England*

VENERATED BY: *Roman Catholic Church, Anglican Communion, US Episcopal Church*

CANONIZED: *Pre-Congregation*

SYMBOLS: *Shown as king, crowned*

O God, who didst call thy servant Alfred to an earthly throne that he might advance thy heavenly kingdom, and didst give him zeal for thy church and love for thy people: Grant that we, inspired by his example and prayers, may remain steadfast in the work thou hast given us to do for the building up of thy reign of love; through Jesus Christ, our Lord. Amen.

EIGHTEENTH-CENTURY PORTRAIT OF ALFRED BY SAMUEL WOODFORDE

Frumemtius

T his remarkable saint is venerated as the evangelizer of Ethiopia and the founder of the Coptic Church in the kingdom of Axum. Ethnically a Syro-Phoenician Greek born in Tyre, he first traveled down the Red Sea from Egypt as a boy, with his brother Aedesius, under the guardianship of their uncle Meropius. Along the way, their ship was hijacked, the crew killed, and the two boys taken to the realm of Axum, an enormously wealthy trading state in northeast Africa. Here they grew up as slaves in the royal household, but were released shortly before the king's death. They remained there for several years, helping to educate his young heir. Eventually the brothers traveled north to Egypt, Aedesius returning to Tyre where he became a priest. Frumentius petitioned St. Athanasius of Alexandria (May 2) to send a mission to Axum. Athanasius encouraged Frumentius himself to return, consecrating him as bishop of Axum circa 330–340. After his return to the kingdom, Frumentius succeeded in establishing a Christian community there.

PATRON SAINT OF:
Ethiopia, Kingdom of Axum

STATUS: *Bishop, missionary*

BORN: *Early 4th century AD, Tyre, modern Lebanon*

DIED: *c. 383, Ethiopia*

VENERATED BY: *Roman Catholic Church, Ethiopian Orthodox Church (Aug. 1), Eastern Orthodox Church (Nov. 30), Coptic Orthodox Church (Dec. 18)*

CANONIZED:
Pre-Congregation

SYMBOLS: *Often shown holding a sword*

Pray for us, dear Frumentius, that we may also "bloom where we are planted." You were just a young boy in a strange and pagan land, but you made the best of the situation and brought truth and life to that desolate land and lost people. We pray that we may bring the light of Christ with us wherever we go in hope of inspiring others to follow him. Amen.

FRUMENTIUS IS REGARDED AS THE FATHER OF THE CHRISTIAN CHURCH IN ETHIOPIA.

Simon the Apostle

Simon, along with Jude, are two of the Twelve Apostles of whom little is known. Both men are referred to as cousins of Zebedee, and may therefore have been fishermen in Galilee before being called to follow Christ. They share this feast day on the slender evidence that they were possibly martyred together in Persia, Beirut, or Edessa. They are often represented together.

Simon is often called "the Canaanite" or "the Zealot" due to his apparently rigid observance of Jewish law. This might also indicate that he was a member of a particular Jewish sect at the time. Nothing is known concerning his calling to be an Apostle and, although he appears on all the major lists of the Apostles, he is not associated with any major events in the Gospels. He is not to be confused with "Simon called Peter," who is often referred to simply as Simon, despite Jesus renaming him Peter upon his calling (June 29). Simon's activities following Pentecost are not mentioned in Acts, but he is thought to have preached in Egypt before possibly traveling north with Jude to evangelize Syria and Mesopotamia.

PATRON SAINT OF: *Sawyers, tanners, curriers*

STATUS: *Apostle, martyr*

BORN: *Early 1st century AD*

DIED: *Mid-1st century AD*

VENERATED BY: *Roman Catholic Church, Eastern Orthodox church (July 1), Christian religions that venerate saints*

CANONIZED: *Pre-Congregation*

SYMBOLS: *Fish, boat, oar, saw (the instrument of his martyrdom)*

O Glorious Saint Simon, you were a cousin of Jesus and a devoted follower as well. You were called "the Zealot," indicating that you were willing to give your life for your religion and your freedom . . . Obtain for us the grace to be willing to give our lives for Christ and to labor for the freedom and peace that only God can give. Help us to spend ourselves for God on earth and be received by him in eternal bliss in heaven. Amen.

Simon by Spanish/Greek Mannerist painter El Greco (c.1541–1614)

29

Narcissus of Jerusalem

PATRON SAINT OF:
Invoked against insect bites

STATUS: *Bishop*

BORN: *c. 99 AD*

DIED: *c. 216 AD*

VENERATED BY: *Roman Catholic Church, Eastern Orthodox Church*

CANONIZED:
Pre-Congregation

SYMBOLS: *Bishop holding a thistle, pitcher of water*

God, You made St. Narcissus an outstanding exemplar of Divine love and the Faith that conquers the world, and added him to the role of saintly pastors. Grant by his intercession that we may persevere in Faith and love and become sharers of his glory. Amen.

Narcissus, likely of Greek orgin, was a patriarch of Jerusalem during the first century and is venerated by both the Eastern and Western Churches. In the Easern Orthodox Church his feast is celebrated on August 7. Little is known of his life, but it is believed to have been a long one; many accounts suggest that he would have been around 117 years old at the time of his death. It is said he was in his 80s when he was made the 30th bishop of Jerusalem, and he was credited with many miracles during his time. On one occasion, Narcissus changed water into enough oil to light every lamp in his church. Later, however, he came under fire for several false allegations that tarnished his reputation. Although he forgave the people who had slandered him, he chose this time to leave Jerusalem and live in isolation, appreciating the chance to dedicate himself to prayer and reflection. When he eventually returned to Jerusalem, much older still, he resumed his position with the aid of St. Alexander as his bishop coadjutor.

Benvenuta of Cividale

Benvenuta Bojani was the youngest of seven sisters, born to a man who had desperately wanted a son. She devoted herself to God from a young age, showing no interest in games or toys or fine clothes that had anything to do with the secular world; she eventually began wearing only a hair shirt and a rope belt as a show of austerity. When, as she grew, the rope belt began to cut into her side and had to be removed, Benvenuta's prayers allowed the rope to fall to her feet. While still an adolescent she became a professed member of the Third Order of St. Dominic and lived the rest of her life at home. She was severe in her piety, and often fell ill as a result of fasting and going without sleep. Eventually, she became bedridden for five years, but was still carried to church each week by one of her sisters. It is said that she was finally healed when, during mass, she experienced a vision of Saint Dominic and Saint Peter. From then on, she received regular visions of both angels and demons and believed she could dispel the demons by invoking the name of Mary. After her death, miracles were attributed to her intercession.

STATUS: *Visionary*

BORN: *May 4, 1254, Venice*

DIED: *October 30, 1292, Venice*

VENERATED BY: *Roman Catholic Church*

CANONIZED: *Pre-Congregation*

SYMBOLS: *Dominican habit, rope*

Lord, you gave Blessed Benvenuta the gifts of penance, prayer and humility. Through self-denial and contemplation on heavenly things may we too live in the Spirit and find rest and glory in you, the one God. We ask this through our Lord Jesus Christ. Amen.

Wolfgang of Regensburg

Wolfgang was descended from the Swabian counts of Pfullingen. He was tutored at home, and later attended the Würzburg cathedral school with his friend Henry of Babenberg. When Henry was made archbishop of Trier in 956, he summoned Wolfgang to teach at the school. After Henry's early death, Wolfgang entered the Benedictine Order at Einsiedeln, Switzerland, and was ordained in 968.

In 955, King Otto I "the Great" defeated the Magyars of Hungary, who had been making incursions into Western Europe. Otto hoped that converting the heathen Magyars would integrate them into the Holy Roman Empire, and Wolfgang was chosen to undertake the task. Just a year later, on Christmas 972, Wolfgang was appointed the new bishop of Regensburg, a post where his intellectual abilities, diplomacy, and piety all came to the fore. He was the highly influential tutor to Henry II (July 13), the last Holy Roman Emperor of the Ottonians, and made reforms to the famous St. Emmeran's Abbey. In his old age, Wolfgang lived as a hermit in Upper Austria. When he died his body was returned to the abbey at Regensburg, where many miracles have been reported at his grave.

PATRON SAINT OF: *Carpenters, wood-carvers; invoked against apoplexy, strokes, paralysis, stomach diseases; Regensburg*

STATUS: *Bishop*

BORN: *934, Swabia, Germany*

DIED: *October 31, 994, Pupping, Austria*

VENERATED BY: *Roman Catholic Church, Eastern Orthodox Church*

CANONIZED: *1052*

SYMBOLS: *Forcing the devil to help build a church; a hermit in the wilderness*

Lead me, holy Counselor, to know what to do with my life, how to make good decisions, and how to live life fully. Amen.

LEGENDS FROM WOLFGANG'S LIFE ARE MEMORABLY COMMEMORATED IN THE ALTARPIECE PANELS BY THE REMARKABLE TYROLEAN PAINTER MICHAEL PACHER (1430–98), NOW IN THE ALTE PINAKOTHEK, MUNICH. HERE HE IS SHOWN TRICKING THE DEVIL INTO HELPING HIM BUILD A CHURCH.

NOVEMBER

November often brings clear, crisp days and dark, chilly nights; it is welcomed in with three major festivals, all associated with the dead.

November 1, the day after Halloween, is All Saints' Day and celebrates those who have enjoyed a beatific experience of Heaven. Widely observed in the West, in the Eastern churches it is celebrated on the first Sunday after Pentecost. On November 2, All Souls' Day commemorates those who have passed on, but may not yet have reached Heaven. Latin Americans honor the lives of their departed loved ones with the Day of the Dead, or "Dia de los Muertos," a two-day festival on November 1 and 2. November 11—for centuries celebrated as Martinmas, the traditional beginning of winter in the European agricultural calendar—is now better known for marking Remembrance (or Veterans) Day, recognizing all those fallen on the field of battle. On a more joyful note, November often includes the first day of Advent.

THE DAY OF THE DEAD IS A MAJOR FESTIVAL THROUGHOUT LATIN AMERICA, WHEN FAMILIES COME TOGETHER TO REMEMBER THEIR DEPARTED LOVED ONES AND ANCESTORS. REVELERS BUILD ALTARS, CREATE CONFECTIONARY IN THE FORM OF SKULLS AND SKELETONS, VISIT GRAVES, AND HOLD PARTIES.

All Saints Day

The his important ecumenical feast (a solemnity in the General Roman Calendar), All Saints' Day celebrates not only every saint recognized by the Church, but also their associates and followers, even if unknown, and indeed all those whose lives displayed demonstrable sanctity. It is also a time to remember all those who have been nominated as suitable for canonization, but whose cases remain under consideration. Further, it reminds Catholics of those en route to full sainthood, who have reached the stage of veneration or beatification, but who have not yet been canonized, or have not been assigned a feast day.

The feast was possibly first introduced in England in the early 8th century, where it was called All Hallows Day, thus the night before was called All Hallow's Eve, shortened to Halloween, a date that promoted fear of the dead. On the other hand, both All Saints' Day and All Souls' Day, November 2, honor the deceased. The feast became established throughout Europe by the 12th century, and is still observed by most Christians around the world, although the Eastern Orthodox churches celebrate this feast on the first Sunday after Pentecost. The Church of the East celebrates it on the first Friday after Easter.

OBSERVANCES:
Church services, praying for the dead, visiting cemeteries

CELEBRATED: *Roman Catholic Church, Eastern Orthodox Church*

We thank you, God, for our blessed saints. They left their mark on the earth for you, for us, for our children to come. Thank you . . . for the tremendous sacrifices made by those who have gone before us. Bless the memories of your saints, God. May we learn how to walk wisely from their examples of faith, dedication, worship, and love. Amen.

THE SOLEMNITY OF ALL SAINTS, ESPECIALLY IN LATIN AMERICA WHERE THE INVOCATION OF SAINTS IS OF PARTICULAR IMPORTANCE, INCLUDES A COMPLEX ICONOGRAPHY. HERE THE BLESSED VIRGIN OF CARMEL GIVES HER INSTRUCTIONS TO THE ARCHANGELS CONCERNING WHO SHOULD BE RAISED FROM PURGATORY.

Victorinus of Pettau

Victorinus was an early Christian theologian and ecclesiastical writer. Likely born in Greece, he lived and wrote during the late 4th century. He apparently spoke Greek better than Latin, which caused St. Jerome to note that his writings in Greek were superior to those in his adopted language, which Jerome said lacked style. A bishop of Pattau (Styria in Austria), Victorinus was the first theologian to use Latin for his exegesis—critical explanations or interpretations of religious texts.

His written works consisted of commentaries on various books of Holy Scripture such as Genesis, Exodus, Leviticus, Isaiah, Ezekiel, St. Matthew, and the Apocalypse, as well as treatises against heresies of the time. All that has survived are his Commentary on the Apocalypse and a short tract entitled On the construction of the world. The Commentary was written not long after the Valerian Persecution, probably around 260 AD. According to St. Jerome, Victorinus died a martyr during the Diocletian persecutions.

STATUS: *Bishop, martyr.*

BORN: *3rd century AD, Likely in Greece*

DIED: *303/304 AD, Pettau*

VENERATED BY: *Roman Catholic Church, Eastern Orthodox Church*

CANONIZED: *Pre-Congregation*

SYMBOLS: *Pontifical vestments, palm*

St. Victorinus, we beseech you for guidance, instruct us on how to read scripture, as you once did, to gain a deeper understanding of increasing faith and devotion and to perceive how we might better follow the path laid out for us by our Heavenly Father. Amen.

VICTORINUS ON A FRESCO IN THE PARISH CHURCH OF NOVA CERKEV, SLOVENIA.

Martin de Porres

PATRON SAINT OF:
*Mixed-race people, barbers,
innkeepers, public health
workers, those seeking racial
harmony*

STATUS: *Priest*

BORN: *December 9, 1579,
Lima, Peru*

DIED: *November 3, 1639,
Lima, Peru*

VENERATED BY: *Roman
Catholic Church, Anglican
Communion, Lutheranism, in
Peru*

CANONIZED: *1962*

SYMBOLS: *Dog, cat, bird,
and mouse eating from same
dish; broom, crucifix, rosary,
heart*

*You have given to the world a
glorious apostle of humility, St
Martin de Porres. Guide us by his
example and strengthen us through
his intercessions in our efforts to
conform our hearts to the humble
heart of Thy crucified Son. Amen.*

Martin was born in Lima, Peru, an illegitimate child of mixed racial heritage. He took after his mother, a freed black slave from Panama, rather than his father, a Spanish hidalgo. He was apprenticed to a barber-surgeon to learn the medical arts. Due to Peruvian law, those of African or Indian descent were barred from taking holy orders, so Martin applied for the position of "donado," a volunteer who performs menial tasks, at the Convent of the Rosary. Eventually the prior allowed him to take vows as a Dominican tertiary. In 1603 he was elevated to a Dominican lay brother and at 34 he was put in charge of the convent infirmary, a position he would hold until his death at 56. He ministered with equal concern to Spanish nobles and African slaves. Once when a ragged, ulcerous beggar reached out to Martin, he took him to his own bed. "Compassion is preferable to cleanliness," he responded to a shocked friar. Martin humbly referred to himself as a "mulatto dog"—after one of the novices scorned his mixed blood—but he was generally revered by his fellow priests and his patients.

Charles Borromeo

Charles Borromeo was one of the most important figures of the Counter-Reformation. He was born to a noble family, educated in Milan and Pavia, studying civil and canon law, and entered the clergy at age 12. Under the patronage of his uncle, Pope Pius IV, he rose rapidly, becoming administrator and then bishop of Milan, then cardinal.

Despite his aristocratic background and wealth, Charles gave most of his money away; he lived frugally and worked actively for his congregation during the plague of 1576. He was determined to re-establish the Catholic faith as a dignified central force in contemporary society. In the face of the Protestant challenge, Charles dedicated himself to implementing the reforms promulgated at the Council of Trent, founding seminaries and schools, and imposing strict discipline on his priests. He even survived an assassination attempt by a lay confraternity in 1569. In 1578 he founded a society of diocesan priests, the Oblates of St. Ambrose, to enforce his reforms.

PATRON SAINT OF: *Bishops, catechists, seminarians, invoked against stomach disorders*

STATUS: *Bishop, Founder*

BORN: *1538, Arona, Italy*

DIED: *1584, Milan, Italy*

VENERATED BY: *Roman Catholic Church*

CANONIZED: *1610*

SYMBOLS: *Usually shown bareheaded and tonsured, barefoot, with a rope or cord, although often in cardinal's robes*

Almighty God, you have generously made known to man the mysteries of your life through Jesus Christ your Son in the Holy Spirit. Enlighten my mind to know these mysteries which your Church treasures and teaches.

Move my heart to love them and my will to live in accord with them. Give me the ability to teach this Faith to others without pride, without ostentation, and without personal gain....

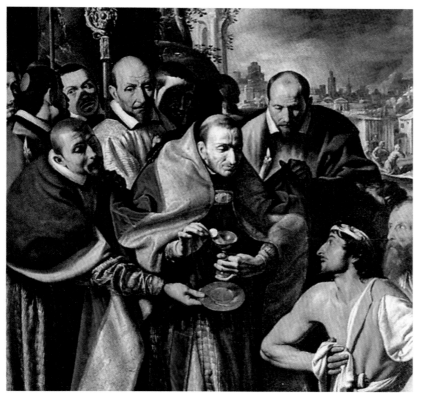

CHARLES OFFERING THE HOST TO A PLAGUE VICTIM. DESPITE BEING SOMETHING OF A MARTINET, CHARLES WAS SELFLESS IN HIS DEVOTION TO HIS FLOCK.

Zechariah and Elizabeth

Though they are sparingly mentioned in the New Testament, the parents of John the Baptist are key figures in the prelude to Christ's ministry. According to the Gospel of St. Luke, Zechariah was a priest in the temple at Jerusalem and married to Elizabeth, who was of the line of Aaron, the Priest families of Israel. Although they were "righteous before God," they had no children: Elizabeth was barren, and they were both quite old. Then Zechariah was visited by the Archangel Gabriel (Sept. 29), who announced that his barren wife was now with child—a son who would become John the Baptist (Luke 1:5–25).

Disbelieving, Zechariah asked for proof, and in punishment, Gabriel struck Zechariah dumb. His speech was miraculously restored, however, following John's birth (June 24) and after Zechariah confirmed the unusual name of the child in writing. Zechariah then spoke the prophetic lines of the Benedictus (Luke 1: 68–79), including "And you, my child, will be called a prophet of the Most High; for you will go on before the Lord to prepare the way for him." Elizabeth also features in Luke 1:42 when she is visited by her cousin—the Visitation of the Blessed Virgin Mary (May 31).

PATRON SAINT OF:
Parents, grandparents

STATUS: *Parents of John the Baptist*

BORN: *Mid-1st century bc*

DIED: *Early 1st century ad*

VENERATED BY: *Eastern Orthodox church*

CANONIZED:
Pre-Congregation

SYMBOLS: *Aged couple, usually at birth of John the Baptist; Elizabeth with Virgin and Child and St. John*

Heavenly Father, just as you answered the many prayers of Zechariah and Elizabeth for a child, I pray You will furnish me with the faith to hold onto my aspirations and that You may one day look upon me with favor and empower me. This I ask in the name of Jesus Christ, our Lord. Amen.

DOMENICO GHIRLANDAIO'S RICH IMAGINING OF ZECHARIAH'S ENCOUNTER WITH THE ANGEL GABRIEL WAS PAINTED IN FLORENCE IN 1490. THE ASSEMBLED CONGREGATION COMPRISES PORTRAITS OF FLORENTINE WORTHIES OF THE TIME, ALL UNAWARE OF THE MIRACULOUS EVENT.

Paul of Constantinople

K nown also as Paul the Confessor, he was a strong defender of the Nicene Creed at a time when the Arian controversy wracked the Roman Empire. Early on he served as a presbyter of Constantinople and as secretary to the aged bishop Alexander. Backed by the Orthodox party, Paul himself was elected bishop of Constantinople in around 336, some ten years after the Council of Nicaea had condemned Arianism—a doctrine that believed that Jesus, although the God the Son, was not co-eternal with God the Father. Unfortunately this elevation occurred just as the Emperor Constantius II, an Arian supporter, gained power. Paul was declared unfit, was rapidly supplanted, but was soon re-elected after he sought the aid of Pope Julius I, who espoused his cause, and that of other displaced bishops.

Imperial pressure resulted in another popular rebellion between Paul and the Arians. The emperor sent a general to expel Paul, but the angry townspeople set fire to his quarters and killed him. Paul was exiled to the shores of the Black Sea, but once again was reinstated, then once again exiled to the Cucusus region in chains. His captors supposedly starved him, but when he refused to die they ended up strangling him.

STATUS: *Bishop, martyr.*

BORN: *c.300, Thessaloniki, Greece*

DIED: *c.350, Cucusus, Armenia*

VENERATED BY: *Roman Catholic Church, Eastern Orthodox Church*

CANONIZED: *Pre-Congregation*

SYMBOLS: *Wearing a robe patterned with crosses, holding a book*

O blessed St. Constantine, let us show the courage and fortitude you displayed when you were declared unfit to serve as bishop, let us find wise solutions, as you did by seeking an advocate for your cause, and let us gracefully accept the outcome if our fortunes do not prosper. This we ask in the name of Jesus Christ, our Lord. Amen.

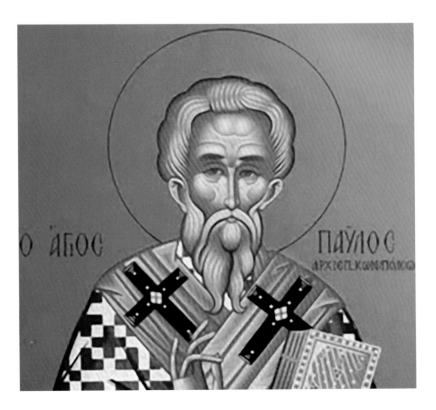

Willibrord of York

Willibrord was the son of Wilgils or Hilgis, a Saxon of Northumbria who became a hermit and was himself canonized. Presented to the Abbey of Ripon as a child by his father, Willibrord was raised under the guidance of St. Wilfrid. He later joined the Benedictines, also known as the Order of Saint Benedict, before relocating to the Abbey of Rath Melsigi in Ireland, a center of European learning, where he remained for twelve years. St. Egbert, the bishop of Lindisfarne, sent him with 11 companions to convert the pagan Frisians of the North Sea coast. During this period, Willibrord made two trips to Rome as a missionary. During the second trip, Pope Sergius I named him bishop of the Frisians. He went on to found several Frisian churches, including a cathedral in Utrecht. He later established the Abbey of Echternach in 698. When Willibrord died in the year 739, it was there he was buried.

PATRON SAINT OF:
Epileptics, invoked against convulsions and epilepsy; Luxembourg, Netherlands, Archdiocese of Utrecht

STATUS: *Apostle to the Frisians, bishop, mercenary*

BORN: *c. 658, Northumbria*

DIED: *November 7, 739, Echternach, Luxembourg*

VENERATED BY: *Roman Catholic Church, Eastern Orthodox Church, Anglican Communion*

CANONIZED:
Pre-Congregation

SYMBOLS: *Depicted dipping staff into cask*

O God, who gave increase to your Church through the zeal for religion and apostolic labors of blessed Willibrord, grant, through his intercession, that she may always receive new growth in faith and in holiness. Through our Lord Jesus Christ, your Son, who lives and reigns with you in the unity of the Holy Spirit, one God, for ever and ever. Amen.

STATUE OF SAINT WILLIBRORD BEHIND THE "ST. WILLIBRORD BASILIKA", ECHTERNACH, LUXEMBOURG

John Duns Scotus

John Duns Scotus, also known as "Duns the Scot," was a Scottish priest, Franciscan friar, philosopher, theologian, and professor. He was renowned for his academic and philosophical work, particularly for his complex and compelling metaphysical arguments in support of the existence of God and the Immaculate Conception of Mary. He also argued for the existence of free will and against skepticism and Illuminationism, a mystic philosophy with Persian influences.

Born in Duns, Scotland, he studied at the universities of Oxford, Cambridge, Paris, and Cologne. He received his doctorate in Paris, where he lectured for many years. Duns was a polarizing figure, and has received a great deal of both praise and criticism over the centuries. The word "dunce," referring to someone incapable of learning, stems from the derogatory use of his name in the 1500s. Yet others have called him "Doctor Subtilis" for the unique subtlety and nuance of his arguments. Either way, Duns' work had a formative effect on Catholic philosophy, laying the groundwork for future discussions for hundreds of years to come.

PATRON SAINT OF: *Academics; apologies; scholars; theologians and philosophers; Cologne, Germany*

STATUS: *Priest, philosopher, professor*

BORN: *c. 1265, Duns, County of Berwick, Kingdom of Scotland*

DIED: *November 8, 1308 (aged 41–42), Cologne, Holy Roman Empire*

VENERATED BY: *Roman Catholic Church*

BEATIFIED: *1993*

SYMBOLS: *Books, vision of the Virgin Mary, a moon on the chest of a Franciscan friar*

Lord God, source of all wisdom, in Blessed John Duns Scotus, priest and champion of the Immaculate Virgin, you have given us a master of life and thought. Grant that, enlightened by his example and nourished by his doctrine, we may remain faithful followers of Christ, who lives and reigns with you in the unity of the Holy Spirit, one God, for ever and ever. Amen.

Theodore of Amasea

S aint Theodore of Amasea has also been referred to as Theodore Tyron, Theodore Tiro, and Theodore the Recruit. He is one of two saints named Theodore who were venerated as warriors saints and great martyrs, the other being Theodore of Heraclea. The details of his life prior to his martyrdom are recorded mostly in legends. He was a soldier of the Roman Army serving in Amasea, in North Turkey, and was once arrested for his refusal to worship pagan gods along with his fellow recruits. Yet he was freed after a warning, perhaps due to his youth. He was then arrested again shortly afterward for setting fire to a pagan temple of the mother goddess Cybele. Condemned to death, after being tortured, he was thrown into a furnace and burned alive. As a warrior saint, it has been frequently recorded that his intercession could help turn the tide of battle, making him popular as a patron saint of soldiers and crusaders. Many illustrations of Theodore also depict him as a dragon slayer, and he is often shown fighting a dragon beside St. George.

PATRON SAINT OF:
Recovery of lost articles, invoked against storms, soldiers: Brindisi

STATUS: *Soldier, martyr*

BORN: *c. 3rd century, Turkey*

DIED: *February 17, 306, Amasea, Turkey*

VENERATED BY: *Roman Catholic Church, Eastern Orthodox Church*

CANONIZED:
Pre-Congregation

SYMBOLS: *Depicted as a soldier or in court dress, spear, temple, torch, dragon, pyre, martyr's wreath*

O Heavenly King, Saint Theodore was a young soldier in the Roman army when he converted to Christianity. Though he was ordered to fight enemies of the empire, he believed that the devil was the only true enemy. Soon, he was killed for being a Christian, thus winning the battle against the demons who wanted to keep him out of Heaven. I ask him to pray for my fight against evil and temptation and to pray for all my loved ones during their battles. . . . Amen.

ST. THEODORE TYRO (ORTHODOX ICON)

Leo the Great

Born to a noble, influential family, Leo served as an emissary for Emperor Valentinian III. Leo was unanimously elected pope in 440. In 445, he obtained from Valentinian a decree that recognized the primacy of the bishop of Rome—that his rulings had the force of ecclesiastical law, and any opposition would be interpreted as treason. Leo quickly asserted his authority, rebuking errant bishops for deviations from Roman practice.

At the Second Council of Ephesus in 449, Leo's representatives delivered his famous Tome, a statement of faith in the Roman Church. He convened the Council of Chalcedon in 451 to condemn heretical teachings. Rome, meanwhile, was increasingly vulnerable to barbarian threats from the East. In 452, Attila the Hun, invaded Italy and threatened Rome. Leo was sent to negotiate with Attila at Mantua. The encounter was successful—perhaps because he offered Attila a large sum of money, or because the Hun's forces were overstretched. Legend claims that as Leo spoke, Attila had a vision of a sword-wielding man in priestly robes threatening him. When the Vandals under Genseric occupied Rome in 455, Leo persuaded them not to pillage the city. He died in 461, leaving letters and writings of great historical value.

STATUS: *Pope, Doctor of the Church*

BORN: *c. 400, Tuscany, Italy*

DIED: *November 10, 461, Rome, Italy*

VENERATED BY: *Roman Catholic Church, Eastern Orthodox Church, Anglican Communion*

CANONIZED: *Pre-Congregation*

SYMBOLS: *Papal vestments, papal tiara,, image of the Virgin, pick-axe, model of St. Maria Maggiore, horse, Attila kneeling*

God our Father, you will never allow the powers of hell

to prevail against your Church, founded on the rock

of the apostle Peter. Let the prayers of Pope Leo the Great

keep us faithful to your truth and secure in your peace.

Through our Lord Jesus Christ, your Son. Amen.

Martin of Tours

Born into a Roman military family, Martin served as a cavalry officer in Amiens. Here, he experienced a pivotal vision. Encountering a beggar at the city gates, he cut his cloak in half and shared it. That night he dreamed he saw Jesus, dressed in the half-cloak, saying, "Here is Martin, the Roman soldier, who is not baptized; he has clad me." Martin's nascent piety was stirred, and he was baptized. Concluding that his faith prohibited him from fighting, he was imprisoned for cowardice, but eventually released. Martin became a disciple of Hilary of Poitiers (Jan. 13) in Tours. When Hilary was sent into exile, Martin returned to Italy, to live the life of a hermit. In 361, Hilary was reinstated; Martin returned to Gaul and established a monastery. He was acclaimed bishop of Tours in 371. Legend says that—unwilling to accept the honor—he took refuge in a stable filled with geese, whose gobbling soon betrayed his whereabouts. Martin began destroying all the pagan temples in Tours and constructing churches. He also founded an abbey at Marmoutier and frequently withdrew there for the tranquil monastic life.

PATRON SAINT OF:
Merovingians, Carolingians (French royal families); beggars, geese, horses, innkeepers, soldiers, tailors, vintners; invoked against poverty, alcoholism

STATUS: *Bishop*

BORN: *316 AD, Savaria, modern Hungary*

DIED: *397 AD, Candes-St.-Martin, France*

VENERATED BY: *Roman Catholic Church*

CANONIZED:
Pre-Congregation

SYMBOLS: *Man on horseback, sharing cloak with beggar; cutting cloak in half; globe of fire; goose*

Glorious Saint Martin, you who worked miracles and prodigies, who with joy, amiability and the most exquisite goodness won over the hearts of all and did not cease to ever work for their wellbeing:

give me your hand and help me to come out of all lack and scarcity which today afflicts me and weighs me down. Amen.

THIS FRESCO, FROM THE LOWER CHURCH OF SAN FRANCESCO AT ASSISI, PAINTED BY SIMONE MARTINI IN 1321, CELEBRATES ST. MARTIN'S RENUNCIATION OF VIOLENCE IN THE BATTLEFIELD.

Didacus of Alcalá

S aint Didacus of Alcalá, also known as Diego de San Nicolás, was a Spanish Franciscan lay brother, missionary, and incorruptible. He spent his early years living as a hermit, wandering under the guidance of another hermit priest. He eventually joined the Order of the Friars Minor and relocated to Lanzarote, where he served as a porter for many years. He also acted as a missionary during this time, introducing the local Guanche people to Christianity. In 1445, due to his zeal and sanctity, he was appointed guardian of Franciscan community on the Canary Island of Fuerteventura, where the Friary of St. Bonaventure was soon founded. In 1450, Didacus was present in Rome for the Jubilee Year when, due to the large number of visitors, an epidemic broke out; he remained in the city for three months to care for the sick, and he quickly gained a reputation for his miraculous healings of those who visited him. He spent his last years in spiritual contemplation in a friary in Alcalá, Spain.

PATRON SAINT OF: *Roman Catholic Diocese of San Diego, Franciscans*

STATUS: *Missionary, Franciscan lay brother*

BORN: *c. 1400 San Nicolás del Puerto, Kingdom of Seville, Crown of Castile*

DIED: *November 12, 1463 Alcalá de Henares, Kingdom of Toledo, Crown of Castile*

VENERATED BY: *Roman Catholic Church*

CANONIZED: *1588*

SYMBOLS: *Cross, lily*

Almighty and eternal God, in whose marvelous ordering of things the weak of this world are singled out to shame the strong, grant, we pray, that by imitating the humility of St. Didacus here on earth, we may be raised up to eternal glory with him in heaven. Through our Lord Jesus Christ, your Son, who lives and reigns with you in the unity of the Holy Spirit, one God, for ever and ever. Amen.

SAN DIEGO DE ALCALÁ BY FRANCISCO DE ZURBARÁN

Frances Xavier Cabrini

Though born in Italy, Frances Cabrini, 13th child of a Lombardy farmer, was the first American to be canonized. In spite of being a sickly child, she graduated from school cum laude, with a teaching certificate. After her parents died in 1870, she applied for admission to the Daughters of the Sacred Heart in Arluno. They told her she was too frail, however. She finally took her religious vows in 1877, adding Xavier to her name to honor the Jesuits. Having run an orphanage in northern Italy for three years, in 1880 she founded the Missionary Sisters of the Sacred Heart of Jesus. Her intention was to do missionary work in China, but Pope Leo XIII requested that she travel to the United States, then already home to millions of Italian immigrants.

Frances arrived in New York in 1889 and immediately began to open orphanages, hospitals, and schools. Her first orphanage, the St. Cabrini Home, was in Ulster County, New York. She became an American citizen in 1909, yet her charitable work was never restricted to the United States. She traveled widely across Central and South America and made numerous return visits to Europe.

PATRON SAINT OF:
Immigrants, hospital administrators

STATUS: *Virgin, Missionary, foundress*

BORN: *July 15, 1850, Lombardy, Italy*

DIED: *December 22, 1917, Chicago, US*

VENERATED BY: *Roman Catholic Church*

CANONIZED:
Pre-Congregation

SYMBOLS: *Ship, heart, book*

You have urged us through your son, Our Lord and saviour Jesus Christ to ask for your assistance in all our needs. Grant me through the intercession of Saint Frances Xavier Cabrini, whom I invoke, that I may obtain the grace I desire . . . according to your holy will. Amen.

Laurence O'Toole
(Lorcán Ua Tuathail)

Laurence was the youngest son of the king Muirchertach Ua Tuathail of Leinster. A 10 the boy was sent as a political hostage to the new over-king from South Leinster, Diarmait Mac Murchada. At some point Laurence was imprisoned and starved, but the intercession of the abbot of Glendalough restored relations between the two kings. This rescue strengthened the boy's wish to become a priest and so he remained with the abbot. He became abbot himself at 26, working to strengthen the bonds between Ireland and Rome. He also protected the community against brigands with prayers and fasting. At 32 he was unanimously elected archbishop of Dublin, the first Irishman to rule the see in a town governed by Danes and Norwegians. He began a policy of church building, laying the foundation stone for Christ Church, and reached out to the poor as well as orphaned or abandoned children.

PATRON SAINT OF: *Archdiocese of Dublin*

STATUS: *Archbishop*

BORN: *1128, Kilkea, County Kildare, Ireland*

DIED: *November 14, 1180, Eu, Normandy, Angevin Empire*

VENERATED BY: *Roman Catholic Church, Church of Ireland*

CANONIZED: *1225*

SYMBOLS: *Bearded man, mitre, archbishop's pallium*

Dear Lord, thank you for those like St. Lawrence who intercede on our behalf and negotiate for the well-being of our country, our families, our lives. We ask that St. Lawrence continue to intercede for us and help us to live our lives in peace and harmony. Amen.

BAPTISTERY WINDOW OF CHRIST CHURCH CATHEDRAL, DUBLIN

Albert the Great

PATRON SAINT OF:
Scientists, the natural sciences, medical technicians, philosophers

STATUS: *Bishop, theologian, Doctor of the Church*

BORN: *c. 1200, Duchy of Bavaria*

DIED: *November 15, 1280, Cologne, Holy Roman Empire*

VENERATED BY: *Roman Catholic Church*

CANONIZED:
Pre-Congregation

SYMBOLS: *Dominican robes, miter, book and quill*

Dear St. Albertus Magnus, Scientist and Doctor of the Church, natural science always led you to the higher science of God. Though you had an encyclopedic knowledge, it never made you proud, for you regarded it as a gift of God. Inspire our scientists of today to use their gifts well in studying the wonders of creation, thus bettering the lot of the human race and rendering greater glory to God. Amen.

One of a group of enormously literate medieval churchmen and scholars—which included his pupil Thomas Aquinas (Jan. 28)—Albert had a profound influence on the doctrinal footings of the Catholic Church.

Little is known of his early years except that he entered the Dominican Order while studying at Padua, and went on to teach at Hildesheim, Regensburg, and Cologne. There he taught Aquinas and reorganized the Dominican studies before moving on to teach in Paris. For three years from 1254, Albert was Dominican Prior Provincial to Germany and personal theologian to Pope Alexander IV. He was appointed bishop of Regensburg (Ratisbon), Germany, in 1260, but retired to Cologne after two years. He pioneered the application of Aristotelian principles to theology, seeking the coexistence of science and religion. Also known as Albertus Magnus, his prolific output, some 38 volumes of treatises on subjects as varied as astronomy and botany as well as theology, led him to be declared a Doctor of the Church in 1931, upon his canonization.

THE APPARITION OF THE VIRGIN TO SAINT ALBERT THE GREAT BY VICENTE SALVADOR GOMEZ

Edmund Rich

Educated at a monastic school in Oxfordshire, Edmund attended the universities of Oxford and Paris, and became a lecturer in mathematics and dialectics, and the first known Oxford Master of Arts. Pious and ascetic, he abandoned his secular career and was ordained some time after 1205. He received a doctorate in theology, and soon gained a reputation as an inspirational preacher. After three years as vicar of Calne, Wiltshire, and treasurer of Salisbury Cathedral, he was appointed archbishop of Canterbury in 1234. A proponent of independence from Rome, Edmund was opposed to the appointment of foreigners in influential ecclesiastical and civil positions. He asserted these views to King Henry III, and persuaded him—under threat of excommunication—to dismiss his councilors. He visited Rome in 1237 to enlist the pope's support for his ecclesiastical reforms. The mission failed, and on returning to England he found his authority seriously undermined. By 1240, he was forced to submit to the pope, paying Rome one-fifth of his revenues. His spirit broke, and in the summer of 1240 he retired to the Augustinian house at Soisy-Bouy.

PATRON SAINT OF: *Abingdon, Diocese of Portsmouth*

STATUS: *Bishop*

BORN: *c.1175, Abingdon, England*

DIED: *1240, Soisy-Bouy, France*

VENERATED BY: *Roman Catholic Church*

CANONIZED: *1246*

SYMBOLS: *Archbishop making vow before or receiving lamb from the Blessed Virgin Mary; with St. Richard of Chichester or St. Thomas of Canterbury*

Illuminate my heart with the grace of your Holy Spirit; grant that I may ever be obedient to your commandments; suffer me not to be separated from you, O God, who lives and reigns with God the Father and the same Holy Spirit for ever and ever. Amen.

THE PIOUS EDMUND RICH RENDERED IN A WOODCUT FROM THE NUREMBERG CHRONICLE.

Elisabeth of Hungary

PATRON SAINT OF:
*Dying children, the homeless,
widows, exiles*

STATUS: *Princess*

BORN: *1207, Pressburg,
Hungary*

DIED: *1231, Marburg,
Hessen (Germany)*

VENERATED BY: *Roman
Catholic Church*

CANONIZED: *1235*

SYMBOLS: *Roses, crown,
basket of food*

*Almighty God, by whose grace
your servant Elizabeth of Hungary
recognized and honored Jesus in
the poor of this world: Grant that
we, following her example, may
with love and gladness serve those
in any need or trouble. In the name
and for the sake of and through
Jesus Christ our Lord. Amen.*

The daughter of King Andrew II of Hungary, Elisabeth was wed to Ludwig IV of Thuringia at only 14, in order to reinforce the political alliance between the two courts. He was crowned ruler in the same year, 1221. At this time Elisabeth came under the influence of a group of Franciscan monks, and started dedicating herself to charitable works. Konrad von Marburg, a harsh and worldly priest, was appointed as her confessor, and began to exert considerable influence over her.

In 1226, when her husband was called to the Imperial Diet in Cremona, Elisabeth assumed control of the affairs of state, building a hospital in Wartburg Castle. A year later Elisabeth was left a widow and she moved to Marburg. Konrad now began to wield sadistic power over his young charge. Elisabeth swore complete obedience to him, taking a vow of celibacy that would prohibit her from remarrying and making a new dynastic alliance. Konrad ruled her with a rod of iron, meting out physical punishments for transgressions, and ordered her to send away her three children. Elisabeth became affiliated with the Third Order of St. Francis, a lay group, and built a hospital at Marburg for the needy. She died at only 24, possibly broken by Konrad's harsh treatment.

A 19TH-CENTURY PAINTING BY CALDERON OF ELISABETH TAKING HER VOW OF CELIBACY, AS THE LOATHSOME KONRAD VON MARBURG LOOKS ON.

Rose Philippine Duchesne

Born in France to a prominent and wealthy family, Rose Philippine Duchesne could have lived her whole life in comfort and ease. Instead, she chose to go against her family's wishes and become a nun, joining the Visitation of the Holy Mary at the age of 18. She became Mother Superior of her monastery by 1804, and later agreed to merge the Visitation with the Society of the Sacred Heart, a community recently founded by Madeleine-Sophie Barat. Duchesne oversaw a new convent and a school in Paris, before traveling to New Orleans in 1818 to establish the congregation's first communities in the United States. As a child she had heard stories at her parish church of the missions in Louisiana and felt a desire to serve the native peoples who lived there. She took a steamboat up the Mississippi to the Missouri Territory, where she established a convent in a log cabin. Duchesne stayed in the United States for the remainder of her life, establishing several schools and convents, and teaching among the Pottawatomies at Sugar Creek, Kansas, until her death at age 83.

PATRON SAINT OF: *Perseverance amid adversity; Diocese of Springfield-Cape Girardeau*

STATUS: *Missionary, nun, educator*

BORN: *August 29, 1769, Grenoble, Dauphiné, Kingdom of France*

DIED: *November 18, 1852, St. Charles, Missouri, U.S.*

VENERATED BY: *Roman Catholic Church, Society of the Sacred Heart*

CANONIZED: *1988*

SYMBOLS: *Nun's habit, map*

Gracious God, you filled the heart of Rose Philippine Duchesne with charity and missionary zeal and gave her the desire to make you known among all peoples. Fill us, who honor her memory today, with that same love and zeal to extend your kingdom to the ends of the earth. We ask this through our Lord Jesus Christ, your Son, who lives and reigns with you and the Holy Spirit, one God for ever and ever. Amen.

Hilda of Whitby

Hilda was a Celtic noble, scholar, teacher, and abbess and a key figure in the Christian conversion of Anglo-Saxon England. Born into a royal family, she was the daughter of Hereric, the nephew of King Edwin of Deira (later Northumbria), and was raised at his court. Paulinus of York, chaplain of Edwin's Christian wife, Aethelburh, eventually baptized the entire court, including young Hilda. She served as the second abbess of Hartlepool Abbey and was responsible for founding Whitby Abbey, or Streoneshalh, in 657.

Perhaps her greatest gift was wisdom—Hilda's shrewd counsel was in such demand that kings came to her directly for advice. Hilda was also a devotee of the arts and of the pursuit of culture. She is known as the patron saint of poetry in particular, largely due to her close relationship with Cædmon, the monastery herdsman. Cædmon, now considered the earliest-named English poet, found himself encouraged by Hilda after receiving a vision while sleeping to sing praises to God. In other legends, it is said that Hilda defeated a plague of snakes by turning each snake to stone.

PATRON SAINT OF:
Learning and culture, poetry; National Cathedral School for Girls in Washington

STATUS: *Abbess*

BORN: *c. 614, Kingdom of Deira*

DIED: *November 17, 680, Hackness*

VENERATED BY: *Catholic Church, Eastern Orthodox Church, Anglican Communion*

CANONIZED:
Pre-Congregation

SYMBOLS: *Crozier, holding a model of Whitby Abbey*

O God of peace, by whose grace the abbess Hilda was endowed with gifts of justice, prudence, and strength to rule as a wise mother over the nuns and monks of her household, and to become a trusted and reconciling friend to leaders of the Church: Give us the grace to recognize and accept the varied gifts you bestow on men and women, that our common life may be enriched and your gracious will be done; through Jesus Christ our Lord, Amen.

Edmund the Martyr

Edmund's life story is mainly derived from the Anglo-Saxon Chronicle. He was likely descended from the kings of East Anglia in the Wuffling line, although legend claims Edmund was the youngest son of Alcmund, a Saxon king. Edmund succeeded to the throne of East Anglia at age 14, in 854. During his reign he was considered an exemplary king, impervious to flattery and bribery, and who treated everyone justly. In 869 Danish invaders marched south from York toward East Anglia. Edmund's forces engaged them at Hoxne, and he was killed. While he probably fell in battle, legend insists he died a martyr—that he refused to renounce his faith even when beaten with cudgels and tied to an oak tree and subjected to a rain of Danish arrows. He was finally beheaded and his remains thrown into the nearby forest. In Abbo of Fleury's 10th century account of his martyrdom, Edmund's subjects searched the forest for his severed head and eventually heard Edmund's voice calling, "Here I am!" They found his head being guarded by a gray wolf, which accompanied Edmund's men back to the town, before disappearing into the forest.

PATRON SAINT OF:
Kings, wolves, pandemics, torture victims

STATUS: *King, martyr*

BORN: *c. 841, probably East Anglia, England or Nuremburg, Germany*

DIED: *869, East Anglia, England*

VENERATED BY: *Roman Catholic Church, Eastern Orthodox Church, Anglican Communion*

CANONIZED:
Pre-Congregation

SYMBOLS: *Crowned and robed as a king; holding orb, scepter, arrow, or sword*

O God of inexpressible mercy, who gloriously enabled the most blessed King Edmund to overcome the enemy by dying for your name, grant, in your mercy, to us your servants that by his intercession we may overcome and extinguish the temptations of the old enemy, through Christ our Lord. Amen.

REPRESENTATIONS OF EDMUND TEND TO FOCUS ON HIS MARTYRDOM AT THE HANDS OF DANISH ARCHERS.

Gelasius I

T he first pope to be called "Vicar of Christ," Gelasius was probably born in
Roman Africa in the period before the Vandal invasion. He was elected Bishop
of Rome in 492 and was likely the third and final pope of Berber descent. A prolific
writer, his style placed him somewhere between the theologians of Late Antiquity and
those of the Early Middle Ages.

As pope, he insisted on strict Catholic orthodoxy and forcefully demanded
respect for papal authority. This increased already simmering tensions between the
Eastern and Western Churches. Unfortunately, Gelasius inherited the discord of his
predecesor Felix III with the Eastern Roman Emperor Anastasius and the Patriarch of
Constantinople. A split with both Emperor and Patriarch seemed inevitable, from the
Western point of view, because they accepted the Monophysite heresy—that Jesus had a
Divine, but not human, nature. In 494, Gelasius penned the highly influential letter,
Due Sunt, to Anastasius on the subject of the relation of Church and state; its political
impact lasted for more than a millennium after its composing.

STATUS: *Pope*

BORN: *c. 5th century, Roman
Africa or Rome*

DIED: *November 19, 496,
Rome, Ostrogothic Kingdom*

VENERATED BY: *Roman
Catholic Church*

CANONIZED:
Pre-Congregation

SYMBOLS: *Depicted in
papal vestments holding cross,
Bible, or model church*

*. . . Lord Jesus Christ, your
resurrection has gathered together
the multitude of believers into a
single community.*

*May your Church of today, like
that of old, have but one heart,
have but one soul.*

*Perfect our conversation as
believers that our discourse may
reflect the unity you share with the
Father and the Holy Spirit as you
live and reign, one God, now and
forever. Amen.*

Cecilia

S t. Cecilia was an early Roman martyr who experienced visions of angels, heard heavenly music, and sang to God as she was dying. She has long been revered as the patron saint of music. It had been generally accepted that Cecilia was a noblewoman of Rome who was martyred, along with her husband and brother-in-law, Maximus, around 230, under the emperor Alexander Severus. Later research, however, indicates that she died in Sicily between 176 and 180, during the rule of Marcus Aurelius.

Legend has it that Cecilia was an ardent Christian who heard heavenly music in her heart as she was married. She went on to convert her husband, Valerian, and his brother, to the Christian faith, and they dedicated themselves to burying Christian martyrs. Following the execution of her husband and his brother, she arranged to have her home preserved as a church. Roman officials attempted to kill Cecilia by suffocating her in a steam bath; they then attempted to behead her three times, but she would not succumb until she had received Holy Communion. It was three days before she finally died.

PATRON SAINT OF:
Music, hymns, musicians, poets

STATUS: *Martyr*

BORN: *c. 200–230 AD, Rome, Italy*

DIED: *222–235, Sicily, Italy*

VENERATED BY: *Roman Catholic Church, Eastern Orthodox Church, Anglican Communion*

CANONIZED:
Pre-Congregation

SYMBOLS: *Playing flute, organ, violin, harp, harpsichord, singing, roses*

Oh Saint Cecilia, you were arraigned before a Roman prefect for the offense of loving Christ. You refused to sacrifice to the pagan Gods and debated your captors with unshakeable faith, even to the point of a death sentence. Bless all those who are not offended by God's scandalous message of grace and forgiveness, and help us overcome every kind of idolatry that keeps us in servitude. Amen.

CECILIA BECAME A POPULAR SAINT IN ROME FROM THE 5TH CENTURY. HER BASILICA IN THE TRASTEVERE DISTRICT WAS REBUILT BY POPE PASCHAL I AROUND 820, AND AGAIN IN 1599.

Clement I

PATRON SAINT OF:
Stonecutters, mariners;
Angono, Rizal

STATUS: *Pope, martyr*

BORN: *c. 35 AD, Rome*

DIED: *c.101, Bosporan*
Kingdom

VENERATED BY: *Roman*
Catholic Church, Eastern
Orthodox Church, Oriental
Orthodox Church, Anglican
Communion, Lutheranism

CANONIZED:
Pre-Congregation

SYMBOLS: *Papal vestments,*
mariner's cross, anchor tied to
his side, martyr's palm

Lord, I believe in you: increase
my faith.

I trust in you: strengthen my trust.

I love you: let me love you more
and more.

I am sorry for my sins: deepen my
sorrow.

I worship you as my first beginning,

I long for you as my last end,

I praise you as my constant helper,

And call on you as my loving
protector. Amen.

Clement of Rome became one of the most important of the early popes and was possibly appointed bishop of Rome by St. Peter himself. In the 3rd or 4th century a tradition arose that identified Clement as the person Paul mentioned in Philipians 4:3, as "a fellow laborer in Christ." He is most noted for his first epistle to Corinthian Christians, dealing with the structure of the Church there. This letter reveals the clear authority of Rome in ecclesiastical matters, and the need for submission to that authority. It also acknowledges the political supremacy of the Roman Empire, at the time under the emperor Domitian, a persecutor of Christians, and accords due respect to the secular powers of the empire.

Voragine's *The Golden Legend* provided little of Clement's background, only that he was known to be a leading figure in the first-century Church of Rome. It also provides Clement with an unsubstantiated martyrdom under the Roman emperor Trajan, in which he was thrown from a ship with an anchor tied to his neck. According to legend, the sea immediately receded for three miles, and a marble temple was discovered, containing his sarcophagus and his remains, still attached to the anchor.

CLEMENT'S LETTERS REMAIN AN IMPORTANT SOURCE FOR UNDERSTANDING THE STATUS OF THE EARLY CHRISTIAN CHURCH IN ROME, AND ESTABLISHED A SIGNIFICANT PRECEDENT FOR THE DEVELOPMENT OF THE PAPAL SEE.

Martyrs of Tonkin

E ven more than in other parts of eastern Asia, Christian missionaries and converts in Vietnam were brutally persecuted from the moment the first Europeans reached the country in 1533, when Christianity was declared illegal by imperial edict. At least 130,000, and possibly as many as 300,000, Christians were executed for their faith; many were tortured beforehand. The killings reached a peak after 1855, when Emperor Tu-Dúc instituted a renewed, even more savage persecution. It was ended in 1862 when France effectively annexed Vietnam, partly in response to the treatment of French missionaries.

In 1988 Pope John Paul II canonized 117 of those executed. Of them, ten were French, members of the Paris Foreign Missions Society; 11 were Spanish Dominicans; and the remaining 96 were Vietnamese, Andrew Dung-Lac (d.1839) being among those most venerated. The martyrs had all suffered a variety of appalling fates, of which beheading was perhaps the most merciful. Many were dismembered, others suffocated, some burned alive. Most had the characters ta dao, meaning "false religion," branded on their faces before they died.

STATUS: *Priests, martyrs*

BORN: *19th century*

DIED: *19th century*

VENERATED BY: *Roman Catholic Church*

CANONIZED: *1988*

PIERRE BORIE OF THE PARIS FOREIGN MISSIONS SOCIETY WAS BEHEADED IN NOVEMBER 1838. ON THE GROUND BEFORE HIM LIES A CANGUE, A PORTABLE, LADDER-LIKE YOKE WORN BY PRISONERS. THE CANGUE BORIE WAS FORCED TO WEAR IS DISPLAYED IN THE SOCIETY'S HEADQUARTERS IN PARIS.

O Vietnamese Martyrs, with the Grace of God, you had victoriously implanted the mustard seed of Faith that grew into the Church of Vietnam. Your courageous sacrifice had reserved your Heavenly rest. United with you, we offer our gratitude and thanks to God and the Holy Mother, for all of your martyrdom and your lives that we now celebrate. We beseech you . . . to follow your Faith in humility, charity and love. When we are in despair and danger, please aid and console us in fulfilling the Father's Will and carry our crosses to Eternal Glory. Amen.

Catherine of Alexandria

PATRON SAINT OF:
*Unmarried girls, potters,
spinners, archivists, lawyers,
jurists, nurses, librarians,
mechanics*

STATUS: *Virgin, martyr*

BORN: *287 AD, Alexandria,
Egypt*

DIED: *305 AD, Alexandria,
Egypt*

VENERATED BY: *Roman
Catholic Church, Eastern
Orthodox Church, Oriental
Orthodoxy, Anglican
Communion, Lutheranism*

CANONIZED:
Pre-Congregation

SYMBOLS: *Breaking wheel,
sword, crown at her feet,
hailstones, bridal veil and ring,
dove, scourge*

*St. Catherine of Alexandria, you
were born into a pagan family,
in a society that was hostile to
Christianity. You did not have
the benefit of an upbringing in the
Faith. But when you received a
vision of the Blessed Mother and
Child Jesus, you knew you wanted
to be part of the Christian Faith.
Pray that I may actively choose to
love God, as you did! This I ask
in the name of Christ, our Lord.
Amen.*

E ven if Catherine's existance is historically doubtful, her importance in the Middle Ages as an exemplar of beauty, intelligence, learning, sanctity, and chastity cannot be overstated. She is also one of the Fourteen Holy Helpers. The daughter of the Roman governor of Alexandria, she was converted to Christianity before age 20 by one of the Egypt's desert hermits. In a vision she found herself united with Christ in a "mystic marriage." She subsequently attempted to convert Roman emperor Maximinus, in the process brilliantly confounding the 50 pagan philosophers he had deputed to argue with her. Many of them converted to Christianity, as did the empress, Caecilia Paulina. Maximinus then had Catherine imprisoned and ordered that she be "broken" on a wheel (hence "Catherine wheel"). After the wheel itself miraculously broke, Catherine was beheaded. In the 6th century, Justinian order the construction of a monastery over her grave site. In about 800, her body was rediscovered—her hair still growing—and so her cult began to develop.

AN IDEALIZED IMAGE OF AN IDEAL SAINT. ST. CATHERINE BY THE EARLY RENAISSANCE VENETIAN PAINTER, CARLO CRIVELLI, C.1470.

Leonard of Port Maurice

Leonard, born Paul Jerome Cazanova, grew up on the northwestern coast of Italy, where his father was a ship's caption. Although Leonard's childhood dream was to become a missionary in China, he rarely traveled outside of his home country. This was due in part to a debilitating illness that he suffered after he was first ordained by the Franciscans in 1703; it took four years for him to fully recover, and from that point on he continued his career as a preacher, missionary, and ascetic writer within Italy. He also emerged as a tireless propagandist who was especially vocal in his advocacy of using the Sacred Heart of Jesus, the Blessed Sacrament, the Immaculate Conception, and, above all, the 14 Stations of the Cross, as aids to contemplation and prayer. During his time as a missionary, Leonard established over 500 Stations of the Cross throughout Italy, including one at the Coliseum in Rome. He continued to preach and carry out missions for over forty years, dedicating huge amounts of time and energy to each cause.

PATRON SAINT OF:
Parish mission preachers

STATUS: *Friar*

BORN: *December 20, 1676 Porto Maurizio*

DIED: *November 26, 1751 Rome*

VENERATED BY: *Roman Catholic Church*

CANONIZED: *29 June 1867*

SYMBOLS: *Stations of the cross*

Almighty and merciful God, who made Saint Leonard an outstanding herald of the mystery of the Cross, grant, by his intercession, that, acknowledging on earth the riches of the same Cross, we may be worthy to attain the fruit of redemption in Heaven. Through our Lord Jesus Christ, your Son, who lives and reigns with you in the unity of the Holy Spirit, one God, for ever and ever. Amen.

James the Persian

Also known as James the Mutilated, he was a high-born Syriac Christian in the Persian Sassanid empire, one considered a "a lord of merit . . . wealthy, knowledgeable, and virtuous." As a favorite of the emperor, Yezdegeherd, he was showered with honors to the point that his head was turned by his worldly success, and he renounced his faith. His mother and his wife, appalled by his apostasy, wrote to him, rebuking James for his fickleness. He at once recognized his foolishness and publicly re-embraced Christianity. His reward was to be put to death by Yezdegeherd's successor, who instituted the second great Persian persecution of Christians in around 420. It was decreed that James be progressively dismembered. One by one, his fingers were severed, then his toes, then his legs, then his arms, then his shoulders. All the while, James staunchly proclaimed his Christian faith. Finally, he was decapitated. "A sweet-smelling fragrance, as of a cypress" was given off by his mutilated corpse.

PATRON SAINT OF:
Lost vocations, torture victims

STATUS: *Martyr*

BORN: *4th century AD, Beth Huzaye, Persia*

DIED: *421 AD, Persia*

VENERATED BY: *Roman Catholic Church, Eastern Orthodox Church, Eastern Catholic Church, Oriental Orthodoxy*

CANONIZED:
Pre-Congregation

Receive, O Lord, the prayers of your humble servant; give strength and courage to the son of your maidservant; make of me a sign of consolation for those who love you, those who suffer, and for those who will suffer persecution for your namesake. And when I will have overcome by your omnipotent grace, thus receiving the crown of the elect, make my enemies see it so they may be confounded, because you have been, Lord, my consolation and my stronghold. Amen.

IN THE CATHOLIC CHURCH, JAMES THE PERSIAN IS KNOWN AS JAMES INTERCISUS, MEANING LITERALLY "CUT TO PIECES."

Catherine Labouré

Catherine Labouré was an illiterate peasant girl who served as a very junior member of a nursing order in Paris, the Daughters of Charity. In 1830 she claimed to have had three visitations by the Virgin Mary. On the first, in July, she was summoned at night to the order's chapel on the rue du Bac, Paris. There she encountered "a most beautiful lady," who issued a series of warnings about the imminent collapse of the restored French monarchy. On the second, in November, the Virgin appeared to her standing on a globe, shimmering with light emanating from the many rings on her fingers. Around her was a glowing oval frame. Slowly the figure rotated and 12 stars appeared around it, as did the letter M, the Sacred Heart of Jesus, and the Immaculate Heart of Mary. The Virgin charged Catherine with having a medal made incorporating these devices. Catherine received a final visitation in December.

Catherine reported the visitations to the order's priest, Father Aladel, who requested permission from his bishop for the medals to be made. They became instantly popular across the Catholic world.

PATRON SAINT OF: *Miraculous medal, the infirm, the elderly*

STATUS: *Mystic*

BORN: *May 2, 1806, Burgundy, France*

DIED: *December 31, 1876, Paris, France*

VENERATED BY: *Roman Catholic Church*

CANONIZED: *1947*

SYMBOLS: *Daughters of Charity habit, Miraculous Medal*

Saint Catherine Labouré, you were the chosen confidant of the Blessed Virgin Mary. She revealed to you her desire that her children wear the Miraculous Medal as a mark of their love for her and in honor of her Immaculate Conception. Intercede for us, that we may follow our heavenly mother's desires. Ask that we may receive those special graces which flow from her motherly hands like rays of light. Amen.

Saturninus of Toulouse

PATRON SAINT OF:
Toulouse, France

STATUS: *Bishop, missionary, martyr*

BORN: *c. 3rd century Patras, Greece*

DIED: *c. 257 Toulouse, Gaul (France)*

VENERATED BY: *Roman Catholic Church, Eastern Orthodox Church*

CANONIZED:
Pre-Congregation

SYMBOLS: *Bishop's mitre, bishop being dragged by a bull*

O God, who gives us the joy of celebrating the feast of blessed Saturninus, your Martyr, grant that we may be helped by his merits. Through our Lord Jesus Christ, your Son, who lives and reigns with you in the unity of the Holy Spirit, one God, for ever and ever. Amen.

L ittle is known of Saturninus' life except that he was bishop of Toulouse; he may have been a Greek from North Africa, possibly the son of the King of Achaea. At the request of Pope Fabian, Saturninus traveled to Gaul in 245, one of seven bishops chosen for the mission. There he worked to convert a large number of locals to Christianity. He was a friend of St. Papulus, and was responsible for the conversion to Christianity of both Saint Honestus and Saint Firminus. He was also credited with many miraculous healings. It was said that after he began his missionary work in Gaul, the oracles of Toulouse stopped receiving visions from their gods. Saturninus was blamed for this and arrested in 257. When ordered to offer sacrifice to appease the pagan gods, he refused and was executed by being dragged through the city by a bull. His body was interred on the spot where the bull finally stopped. He was given a more fitting burial by his successors, Hilary and Exuperius, who erected a wooden oratory over the Roman crypt. The site is now home to the church of Notre-Dame du Taur, which translates to "Our Lady of the Bull."

SAINT SATURNINUS IS DRAGGED TO HIS DEATH BY A BULL. A 19TH CENTURY ENGRAVING FROM SHEA'S PICTORIAL LIVES OF THE SAINTS.

Andrew the Apostle

A fisherman from the northern shores of Lake Galilee, Andrew was the first of the Apostles to be called by Jesus. He was the brother of Simon Peter (St. Peter), and introduced him to Jesus. He is remembered in the Gospels as one of the disciples involved in the miracle of the feeding of the five thousand. After Pentecost, the record of Andrew's ministry and preaching becomes very unclear. The 2nd century apocryphal Acts of Andrew and Matthias describes Andrew rescuing Matthias (May 14) from cannibals, while the Acts of Andrew tells of him performing miracles in Anatolia and Greece. The Old English poem Andreas even saw him visiting Ethiopia. One account cites Andrew as the first bishop of Byzantium, effectively identifying him as the founder of the Eastern Orthodox tradition.

Scholars also disagree on the site of Andrew's martyrdom. Scythia, on the Black Sea, Kiev, and Epirusare are possibilities. The most likely is Patras in Achaea, Greece, where Andrew is said to have been crucified (tied rather than nailed), preaching from the cross for two days before expiring.

PATRON SAINT OF:
Fisherman, ropemakers, singers, miners, butchers, textile workers, protection from sore throats, convulsions, fever

STATUS: *Apostle*

BORN: *5–10 AD, Galilee, Israel*

DIED: *November 30, 60 AD, Patras, Greece*

VENERATED BY: *Roman Catholic Church, all Christian denominations that venerate saints*

CANONIZED: *Pre-Congregation*

SYMBOLS: *Old man with long white hair and beard, holding the Gospel, book, or scroll, sometimes leaning on a saltire, fishing net*

O good Cross, made beautiful by the body of the Lord: long have I desired you, ardently have I loved you, unceasingly have I sought you out and now you are ready for my eager soul. Receive me from among men and restore me to my Master, so that he who, by means of You, in dying redeemed me, may now receive me. Amen.

SAINT ANDREW THE APOSTLE BY ARTUS WOLFFORT

DECEMBER

Advent marks the start of the Christian year in most Western traditions. Derived from the Latin *adventus*, or "coming," the season begins on the fourth Sunday before the celebration of the Nativity of Christ on December 25, occurring on or between November 27 and December 3. With winter closing in, December is a time of hushed expectation, of light in the darkness, as Christmas approaches.

The season's traditions are carried far beyond the portals of the church by Advent candles and calendars, full of the promise of treats and joyous abundance to come. The feast day of the saint most widely associated with Christmas, Nicholas of Myra, remembered in some countries today as Santa Claus, falls some time before Christmas itself, on December 6. The first martyr, Saint Stephen, is commemorated on December 26, and the Massacre of the Holy Innocents by Herod on December 28.

THERE IS A CHARACTERISTIC SIMPLICITY AND HUMANITY IN THE EARLY RENAISSANCE PAINTER GIOTTO'S REPRESENTATION OF THE NATIVITY (C.1310) THAT IS FAR REMOVED FROM THE ELABORATE NARRATIVES WE ARE FAMILIAR WITH TODAY.

Charles de Foucauld

Charles Eugène Vicomte de Foucauld, was among the most remarkable of 20th-century holy men: an aristocrat, immensely rich, and an explorer and soldier, forever disdainful of his superiors, who argued forcefully for the French colonization of North Africa (in which he played a key early role). As a dissipated young man, Charles was so taken by a rare wine he drank in a restaurant that he bought the entire stock for 18,000 francs (at a time when the average laborer in France received perhaps 2,400 francs a year). Yet in 1890, in an utter reversal of his early life, Charles became a Trappist monk, devoting himself to a spartan existence to the point of almost complete destitution. Between 1890 and his ordination in 1901, he spent time not just with Trappists in France and Syria, but also with an order of Poor Clares in Nazareth. He subsequently lived as a hermit in North Africa, first at Béni Abbès, Morocco, and later in even more remote Tamanrasset, deep in southern Algeria, among the desert Tuareg people. In between his devotions, he compiled a scholarly dictionary and grammar of their language.

STATUS: *Trappist Monk, hermit*

BORN: *September 15, 1858, Strasbourg, France*

DIED: *December 1, 1916, Tamanrasset, Algeria*

VENERATED BY: *Roman Catholic Church, in Morocco, Algeria*

BEATIFIED: *2005*

SYMBOLS: *Trappist habit*

Father, I abandon myself into your hands; do with me what you will.

Whatever you may do, I thank you: I am ready for all, I accept all.

Let only your will be done in me, and in all your creatures.

I wish no more than this, O Lord. Amen.

BY 1902, CHARLES HAD REDUCED HIS DIET TO SUCH A DEGREE — BREAD, SOME PORRIDGE, AND TEA — THAT HE WAS ON THE POINT OF DEATH FROM MALNUTRITION. HE TOLD A GROUP OF TRAPPISTS WHO HOPED TO JOIN HIM THAT THEY COULD DO SO ONLY IF THEY WERE "PREPARED TO DIE OF HUNGER."

Chromatius

STATUS: *Bishop, theologian*

BORN: *4th century, Aquileia, Italy*

DIED: *c. 406/407, Italy*

VENERATED BY: *Roman Catholic Church, Eastern Orthodox Church*

CANONIZED: *Pre-Congregation*

SYMBOLS: *White bearded bishop*

Let us pray to the Lord with all our heart and with all our faith, let us pray to Him to deliver us from all enemy incursions, from all fear of adversaries . . . May He protect us with His customary merciful love and bring about for us, what holy Moses said to the Children of Israel—The Lord will fight to defend you and you will be silent. It is He who fights, it is He who wins the victory. And so that He may condescend to do so, we must pray as much as possible. He himself said . . . Call on me on the day of tribulation; I will set you free and you will give me glory. Amen.

C hromatius suffered the loss of his father as an infant and was raised his mother and his large group of older siblings. Follwing a calling to the priesthood, he was ordained around 378, and a decade later was elevated to bishop of the northern Adriatic city of Aquileia in 388. A celebrated prelate and leading theologian of this era, he corresponded with St. Ambrose of Milan (Dec. 7) and St. Jerome (Sept. 30) as well as St. John Chrysostom, bishop of Constantinople (Sept. 13) and noted historian/monk Tyrannius Rufinus. Chromatius was known to encourage the first two to produce learned works, and as a result Jerome dedicated a number of works to him, while Ambrose produced exegetical essays, critical explanations of religious text. In the bitter quarrel between St. Jerome and Rufinus concerning Origenism, although Chromatius rejected the false doctrines of Origen of Alexandria, he attempted to make peace between his two friends. He himself wrote a number of commentaries on St. Matthew's Gospel and a series of 38 sermons. A great opponent of arianism, a deeply divisive heresy, Chromatius zealously rooted it out in his diocese.

A ROMANESQUE FRESCO FROM THE BASILICA AT AQUILEIA CELEBRATING THE CHURCH FATHER CHROMATIUS.

Francis Xavier

The list of countries of which Francis Xavier is the patron surely indicates his importance as the greatest missionary the history of the Catholic Church. Known as the "Apostle of the Indies and Japan," his career developed at an opportune moment. Rome, under pressure from the Reformation north of the Alps, was forced to take decisive action to re-establish its authority, in part by converting as many people as possible across the wider world, one increasingly colonized by European powers.

A well-born Basque, Francis attended the University of Paris, where he met fellow Spaniard Ignatius of Loyola (July 31) and joined him to form the Jesuits. He was ordained in Venice in 1537 and in 1540 set off for Goa, a Portuguese trading settlement on the Indian coast. While attending hospitals and prisons, Francis traveled throughout southern India, working with low-caste Paravas. He also evangelized in Ceylon (Sri Lanka), Malacca, and the Moluccas. His letters to the king of Portugal reveal that he was highly critical of the behavior of colonists toward the indigenous populations.

PATRON SAINT OF: *Missionaries, plague epidemics; Goa, India, Japan, Pakistan, Bangladesh, Indonesia, the Philippines, Mongolia, Borneo*

STATUS: *Priest, missionary*

BORN: *1506, Navarre, Spain*

DIED: *1552, Sancian (Sangchwan), China*

VENERATED BY: *Roman Catholic Church, US Evangelical Lutheran Church*

CANONIZED: *1622*

SYMBOLS: *Bearded and youthful; bearing crucifix, flaming heart, torch, or lily*

Francis, we pray to you for the courage to be missionaries, reaching out and leading others to Jesus. … Francis, may we help those in need, may we live a life rooted in prayer and may we bring Christ to all those we meet. This we ask through your Son, our Lord, Jesus Christ. Amen.

Barbara

Whatever the doubts as to her existence, the legend of St. Barbara, one of the most popular saints in the Middle Ages and one of the Fourteen Holy Helpers, is among the most appealingly vivid of any saint. She is said to have been the daughter of a pagan, Dioscorus, who confined her in a tower, where in her enforced solitude she became a Christian. Her father discovered her conversion after she had three windows installed in a bathhouse in honor of the Trinity. When, in his rage, he attempted to kill her, she escaped after an opening miraculously appeared in the wall. A shepherd who then betrayed her was turned to stone and his sheep to locusts. Though she was tortured, her wounds healed instantly. She was beheaded by her father, who was subsequently struck by lightning.

PATRON SAINT OF:
Artillerymen, gunpowder makers, mathematicians, miners, stonecutters, those afraid of lightning, fever

STATUS: *Virgin, martyr*

BORN: *c. 273 AD, Nicomedia, Turkey*

DIED: *c. 306, Nicomedia, Turkey*

VENERATED BY:
Roman Catholic Church, Eastern Orthodox Church

CANONIZED:
Pre-Congregation

SYMBOLS: *Chalice, lightning, martyr's crown/ palm, three-windowed tower*

Saint Barbara, your courage is much stronger than the forces of hurricanes and the power of lightening. Be always by our side so that we, like you, may face all storms, wars, trials and tribulations with the same fortitude with which you faced yours. Amen.

BARBARA AND HER TOWER PORTRAYED IN A 16TH-CENTURY FRENCH STATUE.

THE 14 HOLY HELPERS
During the Middle Ages, this group of largely traditional, Pre-Congregational saints became enormously popular in Central Europe and Germany. Their intercession was invoked on an almost daily basis for everyday problems, and their cultural legacy remains recognized even today.

HELPER:	PATRONAGE
Agathius (May 8)	Headache
Barbara (Dec. 4)	Fever, sudden death, lightning
Blaise (Feb. 3)	Throat ailments, pets
Catherine (Nov. 25)	Sudden death
Christopher (July 25)	Traveling, plague
Cyriacus (Aug. 8)	Temptation on the deathbed
Denis (Oct. 9)	Headache
Erasmus/Elmo (June 2)	Stomach ailments
Eustace (Sept. 20)	Family discord
George (April 23)	Pets
Giles (Sept. 1)	Plague, the infirm, good confession
Margaret of Antioch (July 20)	Childbirth, possession by devils
Pantaleon (July 27)	Cancers and tuberculosis
Vitus (June 15)	Epilepsy, lightning

Sabas the Sanctified

S abas was the son of a military commander; left with an uncle at age five when his parents journeyed to Alexandria, at eight the boy sought refuge in the monastery of Bishop Flavian of Antioch. There, he quickly became an expert on the Holy scriptures. When his family asked him to return to the world and accept an arranged marriage, he refused. He received his monastic tonsure at the age of 17 and remained in the monastery for 10 years. He subsequently traveled to the Holy Land and served in Palestine under Euthymius the Great, then under his disciple, Theoctistus. He spent several years as a hermit until his fame as a holy man grew to the point that he was persuaded to found monastic communities of his own.

Sabas played a critical role in the early monastic tradition as it developed in the Middle East and North Africa. He founded a number of monasteries, most famously that which bears his name, Mar Saba, outside Jerusalem. In 491, the patriarch of Jerusalem, Salustius, ordained him and appointed him head, or archimandrite, of all of Palestine's monasteries.

PATRON SAINT OF:
Monastic life

STATUS: *Monk, hermit*

BORN: *439 AD,*
Cappadocia, Turkey

DIED: *December 5, 532,*
Jerusalem, Palestine

VENERATED BY: *Roman*
Catholic Church, Eastern
Orthodox Church,
Lutheranism

CANONIZED:
Pre-Congregation

SYMBOLS: *Monk with*
abbot's staff

O wondrous and laudable Saint of God, venerable Father Sabbas, despise not our petitions, but hear us who entreat thee, and keep us under thy protection and defense, undisturbed by enemies visible and invisible, that we may be vouchsafed to complete our life in repentance, and obtain the eternal good things in the Kingdom of Christ. Amen.

Nicholas of Myra

Possibly the most widely known and beloved saint in his role as "Santa Claus," or "Father Christmas," Nicholas of Myra was an exceedingly popular saint long before the commercialization of Christmas in the 19th century. Nicholas was probably born in Lycia in southwest Asia Minor (Turkey), and became bishop of Myra, the provincial capital. During the Diocletian persecution he was imprisoned, but was released unharmed. Twenty years later, he attended the Council of Nicaea (325) to denounce Arianism. He may have been martyred. One legend, which enforces the tradition of giving presents to children at Christmas, involves three girls, to whom he purportedly gave bags of gold as dowries to prevent them becoming prostitutes.

At some point, Nicholas's cult in northern Europe became entwined with Nordic myths, especially those of Odin, reinforcing his association with winter's attributes such as snow and holly. In 1087 the city of Bari in southern Italy, keen to build a reputation as a pilgrimage center, endorsed a raid on Myra and looted Nicholas's relics. Tradition tells us that the relics were later removed from Bari to Jerpoint Abbey, in County Kilkenny, Ireland.

PATRON SAINT OF:
Children, archers, sailors, merchants, pawnbrokers; Amsterdam, Moscow

STATUS: *Bishop*

BORN: *Late 3rd century, Patara, modern Turkey*

DIED: *Mid-4th century, Myra, modern Turkey*

VENERATED BY: *Roman Catholic Church, Eastern Orthodox Church*

CANONIZED:
Pre-Congregation

SYMBOLS: *Often shown bearing three moneybags or golden balls; more commonly, since late 19th century portrayed as Santa Claus*

Glorious St. Nicholas, from thy throne in glory, where thou dost enjoy the presence of God, turn thine eyes in pity upon me and obtain for me from our Lord the graces and helps that I need in my spiritual and temporal necessities. Comfort the afflicted, provide for the needy, strengthen the fearful, defend the oppressed, give health to the infirm; cause all men to experience the effects of thy powerful intercession with the supreme Giver of every good and perfect gift. Amen.

Ambrose

With his contemporaries Sts. Jerome (Sept. 30), Augustine of Hippo (Aug. 28), and Gregory the Great (Sept. 3), Ambrose is one of four Latin Doctors of the Church, who lived at a time when Christianity had only recently been adopted as the imperial religion by Constantine. A prolific writer, Ambrose emerged as the most politically astute of his peers in both ecclesiastical and lay matters.

Born to Roman nobility and extremely well educated, in 370 he was appointed governor of Aemilia and Liguria in Italy. Upon the death in 374 of the Arian bishop of Milan, street fighting erupted between Christian factions, and Ambrose, whose intercession calmed the mobs, was declared bishop. Although reluctant to accept, he was rapidly baptized and consecrated, and distributed his wealth to the poor. With his political background he was an astute advocate of the distinction between Church and State: he advised the emperor Gratian about Arianism, and pointed out to Gratian's successor, Valentinian, that the emperor was part of, but not above, the Church. Ambrose was a thoughtful promoter of monasticism, nunneries under the Marian cult, the performance of the Eucharist, clerical ethics, and the use of hymns during acts of worship.

PATRON SAINT OF:
Beekeepers

STATUS: *Bishop, Doctor of the Church*

BORN: *c. 339 AD, Trier, Germany*

DIED: *397 AD, Milan, Italy*

CANONIZED:
Pre-Congregation

SYMBOLS: *In bishop's robes, with book or miter; with a scourge; with a bee, or beehive*

O Lord, who has mercy upon all, take away from me my sins, and mercifully kindle in me the fire of your Holy Spirit. Take away from me the heart of stone: give me a heart of flesh, a heart to love, to adore you, Lord, a heart to delight in you, to follow, to rejoice in you, for the sake of Jesus Christ. Amen.

ST. AMBROSE RECEIVING THE PENANCE OF THEODOSIUS BY ANTHONY VAN DYCK (1599–1641).

Macarius of Egypt

Also known as Macarius the Great and the Lamp of the Desert, Macarius was born in Lower Egypt, perhaps in the village of Shabsheer (Shanshour). It is told that while pursuing asceticism, he took to smuggling saltpeter in the region of Nitria, which gave him the skills to survive and travel the vast wastes of the North African desert. He was known for his wisdom, called by his kin and close friends, Paidarion Geron, or "old young man"—a young man with an elder's wisdom.

Heeding the wishes of his parents Macarius entered into marriage, but was soon widowed. When his parents died as well, Macarius distributed all his money among the needy. He found a teacher in an older hermit, who lived in the desert. This elder guided him in the spiritual science of watchfulness, fasting, and prayer, and taught him the handicraft of weaving baskets.

When a pregnant woman accused him of having defiled her, Macarius did not defend himself, accepting the slander in silence. As the woman's delivery drew near, however, her labor became exceedingly difficult, and she not give birth until admitting Macarius's innocence.

PATRON SAINT OF:
Cooks, candymakers

STATUS: *Monk, hermit*

BORN: *c. 300 AD, Shabsheer, Egypt*

DIED: *c. 391 AD, Scetes, Egypt*

VENERATED BY: *Roman Catholic Church, Eastern Orthodox Church, Oriental Orthodoxy*

CANONIZED:
Pre-Congregation

SYMBOLS: *Depicted with long white beard, desert setting*

O Lord, Who in Thy abundant goodness and Thy great compassion hast granted me, Thy servant, to pass the time of this night without the temptation of any opposing evil, Lord and Creator of all, by Thy true light and with an enlightened heart grant me to do Thy will, now and ever, and to the ages of ages. Amen.

Juan Diego

Juan Diego Cuauhtlatoatzin was a Chichimec peasant, a Marian visionary, and one of the first Aztecs to convert. He lived simply, caring for his sick uncle and praying at the local shrine to the Virgin Mary. He became well known, however, for the four visions of the Virgin Mary he received in December of 1531, three at the hill of Tepeyac. The Virgin told him to convince the bishop of Mexico, Don Juan de Zumárraga, to erect a chapel in her honor. Each time the bishop turned him down, Diego received another vision encouraging him. Eventually, the she agreed to offer a sign to prove that his visions were real. Diego collected a sack of flowers that the Virgin Mary arranged for him, which he then spilled at the bishop's feet. The flowers formed an image of the Virgin, convincing the bishop immediately that Diego was telling the truth. Once the chapel was built, Diego spent his life serving there.

PATRON SAINT OF: *Indigenous peoples of the Americas*

STATUS: *Visionary*

BORN: *1474 Cuauhtitlán, Tenochtitlan, Aztec Empire*

DIED: *1548 Tepeyac, Mexico City, New Spain*

VENERATED BY: *Roman Catholic Church*

CANONIZED: *2002*

SYMBOLS: *Tilma (cloak) with image of Virgin Mary, roses*

O St. Juan Diego, help me to always bear in mind the words to you of our heavenly Mother and in so doing be drawn closer to Her and Jesus as you were. Amen.

SAINT JUAN DIEGO BY MIGUEL CABRERA, 1752

Eulalia de Mérida

E ulalia was an adolescent martyr, who died during the persecutions of Roman emperor Diocletian or possibly those of Trajan Decius. There is some debate over whether she is the same person as St. Eulalia of Barcelona, who has a similar story.

Although she was hidden in the countryside by her Christian mother to avoid the persecutions of the emperor, when Christians were forced to apostatize or face death, Eulalia escaped from confinement and presented herself at the court of the Roman governor Dacian at Emirita. She openly declared her Christian faith, insulted both the pagan gods and the emperor, and dared the governor to martyr her. In spite of the judge's entreaties to the young girl, he was eventually forced to condemn her. Eulalia was stripped, tortured with torches and hooks, and finally tied to a cross and burned. Throughout these imprecations she taunted her enemies and continued to avow her faith. When she finally expired—her death likely caused by suffication—a dove flew out of her mouth, and snow miraculously fell to cover her nakedness.

PATRON SAINT OF:
Torture victims, runaways, widows; Mérida, Oviedo

STATUS: *Virgin, martyr*

BORN: *c.290 AD, Mérida, Spain*

DIED: *December 10, 304 AD, Mérida, Spain*

VENERATED BY: *Roman Catholic Church, Eastern Orthodox Church*

CANONIZED:
Pre-Congregation

SYMBOLS: *Stake, dove, cross, martyr's palm*

Blessed martyr St. Eulalia, I come before you seeking your intercession on behalf of a dear youth who has run away or is missing. I ask that you cast a spirit of protection over this youth and pray that the parents be freed from fear and anxiety. . . . Eulalia, I have confidence in your intercession and trust in a favorable outcome. Amen.

Damasus I

D amasus's life conincided with the rise of Constantine I, Holy Roman emperor, and the reunion and re-division of the Eastern and Western Roman Empires associated with the advent of Christianity as the official religion. Damasus was elected pope in 366, during the reign of Gratian, in an atmosphere of violence and uncertainty. His claims to the papacy were bitterly disputed by Ursinus, deacon to the previous pope, Liberius, who simultaneously declared himself pope. It was a conflict in which supporters of Damasus were claimed to have massacred 137 supporters of Ursinus. Only in 378, with the exile of Ursinus, was Damasus able to assert his sole authority.

Damasus proved a sturdy champion of the Latin Church, condemning various heretical movements, including Arianism—which recognized Jesus as the Son of God, but not his equal—and overseeing the translation of the Bible into Latin by his secretary, St. Jerome (Sept. 30). This most significant work, known as the Vulgate Bible, would become the standard Latin Bible around the world. He also restored numerous churches and monuments, particularly those commemorating early martyrs.

PATRON SAINT OF:
Archeologists, invoked against fever

STATUS: *Pope*

BORN: *c.305, Vimiranes, Portugal*

DIED: *December 11, 384, Rome, Italy*

VENERATED BY: *Roman Catholic Church, Eastern Orthodox Church*

CANONIZED:
Pre-Congregation

SYMBOLS: *Pope holding patriarchal cross and model of church*

O Saint Damasus, Bishop of Rome . . . You who sought so diligently to preserve the memory of the martyrs lest it should pass away, and the Cross of Christ with it, pray that today, too, the Church will remember its root, the root of Jesse and His sacrifice, and that as she grows our Mother on earth will be well understood by those called into her walls. Pray that the martyrs pray for us, that in their blood we will always find our growth. Amen.

DAMASUS, HERE DEPICTED IN THE PORTICO OF ST. PETER'S, WAS POPE AT A TIME WHEN CHRISTIANITY HAD ONLY RECENTLY BECOME THE OFFICIAL RELIGION OF THE ROMAN EMPIRE. IT WAS A DEVELOPMENT HE SUCCESSFULLY EXPLOITED, ENGINEERING A SIGNIFICANT STRENGTHENING OF THE CHURCH.

Finian of Clonard

PATRON SAINT OF:
Diocese of Meath

STATUS: *Abbot*

BORN: *470 AD, Myshall, Ireland*

DIED: *December 12, 549, Clonard, Ireland*

VENERATED BY: *Roman Catholic Church, Eastern Orthodox Church, in Ireland*

CANONIZED:
Pre-Congregation

As one who labored with zeal in the vineyard of God, by ascetic struggles and toils thou didst ascend from glory to glory, O God-bearing saint. Wherefore, joining chorus now with all the venerable on high, thou standest with boldness before the throne of the King of all, Whom do thou beseech, O Finian most wise, that He have mercy and save our souls. Amen.

Finian, called the father of Irish monasticism, was born in the Kingdom of Leinster, a member of an ancient tribe, Clanna Rudhraighe. After being baptised by Abban, a traditional early Irish saint, the boy was placed under the care of Bishop Fortchern of Trim. There he spent many hours in study and prayer. Some sources claim he studied for a time at the monastic center of Martin of Tours in Gaul. Finian then went to Wales to preach and supposedly stayed for 30 years.

Finian was a follower of Sts. Patrick (March 17), Cadoc, and Gildas. He established monasticism in Ireland—founding Clonard Abbey in County Meath—and forged strong links with the emerging monasteries in England, Wales, Northumbria, and Scotland. Among his many pupils and disciples were St. Ciaran, as well as the missionaries Columba of Iona (June 9), and Brendan the Navigator (May 16). Finian was reputed to have lived 140 years, but he likey died in his sixties and was buried at Clonard. He should not be confused with his near contemporary, St. Finnian of Moville (Sept. 10, d.c.579), who established a thriving monastic school in his native Ulster.

FINIAN AND HIS PUPILS IN A STAINED GLASS WINDOW AT THE CHURCH OF ST. FINIAN IN CLONARD

Lucy (Lucia)

Lucy was likely the offspring of wealthy Roman parents. Her mother suffered a bleeding disorder, and, fearing for Lucy's future, betrothed her to a wealthy pagan suitor. When Lucy traveled to the shrine of St. Agatha at Catania to seek aid for her mother, Agatha spoke to her in a dream, assuring her that her mother would be cured due to Lucy's piety and that Lucy would become "the glory of Syracuse."

In thanks, Lucy planned to distribute her inheritance to the poor. When news of this reached her betrothed, he revealed her Christian beliefs to the authorities at the height of the Diocletian persecutions. Threatened with rape while in prison, she apparently tore out her own eyes rather than submit, offering her eyes to her tormentor. She was tried by the Sicilian governor, Paschasius, who implored her to recant, which she refused to do. She was executed by a sword thrust to the neck. Her relics were taken to Constantinople, but are now claimed by Venice.

PATRON SAINT OF: *Peddlers, light; the blind, sufferers from diseases of the eye*

STATUS: *Virgin, martyr*

BORN: *c. 283 AD, Syracuse, Sicily*

DIED: *c. 304 AD, Syracuse, Sicily*

VENERATED BY: *Roman Catholic Church, Eastern Orthodox Church, Anglican Communion, Lutheranism*

CANONIZED: *Pre-Congregation*

SYMBOLS: *Holding a dish containing her eyes*

O St Lucy, you preferred to let your eyes be torn out instead of denying the faith and defiling your soul; and God, through an extraordinary miracle, replaced them with another pair of sound and perfect eyes to reward your virtue and faith, appointing you as the protector against eye diseases. I ask that you protect my eyesight and heal the illness in my eyes . . . .

Amen.

THE NARRATIVE OF LUCY'S TRIAL AND MARTYRDOM IS CAPTURED HERE BY AN UNKNOWN FLEMISH PAINTER OF THE LATE 15TH CENTURY.

John of the Cross

Born Juan de Yepes y Alvarez, John was the orphaned son of peasants who took to tending the sick and poor. He was admitted to the Carmelite Order in 1563 and then studied at Salamanca University. He was ordained in 1567. Under the influence of St. Teresa (Oct. 15), John joined her reform movement, the Discalced Carmelites, after being trained by Jesuits, and became spiritual director at her priory in Ávila. When other Carmelites' opposition to their reforms led to his arrest and imprisonment in the Carmelite priory in Toledo, he was held in dark, solitary confinement for nine months. He was occasionally brought to the refectory, where he would be abused and scourged, but it was also here he wrote some of his finest mystical poetry. John escaped in 1578 and was appointed confessor to the Discalced Nuns at El Calvario near Baeza, where he wrote extensively. His works from this period include *The Ascent of Mount Carmel* and *The Dark Night of the Soul*.

PATRON SAINT OF:
Mystics, Spanish poets

STATUS: *Priest, mystic, Doctor of the Church*

BORN: *1542, Fontiveros, Spain*

DIED: *1591, Ubeda, Spain*

VENERATED BY: *Roman Catholic Church, by Discalced Carmelites; in Spain*

CANONIZED: *1726*

SYMBOLS: *In Carmelite habit, barefooted, writing*

O Blessed Jesus, grant me stillness of soul in Thee. Let Thy mighty calmness reign in me. Rule me, O thou King of gentleness, King of peace. Give me control, control over my words, thoughts and actions. From all irritability, want of meekness, want of gentleness, O dear Lord, deliver me. By thine own deep patience give me patience, stillness of soul in Thee. Make me in this, and in all, more and more like Thee. Amen.

Maria Di Rosa

Originally named Paola Francesca Di Rosa and later known as Maria Crocifissa Di Rosa, Maria di Rosa was one of nine children born to a wealthy family. Her mother was a countess and her father was a successful industrialist. Her early education was at the convent of the Visitation Sisters, but after her mother's death, she left school and began working at her father's spinning mill. Here, she took notice of the poor working conditions around her. By the time she turned nineteen, she was managing the spinning mill and began making efforts to improve the living and working conditions of the female employees. She also saw to their spiritual needs, something her father encouraged. Still, he began looking for suitors for her, thinking she should marry, but she turned them all down. She asked her priest to speak to her father, letting him know she had another vocation in mind. When a cholera epidemic swept Brescia, she tended the ill at a local hospital. She founded a school for the deaf and later established a religious order, the Ancelle della carità (Handmaids of Charity) in 1840, which was devoted to caring for the sick and the poor.

PATRON SAINT OF: *Ancelle della carità*

STATUS: *Nun, founder of the Ancelle della carità*

BORN: *November 6, 1813, Brescia, Napoleonic Kingdom*

DIED: *December 15, 1855, Brescia, Kingdom of Lombardy–Venetia*

VENERATED BY: *Roman Catholic Church*

CANONIZED: *1954*

SYMBOLS: *Nun's habit*

Lord, hear the prayers of those who recall the devoted life of the virgin Saint Maria Crocifissa di Rosa. Guide us on our way and help us to grow in love and devotion as long as we live. We ask this through Jesus Christ, your Son who lives and reigns with You and the Holy Spirit, one God, forever and ever. Amen.

Honorat KoĐmiĐski

H onorat KoĐmiĐski experienced a religious crisis at the age of eleven, and was not observant for much of his youth. It was only after his arrest in 1846—when Russian soldiers suspected him of being a member of a secret organization—and subsequent imprisonment in Warsaw Citadel that he found his faith once again. He was released from prison a year later after contracting typhus, and chose to enter the Order of Friars Minor Capuchin in Lubartów only a year after that.

After he was ordained, he worked as a teacher from 1853 to 1855, then went on to help found the Felician Sisters congregation. Russia decreed the abolition of religious orders in 1863, and so the presence of occupying Russian soldiers forced KoĐmiĐski to manage his numerous communities in secret. Despite government pressure, KoĐmiĐski oversaw the survival of the Polish Church during the period of Russian repression following the Polish revolt of 1864. He founded an astounding total of 24 religious congregations during his lifetime (eight of which were later disbanded), and still he had time to author 42 volumes of sermons and 21 volumes of letters.

STATUS: *Priest*

BORN: *October 16, 1829, Biała Podlaska, Congress Poland*

DIED: *December 16, 1916, Nowe Miasto nad PilicĐ, Mazowieckie, Vistula Land*

VENERATED BY: *Roman Catholic Church*

BEATIFIED: *1988*

SYMBOLS: *Franciscan habit*

O God, You willed to give to your priest, Blessed Honoratus, a spirit of tender love for souls to reconcile them with You.

Through his intercession may we taste the sweetness of your forgiveness and be joined with You in perfect charity.

We ask this through our Lord Jesus Christ, your Son, who lives and reigns with you and the Holy Spirit, one God, for ever and ever. Amen.

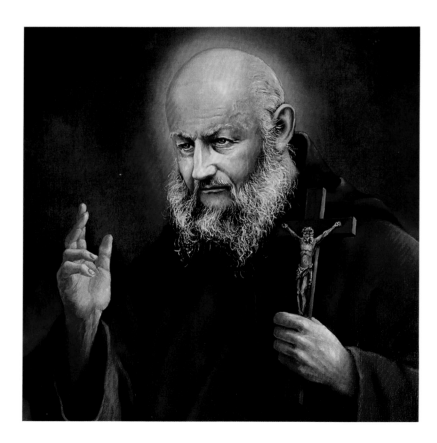

John of Matha

Legend has it, while celebrating his first Mass after his ordination in 1197, John of Matha had a vision of an angel with two captives, one a Christian, the other a Moor. This led to his founding the following year, with the hermit Felix of Valois, the Order of the Most Holy Trinity (the Trinitarians). Its purpose was to free Christians from "the captivity they groaned under among the infidels," in other words, to free those Crusaders held prisoner by the Muslims. (In addition to the Crusades, from the 8th to the 15th century Christians were at risk of capture or kidnapping from annual Muslim raids around the Mediterranean. As a result a number of "rescue" orders were formed during these times.)

The Order, still active today and still ministering to those in prison, expanded rapidly from its first home north of Paris. One-third of all its revenues were set aside to ransom prisoners. An initial visit to Tunis in 1201 made by members of the Order saw the release of 186 captives. John himself journeyed to Tunis in 1202 and 1210, returning respectively with 110 and 120 prisoners.

PATRON SAINT OF:
Prisoners

STATUS: *Priest, founder*

BORN: *June 23, 1160, Provence, France*

DIED: *December 17, 1213, Rome, Italy*

VENERATED BY: *Roman Catholic Church*

CANONIZED: *1666*

SYMBOLS: *Depicted in white Trinitarian habit with blue and red cross*

O God, You were pleased to institute by heavenly direction, through St. John, the order of the Holy Trinity, for redeeming captives from the power of the Saracens; grant, we implore You, that by the suffrage of his merits, we may be delivered by Your grace from captivity of soul and body. This we ask through our Lord Jesus Christ, Your Son. Amen.

Flannan of Killaloe

18

PATRON SAINT OF:
Killaloe, County Clare

STATUS: *Bishop.*

BORN: *c. 8th century, County Clare, Ireland*

DIED: *778*

VENERATED BY: *Roman Catholic Church*

CANONIZED:
Pre-Congregation

SYMBOLS: *Mitre, staff, hooded robe*

O God, strengthen our faith so that our lives may more eloquently bespeak Your Holy Word. May our lives, like St. Flannan's preaching, bring conversion of mind and heart to others. This we ask through Christ our Lord. Amen.

Saint Flannan (Flannán mac Toirrdelbaig), who is venerated by both Ireland and Scotland, was the son of Turlough, an Irish chieftain. He was educated by the monk, St. Molua, who taught him how to "till, sow, harvest, grind, winnow, and bake for the monks." Despite his family's disapproval, he later went on to become a monk himself at Molua's monastery. Flannan then set off on a pilgrimage to Rome by sea; some legends state that he floated all the way to Rome on a millstone. Pope John IV consecrated him upon his arrival, naming him the first bishop of Killaloe. From then on, he traveled the countryside as a teacher and missionary . . . working the occasional miracle, all in the style of a classic Celtic saint. In fact, his preaching was so convincing that even Flannan's elderly father decided to become a monk under Saint Colman's guidance. When Colman blessed Turlough, he noted that seven of his descedants would be kings. Flannan, fearing such a fate, prayed to be spared, and disfiguring scars appeared on his face. Flannan was also known for his peacemaking efforts; he often intervened between opposing chieftains to keep their clan wars from escalating unnecessarily.

A STAINED GLASS DEPICTION OF
FLANNAN OF KILLALOE

Anastasius I

Very little is known of the life of Pope Saint Anastasius I, and even less is known of his youth. It is said that Anastasius was a very pious child, and that this trait followed him into his adult life. He had no interest in wealth or material possessions. He was married, however, and had a son at a relatively young age, but never remarried after the death of his wife. He became pope on the 27th of November, 399, and became one of the first public figures in the church to argue against the heretical writings of Egyptian theologian, Origen. During his reign Anatasius also encouraged Catholics in North Africa to fight Donatism, a heresy that maintained Christian clergy must be faultless for their ministry to be effective and their prayers and sacraments to be valid. It was Anastasius' decree that clerics should stand and bow their heads during the reading of the Gospel during Mass. He served for only two years before his death in 401, and—unusually—was succeeded by his son, Innocent I.

STATUS: *Pope*

BORN: *c. 4th century Rome*

DIED: *December 19, 401, Rome*

VENERATED BY: *Roman Catholic Church*

CANONIZED: *Pre-Congregation*

SYMBOLS: *Papal regalia*

O God, in Your goodness and wisdom You raise up leaders for Your Church who are rooted in Your Word and Your Will. Through the intercession of Your servant, St. Anastasius I, may we be loyal to our Faith in following their directions. This we ask through Christ our Lord. Amen.

IVORY CARVING OF ANASTASIUS I

Dominic of Silos

Dominic was born to a family of peasants and worked as a shepherd in his youth. After joining the Benedictines at the Monasteries of San Millan de la Cogolla, he was eventualy ordained as a priest. He rose to became master of novices and then prior, but after opposing the intention of King Garcia Sanchez III of Navarre to annex the monastery lands, he and two fellow monks were driven out. Under the protection of King Ferdinand I of Leon, he took refuge in Silos at the decaying Abbey of St. Sebastion. With the inspiration of the reforms taking place at Cluny, he chose to rebuild the monastery, in both the physical and spiritual sense. The cloisters were constructed in the Romanesque style and a new scriptorium turned the monstary into a center of book design and scholarship. The proceeds from a gold and silver workshop were offered to charity. The monastery soon became one of the centers of the Mozarabic (an Andalusi Romance language) liturgy and was also able to preserve the Visigothic script of ancient Spain.

PATRON SAINT OF:
Captives, pregnant women, shepherds, invoked against rabies, insects

STATUS: *Abbot*

BORN: *c. 1000 AD, Spain*

DIED: *December 20, 1073, Santo Domingo de Silos, Spain*

VENERATED BY: *Roman Catholic Church*

CANONIZED: PRE-CONGREGATION

SYMBOLS: *Abbot surrounded by the Seven Virtues; mitred abbot enthroned with a book, a veil tied to his crozier*

O God, we ask that blessed St. Dominc of Silo intercede for us as we prepare for our academic challenges. Help us complete the tasks needed to move forward to a successful outcome with the encouragement and guidance of the saint who turned a decaying abbey into a center of learning, and who valued both scholarship and spiritual growth. This we ask in the name of Jesus Christ, your Son. Amen.

SAINT DOMINIC ENTHRONED AS ABBOT BY BARTOLOMÉ BERMEJO (15TH CENTURY)

Peter Canisius

The first Dutchman to become a Jesuit, Canisius was a key figure in the Counter-Reformation, a tireless and resourceful teacher, preacher, diplomat, and, above all, theologian on behalf of what had, for a time, looked a seriously beleaguered Catholic Church.

Canisius was ordained in Rome in 1547, and then helped to establish Cologne's first Jesuit outpost. By 1549, he was teaching theology at Ingolstadt in south Germany. In 1552, he was sent to Vienna, where again he taught theology. His impact was such that a year later he was asked to become the city's bishop. He refused, continuing instead on a near endless series of journeys across central Europe, buttressing Catholic teaching and preaching, and founding four Jesuit colleges.

Canisius's most lasting legacy was a catechism in German, first published in 1558 and issued in 200 editions in Canisius's lifetime alone. When in Fribourg, he claimed he had a vision of the 4th-century saint, Nicholas of Myra (Dec. 6), who instructed him to give up his life of travel and remain in the city. Canisius obeyed, and wrote voluminously for the remaining 20 years of his life.

PATRON SAINT OF: *The Catholic press; Germany*

STATUS: *Priest, Doctor of the Church*

BORN: *1521, Nijmegen, Holland*

DIED: *1597, Fribourg, Switzerland*

VENERATED BY: *Roman Catholic Church, by Jesuits*

CANONIZED: *1925*

SYMBOLS: *Sun with rays*

O God, who for the defense of the Catholic faith made the priest Saint Peter Canisius strong in virtue and in learning, grant, through his intercession, that those who seek the truth may joyfully find You, their God, and that your faithful people may persevere in confessing You. Through our Lord Jesus Christ, your Son, who lives and reigns with you in the unity of the Holy Spirit, one God, for ever and ever. Amen.

A MINIATURE OF CANISIUS PAINTED AFTER HIS DEATH BY AN UNKNOWN ARTIST. CANISIUS REMAINS ONE OF ONLY TWO FIGURES TO HAVE BEEN DECLARED A DOCTOR OF THE CHURCH ON THE SAME DAY AS HIS CANONIZATION.

Anastasia

Anastasia is a shadowy figure, about whom numerous legends abound. She nevertheless remains widely venerated, especially in southeast Europe. She is said to have been married to a Roman nobleman, Publius. When Publius discovered that Anastasia was a Christian, secretly baptized by her mother, he ordered her to be treated like a slave. She rejoiced at this opportunity to serve Christ. Publius died on a mission to Persia, and she subsequently devoted her life to ministering to those Christians imprisoned for their faith, performing numerous works of charity.

Despite a number of miraculous interventions during Anastasia's trial, she appears to have been martyred during the Diocletian persecution in 304. In 460, her relics may have been transferred to Constantinople. An account that she was beheaded on the island of Palmaria is purely legendary. All that is certain is that a woman named Anastasia was martyred in Sirmium and that her memory was kept alive in that city.

PATRON SAINT OF:
Housewives, female slaves, widows

STATUS: *Martyr*

BORN: *2nd century, possibly Rome, Italy*

DIED: *December 25, 304 AD, Sirmium, modern Serbia*

VENERATED BY: *Roman Catholic Church, Eastern Orthodox Church, Eastern Catholic Church, Coptic Orthodox Church*

CANONIZED:
Pre-Congregation

SYMBOLS: *Shown With a martyr's cross*

St. Anastasia, you were born in a society that was hostile to the Christian Faith. Though Christians were often persecuted, your mother ensured that you were raised in the Faith that she loved. . . The education in the Faith you received as a child laid the foundation for your virtuous, holy life that eventually ended in martyrdom. Pray for me, that my love and gratitude for the Faith may never waver. Pray that I may live a life of faithfulness, as you did. Amen.

One legend tells of Anastasia traveling to Aquileia to tend to the sick, and she is regarded as having healing properties by the Eastern churches.

John of Kanty

Despite his low birth, John was immensely learned. He attended Kraków Academy, becoming a Doctor of Philosophy in 1418, and after his ordination, was made rector of the school of the Canons Regular of the Most Holy Sepulcher in Miechow. He accepted a professorship at the university and eventually became director of the theology department. In physics, he helped develop Jean Buridan's theory of impetus, thus anticipating the work of Galileo and Newton.

John was a man of great sanctity and simplicity with no interest in material goods, giving to the poor much of what little he had. His obvious brilliance combined with long-suffering humility aroused considerable jealousy in some segments of the university. In 1431, these enemies succeeded in having him made parish priest of an obscure Bohemian town. When he was recalled to Kraków eight years later, his parishioners, who had initially deeply suspicious of John, begged him to stay. He slept on the bare floor and eschewed meat, and made four pilgrimages to Rome—all on foot—and one to the Holy Land. "Fight all error," he said, "but do it with good humor, patience, kindness, and love."

PATRON SAINT OF: *Kraków University; Lithuania, Poland*

STATUS: *Priest, theologian*

BORN: *June 1390, Kanty, Poland*

DIED: *December 24, 1473, Kraków, Poland*

VENERATED BY: *Roman Catholic Church, in Poland*

CANONIZED: *1767*

SYMBOLS: *Professor's gown, giving clothes to the poor*

Grant, we pray, almighty God, that by the example of the Priest Saint John of Kanty we may advance in knowledge of holy things and by showing compassion to all, may gain forgiveness in your sight. Through our Lord Jesus Christ, your Son, who lives and reigns with you in the unity of the Holy Spirit, one God, for ever and ever. Amen.

Tarsilla and Emiliana

These nobly born Roman sisters, Tarsilla and Emiliana, were two of the three paternal aunts of St. Gregory the Great . . . and it was he who touchingly preserved their story. They are venerated as virgins, as they took vows of chastity together and resolved to dedicate themselves to lives of prayer and austerity. They renounced all worldly things from a very young age and remained in their father's house, which they treated as a convent. It is said that they spent so much time praying that their knees and elbows became arthritically stuck, bent in the position of prayer. The sisters fasted regularly and were well known for their intense levels of self-deprivation. It is believed that Tarsilla saw a vision of their ancestor, St. Felix III, welcoming her into heaven—"a palace of marvelous beauty"— shortly before her death. Tarsilla herself then appeared to Emiliana in a vision to call her into heaven, and Emiliana died only a few days later.

PATRON SAINT OF:
Single laywomen

STATUS: *Virgins, hermits*

BORN: *c. 6th century, Rome*

DIED: *December 24 c. 550 (Tarsilla); January 5, c. 550 (Emiliana), Rome*

VENERATED BY: *Roman Catholic Church*

CANONIZED:
Pre-Congregation

SYMBOLS: *Two sisters praying*

Lord, Just as Tarsilla and Emiliana made of their home a holy sanctuary for prayer and contemplation, let me find the same peace in my surroundings, seeking a quiet spot where I may offer my thanks for your benevolence and your many blessings. Amen.

Birth of Jesus

Tthis very significant feast day is reserved for the celebration of the birth of Christ to the Blessed Virgin Mary. It has no saints associated with it and is preceded by Advent, which begins on the fourth Sunday before this date. The Christmas feast starts on the evening of December 24 and continues until Epiphany, January 6.

The birth of Christ probably occurred in 5 BC, as Herod the Great died in 4 BC. For the Western churches, December 25 was selected during the 4th century revision of the liturgical calendar, as the exact date is unknown. It may have been chosen to counter various pagan festivals that celebrated the return of the Sun after the winter solstice in the Northern Hemisphere. In the Eastern Orthodox churches, Nativity and Epiphany were celebrated together on January 6. Yet December 25 has now become an almost global day of peace, celebration, and meditation. Much symbolism associated with Christmas—decorated trees, Santa Claus, carol singing, and gift giving—derives from German traditions popularized in the 19th century.

The story of the Nativity *(captured brilliantly below by the Dutch painter Geertgen tot Sint Jans).* derives mainly from the Gospel of St. Luke. Having traveled from their home in Nazareth to Bethlehem in order to enroll in a census, Joseph and the heavily pregnant Mary find no rooms, but are lodged in a stable. Christ is born and laid in a manger, with angels in attendance.

STATUS: *Son of God*

BORN: *5 BC, Bethlehem, Israel*

DIED: *28 AD, Jerusalem, Israel*

VENERATED BY: *By all Christian denominations*

SYMBOLS: *Cross, crown of thorns, dove, shown with Apostles and children, preaching, stigmata*

Deliver us from evil by the blessing which Christ brings, and teach us to be merry with clear hearts. May the Christmas morning make us happy to be thy children, and Christmas evening bring us to our beds with grateful thoughts, forgiving and forgiven, for Jesus' sake. Amen.

Stephen

S tephen is celebrated as the first Christian martyr, or protomartyr, but little is known of his early life. He was likely born a Greek-speaking Jew in Jerusalem, and he probably converted to Christianity after the Crucifixion. According to the Acts of the Apostles he was one of the Seven Deacons of the early church appointed by the Apostles to help and serve them, among other tasks distributing alms to the poor and Greek-speaking widows (Acts 6–7). Early Hellenic Christians like Stephen were instrumental in attempting to divorce Christianity from the Jewish Temple and Mosaic Law, and to open the faith to Gentiles, an initiative that would later be supported by St. Paul (Jan. 25). Stephen advocated this before the Jewish council of the Sanhedrin (Acts 7:2–53), also accusing the Jewish orthodoxy of conspiring in the murder of Jesus. Enraged by what they considered his blasphemy, the councilors demanded that he be immediately stoned to death without trial. Stephen prayed that the Lord would receive his spirit and that his killers would be forgiven, then sank to his knees and "fell asleep."

PATRON SAINT OF:
Deacons, stonemasons, coffinmakers, horses, sufferers from headaches

STATUS: *Deacon, Martyr*

BORN: *c. 5 AD, Jerusalem, Israel*

DIED: *c. 35 AD, Jerusalem, Israel*

VENERATED BY: *Roman Catholic Church, Eastern Orthodox church, Oriental Orthodoxy, Church of the East, Lutheranism*

CANONIZED:
Pre-Congregation

SYMBOLS: *Palm of martyrdom, pile of rocks*

Stephen, Stephen, I pray that you hear me. Truly my need is great when it impels me to ask for help even of those by whom I deserve to be punished. But you and all the saints are so full of such wealth from the unending fount of all goodness, that you delight rather to free by your goodness those whom by justice you are able to condemn. Amen.

THE MARTYRDOM OF ST. STEPHEN, ALTHOUGH WELL KNOWN, WAS NOT A WIDELY ILLUSTRATED SUBJECT BEFORE THE COUNTER-REFORMATION, WHEN THE PASSION OF THE SUBJECT PROVIDED IDEAL MATERIAL FOR PAINTERS SUCH AS PETER PAUL RUBENS AND REMBRANDT VAN RIJN (ABOVE, 1625).

John the Evangelist

The son of Zebedee and brother of James the Greater (July 25), John was a fisherman in Galilee, until he and James became Jesus' disciples. John accompanied Jesus throughout His ministry, becoming known as the "Beloved Disciple." At the Last Supper, John asked Jesus who would betray Him, and John was the only one not to desert Him during the Passion, remaining at the foot of the Cross. Jesus appointed John guardian of the Blessed Virgin Mary, and he cared for her after both the Crucifixion and the Ascension. John was also the first disciple to meet Jesus after the Resurrection. Jesus called John and James "the Sons of Thunder," and they both played leading roles in the first Christian community in Jerusalem. John is often viewed as second only to Peter in seniority among the Apostles. Peter and John were arrested for preaching in the Temple and went on a missionary journey to Samaria together. John made later journeys to Ephesus to establish the Church there.

PATRON SAINT OF:
Love, loyalty, friendships, authors, literature

STATUS: *Apostle, evangelist*

BORN: *c. 15 AD, Bethesda*

DIED: *c. 100 AD*

VENERATED BY: *All Christian churches that venerate saints*

CANONIZED:
Pre-Congregation

SYMBOLS: *Eagle, chalice, scrolls*

O Glorious Saint John, you were so loved by Jesus that you merited to rest your head upon his breast, and to be left in his place as a son to Mary. Obtain for us an ardent love for Jesus and Mary. Let me be united with them now on earth and forever after in heaven. Amen.

"St John the Evangelist" by Domenichino (Domenico Zampieri), 1620s

20,000 Martyrs of Nicomedia

PATRON SAINT OF:
Persecuted Christians

STATUS: *Martyrs*

BORN: *Late 3rd century*

DIED: *Between 303 and 311*

VENERATED BY: *Roman Catholic Church, Eastern Orthodox Church, Orientaly Orthodoxy, Anglican Communion, Lutheranism*

CANONIZED:
Pre-Congregation

SYMBOLS: *Martyr's crown, martyr's palm*

In the name of the great and mighty power of God I invoke the sublime influence of the Martyrs of Nicomedia; answer the resolve of my devotion with success in all that I do. Make level the path before me and clear every obstacle in my way. I bare my heart to you and place all worry and care into your holy hands. Free me from all evil. Smite those who would do me harm. In the night be my lantern and my solace. In the daylight be my guide and my protector. Through the intercession of the martyrs of Nicomedia, in Christ Jesus hear my prayers. Amen.

Nicomedia was an ancient city in western Anatolia, located near to Byzantium (later Constantinople). It was the capital of the Roman province of Bithynia (modern Izmit, Turkey) and Pontus, and Diocletian chose it as his eastern capital when he divided the empire in 293. In 303, the imperial palace burned down, and Diocletian's co-ruler Galerius insisted that Christians were responsible. Hitherto relatively tolerant toward Christians, Diocletian unleashed what has become known as the Great Persecution. In Nicomedia, according to some scholars, the event took place because then emperor Maximian, returning in victory over the Ethiopians, demanded sacrifices to thank the gods. The Christians refused and so Maximium and his soldiers supposedly entered a church where 20,000 worshippers were celebrating Christmas. The Christians again refused, and the church was set alight. Those that survived were tortured to death.

This feast day is another example of the demonizing of pagans by Christian hagiographers, as a total of 20,000 victims, even spread over several years, is almost certainly an exaggeration. Historians believe it is more likely that between 3,000 and 3,500 Christians were put to death in this period.

MINIATURE FROM THE MENOLOGION OF BASIL II HONORING THE MARTYRS OF NICOMEDIA

Thomas Becket

Probably the most significant English saint, Thomas Becket embodies the clash between Church and State that was to dominate the English Reformation 400 years later. Thomas was born to a prosperous mercer in Cheapside, London, and was educated at Merton Priory in England and in Paris. After being ordained a deacon, he studied at Bologna and Auxerre, qualifying as a civil and canon lawyer. He was appointed Archdeacon of Canterbury in 1154, the same year 21-year-old Henry II came to the English throne. Henry made Thomas chancellor in 1155. They became close friends and confidants, and Thomas lived the privileged life of a royal favorite.

In 1162 Henry appointed a resisting Thomas Archbishop of Canterbury. Yet after a confrontation at a royal council in Northampton in 1164, Thomas fled to France, remaining in exile for six years. When the Archbishop of York crowned Henry's son, Prince Henry, heir to the throne, specifically defying Thomas's coronation rights as Archbishop of Canterbury, Thomas excommunicated him. On December 29, four of Henry's knights rode to Canterbury and cut Thomas down as he was performing a service in the cathedral.

PATRON SAINT OF:
Secular clergy

STATUS: *Bishop, martyr*

BORN: *December 21, 1118, Cheapside, London*

DIED: *December 29, 1170, Canterbury, England*

VENERATED BY: *Roman Catholic Church, Anglican Communion, in France*

CANONIZED:
1173

SYMBOLS: *Sword, miter, chains of office*

Father, you confirm the true faith with the crown of martyrdom. May the prayers of St Thomas Becket give us the courage to proclaim our faith by the witness of our lives. Through our Lord Jesus Christ, your Son, who lives and reigns with you in the unity of the Holy Spirit, one God, for ever and ever. Amen.

BECKET WAS SLAIN BY HENRY II'S KNIGHTS WHILE CONDUCTING A SERVICE IN CANTERBURY CATHEDRAL DURING THE FEAST OF CHRISTMAS. THIS IMAGE IS FROM A GERMAN DEVOTIONAL CYCLE BY MEISTER FRANCKE CELEBRATING THOMAS'S LIFE AND MARTYRDOM (C.1450).

30

PATRON SAINT OF:
Evesham Abbey

STATUS: *Bishop*

BORN: *Mid-7th century,
Worcester, England*

DIED: *December 30, 717,
Evesham, England*

VENERATED BY: *Roman
Catholic Church, Easstern
Orthodox Church, by
Benedictines*

CANONIZED:
Pre-Congregation

SYMBOLS: *A fish and a key*

*In the face of opposition even from
your peers you stood strong in your
faith and stood up for your beliefs
through God. May we do the same
with your help when faced with
adversity, especially as it relates to
God and our faith. Amen.*

Egwin

E gwin was born in Worcester and was of noble, even royal, blood, being a
descendant of Mercian kings. He may have been nephew to King Aethelred of
Mercia. Once he had become a monk, scholars claim that the king, the clergy, and the
people all demanded his elevation to bishop. And so he was consecrated in 693. As
a bishop he was known as a protector of orphans and widows and a fair judge. Yet he
struggled with the local population over the acceptance of Christian morality, especially
Christian marriage and clerical celibacy. His zeal as a reformer created enemies, and
he was denounced to the king and the archbishop of Canterbury and was forced to
step down. Seeking vindication, he vowed to make a pilgrimage to the pope in Rome
and prepared by locking shackles on his feet and throwing the key into the River Avon.
Later, a fish was caught in the River Tiber and in its mouth was the same key. When it
was brought to Sylvester, and it miraculously proved to unlock his shackles, the Pope
absolved him of any crimes. Returning to England, he founded Evesham Abbey, one
of medieval England's great Benedictine houses.

SCENES FROM THE LIFE OF SAINT EGWIN, ST LAWRENCE'S CHURCH, EVESHAM. THE GLASS IS BY
GEOFFREY WEBB FROM 1943.

Sylvester I

Pope Sylvester's pontificate lasted 21 years (314–35) and is one of the longest, certainly in the early years of the papacy. It lay entirely within the imperial reign of Constantine (306–37), and Sylvester benefited from Constantine's introduction of Christianity as the official religion of the Roman empire under the Edict of Milan in 313. At this critical and advantageous stage, however, Sylvester apparently did little apart from beginning to consolidate the central position of the Church of Rome. Nevertheless, the Holy City gained considerably from Constantine's patronage. Sylvester oversaw the foundation of the first basilica of St. Peter and of the Basilica Constantiniana, which became the pope's palace and cathedral, now St. John Lateran, the second most important basilica in Rome. Two myths attach to Sylvester: that Constantine conferred primacy on Sylvester over all other patriarchs, although the document, the Donation of Constantine, proved to be a forgery; and, secondly, that Sylvester baptized Constantine (who was in fact baptized on his death bed, three years after Sylvester's death). This baptism became a popular subject in art.

PATRON SAINT OF: *Benedictines, Sylvestrines; Feroleto Antico, Nonatola*

STATUS: *Pope*

BORN: *285 AD, Rome, Italy*

DIED: *December 31, 335 AD, Rome, Italy*

VENERATED BY: *Roman Catholic Church, Eastern Orthodox Church (January 2), Anglican Communion, Lutheranism, Armenian Apostolic Church*

CANONIZED: *Pre-Congregation*

SYMBOLS: *Chained dragon or bull, miter*

Come, O Lord, to the help of your people, sustained by the intercession of Pope Saint Sylvester, so that, running the course of this present life under your guidance, we may happily attain life without end.

Through our Lord Jesus Christ, your Son. Amen.

POPE SYLVESTER I BEING GIVEN THE DONATION BY CONSTANTINE. THE EVENT PROVED TO BE A FABRICATION, AND THE DOCUMENT A FORGERY.

GLOSSARY OF EMBLEMS, SYMBOLS, AND ATTRIBUTES

A

Acorns Brigid of Kildare

Alms box John of God

Ampulla Remigius of Reims

Anchor Clement I

Angel (winged person) Matthew the Evangelist

Apples Swithun (with raindrops)

Apron with bread and flowers Casilda

Armor Alexander Nevsky, George, Joan of Arc, Louis, Martin, Wenceslaus. *See also* Soldier

Arrow(s) Edmund, Giles, Sebastian, Canute IV

Axe Alphege (sometimes cleaving skull), Boniface (with oak), Cyprian of Carthage (with crown), Jude, Matthias the Apostle

B

Balls, three Nicholas of Myra

Baptismal font *See* Font (baptismal)

Basket with food Elisabeth of Hungary, Elizabeth of Portugal, John of God, Dorothy Frances of Rome

Bear Columban, Seraphim of Sarov

Bees, Beehive Ambrose (with scourge), Bernard (honey-tongued), Isidore of Seville, John Chrysostom

Bell Antony (with pig), Pedro de San José Betancur, Peter Nolasco

Birds Francis

Blackbirds Kevin of Glendalough

Blood, drops of Rita of Cascia (on forehead). *See also* Stigmata

Boar Quiricus and Julitta

Boat Jude the Apostle, Simon the Apostle. *See also* Ship

Book Often with a pen or quill, generally associated with scholars and writers. Hilary of Poitiers (with quill), Paul the Apostle (with sword). The four Evangelists are usually shown brandishing or writing their respective Gospels, frequently with an indication of divine inspiration, and often accompanied by other identifying emblems: Matthew (with spear, sword or halberd, or moneybags); Mark (with lion); Luke (with ox); John (with eagle, chalice, or snake). *See also* Pen, Scroll

Bowl John of God (two around neck)

Bread Nicholas of Tolentino. *See also* Loaves of bread

Breasts, on a dish Agatha

Bridge Botolph (bridge often represented by a chevron), Swithun

Building Founders of basilicas, churches, monasteries, abbeys, and other institutions are often shown holding a small building. Willibald often shown overseeing construction of a building

Bull Blandina, Eustace, Fermín/Ferminius, Saturninus, Sylvester I. *See also* Cattle

C

Candles Blaise (two, crossed), Brigid of Kildare, Gudula

Cannon Barbara

Capstan Erasmus (Elmo)

Captives *See* Prisoners

Cardinal's hat Bonaventure, Robert Bellarmine, Jerome

Carpenter's square Joseph, Thomas the Apostle (with spear)

Cattle Perpetua and Felicity (heifers), Walston (pair of calves)

Cauldron Vitus

Cave(s) Often associated with hermits. Thecla chose to be immured in one, her hand protruding from fissure

Centurion's uniform Longinus

Chains Leonard

Chalice Barbara, James of the Marches (with snake), John the Evangelist (with snake), Bonaventure (with cross), John Chrysostom (with book). *See also* Ciborium, Holy Grail

Chasuble Ignatius of Loyola

Children John Baptiste de la Salle, Quiricus (as child)

Choughs Thomas Becket

Church *See* Building

Ciborium Bonaventure, Clare, Dunstan, Norbert

Cloak Angela Merici, James the Greater (pilgrim's cloak), Martin (cut by sword)

Club Fidelis (with nails), Gervase and Protase, James the Less (a fuller's club), Timothy (with stones)

Cobbler's last Crispin and Crispinian

Cockleshell James the Greater

Comb Blaise

Coracle Brendan, Maughold

Corn Walburga

Crocodile Pachomius (on its back)

Crosier Often associated with archbishops and bishops, abbots. Augustine of Canterbury, Augustine of Hippo, Benedict of Nursia. *See also* Staff, Shepherd's crook

Cross Appears in various forms as part of the emblems of innumerable saints: Helena, finder of the "True Cross"; bottony with roundels, Philip the Apostle; inverted, Peter the Apostle; Iona, Columba; Maltese, John, James the Greater, Elizabeth (with withered leaves and heart); red on white, George, Ursula; saltire, Andrew (blue on white), Patrick (green on white); Tau, Antony of Egypt; with rope, Julia of Corsica; with thorns and tears, Joseph of Arimathea

Crown Generally associated with royal saints, kings, queens

Crown of thorns Francis de Sales (with heart), John of God, Louis (with fleur-de-lis), Veronica Giuliani

Crowns (triple) Elisabeth of Hungary, Etheldreda, Eric of Sweden (with waves). *See also* Tiara (triple crown)

Crown with arrows Edmund

Cup Benedict of Nursia (fractured)

D

Daffodil David

Dalmatic Stephen, Vincent of Saragossa

Demons Antony of Egypt

Devil Juliana (winged), Bernard of Montjoux (on chain), Wolfgang (building a church)

Doe, shot by arrow Giles

Dog Bernard of Montjoux, Dominic (with star or taper in mouth), Margaret of Cortona (lapdog), Roche (with bread in mouth), Vitus

Dolphin Lucien of Antioch

Dove Catherine of Alexandria, David, Dunstan, Eulalia, Gregory the Great (perched on shoulder), Joseph (perched on flowering branch or rod), John Chrysostom, Quentin (flying from severed head), Scholastica

Dragon David, Margaret of Antioch (being trampled or with cross in mouth), George, Juliana, Archangel Michael, Perpetua (with ladder), Sylvester I (chained)

E

Eagle John the Evangelist, Wenceslaus (on red banner)

Eggs Swithun (broken)

Epigonation Gregory Nazianzus

Escarbuncle Victor of Marseille

Eucharist Ignatius of Loyola

Eyes, on a dish Lucy

F

Fish Egwin (with key), Simon the Apostle, Archangel Raphael

Fishing net Andrew the Apostle, Wilfrid

Flame Brigid of Kildare

Flaming fire Polycarp, Teresa Benedicta (Edith Stein)

Flayed, flaying knife Bartholomew

Fleur-de-lis Blessed Virgin Mary

Font (baptismal) Birinus, Francis Xavier

Forceps Apollonia (holding tooth)

Fox Boniface

G

Giant/gigantic Christopher

Golden balls Nicholas of Myra

Goose Martin

Greyhound Ferdinand III

Gridiron/griddle Lawrence, Vincent of Saragossa

H

Halberd Jude, Matthias the Apostle, Matthew the Evangelist

Harp Cecilia

Head, severed Denis, John the Baptist, Quentin, Sigfrid of Sweden (usually three in a basket), Winfred (with well)

Heart Augustine of Hippo (often flaming, pierced by crossed arrows), Blessed Virgin Mary (winged, often pierced by sword), Catherine of Siena (with cross in it), Francis de Sales (with crown of thorns), Ignatius of Antioch, Teresa (pierced by arrow), Valentine (with arrow); the most frequent *ex-voto* symbol

Hind Eustace, Giles, Hubert, Neot

HIS Inscription usually associated with members/ founders of Society of Jesus (Jesuits), especially Ignatius of Loyola; also Bernardine of Siena

Holy Grail Joseph of Arimathea

Horn Cornelius

Horse/on horseback George, Longinus

J

Jar of ointment Mary Magdalene

K

Keys Egwin (with fish), Peter the Apostle (crossed), Zita (in a bunch)

Knife (flaying) Bartholomew

L

Ladder Angela Merici, Joseph, Perpetua (spiked, with dragon), Romuald

Lamb Agnes, John the Baptist (with shepherd's crook or flag)

Lamp/lantern Brigid of Kildare, Christopher, Frances of Rome, Gudula, Lucy, Nilus

Lance Maurice, Canute IV

Leek David

Levitating John Joseph of the Cross, Joseph of Cupertino

Lightning Barbara

Lily Blessed Virgin Mary and those devoted to or closely associated with her: Aloysius Gonzaga, Anne, Anthony of Padua (with book), Casimir, Catherine of Siena, Francis Xavier, Gertrude the Great, Joseph (with carpenter's square), Kateri Tekakwitha, Margaret of Hungary

Lion(s) Cuthbert (rampant with cross), Denis (rampant with cross), Ignatius of Antioch, Jerome, Mark the Evangelist (winged), Sabbas, Vitus

Loaves of bread Agatha, Anthony of Padua, Mary of Egypt, Philip the Apostle, Sigfrid of Sweden (in fact heads of his companions)

Lozenges Wilfrid (seven)

M

Martlets Edward the Confessor (with cross)

Medicine box Pantaleon, Cosmas and Damian

Millstone Florian

Miter Generally associated with popes, bishops, and other high-ranking church officials. Three miters with a book, Bernard of Clairvaux, or Bernardine of Siena

Moneybags Matthew the Apostle, Cyril of Jerusalem, Nicholas of Myra

Monstrance Clare of Assisi, Norbert, Paschal Baylon

Moon, crescent Blessed Virgin Mary

Musical instruments Cecilia

O

Oak Boniface, Brigid of Kildare (with wreath of acorns)

Oar Jude, Simon the Apostle

Ointment, pot/jar of Mary Magdalene, Rémy, Walburga

Old/in old age A frequent characteristic, denoting sagacity and wisdom. As a specific attribute: Alferius de la Cava

Olive branch Barnabas the Apostle

Oranges/orange branch Frances of Rome

Ox, winged Luke the Evangelist

P

Pallium/Pall Athanasius (with triangle), Augustine of Canterbury (with four black crosses)

Palm Generally associated with martyrdom. Stephen (with stones)

Pens Cyril of Alexandria, Hilary of Poitiers (with books), Justin (with sword)

Pickax, with miter Leo

Pig, with bell Antony of Egypt

Pillar Simeon Stylites, Simeon Stylites the Younger, stylite hermits generally

Pincers Apollonia (holding tooth)

Pitcher Venerable Bede (gold), Florian (containing water)

Plague sores (buboes) Roch

Pomegranate John of God

Prisoners Peter Claver, Vincent Ferrer

Pulpit Vincent Ferrer

Pyx Clare of Assisi

Q

Quills *See* Pens

R

Raindrops Swithun (with apples)

Raising from the dead Lazarus, Stanislaus

Raven Benedict of Nursia, Boniface, Paul the Hermit

Ring Edward the Confessor

Rod Joseph (flowering)

Rooster Vitus

Rope Judas Iscariot (with pieces of silver)

Rosary Aloysius Gonzaga

Rose(s) Blessed Virgin Mary, Barnabas the Apostle, Cecilia, Elisabeth of Hungary, Rita of Cascia, Thérèse of Lisieux

S

Salmon with ring Kentigern

Salt cellar Rupert of Salzburg

Sari Mother Teresa

Saw James the Lesser, Simon the Apostle

Scourge Ambrose, Catherine of Alexandria, Gervase and Protase

Scroll Symbol frequently associated with significant early Church writers such as the Evangelists, the Christian Fathers, and Doctors of the Church, especially Gregory the Great. *See also* Book

Scythe Walston

Shamrock Patrick

Sheep Geneviève (tending). *See also* Shepherd's crook

Shepherd's crook A frequent symbol for an archbishop, bishop, or abbot; also, specifically, Irenaeus, Paschal

Shield Archangel Gabriel (with spear)

Ship Anselm, Bertin, Brendan, Pedro González, Wilfrid. *See also* Boat

Shoes Crispin, Crispinian

Sickle Isidore the Farmer

Skin Bartholomew, often shown carrying his own

Skull Aloysius Gonzaga, Bruno, Francis Borgia (with crown), Odilo (with crossbones)

Slaves Peter Claver

Snake Patrick, Hilda (three, coiled), James of the Marches (escaping from a chalice), John the Evangelist (with chalice)

Soldier Many saints are shown as soldiers, including George, James the Greater, Joan of Arc, Longinus, Louis, Michael the Archangel, Martin, and Pancras

Spade Fiacre

Spatula Pantaleon

Spear Archangel Gabriel (often with shield), Longinus

Staff Generally used (in the

form of a shepherd's crook) for bishops, abbots, abbesses, or missionaries and pilgrims. Archangel Raphael (with wallet), Bridget of Sweden, Christopher (with lamp), Francis of Paola (with cloak), Gertrude of Nivelle (with mouse), James the Greater (with pilgrim's hat and cloak)

Stag Eustace, Hubert. *See also* Hind

Stake Eulalia

Star(s) Thomas Aquinas, Bruno (seven)

Stigmata Francis of Assisi, Catherine of Siena, Charles of Sezze, Padre Pio

Stones Stephen (with palm), Timothy (with club)

Sun Thomas Aquinas (Sun in Splendor with an eye)

Surgical implements Cosmas and Damian

Swan Hugh of Lincoln, Ludger of Münster

Sword Generally associated with martyrdom (a sword stroke to the neck was the most common Roman method of capital punishment), or fighting for the Church (often in the form of a cross). Frumentius, Justin (with quill), Gervase and Protase, James the Greater (red, in form of cross), Kilian, Paul the Apostle (crossed, or with book); multiple swords: Felicitas, Archangel Michael, Peter of Verona, Stanislaus

T

Table, with food and drink Martha

Taper Gertrude the Great

Tears Our Lady of Sorrows, Joseph of Arimathea, Mary Magdalene

Thorn Jerome, Joseph of Arimathea (thorned cross)

Tiara (triple crown) Generally associated with popes

Tongs Dunstan

Tonsure Usually indicates a deacon of the Church (such as Stephen, Maurice, or Lawrence), or a friar (especially Franciscans)

Tooth Apollonia

Torch, flaming Aidan, Dorothy

Tower Barbara

Trampling Bernard of Clairvaux (demons/the devil), Fidelis (heretics), Archangel Michael (the devil), James the Greater (devils, Moors)

Turtle Kateri Tekakwitha

V

Veil Veronica

W

Walking stick Pedro de San José Betancur. *See also* Staff

Waves Botolph, Eric of Sweden (with crowns)

Well Winfred

Whale Brendan

Wheel Catherine of Alexandria, Quentin (broken)

Widow's clothing Monica

Windlass Erasmus (Elmo)

GLOSSARY OF PATRONAGE

A

Abortions, victims of Catherine of Sweden, Vincent of Saragossa

Accidents Christopher

Accountants Matthew the Apostle

Adultery, victims of Elizabeth of Portugal

Advertisers Bernardine of Siena

Advocates Fidelis

African Americans Peter Claver

Agricultural workers Benedict of Nursia

AIDS/HIV sufferers Aloysius Gonzaga, Damien of Molokai, Marianne Cope

Alcoholics John of God, Martin, Matthias the Apostle, Matt Talbot

Alpine travelers Bernard of Montjoux

Amputees Antony of Egypt

Animals Anthony of Padua, Francis of Assisi, Nicholas of Tolentino

Apologists Catherine of Alexandria

Apoplexy sufferers Wolfgang of Regensburg

Apothecaries Cosmas and Damian, James the Greater, Roch

Apprentices John Bosco

Archaeologists Jerome

Archers George, Nicholas of Myra, Sebastian

Architects Thomas the Apostle

Archivists Jerome

Armorers George

Art dealers John the Evangelist

Arthritis sufferers Alphonsus Liguori, James the Greater

Artillerymen Barbara

Astronauts Joseph of Cupertino

Astronomers Dominic

Athletes Sebastian

Authors John the Evangelist

Automobile drivers Christopher, Frances of Rome

Aviators Joseph of Cupertino

B

Bachelors Benedict Joseph Labre, Casimir, Gerald of Aurillac, Pantaleon, Roch

Bakers Agatha

Bankers Matthew the Apostle

Barbers Cosmas and Damian, Louis IX of France

Basketmakers Antony of Egypt

Beekeepers Ambrose of Milan, Bernard of Clairvaux, Valentine

Beggars Giles of Provence, Martin

Betrothed, the Agnes, Valentine

Bishops Charles Borromeo

Blacksmiths Dunstan

Blindness, the blind Cosmas and Damian, Leger, Lucy, Lutgardis, Parasceva

Blood banks Januarius

Boatmen Francis of Paola

Booksellers John of God

Breast cancer sufferers Agatha

Brewers Amand, Augustine of Hippo, Boniface

Brides Dorothy, Elizabeth of Portugal

Builders Vincent Ferrer

Burn victims John the Evangelist

C

Cab drivers Fiacre, Frances of Rome

Cabinetmakers Joseph

Cancer victims Giles of Provence

Canon lawyers Raymond of Peñafort, Robert Bellarmine

Carpenters Joseph, Matthias the Apostle, Wolfgang of Regensburg

Catechists Charles Borromeo, Robert Bellarmine

Catholic lawyers Thomas More

Catholic press, the Peter Canisius

Catholic publishers John Bosco

Catholic universities Thomas Aquinas

Cattle Felicity

Cavers Benedict of Nursia

Chaplains Quentin

Charity, charity workers Elizabeth of Portugal, Vincent de Paul

Chastity Agnes, Maria Goretti, Mary of Egypt

Chefs/cooks Lawrence

Chest problems, protection from Bernardine of Siena

Childbirth Boniface, Gotthard, Juliana, Lutgardis, Margaret of Antioch

Childless, the Anne and Joachim

Children Clotilde, Nicholas of Myra, Pancras; **abandoned** Jerome Emiliani; **adopted** William of Rochester; **choirs of** Dominic Savio; **death of, dying** Elisabeth of Hungary, Frances of Rome, Perpetua and Felicity; **sick/ill** Quiricus and Julitta; **sons, birth of** Perpetua; **with convulsions** Scholastica

Circus people/performers Julian the Hospitaller

Clairvoyance Clare of Assisi

Cobblers Crispin and Crispinian

Coffinmakers Stephen

Comedians Lawrence

Confessors Alphonsus Liguori, Jean-Baptiste Vianney

Construction workers Thomas the Apostle, Vincent Ferrer

Converts Alban

Counts Gerald of Aurillac

Crops, protection
Agnes, Walburga

Curriers Simon the
Apostle

Customs officials
Matthew the Apostle

D

Dancers Vitus

Dauphins Petronilla

Deacons Stephen

Deafness, the deaf
Cornelius, Francis de Sales

Demons, against Mary
of Egypt

Dentists Apollonia

Disabled, the Gerald of
Aurillac, Giles of Provence,
Lutgardis

Dogs Roch, Vitus

Dyers Lydia Purpuraria

Dying, the Benedict of
Nursia, James the Less, John
of God, Margaret of Antioch

Dysentery sufferers
Polycarp

E

Earache sufferers
Polycarp

Earthquakes, against
Francis Borgia

Ecologists Kateri
Tekakwitha

Ecumenism Cyril and
Methodius

Educators Ignatius of
Loyola, John Baptiste de la
Salle

Embroiderers Clare of
Assisi

Engineers Ferdinand III
of Castile, Patrick

**Environment/
environmentalists**
Francis of Assisi, Kateri
Tekakwitha

Epileptics Antony
of Egypt, Apollinaris,
Christopher, Cornelius,
Giles of Provence, Vitus

Ergotism, against
Antony of Egypt

**Eucharistic
confraternities** Paschal
of Baylon

Exiles Clotilde, Elisabeth
of Hungary, Kateri
Tekakwitha, Margaret of
Antioch

**Eye affliction
sufferers** Augustine of
Hippo, Clare of Assisi, Lucy

F

Fallen women Mary
Magdalene

Falsely accused, the
Dominic, Dominic Savio,
Margaret of Antioch,
Margaret of Cortona

Families Eustace,
Quiricus and Julitta

Farmers Botolph, George,
Isidore the Farmer, Walston

Ferrymen Julian the
Hospitaller

Fever sufferers Barbara,
Geneviève, Mary of Egypt,
Petronilla

Filemakers Theodosius
the Cenobiarch

Fire, protection from
Florian

Firefighters Agatha,
Eustace, Florian, John of
God

Fish Neot

Fishermen Andrew the
Apostle, Anthony of Padua,
Peter the Apostle

Florists Dorothy, Rose
of Lima

Forests Giles of Provence

Foresters John Gualbert

**Frenzy, protection
from** Denis

G

Gallstone sufferers
Benedict of Nursia

**Gamblers/gambling
addicts** Bernardine of
Siena, Cajetan, Camillus de
Lellis

Gardeners Agnes,
Christopher, John the
Gardener

Geese Martin

Gentiles Paul the Apostle

Geometricians Thomas
the Apostle

Girls Agnes;
unmarried Catherine of
Alexandria; **teenage** Maria
Goretti

Glassblowers Mark the
Evangelist

Glaziers Mark the
Evangelist

Goiter sufferers Mark
the Evangelist

Goldsmiths Anastasius
the Persian, Clare of Assisi

Gout sufferers
Apollinaris, Gotthard

Governors Ferdinand III
of Castile

Grandparents Anne
and Joachim, Zechariah and
Elizabeth

Gravediggers Antony of
Egypt

Guides Bona of Pisa

Gunpowder makers
Barbara

H

**Hailstorms,
protection from**
Barnabas the Apostle

Handicapped, the
Angela Merici

Hatmakers James the
Greater

Haymakers Gervase and
Protase

Headache sufferers
Agathius, Anastasius the
Persian, Denis, Pancras,
Stephen, Teresa of Ávila

Hemorrhoid sufferers
Fiacre

**Heresy, fighters
against** Fidelis

Hermits Antony of Egypt,
Giles

Hernia sufferers
Conrad of Piacenza, Cosmas
and Damian

Historians The
Venerable Bede

**Homelessness/the
homeless** Elisabeth
of Hungary, Margaret of
Cortona, Benedict Joseph
Labre

Horses Anthony of Padua,
Giles, Martin, Pontian
and Hippolytus, Stephen,
Vincent de Paul

Horsemen James the
Greater

Hospitals Camillus

de Lellis, John of God, Jude the Apostle, Vincent de Paul; **hospital administrators** Frances Xavier Cabrini

Housewives Anastasia, Anne and Joachim

Hunters/hunting Eustace, Hubert

Hydrophobics Denis

I

Immigrants Frances Xavier Cabrini

Infants Blaise

Innkeepers Julian the Hospitaller, Martin

Insanity, the insane Margaret of Cortona, Theodosius the Cenobiarch

Insect bite sufferers Mark the Evangelist

Internet, the Isidore of Seville

J

Jurists John of Capistrano

Juvenile delinquents Dominic Savio

K

Kidnapping victims Alphege

Kidney disease sufferers Margaret of Antioch

Knights George

Knights Hospitaller John the Almsgiver

L

Laborers Isidore the Farmer, James the Greater, John Bosco, Joseph

Lacemakers John Francis Regis

Launderers Clare of Assisi, Veronica

Lawyers Catherine of Alexandria, Fidelis, Mark the Evangelist

Lay people Frances of Rome

Leatherworkers Bartholomew, Crispin and Crispinian

Leprosy sufferers Damien of Molokai, George, Marianne Cope, Vincent de Paul

Librarians Catherine of Alexandria, Jerome, Lawrence

Light Lucy

Lightning, protection from Barbara

Lions Mark the Evangelist

Locksmiths Dunstan, Quentin

Lost causes Jude the Apostle, Rita of Cascia

Lost objects/ possessions Anthony of Padua, Vincent de Paul

Lovers Valentine

M

Magistrates Ferdinand III of Castile

Mariners Erasmus (Elmo), Francis of Paola, Nicholas of Tolentino

Marital difficulties Edward the Confessor, Marguerite d'Youville, Rita of Cascia

Marriage John Francis Regis

Martyrs Teresa Benedicta of the Cross

Mathematicians Barbara

Mental illness Benedict Joseph Labre, Giles of Provence

Mentally handicapped Joseph of Cupertino

Merchants Nicholas of Myra

Migrants Joseph

Military chaplains John of Capistrano

Millers Leger

Milliners Catherine of Alexandria

Miners Barbara

Miscarriages Catherine of Sweden

Missions Thérèse of Lisieux

Missionaries Francis Xavier, Stephen of Perm

Monks Antony of Egypt, Benedict of Nursia

Moral order Stanislaus

Moralists Alphonsus Liguori

Mothers Monica; **single** Margaret of Cortona; **with babies** Nicholas of Tolentino

Mountain travelers Petronilla

Mountaineers Bernard of Montjoux

Music/Musicians Benedict Biscop, Cecilia, Dunstan

Mystics John of the Cross

N

Natural sciences Albert the Great

Naval officers Francis of Paola

Needleworkers Clare of Assisi

Nettle rash sufferers Benedict of Nursia

Nightwatchmen Peter of Alcántara

Notaries Mark the Evangelist

Nurses Agatha, Camillus de Lellis, Catherine of Alexandria, Cosmas and Damian, John of God

O

Orphans Angela Merici, Jerome Emiliani, Marguerite Bourgeoys, Mariana Paredes y Flores, Mary of the Incarnation, Teresa Benedicta of the Cross, Zoticus

Outcasts Marianne Cope

Oversleeping Vitus

P

Painters Benedict Biscop, John of Fiesole (Fra Angelico), John the Evangelist, Luke the Evangelist

Pandemics, against Edmund

Papacy/Papal Peter the Apostle

Paralysis, protection from Wolfgang of Regensburg

Parents Clotilde, Zechariah and Elizabeth;

loss of Mariana Paredes y Flores

Parish priests Jean-Baptiste Vianney

Parks, park rangers John Gualbert

Pawnbrokers Nicholas of Myra

Peacemakers Barnabas the Apostle, Oliver Plunkett (in Ireland)

Peddlers Lucy

Perjury, protection from Pancras

Pestilence, against Catherine of Siena, Cosmas and Damian

Pets Blaise, George

Philanthropists Katharine Drexel

Philosophers Catherine of Alexandria, Justin

Photographers Veronica

Physicians Cosmas and Damian, Luke the Evangelist, Pantaleon

Piety, people ridiculed for Frances of Rome

Pigs Antony of Egypt

Pilgrims Bona, James the Greater, Roch

Plague, against Christopher, Francis Xavier; **victims** George, Roch, Sebastian

Plowmen, plowboys Fiacre

Plumbers Vincent Ferrer

Poets Cecilia, David, John of the Cross

Poison victims John the Evangelist

Possession, deliverance from Denis, Margaret of Antioch

Poverty, the poor, paupers Anthony of Padua, Ferdinand III of Castile, Marguerite Bourgeoys, Martin, Mary of the Incarnation, Zoticus

Preachers Catherine of Alexandria

Pregnancy/pregnant mothers Dominic of Silos, Joseph, Margaret of Antioch

Printers Augustine of Hippo, John of God, Louis IX of France

Prison guards/wardens Hippolytus

Prisoners Charles of Blois, Dominic of Silos, Ferdinand III of Castile, Germanus, John of Matha, Leonard, Mark the Evangelist, Vincent de Paul

Prostitutes (penitent) Margaret of Cortona, Mary Magdalene

Publishers John of God, John the Evangelist

R

Rabies sufferers Denis, Walburga

Racial justice Katharine Drexel

Rape victims Agnes, Maria Goretti

Refugees Alban

Repentant, the Mary Magdalene

Rheumatism sufferers James the Greater, Kilian

Roasters Lawrence

Runaways Eulalia

S

Sailors Erasmus (Elmo), Nicholas of Myra, Pedro González, Walburga

Salmon Kentigern

Sawyers Simon the Apostle

Scholars Catherine of Alexandria

Schools José de Calasanz

Schoolchildren Benedict of Nursia, John Bosco, José de Calasanz

Scientists Albert the Great

Scrofula sufferers Mark the Evangelist

Secular clergy Thomas Becket

Security guards Matthew the Apostle

Seminarians Charles Borromeo, Gabriel of Our Sorrows

Sexual temptation, sufferers from Margaret of Cortona, Mary of Egypt

Shepherds Dominic of Silos, Paschal of Baylon

Shipwrights Peter the Apostle

Sickness, the sick Angela Merici, Camillus de Lellis, Catherine de' Ricci, Catherine of Siena, Hugh of Lincoln, Jacinta and Francisco Marto, John of God, Mariana Paredes y Flores, Teresa of Ávila, Teresa of the Andes, Theodosius the Cenobiarch

Silversmiths Dunstan

Skiers Bernard of Montjoux

Skin disease sufferers Antony of Egypt, Charles Borromeo, Mary of Egypt

Slaves Anastasia (female), Germanus, Peter Claver

Smallpox, protection from Matthias the Apostle

Snakebite sufferers Vitus

Social workers John Francis Regis, Rose of Lima (in Peru)

Soldiers George, Ignatius of Loyola, Martin, Sebastian

Sore throat sufferers Blaise, Etheldreda

Souls in purgatory Nicholas of Tolentino, Odilo

Stained-glass window makers Mark the Evangelist

Statesmen Thomas More

Stockbrokers Matthew the Apostle

Stomach disease sufferers Erasmus (Elmo), Wolfgang of Regensburg

Stonemasons/stonecutters Barbara, Louis IX of France, Peter the Apostle, Stephen

Storms, against Vitus, Walburga

Stroke sufferers Wolfgang of Regensburg

Students Gabriel of Our Sorrows, Jerome, José de Calasanz, Joseph of Cupertino, Lawrence, Ursula

Sudden death, protection from Barbara, Catherine of Alexandria, Christopher

Surgeons Cosmas and Damian, Luke the Evangelist, Quentin

Surveyors Thomas the Apostle

Swans Hugh of Lincoln

Swordsmen George

Syphilis sufferers Fiacre, George

T

Tailors Martin, Matthias the Apostle

Tanners Bartholomew, Lawrence, Simon the Apostle

Tax collectors Matthew the Apostle

Teachers Catherine of Alexandria, Gregory the Great, John Baptiste de la Salle

Television Clare of Assisi

Temptation, sufferers from Benedict of Nursia, Cyriacus

Theft/thieves, discovery of Gervase and Protase

Theologians Alphonsus Liguori, Augustine of Hippo, Catherine of Alexandria, Thomas the Apostle

Tile makers Fiacre

Toothache sufferers Apollonia, Christopher

Torture victims Alban, Edmund, Eulalia, Pantaleon

Translators Jerome

Travelers Botolph, Christopher, Gertrude of Helfta, Rainerius, Sebastian of Aparicio

Traveling merchants Gotthard

Tuberculosis, sufferers from Pantaleon

U

Unemployed, the Cajetan

Unfortunate, the Jude the Apostle

Unmarried laywomen Gudula

US Special Forces Philip Neri

V

Vegetarians David

Venereal disease sufferers Fiacre

Veterinarians James the Greater

Vinegar merchants Vincent of Saragossa

Violations Vincent of Saragossa

Viticulture/ winemakers Amand, Martin, Vincent of Saragossa

Vocations Alphonsus Liguori, Junípero Serra

Volcanoes, deliverance from Januarius

Volunteers Vincent de Paul

W

Water, protection from Florian

Wax makers Bernard of Clairvaux

Weather Swithun

Wheelwrights Catherine of Alexandria

Widows Anastasia, Bridget of Sweden, Elisabeth of Hungary, Frances of Rome, Marguerite d'Youville, Mary of the Incarnation, Monica, Perpetua

Wild animals Blaise, Francis of Assisi, Theodora of Alexandria

Wine merchants Martin, Vincent of Saragossa

Wives Monica

Wolves Edmund

Woodworkers Joseph

Workers Joseph

Writers of English The Venerable Bede

Y

Youth/the young Aloysius Gonzaga, Casimir

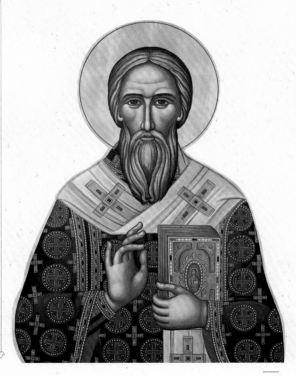

INDEX

George	Apr 23	John of Ávila	May 10	Margaret of Hungary	Jan 18
Gerard Sagredo	Sept 24	John of Beverley	May 7	Marguerite Bourgeoys	Jan 12
Gilbert of Sempringham	Feb 4	John of Capistrano	Oct 23	Maria Di Rosa	Dec 15
Giles of Provence	Sept 1	John of God	Mar 8	Maria Goretti	Jul 6
Giovanni Dominici	Jun 10	John of Kanty	Dec 23	Marian and James	May 6
Godric of Finchale	May 21	John of Matha	Dec 17	Marianne Cope	Jan 23
Gregoria Barbarigo	Jun 18	John of the Cross	Dec 14	Marie Rose Durocher	Oct 6
Gregory of Nyssa	Jan 10	John the Baptist	Jun 24	Maria Soledad	Oct 11
Gregory the Great	Sept 3	John the Evangelist	Dec 27	Mark the Evangelist	Apr 25
Hedwig of Poland	Jul 17	John Theristus	Feb 24	Martha, Mary, and Lazarus	Jul 29
Helena, Mother of Constantine	Aug 18	Jonas and Barachisius	Mar 29	Martin I	Apr 13
Henry II	Jul 13	Josemaría Escrivá de Balaguer	Jun 26	Martin de Porres	Nov 3
Hilarius	Feb 28	Joseph	Mar 19	Martin of Tours	Nov 11
Hilary of Arles	May 5	Josephine Bakhita	Feb 8	Martyrs of Tonkin	Nov 24
Hilary of Poitiers	Jan 13	Joseph of Cupertino	Sept 18	Mary	Jan 1
Hilda of Whitby	Nov 19	Juan Diego	Dec 9	Mary Bertilla Boscardin	Oct 20
Hildegard of Bingen	Sept 17	Juliana	Feb 16	Mary Magdelene	Jul 22
Honorat Koðmiðski	Dec 16	Julian of Norwich	May 13	Mary of Egypt	Apr 3
Hugh of Châteauneuf	Apr 1	Julie Billiart	Apr 8	Mary of the Incarnation	
Ignatious of Antioch	Oct 17	Junipero Serra	Jul 1	(Carmelite)	Apr 18
Ignatious of Loyala	Jul 31	Justin	Jun 1	Matilda of Ringelheim	Mar 14
Irenaeus	Jun 28	Kateri Tekakwitha	Jul 14	Matthew the Apostle	Sept 21
Isabelle of France	Feb 26	Katherine Drexel	Mar 3	Matthias the Apostle	May 14
Isidore of Seville	Apr 4	Kilian	Jul 8	Maximilian Kolbe	Aug 14
Isidore the Laborer	May 15	Laurence Giustiniani	Jan 8	Methodius of Constantinople	Jun 14
James the Greater	Jul 25	Laurence O'Toole	Nov 14	Monica	Aug 27
James the Persian	Nov 27	Lawrence	Aug 10	Mother Teresa	Sept 5
Jane Frances de Chantal	Aug 12	Lawrence of Brindisi	Jul 21	Mungo	Jan 14
Januarius	Sept 19	Leander of Seville	Mar 13	Narcissus of Jerusalem	Oct 29
Jean Baptist de la Salle	Apr 7	Leo IX	Apr 19	Nicholas of Myra	Dec 6
Jean-Baptiste Vianney	Aug 4	Leobinus of Chartres	Sept 15	Nicholas von Flüe	Mar 21
Jean Eudes	Aug 19	Leodegar	Oct 2	Nicodemus of Mammola	Mar 25
Jeanne Delanoue	Aug 17	Leonard of Port Maurice	Nov 26	Norbert of Xanten	Jun 6
Jeanne Jugan	Aug 30	Leo the Great	Nov 10	North American Martyrs	Oct 19
Jerome	Sept 30	Longinus	Mar 15	Notburga	Sept 14
Joan de Lestonnac	Feb 2	Louis IX of France	Aug 25	Odilo of Cluny	May 11
Joan of Arc	May 30	Louise de Marillac	Mar 12	Onouphrios (Onofrio)	Jun 12
John I	May 18	Lucy (Lucia)	Dec 13	Oscar Romero	Mar 24
John XXIII	Jun 3	Ludger of Münster	Mar 26	Osmund	Jul 16
John Bosco	Jan 31	Luigi Monza	Sept 29	Oswald of Northumbria	Aug 5
John Coleridge Patteson		Luke the Evangelist	Oct 18	Oswald of Worcester	Feb 29
and Pacific Martyrs	Sept 20	Lutgardis	Jun 16	Pachomius the Great	May 9
John Chrysostom	Sept 13	Lydia Purpuraria	Aug 3	Padre Pio of Pietrelcina	Sept 23
John Climacus	Mar 30	Macarius of Egypt	Dec 8	Pancras of Rome	May 12
John Duns Scotus	Nov 8	Macrina the Younger	Jul 19	Panteleon	Jul 27
John Francis Regis	Sept 10	Margaret Mary Alacoque	Oct 16	Paschal of Baylón	May 17
John Joseph of the Cross	Mar 5	Margaret of Antioch	Jul 20	Patrick	Mar 17
John Nepomucene Neumann	Jan 5	Margaret of Cortona	Feb 22	Paul Miki and Companions	Feb 6

PUBLISHER'S ACKNOWLEDGMENTS

For information on any photographs other than sourced from Wikimedia Commons or public domain websites,
please contact: info@moseleyroad.com

Books
Donald Attwater *The Penguin Dictionary of Saints* (Harmondsworth, 1979)
David Hugh Farmer *The Oxford Dictionary of Saints* (Oxford, 1978)
John Foxe *The Book of Martyrs* (London, ed. Henry Southwell)
James Hall *Hall's Dictionary of Saints* (Cambridge, 1870)
Michael McMahon *Saints* (Northampton, 2006)
Mary Sharp *Saints in Europe* (London, 1964)
Edith Simon *The Saints* (Harmondsworth, 1972)
Richard P. McBrien *Lives of the Saints* (San Francisco, 2004)
Richard P. McBrien *Pocket Guide to the Saints* (San Francisco, 2006)
W. Ellwood Post *Saints, Signs and Symbols* (London, 1974)
Lectionary of Common Worship 2009 (London, 2008)

Websites
www.catholic-forum.com
www.catholic.org
www.americancatholic.org
www.saints.sqpn.com